Statistics for Social and Health Research
With a Guide to SPSS

This book is dedicated to
my mother
my late father
Alex, Tasos, Effi, Ann, Elli, Mimi, Costa, Anna
Erin, Ben, Luke, Sophie, Elli Rose, Jordan
Pamela, Ryan, Michelle
Timothy, Alana
Danielle, Christine, Leanne, Marie
Amanda, Lisa
Alexandra, Andrea, Christopher
Stacey, Chloe, Billy
Alexandra, Katherine, Evelyn

Statistics for Social and Health Research

With a Guide to SPSS

George Argyrous

SAGE Publications

London • Thousand Oaks • New Delhi

SAGE Publications Ltd
6 Bonhill Street
London EC2A 4PU

SAGE Publications Inc.
2455Teller Road
Thousand Oaks, California 91320

SAGE Publications India Pvt Ltd
32, M-Block Market
Greater Kailash – I
New Delhi 110 048

British Library Cataloguing in Publication data

A catalogue record for this book is available from the British Library

ISBN 0 7619 6817 2
ISBN 0 7619 6818 0 (pbk)

Library of Congress catalog record available

Typeset in Times
Printed in Great Britain by The Gromwell Press Ltd, Trowbridge, Wiltshire

SPSS and associated proprietary computer software are the trademarks of SPSS Inc.

Statistics for Social and Health Research is not sponsored or approved or connected with SPSS Inc. All references in the text of this book to SPSS products are to the trademarks of SPSS Inc.

All names of computer programs are hereby acknowledged as trademarks (registered or otherwise), whether or not the symbol appears in the text.

Contents

Part 4 Inferential Statistics: Two or More Independent Samples

Preface

This book is aimed at students and professionals who do not have any existing knowledge in the field of statistics. It is not unreasonable to suggest that most people who fit that description come to statistics reluctantly, if not with hostility. It is usually regarded as 'that course we had to get through'. I suspect that a sense of dread is also shared by many instructors when confronted with the prospect of having to teach the following material.

  This book will hopefully ease some of these problems. It is written by a non-statistician for non-statisticians, for students who are new to the subject, and for professionals who may use statistics occasionally in their work. It is certainly not the only book available that attempts to do this. One might in fact respond with the statement 'not another stats book!' There are important respects, however, in which this book is different to the numerous other books in the field.

Communication of ideas This book is written with the aim of communicating the basic ideas and procedures of statistical analysis to the student and user, rather than as a technical exposition of the fine points of statistical theory. The emphasis is on the explanation of basic concepts and especially their application to 'real-life' problems, using a more conversational tone than is often the case. Such an approach may not be as precise as others in dealing with statistical theory, but it is often the mass of technical detail that leaves readers behind, and turns potentially users of statistical analysis away.

Integrated use of SPSS This book integrates the conceptual material with the use of the main computer software package, **SPSS**. The development and availability of this software has meant that for most people 'doing stats' equals using a computer. The two tasks have converged. Unfortunately, most books have not caught up with this development and adequately integrated the use of computer packages with statistical analysis. They concentrate instead on the logic and formulas involved in statistical analysis and the calculation 'by hand' of problem solutions. At best other books have appendices which give brief introductions and guides to computer packages, but this does not bridge the gap between the hand calculations and the use of computer software. This book builds the use of SPSS into the text. The logic and application of various statistical techniques are explained, and then the examples are reworked on SPSS. Readers can link explicitly the traditional method of working through problems 'by hand' and working through the same problems on SPSS. Exercises also explicitly attempt to integrate the hand calculations with the use and interpretation of computer output.

To help readers along, a CD with all the data necessary to generate the results in the following chapters is included with this book, so that all the procedures described there can be replicated. These files were generated on Version 9.0 of SPSS for Windows (which is also now available for Apple Macintosh computers that can run an emulation program such as Virtual PC or SoftWindows). But users of any version of SPSS after Version 5.0 will be able to open these files and reproduce the results printed in the text. There are slight differences in the appearance of some windows, but the basic menu structure is the same for all of these versions of the program.

It is necessary, however, to point out that this is not a complete guide to SPSS. This book simply illustrates how SPSS can be used to deal with the basic statistical techniques that most researchers commonly encounter. It does not exhaust the full range of functions and options available in SPSS. For the advanced user, nothing will replace the *User's Guide* published by SPSS Inc. But for most people engaged in social research, the following text will allow them to handle the bulk of the problems they will encounter.

For users of other statistics packages such as Microsoft Excel, the files are also saved in ASCII and Excel format so that they can be imported to these programs, along with a **Readme** file that explains the data definitions. All the files, and periodic minor updates and corrections, can be obtained at the following web site:

ftp://ftp.arts.unsw.edu.au/Pub/

Clear guide to choosing the appropriate procedures This book is organized around the individual procedures (or sets of procedures) needed to deal with the majority of problems people encounter when analyzing quantitative data. Other texts flood the reader with procedure after procedure, which can be overwhelming. How to choose between the options? This book concentrates on just the most widely used techniques, and sorts through them by building the structure of the book around these options. Entire chapters are devoted to individual tests so that the situations in which a particular test is applied will not be confused with situations that call for other tests. Thus after working through the text, readers can turn to individual chapters as needed in order to address the particular problems they encounter.

Having noted the main features of this book as compared to others in the field, it is also worth noting what this book is not. This book looks at the analysis of quantitative data, and only the analysis of quantitative data. It makes no pretence to being a comprehensive guide to social or health research. Issues relating to the selection of research problems, the design of research methods, and the procedures for checking the validity and reliability of results are not covered. Such a separation of statistics from more general considerations in the design of research is a dangerous practice since it may give the impression that statistical analysis *is* research. Yet, nothing could be further from the truth. Statistical analysis is one way of processing information, and not always the best. Nor is it a way of proving anything (despite the rhetorical language it employs). At best it is evidence in an ongoing persuasive argument. The separation of statistics from the research process in general may in fact be responsible for the over-exalted status of statistics as a research tool.

Why then write a book which reinforces this separation? First, there is the simple fact that no single book can do everything. Indeed, other books exist which detail the issues involved in research, and the place of statistical analysis in the broader research process. Rather than duplicating such efforts this book is meant to sit side by side with such texts, and provide the methods of statistical analysis when required. Second, statistical analysis is hard. It raises distinct issues and problems of its own which warrant a self-contained treatment.

The first edition of this book, entitled *Statistics for Social Research*, was originally published by Macmillan Education Australia. I want to acknowledge again all those people mentioned there for their assistance. To that list I would like to add Anna Bulman for her assistance with the design and layout of the figures. This edition has much new material, reordered many chapters in what I hope is a more coherent manner, and tried to broaden its appeal to the health sciences through the inclusion of examples and exercises suited to their interests, but which are still intelligible to a non-specialist. The main difference, though, is conceptual. As I encounter more and more examples of statistical analysis, I am increasingly convinced that the difference between 'good' and 'bad' statistics is determined by the clarity of the research question that is being investigated. A clear awareness of what the research is meant to investigate can pre-empt many problems and allow researchers to cut through the wealth of data they may accumulate and the myriad of procedures they could apply to it. As will become clear in the text, there are many techniques that *could* be applied to any given set of data; what *should* be applied is decided by its relevance to the research question under investigation.

I am indebted to the Longman Group UK Ltd, on behalf of the Literary Executor of the late Sir Ronald Fisher and Dr Frank Yates FRS, for permission to reproduce Tables III, IV, and V from *Statistical Tables for Biological, Agricultural, and Medical Research*, 6/e (1974) in the Appendix, and to Professor A. Hald for permission to reproduce in amended form Table 1 of *Statistical Tables and Formulas 1952* in the Appendix.

Lastly, to the reader, I welcome any comments and criticisms, which can be passed on to me at the following address:

School of Social Science and Policy
University of New South Wales
NSW 2052, Australia
email: g.argyrous@unsw.edu.au

PART 1

Univariate Descriptive Statistics

1

Variables and their Measurement

Social and health science research involves the investigation of countless questions from fields as wide as economics, political science, sociology, psychology, public health, nursing, and marketing. These various fields of study throw up questions like:

'What are the *incomes* of households in a local community?'
'What are the *ages* for members of a local community?'
'What is the prevalence of *respiratory illness* across *occupational groups*?'
'Has there been a change in the level of *violent crime* in the past 20 years?'
'What are people's *attitudes to violence on television*?'

Despite the diversity of the subject matter contained in these questions, there is one thing that unifies them: they all involve the investigation of one or more **variables**.

A **variable** is a condition or quality that can vary from one case to another.

Age is clearly a variable since it can be different from person to person. The opposite notion to a variable is a **constant**, which is simply a condition or quality that does not vary between cases. The number of cents in a United States dollar is a constant: every dollar coin will always exchange for 100 cents. Most research, however, is devoted to understanding variables – whether (and why) a variable takes on certain traits for some cases and different traits for other cases. The task of recording the way in which a variable 'appears' across different cases is called the process of **measurement** or **observation**.

Measurement is the process of determining and recording which of the possible traits of a variable an individual case exhibits or possesses.

The variable 'sex' has two possible traits, female and male, and measurement involves deciding which of these two categories a given person falls into.

These measurements, or observations, of a variable are the raw data of research and are taken from units of analysis we term **cases**.

A **case** is an entity that displays or possesses the traits of a variable.

Although in research cases are often individual people, this is not always so. For example, if I am interested in retention rates for high schools in a particular area, the cases are high schools. It is individual high schools that are 'stamped' with a label indicating the particular retention rate that applies to them. In this example, the list of all the high schools in the region constitutes my target **population** (sometimes called a **universe**).

A **population** is the set of all cases of interest.

In everyday terms the word 'population' means the people living in a certain country or region at a certain date. Yet just as individual cases can be entities other than people, so too can the population be made up of elements other than individual people.

For reasons we will investigate later, we may not be able to or not want to investigate the entire population of interest. Instead we may take measurements from only a sub-set of the population, and this sub-set is called a **sample**.

A **sample** is a set of cases that does not include every member of the population.

For example, it may be too costly or time consuming to investigate every high school in the area. We select instead only 10 schools to investigate and take our measurements of retention rates from them.

To summarize these basic concepts (Table 1.1) let us look at one of the examples of a research question we listed above: 'What are the *incomes* of households in a local community?'

Table 1.1 Summary

Variable	Income
Cases	Individual households
Measurement	Determining the income of individual households
Population	All the households in the defined region at a given date
Sample	The set of households in the region from which we actually take a measurement of income

Having broken down the research question this way, we are now confronted with the practical research issue: how do we actually measure household income? What 'instrument' are we to use to determine how households vary in terms of their respective incomes? In order to take measurements of a variable for a set of cases, we confront the process of conceptualization and operationalization.

The conceptualization and operationalization of variables

Where do variables come from? Why do we choose to study particular variables and not others? The choice of variables to investigate is affected by a number of complex factors, three of which I will emphasize here.

Theoretical framework   Theories are ways of interpreting the world and reconciling ourselves to it, and even though we may take for granted that a variable is worthy of research, it is in fact often a highly charged selection process that directs one's attention to it. We may be working within an established theoretical tradition that considers certain variables to be central to its world-view. For example, Marxists consider 'economic class' to be a variable worthy of research, whereas another theoretical perspective might consider this variable to be uninteresting. Analyzing the world in terms of economic class means not analyzing it in other ways, such as social groups. This is neither good nor bad: without a theory to order our perception of the world, research will often become a jumble of observations that do not tie together in a meaningful way. But the theoretical preconceptions upon which the choice of variables to investigate is often based should be acknowledged.

Pre-specified research agenda   Sometimes the research question and the variables to be investigated are not determined by the researchers themselves. For example, a consultant may contract to undertake research that has terms of reference set in advance by the contracting body. In such a situation the person or people actually doing the research might have little scope to choose the variables to be investigated and how they are to be defined, since they are doing work for someone else.

Curiosity-driven research   Sometimes we might not have a clearly defined theoretical framework to operate in, nor clear directives from another person or body as to the key concepts to be investigated. Instead we want to investigate a variable purely on the basis of a hunch, a loosely conceived feeling that something useful or important might be revealed by looking at a particular variable. This can be as important a reason for undertaking research as the imperatives of social theories. Indeed, when moving into a whole new area of research, into which existing theories have not ventured, simple hunches can be very fruitful motivations.

These three motivations are obviously not mutually exclusive. For example, even if the research agenda is specified by another body, that body will almost certainly be operating within some theoretical framework. Whatever the motivation, though, social inquiry will initially direct us to particular variables to be investigated. At this initial stage a variable is given a **conceptual definition**.

The **conceptual definition** (or **nominal definition**) of a variable uses literal terms to specify the qualities of a variable.

A conceptual definition is much like a dictionary definition; it provides a working definition of the variable so that we have a general sense of what it 'means'. For our example of measuring 'income', I might define income conceptually as 'an individual's legal claim over goods and services'.

It is clear, though, that if I now instructed researchers to go out and measure people's 'legal claims over goods and services', they would leave scratching their heads. I also need to provide a set of instructions that will allow the researchers actually to record how such claims over goods and services will vary from one person to the next. In other words, defining a variable of interest at only a conceptual level is only the beginning; we then need a set of rules and procedures – operations – that will allow us actually to 'observe' a variable in the world. What will we look for to identify someone's income? This is the problem of **operationalization**.

The **operational definition** of a variable specifies the procedures and criteria for taking a measurement of that variable for individual cases.

To observe a given person's income I need to decide on the things to look for that will allow me to measure it. A statement like 'income is the sum of all cash payments, such as wages, salaries, and welfare payments, received in the previous year' provides an operational definition of income. With this definition in hand a researcher can now go out into the world and start measuring the income of individuals by adding up all the money received through various sources over the past year.

This process of definition is a major, if not *the* major, source of disagreement in research. Any given conceptual definition can usually be operationalized in many different ways, and no one of these may be perfect. For example, operationalizing income in terms of the sum of cash payments a person receives leaves out other sources of income, such as payments of goods in kind; rather than just being paid in money a person may be paid in goods that can be directly consumed.

What criteria should be used in deciding whether a particular operational definition is adequate? In the technical literature this is known as the problem of **construct validity**. Ideally, we are looking for an operationalization that will vary when the underlying variable we think it 'shadows' varies. A mercury thermometer is a good instrument for measuring changes in daily temperature because when the underlying variable (temperature) changes the means of measuring it (the height of the bar of mercury) also changes. If the thermometer is instead full of water rather than mercury, variations in daily temperature will not be matched by changes in the thermometer. Two days might actually be different in temperature, without this variation being 'picked up' by the instrument. Coming back to our example of income, and relying on an operational definition that just includes cash payments, we might record two people as having the same income, when in fact they differ. Imagine two people who receive the same amount of cash in payment for their work, but one of them also has their children's school fees paid by their employer and a company car thrown in. Clearly there is variation between the two people in terms of their income – their respective command over goods and services. But this variation will not be recorded if we rely on an operational definition based on just the sum of cash payments.

To illustrate further the 'slippage' that can occur in moving from a conceptual to an operational definition of a variable, consider the following example. A study is interested in people's 'criminality'. We may define criminality conceptually as non-sanctioned acts of violence against other members of society or their property. How can a researcher identify the pattern of variation in this variable? A number of operational definitions could be employed:

- counting a person's number of criminal arrests from official records;
- calculating the amount of time a person has spent in jail;
- asking people whether they have committed crimes;
- recording a person's hair color.

Clearly, it would be very hard to justify the last operationalization as a valid one: it is not possible to say that if someone's level of criminality changed so too would their hair color! The other operational definitions seem closer to the general concept of criminality, but each has its own problems: asking people if they have committed a crime may not be a perfect measure because people might not be truthful about such a touchy subject. Counting the number of times a person has been arrested is not perfect – two people may actually have the same level of criminality, yet one might have more recorded arrests because they are a member of a minority group that the police target for arrest. This operationalization may thereby actually be measuring a different variable from the one intended: the biases of police rather than 'criminality'. Using any of these operational definitions to measure a person's criminality may not perfectly mirror the result we would get if we could 'know' their criminality.

A number of factors can generate problems in arriving at an operational definition of a variable with a high construct validity.

The complexity of the concept   Some variables are not very complex: a person's sex, for example, is determined by generally accepted physical attributes. However, most variables are rarely so straightforward. We have seen that income has a number of dimensions such as cash payments and payments in kind. Indeed each of these dimensions of income are conceptual variables in themselves, and raise problems of operationalization of their own. Any single operationalization that focuses on one dimension, by only considering cash payments for example, will miss out on the other dimensions.

Availability of data We might have an operationalization that seems to capture perfectly the underlying variable of interest. For example, we might think that number of arrests is a flawless way of 'observing' criminality. The researchers, though, may not be allowed, for privacy reasons, to review police records to compile the information. Clearly, a less than perfect operationalization will have to be employed, simply because we cannot get our hands on the 'ideal' data.

Cost and difficulty of obtaining data Say we were able to review police records and tally up the number of arrests. The cost in doing so, though, might be prohibitive, in terms of both time and money. Similarly, we might feel that a certain measure of water pollution is ideal for assessing river degradation, but the need to employ an expert with sophisticated measuring equipment might bar this as an option, and instead a subjective judgment of water 'murkiness' might be preferred as a quick and easy measure.

Ethics Is it right to go looking at the details of an individual's arrest record, simply to satisfy one's own research objectives? The police might permit it, and there might be plenty of time and money available, but does this justify looking at a document that was not intended to be part of a research project? The problem of ethics – knowing right from wrong – is extremely thorny, and I could not even begin to address it seriously here. It is simply raised as an issue affecting the operationalization of variables that regularly arises in social and health research dealing with the lives of people. (For those wishing to follow up on this important issue, a good starting point is R.S. Broadhead (1984) Human rights and human subjects: Ethics and strategies in social science research. *Sociological Inquiry*, 54, 107–123.)

For these (and other) reasons a great deal of debate about the validity of research centers around this problem of operationalization. In fact, many debates surrounding quantitative research are not actually about the techniques or results of the research but rather whether the variables have been 'correctly' defined in the first place. Unless the operational criteria used to measure a variable are sensitive to the way a variable changes between cases, they will generate misleading results.

An operational definition of a variable will usually specify a range of **categories** or **values** (sometimes called **scores**) for a variable into which individual cases will fall. *These categories or values are meant to capture the possible range of variation that could arise in the process of measurement.* The categories of male and female specify, for example, the full range of variation that individual cases can display for the variable 'sex'. In specifying this range, an operational definition must satisfy the following rule.

An operational definition must allow a researcher to assign each case into one, and only one, of the categories of the variable.

This statement actually embodies two separate principles of measurement. The first is the **principle of exclusiveness**, which states that no case should have more than one value for the same variable. For example, someone cannot be both 18 years of age and 64 years of age. Measurement must also follow the **principle of exhaustiveness**, which states that every case can be classified into a category. For example, a scale for measuring family status must allow for every possible type of family status that can arise. If we did not include a category for 'never married' then this will provide a crack through which some cases will fall and not be detected in the measurement process.

Levels of measurement

An operational definition of a variable, in specifying the range of categories or values that can be assigned to individual cases, will imply a certain **level of measurement**. There are four different levels at which we may undertake the process of measurement:

- nominal
- ordinal
- interval
- ratio

These levels of measurement are a fundamental distinction in statistics, since they determine much of what we can do with information gathered. In fact, when considering which of the myriad of statistical techniques we will choose to analyze information, usually the first question to ask is the level at which a variable has been measured. As we shall see there are things we can do with data collected at the interval level of measurement that we cannot do with data collected at the nominal level. We speak of *levels* of measurement because *the higher the level of measurement the more information we have about a variable*.

Nominal data

We begin by considering the lowest level of measurement, which is the **nominal** scale.

A **nominal** scale of measurement only indicates the category of a variable that a case falls into.

For example, assume I am interested in people's religion. Operationally I define a person's religion as the established church to which they belong, providing the following range of categories: Muslim, Hindu, Jewish, Christian, Other.

Notice that to ensure the scale is exhaustive this nominal measure, like most nominal measures, has a catch-all category of 'Other'. Sometime these catch-all categories are labeled 'miscellaneous' or 'not elsewhere counted', and such categories provide a quick way of identifying a nominal scale of measurement.

Another easy way to detect a nominal scale is to rearrange the order in which the categories are listed and see if the scale still 'makes sense'. For example, either of the following orders for listing religious denomination are valid:

Christian	Muslim
Muslim	Jewish
Jewish	Hindu
Hindu	Christian
Other	Other

Obviously, the order in which the categories appear does not matter, as long as the rules of mutual exclusivity and exhaustiveness are followed. This is because there is no sense of rank or order of magnitude: one cannot say that a person in the 'Christian' category has more or less religion than someone in the 'Hindu' category. In other words, *a variable measured at the nominal level varies qualitatively but not quantitatively*: someone in the Christian category is qualitatively different to someone in the Hindu category, with respect to the variable 'Religion', but they do not have more or less Religion.

It is important to keep this in mind, because *for convenience* we can assign numbers to each category as a form of shorthand (a process that will be very useful when we later have to enter data into SPSS). Thus I may **code** – assign numbers to – the categories of religion in the following way:

1 = Muslim
2 = Jewish
3 = Hindu
4 = Christian
5 = Other

These numbers are simply category labels that have no quantitative meaning as such. The numbers simply identify different categories, but do not express a mathematical relationship between those categories. They are simply used for convenience in analyzing and describing data. I could just as easily have used the following coding scheme to assign numerical values to each category:

1 = Muslim
5 = Jewish
6 = Hindu
8 = Christian
9 = Other

Ordinal data

An ordinal scale of measurement also categorizes cases. Thus nominal and ordinal scales are sometimes collectively called categorical scales. However, an ordinal scale provides additional information.

An **ordinal** level of measurement, in addition to the function of classification, allows cases to be ordered by degree according to measurements of the variable.

Ordinal scales, that is, enable us to **rank** cases. Ranking involves ordering cases in a quantitative sense, such as from 'lowest' to 'highest', from 'less' to 'more', or from 'weakest' to 'strongest'. Ordinal scales are particularly common when measuring attitude or satisfaction in opinion surveys.

For example, assume that in trying to measure income I settle on the following scale:

> *low income   middle income   high income*

where low income includes people whose annual income is $15,000 or less, middle income includes people who earn between $15,001 and $50,000 a year, and high income includes people who earn more than $50,000 a year. This scale clearly does the task of a nominal scale, which is to assign cases into categories. In addition to this, being an ordinal scale, it allows me to say that someone who is in the middle income category *has more income* than someone in the low income category. Put another way, the middle income earner is **ranked above** the low income earner. Unlike nominal data, a case in one category is not only different to a case in another, it is 'better', or 'stronger', or 'bigger', or more 'intense': *there is directional change*.

Here we *cannot rearrange the categories* without the scale becoming senseless. Thus, if I construct the scale in the following way, the ranking of cases according to income is lost:

> *middle income   high income   low income*

As with nominal data, numerical values can be assigned to the categories as a form of shorthand, but with ordinal scales these numbers also need to preserve the sense of ranking. Thus either of the following sets of numbers can be used:

> 1   2   3
> *low income   middle income   high income*

> or

> 23   88   105
> *low income   middle income   high income*

Either coding system allows the categories to be identified and ordered with respect to each other, but the numbers themselves do not have any quantitative significance beyond the function of ranking.

Interval/ratio data

Ordinal scales permit us to rank cases in terms of a variable; we can say that one case is 'better' or 'stronger' than another, for example. But an ordinal scale does not allow us to say *by how much* a case is better or stronger when compared with another. If I use the above income scale, I cannot say how much more income someone in the high income category has relative to someone in the middle income category. It would be misleading for me to use the second of the coding schemes above and say that a high income earner has 17 more units of income than a middle income earner (i.e. $105 - 88 = 17$). The distances – **intervals** – between the categories are unknown.

Consider, however, if we measure income in an alternative way, by asking each person how much they earned in the previous year *in dollars*. Clearly, I can perform the task of assigning people into categories based on the dollar amount of their annual incomes. I can also perform the task of rank ordering cases according to these measurements by indicating who has more or less income than another person. Unlike nominal and ordinal scales, however, I can also measure the *amount difference* in income between cases. In this measurement scale the numbers we get do really signify a quantitative value: an amount of dollars.

It is this ability to measure the distances between points on the scale that makes this method of observing income an **interval/ratio** scale.

An **interval** scale has units measuring intervals of equal distance between values on the scale.

A **ratio** scale has a value of zero that indicates cases where no quantity of the variable is present.

In other words, not only can we say that one case has more (or less) of the variable in question than another, but we can also say how much more (or less). Thus someone who has an annual income of $30,000 has $10,000 more income than someone earning $20,000 a year; we can measure the interval between them. Moreover, *the intervals between points on the scale are of equal value over its whole range*, so that the difference in income between $20,000 and $30,000 is the same as the difference in income between $120,000 and $130,000.

Clearly the numbers on an interval scale do have significance, since they indicate a measurable quantity. Hence these numbers are termed the **values** for the variable. (In the following chapters we will often also refer to the numbers used to represent the categories of nominal and ordinal data as 'values' or 'scores', so that the terms 'values', 'scores' and 'categories' are used interchangeably. For the reasons we have just outlined this is, strictly speaking, incorrect. However, if we take note that for nominal and ordinal data such values are simply category labels without real quantitative significance, such terminology is not too misleading.)

Notice that an observation of $0 represents a case which possesses no quantity of the variable 'income'. Such a condition is known as a **true zero point** and is the defining characteristic of ratio data, as opposed to interval data. For example, heat measured in degrees Celsius does not have a true zero. There is a zero point, but 0°C does not indicate a case where no heat is present – it is cold but not that cold! Instead, 0°C indicates something else: the point at which water freezes. However, this distinction between interval and ratio scales of measurement is a fairly subtle one, and not important for what is to follow. We can generally perform the same statistical analyses on interval data that we can perform on ratio data, and for this reason, we combine them into the one interval/ratio level of measurement.

Discrete and continuous variables

Another important distinction that affects the process of measurement is the distinction between **discrete** and **continuous** variables.

A **discrete variable** has a countable number of values.

For example, sex is a discrete variable with only two possible categories (male/female). With discrete variables measured at the interval/ratio level there is often a unit of measurement that cannot be subdivided. Consider the number of children per household. It makes no sense to talk of 1.7 children per household, since children do not come in units of less than one! We have to 'jump' from one whole value of the variable to the next. Other examples are the number of prisoners per jail cell, the number of welfare agencies in a district, and the number of industrial accidents in the previous year.

Consider, on the other hand, the variable 'satisfaction with library service'. Satisfaction levels between library users can be ever so slightly different, so that they can conceivably change in a *gradual* way from person to person or for the same person over time. This is an example of a continuous variable.

A **continuous variable** can vary in quantity by infinitesimally small degrees.

Continuous variables are often measured by units that can be subdivided infinitely. Age is an example of a continuous variable, since there is no basic unit with which age is measured. We may begin by measuring age in terms of years. But a year can be divided into months, and months into weeks, weeks into days, and so on. The only limit is exactly how precise we want to be: years are not as accurate as months, and months not as accurate as weeks.

Theoretically, with a continuous variable we can move gradually and smoothly from one value of the variable to the next without having to jump. Practically, though, we will always have to 'round off' the measurement and treat a continuous variable *as if* it is discrete, and this causes the scale of measurement to 'jump' from one value to the next. For example, we may settle on measuring satisfaction with library services by asking people if they are Very Satisfied, Satisfied, Unsatisfied, or Very Unsatisfied. The *scale* is discrete, even though the underlying variable is continuous. Similarly with age: though we may measure age in discrete *units* such as years or months, the variable itself increases in a continuous way.

The use of these discrete measurement scales causes us to cluster cases together into discrete groups. The discrete points on the scale, in other words, act like centers of gravity pulling in all the slight variations close to them in the variable that we do not want to worry about. When we say that two people are 18 years of age, they may in fact be different in terms of age, unless they are born precisely at the same time. But the slight difference that may exist between someone whose age is 18 years, 2 months, 5 days, 2 hours, 12 seconds... and someone whose age is 18 years, 3 months, 14 days, 7 hours, 1 second... might be irrelevant for the research problem we are investigating and we treat them the same in terms of the variable, even though they are truly different.

Summary

The importance of the distinction between nominal, ordinal, and interval/ratio data is the amount of information each level provides (Table 1.2).

Table 1.2 Levels of measurement

Level of measurement	Examples	Measurement procedure	Operations permitted
Nominal (lowest level)	Sex Race Religion Marital status	Classification into categories	Counting number of cases in each category; comparing number of cases in each category
Ordinal	Social class Attitude and opinion scales	Classification plus ranking of categories with respect to each other	All above plus judgments of 'greater than' or 'less than'
Interval/ratio (highest level)	Age in years Number of children	Classification plus ranking plus description of distances between scores in terms of equal units	All above plus other mathematical operations such as addition, subtraction, multiplication, etc.

Source: J.F. Healey (1993) *Statistics: A Tool for Social Research*, Belmont, CA: Wadsworth, p. 14.

Table 1.2 summarizes the amount of information provided by each level of measurement and the tasks we are thereby allowed to perform with data collected at each level. Nominal data have the least information, ordinal data give more information because we can rank cases, and interval/ratio data capture the most information since they allow us to measure difference.

This chapter discussed the preliminaries that need to be taken into account before statistical information can be analyzed. This was done fairly generally, since the rest of this book is concerned with the process of analysis – what do we do with data once they have been collected? Having collected data we can then proceed to analyze them, and the first step in analysis is usually to describe the data. The process of description will be discussed in the next few chapters.

Exercises

1.1 Consider the following ways of classifying respondents to a questionnaire.
   (a) Voting eligibility:
      • Registered voter
      • Unregistered but eligible to vote
      • Did not vote at the last election
   (b) Course of enrollment:
      • Physics
      • Economics
      • English
      • Sociology
      • Social sciences
   (c) Reason for joining the military:
      • Parental pressure
      • Career training
      • Conscripted
      • Seemed like a good idea at the time
      • No reason given
   Do these violate the principles of measurement? If so, which ones and how?

1.2 What is the level of measurement for each of the following variables?
   (a) The age in years of the youngest member of each household
   (b) The color of a person's hair
   (c) The color of a karate belt
   (d) The price of a suburban bus fare
   (e) The years in which national elections were held
   (f) The postcode of households
   (g) People's attitude to smoking

(h) Academic performance measured by number of marks
(i) Academic performance measured as fail or pass
(j) Place of birth, listed by country
(k) Infant mortality rate (deaths per thousand)
(l) Political party of the current Member of Parliament or Congressman or Congresswoman for your area
(m) Proximity to the sea (coastal or non-coastal)
(n) Proximity to the sea (kilometers from the nearest coastline)
(o) Relative wealth (listed as 'Poor' through to 'Wealthy')
(p) The number on the back of a football player

1.3 Find an article in a journal that involves statistical analysis. What are the conceptual variables used? How are they operationalized? Why are these variables chosen for analysis? Can you come up with alternative operationalizations for these same variables? Justify your alternative.

1.4 For each of the following variables describe briefly a means of measurement:
(a) Racial prejudice
(b) Household size
(c) Height
(d) Drug use
(e) Voting preference
(f) Economic status
(g) Aggressiveness
For each operationalization state the level of measurement. Suggest alternative operationalizations that involve different levels of measurement.

1.5 Which of the following are discrete variables and which are continuous variables?
(a) The numbers on the faces of a die
(b) The weight of a new-born baby
(c) The time at sunset
(d) The number of cars in a parking station
(e) The amount of water consumed by a household per day
(f) Attitude to the use of nuclear power

1.6 The following is a question from a national survey of attitudes toward unemployment:

What is your impression of the government's efforts to address the current unemployment situation? Please circle one of the following:

1 The government is doing nothing to tackle the problem
2 The government is addressing the problem, in an unsatisfactory manner
3 The government is addressing the problem, in a satisfactory manner

4 The government is doing everything it can to solve the problem
5 No opinion

What variable is this question trying to measure? Do you see any problems with the range of responses provided?

2

Setting up an SPSS Data File

Chapter 1 introduced the conceptual issues involved in the process of measurement. This chapter will introduce SPSS, the main statistical package for analyzing data. In setting up an SPSS file to undertake statistical analysis we encounter many of these conceptual issues in a very practical way.

In Table 2.1 we present the results of a hypothetical survey of 20 people, which we will use to illustrate the way in which an SPSS data file is created. In this hypothetical survey I am interested in three separate variables: age, sex, and health level. Sex is measured by classifying cases into male or female (nominal). The survey respondents are also asked to rate their own health levels as 'Very healthy', 'Healthy', or 'Unhealthy' (ordinal). Finally, age is measured by asking people their age in whole years on their last birthday (interval/ratio).

Table 2.1 Results of a survey of 20 people

Case number	Sex	Health rating	Age in years
1	Male	Very healthy	18
2	Male	Very healthy	21
3	Female	Healthy	20
4	Male	Unhealthy	18
5	Female	Very healthy	19
6	Male	Unhealthy	18
7	Female	Unhealthy	22
8	Male	Very healthy	19
9	Female	Healthy	18
10	Male	Healthy	20
11	Male	Unhealthy	18
12	Female	Very healthy	19
13	Male	Very healthy	22
14	Male	Very healthy	19
15	Female	Unhealthy	20
16	Female	Healthy	18
17	Male	Unhealthy	21
18	Female	Unhealthy	19
19	Male	Healthy	18
20	Male	Very healthy	20

The rest of this chapter will detail how we can record this information in SPSS so that we can use it as an example when we learn the techniques for statistical analysis in later chapters.

The SPSS Data Editor window

To begin an SPSS session you need to run the program (Figure 2.1). Assuming the program has been installed correctly, you will be able to run SPSS from the **Start/Programs** button on the bottom left of your screen.

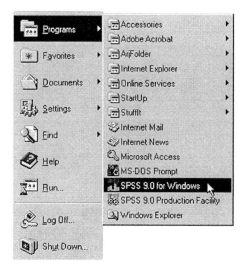

Figure 2.1 Launching the SPSS program

Launching SPSS will bring up the **Data Editor** window (Figure 2.2). (If a window first appears asking you "What would you like to do?" select **Type in data** and then **OK**.). This is the 'data page' on which all the information will be entered. Think of it as a blank table, like Table 2.1 before any information was typed into it. The **Data Editor** window is made up of a series of columns and rows, which form little rectangles called **cells**. As with Table 2.1 above, each column will contain the information for each one of the variables, and each row will contain the information for each case. The first row of cells (the ones at the top of each column) are shaded and contain a faint **var**. This row of shaded cells will act like the first row of Table 2.1, which contains the names of the variables whose information is stored in each column. Similarly, the first column is shaded and contains faint numbers 1, 2, 3, and so on. This is analogous to the first column in Table 2.1, which contains the numbers (1–20) that have been assigned to each person surveyed. These are sometimes called **case numbers**.

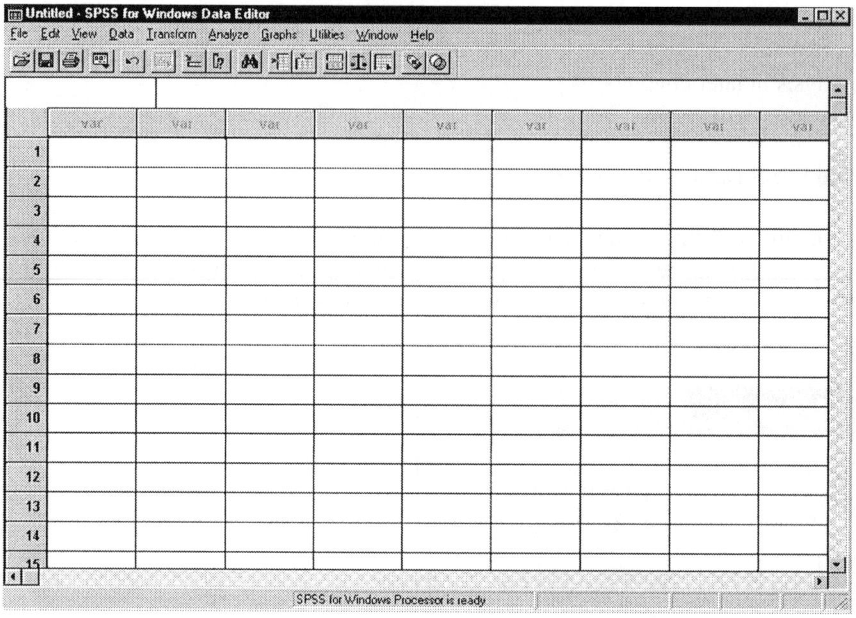

Figure 2.2 The SPSS **Data Editor** window

At the top of the window is a **menu bar** (Figure 2.3).

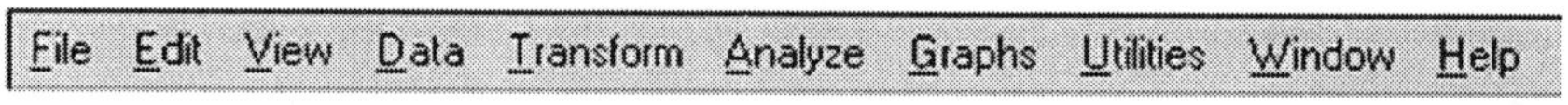

Figure 2.3 The menu bar

We define and analyze data by selecting commands from this menu. Usually selecting commands from the menu will bring up on the screen a small rectangular area, which we call a **dialog box**, from which more specialized options are available, depending on the type of procedure we want to undertake. By the end of this and later chapters (hopefully) this way of hunting through the SPSS menu for the appropriate commands will be very familiar. In fact, it is very similar to many other software applications that readers have encountered, such as word processing and spreadsheet software.

Below the menu bar is a **tool bar** which provides an *alternative* means for activating many of the commands contained within the menu (Figure 2.4).

Figure 2.4 The tool bar

Generally we will concentrate on using the **menu bar** to activate SPSS commands, even though sometimes clicking on the relevant button on the **tool bar** may be quicker. We will concentrate just on the use of menu options simply to ensure that we learn one method consistently; after some level of proficiency readers can then decide whether selecting commands through the menu or by clicking on the buttons is preferable.

Those of you working with a version of SPSS older than Version 9.0 may notice a slight difference between the menu bar on your screen and that in Figure 2.3. Rather than **Analyze** appearing between **Transform** and **Graph** you will see **Statistics**. This is where we find the commands for most of the procedures we will learn in the following chapters. Thus, in later chapters where you are asked to select the **Analyze** command, users of older versions of SPSS should instead select **Statistics**. Other than this there is no major difference between the different versions of the program.

You should also observe that the unshaded cell at the top left of the page has a heavy border, which indicates that it is the **active cell** (Figure 2.5).

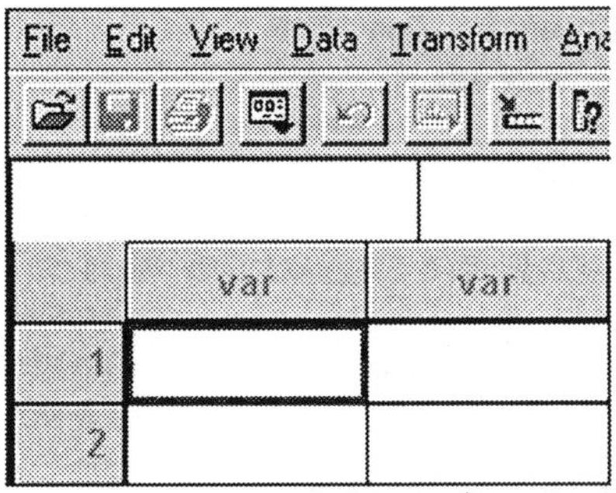

Figure 2.5 The active cell

The active cell is the cell in which any information will be entered if I start typing. Any cell can be made active simply by pointing the cursor at it and clicking the mouse. You will then notice a heavy border around the cell you have just clicked on, indicating that it is the active cell.

The process of data entry involves three basic steps, which we will work through in sequence.

- Attaching a variable name and label to the top of each column in which data will be stored.
- Specifying the meaning of the values that will be entered in the cells.
- Entering the data into the cells.

We will go through each of these steps for each of the variables we are working with.

The <u>D</u>efine Variable command

The first step in setting up an SPSS data file is to define the variables to be analyzed using the **<u>D</u>ata/<u>D</u>efine Variable** command. We will begin with the first variable for which we have collected data, which is the sex of each respondent.

As mentioned earlier a single column stores data for a single variable. We will enter the data for respondents' sex in the first column. The first step is to bring up the **<u>D</u>efine Variable** dialog box. This is done in one of two ways:

1. by making a cell in the first column active by clicking on it and selecting the **<u>D</u>ata/<u>D</u>efine Variable** command (Figure 2.6(a)),

or

2. by pointing the cursor at the shaded cell at the top of the relevant column and double-clicking the mouse button (Figure 2.6(b)).

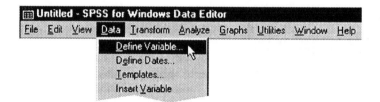

Figure 2.6(a) Selecting <u>D</u>efine Variable command from the menu

Figure 2.6(b) Selecting <u>D</u>efine Variable command by clicking the column head

Try both methods to see that the result will be the same: a dialog box headed **Define Variable** 'floats' in front of the **Data Editor** window (Figure 2.7). This dialog box acts as a 'launching pad' for undertaking the various tasks we need to do to set up a column for data entry. We select in turn each of the buttons in the area headed **Change Settings** and make the necessary changes. The changes we make will be displayed in the area headed **Variable Description**.

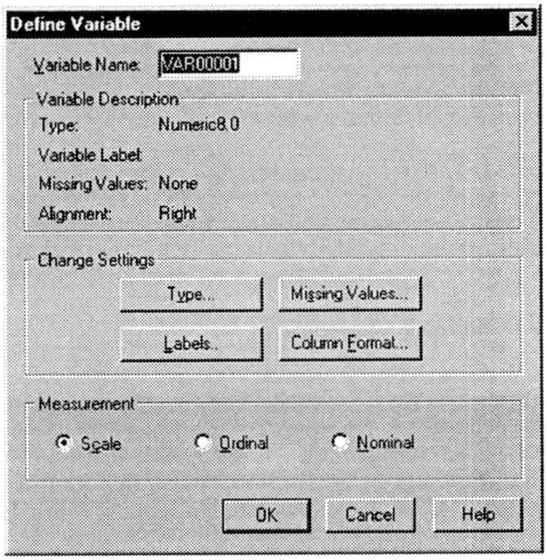

Figure 2.7 The **Define Variable** dialog box

Assigning a variable name

The first task is to give the variable a name. You will notice that next to
Variable Name: VAR00001 is shaded. VAR00001 is the name that SPSS will
give the variable in column 1 unless we tell it otherwise. We want to use a
more meaningful name so we type **sex** in this area.

There are some limitations imposed by SPSS on the names we can assign to
our variables:

- A variable name can only have a maximum of <u>eig</u>ht characters made up of
  letters and/or numbers.
- A variable name must begin with a letter.
- A variable name cannot end with a period.
- A variable name cannot contain blanks or special characters such as &, ?, !,
  ', *.
- A variable name must be unique. No other variable in a given data file can
  have the same name.
- A variable name will appear in lower-case letters, regardless of the case in
  which is typed.

Given these specific limitations, in general you will find that one of two
schemes is adopted in naming variables in SPSS. One uses **sequential names**
indicating where on the research instrument (the questionnaire, interview
schedule, record sheet, etc.) the variable appears. An example of this might be
to name variables Q1, Q2, Q3A, Q3B, and so on, to indicate which question

number on a questionnaire generated the data for a given variable. This provides a quick and easy way of assigning variable names and allows you to link a name directly to the research instrument on which the data are recorded. Its disadvantage is that the individual variable names do not give an impression of the contents of the variable.

The other variable naming scheme that is commonly adopted, and which we are using here, is to use **descriptive names**. This is a more time-consuming method, but the individual variable names, such as **sex,** give an immediate impression as to what the data in a given column are about.

Setting the data type

We next click on the **Type** button, which brings up another dialog box. This defines the type of data that we will be entering for this variable. We plan to type in numbers which stand for each of the two categories of the variable (1 for female and 2 for male). This is known as **numeric** data and is the pre-chosen ('default') setting. Since most data are of a numeric type, SPSS sets this as the default so we don't need to change it. There are a number of other choices available, which we will not go into here, but which may be useful for special kinds of data such as dates or currencies.

We can also specify the width of the data, which is the maximum number of characters that can be entered as data for each case; the default is eight, so if we had values for a variable with more than eight digits we would need to change this. For example, if we were entering the populations of various countries, we would not be able to include data for countries such as the USA or China with populations greater than 99,999,999 unless we change the default setting. We would need to type over 8 in the **Width** box with a higher number such as 10.

Lastly we can specify the number of decimal places that the data are to be rounded to. Here we will just be typing in 1 or 2, so we are using no decimal places. The default setting is for 2 decimal places, so unless we change this our column of numbers will be made up of 1.00 and 2.00. This does not actually affect any of the analysis in any way, but for appearance sake we change the number of decimal places to zero by highlighting over 2 and typing 0.

If we follow all these procedures the dialog box will look like Figure 2.8.

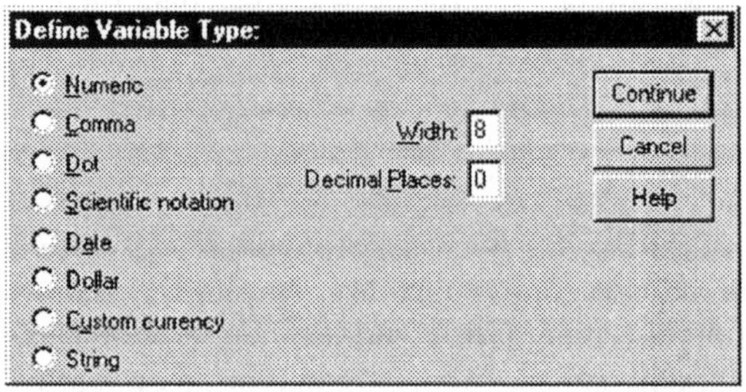

Figure 2.8 The **Define Variable Type:** dialog box

If this is what you see on your screen click on **Continue**, which will return you to the **Define Variable** dialog box.

Defining variable and value labels

We next click on the **Labels** button, which brings up the **Define Labels** dialog box. In this box we provide variable and value labels. The cursor will be flashing in the area next to **Variable Label:**. A variable label is a longer description (up to 120 characters) of the variable than can be included in the short eight-character variable name we have already introduced. For example, with the variable 'Health rating' we obviously cannot type this in as the variable name since it exceeds the eight-character limit. We need to think of some abbreviation for 'health rating' instead. We will use **health**. A problem might arise, however, if we rely solely on abbreviated variable names, especially when working with lots of variables. If we generate results and the output contains information about a variable called **health**, we may have forgotten by that point what that abbreviation really stands for. Similarly, I might remember what **health** really refers to, but others looking at the results will be left scratching their heads. To guard against this, SPSS allows us to enter a 'long' variable name, called a **variable label**, if we have used an abbreviation as the title of a column. The long name will not appear on the data page, but will be printed with any results generated, so that in any output we will see that the brief variable name **health** is really a shorthand way of writing 'health rating'. In other words, this variable label will appear with any output we may generate and acts as an explanation of the variable. With interval/ratio data it is also a useful way of including the unit of measurement. Although the short variable **sex** is fairly self-explanatory, to get into the habit of typing in variable labels we will type **sex of respondent**.

Having labeled the variable we are interested in, we can now proceed to define the range of scores or categories that the variable can take. The categories of nominal and ordinal variables are initially described in words, called **value labels**. Thus sex has two value labels: female and male. To perform statistical analysis, and to make data entry quicker, it is best to link each label to a specific number or **value**. Thus we assign a number to each value label, and enter these numbers into the data file. For example, with the variable 'sex' we will arbitrarily code female responses as 1, and male responses as 2. Instead of typing in male or female for each case, we type in the number assigned to each of these labels – a much faster procedure.

With a nominal scale such as 'sex' the actual numerical code given to each value label is arbitrary: we can just as easily reverse the order and assign 1 to male and 2 to female. In fact, we could assign 3 to female and 7 to male, or any other combination of values. But, generally, the simpler the coding scheme the better. The procedure for defining the value labels for sex is provided in Table 2.2 and Figure 2.9.

Table 2.2 The **Value Labels** command on SPSS

SPSS command/action	Comments
1 Double-click on the shaded cell with **sex** contained in it	This brings up the **Define Variable** window
2 Click on **L**abels	This brings up the **Define Labels:** window
3 In the box next to **Val<u>ue</u>:** type **1**	
4 In the box next to **Valu<u>e</u> Label:** type **female**	You will notice that as soon as you start typing **Add** suddenly darkens, whereas it was previously faint
5 Click on **A**dd	This pastes the information into the adjacent area so that **1="female"**. The cursor will automatically jump back to the box next to **Value:**
6 Type **2**	
7 In the box next to **Valu<u>e</u> Label:** type **male**	
8 Click on **A**dd.	This value and value label will now be added to the list, so that **2="male"**
9 Click on **Continue**	

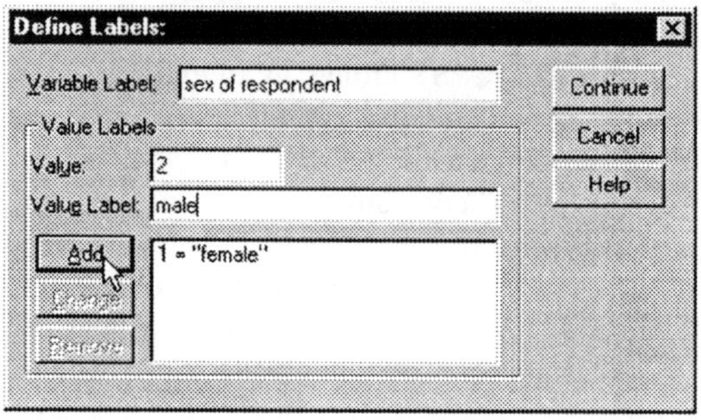

Figure 2.9 The **Define Labels:** dialog box

If you get an error message when you click on **Continue** stating 'Any pending Add or Change operations will be lost', it is because you have forgotten to click the **A**dd button after typing in a value and value label. If this happens click on **OK** which will return you to the **Define Labels:** dialog box and click on **A**dd.

Setting missing values

The next option we will use in the **Define Variable** box is the **Mi**s**sing Values** option. A missing value is a number that indicates to SPSS that the response is not 'useable' and should not be included in the analysis. Missing values can arise for many reasons. Someone may not have chosen to fill in the part of the questionnaire that asked for their sex, or else they may have written with such poor handwriting that we cannot decipher their response to a particular question. When we do not have a useful datum for an individual case for a specific variable we need to enter a missing value into the relevant cell, indicating that a valid response was not provided in that instance and therefore should not be included in any analysis of that variable.

SPSS has a default setting called the **system missing value** which is simply a space typed in the cell where no valid response occurs. We can also provide **user-defined missing values**, whereby we specify a particular number to indicate invalid responses. In selecting a number to be the missing value we need to be careful to select a value that the variable cannot possibly take. In this example, we can choose 9 to be the missing value, since it is impossible for the variable 'sex' to take on this value. Obviously if we were measuring the age of school children, 9 would not be an appropriate choice for the missing value; 99 might be better because it is highly unlikely that such a score could actually represent a real case. The SPSS procedures for assigning user-defined missing values are presented in Table 2.3 and Figure 2.10.

Table 2.3 Assigning user-defined missing values on SPSS

SPSS command/action	Comments
1 Click on **Missing Values**	This brings up the **Define Missing Values:** window. Next to **N**o **missing values** there is a small circle with a black dot. This indicates that the default setting is for no missing values to be specified
2 Click on the small circle next to **D**iscrete missing values	The circle to the left of **D**iscrete **missing values** will now contain the black dot, and the cursor will be flashing in the adjacent rectangle
3 Type **9**	
4 Click on **Continue**	

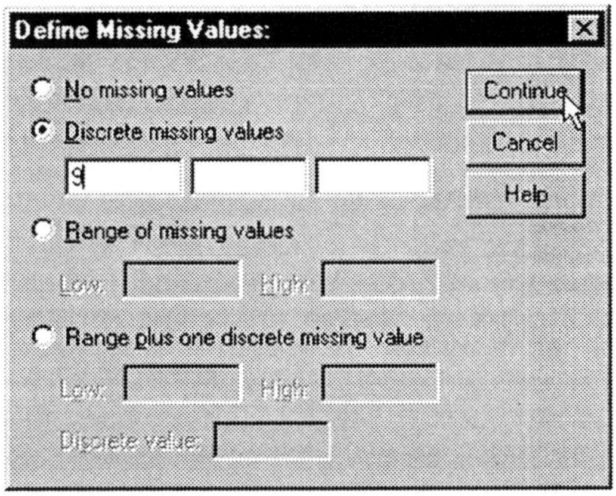

Figure 2.10 The **Define Missing Values:** dialog box

Having defined the missing value when we set up the data file, we can then enter 9 during the data entry process if we encounter a respondent for whom their sex cannot be determined.

Setting the column format

We should now be back to the **Define Variable** box. The last button to click is the **Column Format** button. This option is basically cosmetic, in so far as it only affects the appearance of the **Data Editor** without affecting the type of analysis we can do. It changes two particular settings. The first is the column width as it appears in the **Data Editor**, and the other is the alignment of the data contained in each column. We will not bother making any changes to this.

Specifying the level of measurement

The last step in setting up a column for data entry is to specify the level of measurement for the variable. In this example, sex is a nominal variable, so in the area headed **Measurement** in the **Define Variable** box we click on **Nominal**, filling the small circle (called a 'radio button') next to it.

If all these procedures are followed the dialog box will look like Figure 2.11.

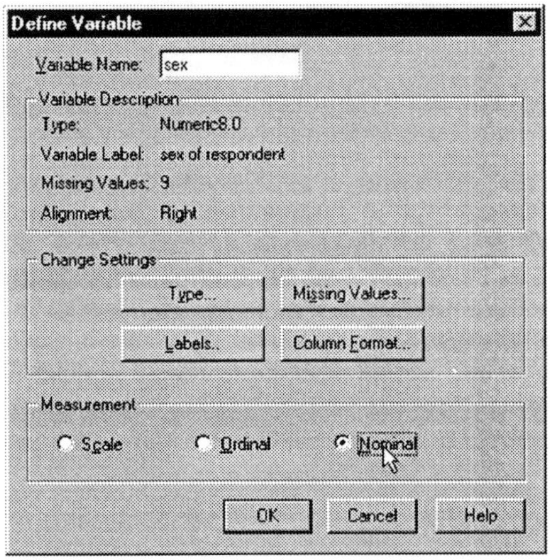

Figure 2.11 Setting the level of measurement

We can now go through the same variable definition procedure for our remaining two variables. I leave it to you to go through the steps we have just followed for the variable sex, but adapting them to record the relevant information for Health rating and Age. To help you along you should follow the coding scheme in Table 2.4. In fact, before undertaking data entry it is very helpful to write out a coding scheme such as this to clarify the definitions that you will follow. Constructing a coding scheme is especially helpful if more than one person is involved in the data entry process, so that everyone follows the same scheme.

Table 2.4 Coding scheme

Variable	Variable label (optional)	Value	Value label	Missing value	Level of measurement
sex	Sex of respondent	1 2	Female Male	9	Nominal
health	Health rating	1 2 3	Unhealthy Healthy Very healthy	9	Ordinal
age	Age in years	18, 19, 20, 21, 22	(unnecessary since the values refer to a real quantity)	99	Interval/ratio

Some specific points need to borne in mind when defining these last two variables:

- With an ordinal scale such as Health rating the values need to preserve the ranking of cases that ordinal scales are meant to reflect, *with higher numbers indicating an increase in the quantity or intensity or strength of the variable*. Thus, we will assign 1 to 'Unhealthy', 2 to 'Healthy', and 3 to 'Very healthy'.
- With interval/ratio data it is helpful to use the **Variable Label:** command to specify the units of measurement. Thus, although age is already a self-explanatory name that does not seem to warrant a variable label, it will prove helpful to type **Age in years** under the **Variable Label:** command.
- We only use value labels for nominal and ordinal data, not for interval/ratio data. In other words, for nominal and ordinal data, each point on the scale is described twice: once using words and again using numbers. With interval/ratio data, on the other hand, this dual system of coding – one in words, one in numbers – is unnecessary because the actual values quantify the variable. When defining the variable label for age we specified the unit of measurement: 'Age in years', so that we know the quantity these values refer to. Thus the number assigned to any given case will indicate the number of units; for example, '19' indicates 19 years, '20' indicates 20 years, and so on. We do not need then to provide value labels for each of these numerical codes, since their meaning is self-evident.
- Under **Measurement** you will notice that **Scale** is automatically selected. This is SPSS's (unfortunate) term for what we have been referring to as interval/ratio data. This is the appropriate level for age measured in years, so that for this variable we leave the setting as we find it.

Generating the variable definitions on SPSS

Once we have defined our variables we can ask SPSS to provide the coding scheme we have used in the variable definitions by selecting from the menu **Utilities/File Info** (Figure 2.12). This will generate information in the output window (Figure 2.13) that can be printed off for reference during the analysis.

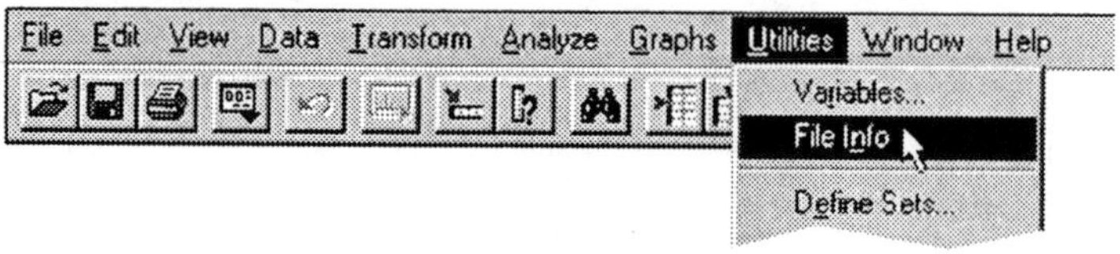

Figure 2.12 Generating file information

File Information

```
              List of variables in the working file

Name
          Position

SEX       Sex of respondent                                     1
          Measurement Level: Nominal
          Column Width: Unknown     Alignment: Right
          Print Format: F8
          Write Format: F8
          Missing Values: 9

          Value      Label
              1      female
              2      male

HEALTH    Health rating                                         2
          Measurement Level: Ordinal
          Column Width: Unknown     Alignment: Right
          Print Format: F8
          Write Format: F8
          Missing Values: 9

          Value      Label
              1      Unhealthy
              2      Healthy
              3      Very healthy

AGE       Age in years                                          3
          Measurement Level: Scale
          Column Width: Unknown     Alignment: Right
          Print Format: F8
          Write Format: F8
          Missing Values: 99

          Value      Label
              1      female
              2      male
```

Figure 2.13 SPSS **File Info** output

The numbers under `Position` on the right-edge of the page indicate the column in which the variable appears. Printing out this file information and having it close at hand can be very useful when actually analyzing data.

The SPSS Viewer window

You will notice that SPSS printed the file information we requested on a separate **Viewer** window (Figure 2.14).

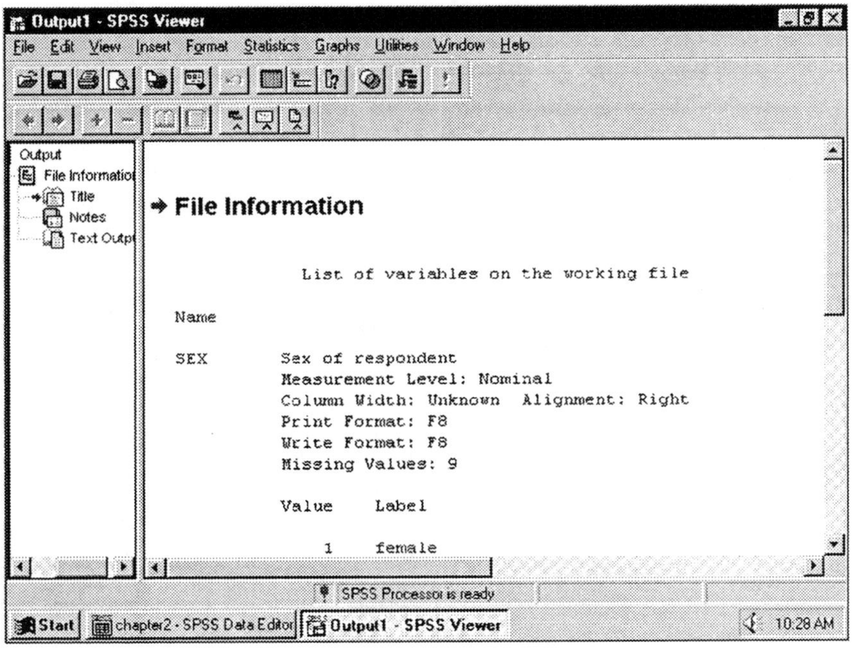

Figure 2.14 The SPSS **Viewer** window

You will become familiar with this process of requesting output from the menu, based on the data in the **Data Editor**, and viewing the output in the **Viewer** window. To switch back and forth we simply select the relevant 'page' from the **Window** option on the menu bar.

The major part of the **Viewer** window is a frame that contains the information we have requested. Often all the information cannot fit on one screen and we need to scroll up and down the frame by using the scroll bar on the right of the **Viewer** window.

SPSS does not print over existing output whenever we request new information. Instead it adds new output to the bottom of the existing output. When undertaking a lot of analysis this can create a lengthy output page. To make it easier to navigate through the output in the **Viewer** window, on the left-hand side of the output frame is a narrower frame that provides a 'Table of contents'. This is a list of the output we have generated during the course of an SPSS session. We can use this list on the left-hand side to jump to the relevant bit of output we are after simply by clicking on the brief description of that output in the list.

The other important thing to know about the **Viewer** window is that 'old' output is not automatically updated whenever we change information on the **Data Editor** window. For example, if we went back and changed the value labels for the variables we are working with, the variable information we have just generated will no longer apply, but will still be recorded on the **Viewer** window. We will need again to run the **Utilities/File Info** command to generate the information for the updated variable labels.

Data entry

Once the variables and values have been defined, the data from the survey can be entered. We will begin with the information on the sex of each student.

Table 2.5 Data entry on SPSS

SPSS command/action	Comments
1 Click on the cell next to the shaded cell **1** and below the shaded cell **sex**	This will be the active cell where any information typed will be pasted
2 Type **2**	This indicates that case no. 1 is male, according to the coding scheme specified in the **Value Labels** command
3 Press **return**	The value label **2** appears in the first cell, and the cell for case no. 2 will now be active
4 Type **2**	This indicates that case no. 2 is also male
5 Press **return**	The label **2** should appear in the second cell, and the cell for case no. 3 will now be active
6 Continue this procedure until the first 20 rows of this column contain either **1** or **2**.	

Think how time consuming this data entry process would have been if we had to type male or female into each cell, rather than just 1 or 2: this should indicate the advantage of using the **Value Labels** command when setting up the data file.

You may notice that, as you type, the data initially appear on the bar just above the data fields (Figure 2.15).

1:sex	1

Figure 2.15 The **Cell** editor

This is where information is entered until you hit the **return** key, which then places the data into the active cell. The 'address' of the active cell is indicated on the left of the **Cell** editor. This address is defined by the combination of the row number and column name that intersect at the active cell. If at any point we make a mistake, or we need to change the information in any particular cell, we simply make that cell active and type in the new information. On hitting the **return** key the new value will replace the old.

To enter the data for health rating we need to make the first cell in the second unshaded column active by pointing the cursor to it and clicking. The person who has been assigned to be case 1 is 'Very healthy'. According to our coding scheme we therefore enter **3** into this cell by typing this number and pressing the **return** key. Case 2 also is 'Very healthy', so we repeat the procedure, and so on down to case 20.

Finally we make the first cell in the third column active and begin typing in each person's age.

If all these procedures are followed the **Data Editor** will look very much like Table 2.1 at the start of this chapter (Figure 2.16).

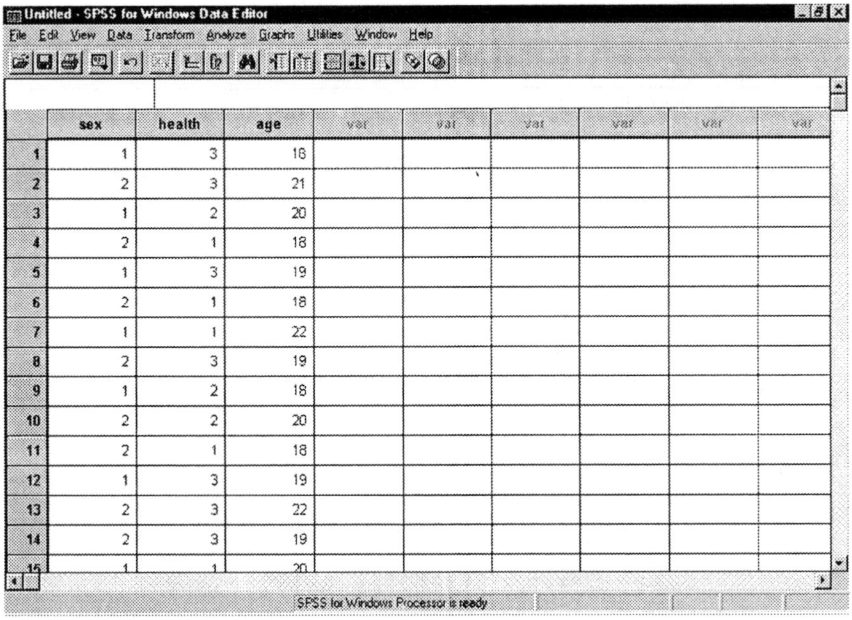

	sex	health	age	var	var	var	var	var	var
1	1	3	18						
2	2	3	21						
3	1	2	20						
4	2	1	18						
5	1	3	19						
6	2	1	18						
7	1	1	22						
8	2	3	19						
9	1	2	18						
10	2	2	20						
11	2	1	18						
12	1	3	19						
13	2	3	22						
14	2	3	19						
15	1	1	20						

Figure 2.16 The SPSS **Data Editor** after data entry

We can ask SPSS to display the value labels rather than the values on the data page by selecting **View** from the menu and scrolling down to **Value Labels** (Figure 2.17).

Figure 2.17 The **Value Labels** command

This will transform the data page so that it has value labels appearing. To bring back the values we simply repeat the procedure.

Saving a data file

The last action we need to take in setting up the data file is to save the file (Table 2.6, Figure 2.18).

Table 2.6 Save As command on SPSS

SPSS command/action	Comments
1 From the menu select **File**	
2 From the pull-down menu select **Save As**	
3 In the area next to **File name:** type **chapter2**	The limits on the length of the filename will depend on the type and version of your operating system. Here I will call the file **chapter2**
4 Click on the down arrow on the right of the area next to **Save in:**	A drop-down menu will appear with a list of areas on your computer to save the file
5 Specify a location on your computer or network to the store the file.	
6 Click on **Save**	

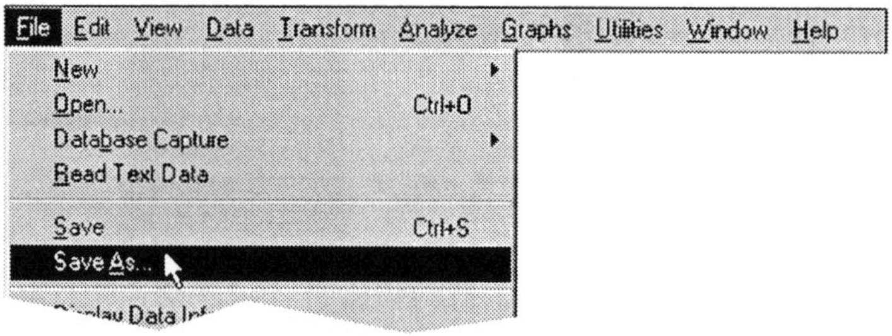

Figure 2.18(a) The **Save As** command

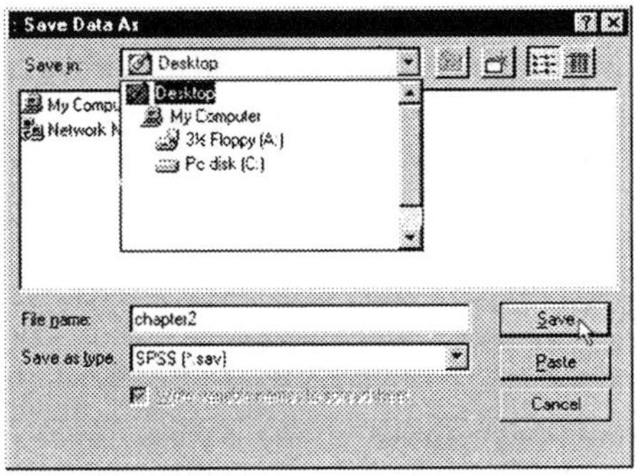

Figure 2.18(b) The **Save Data As** dialog box

We need to decide where we want to store the file. This is usually a choice between somewhere on the computer's hard drive, or on a floppy disk that we place in the disk drive. We will store the file we have just created on the computer's desktop, but wherever you choose to store data it is very important to *make a regular backup*. No storage medium is immune to errors. Get into the habit of making a copy of your data files to guard against any unforeseeable problems.

Once this has been done the name of the active data file will appear in the bar at the top of the **Data Editor** (Figure 2.19).

Figure 2.19

After using the **File/Save As** command, a file can be quickly resaved in the same location and with the same name, by using the **File/Save** command instead of **File/Save As** (Figure 2.20).

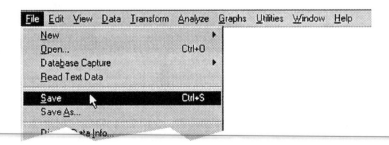

Figure 2.20 The **Save** command

In fact, you should not wait until the end of your data entry session to save the file. Mishaps can happen, often at the worst time. Losing data, after spending a considerable amount of time entering them, can be very demoralizing. We should get into the habit of saving work every 15 minutes or so.

Summary

We have worked through the process of setting up an SPSS data file. Needless to say we have only skimmed the surface with respect to the full range of options available. But it would be fair to say that the procedures we have covered here involve the majority of data entry situations. I leave it to the reader to play around with SPSS and learn the full range of features that it provides. The program comes with its own tutorial and sample data files that will guide you through the various features. The program also comes with a very useful help facility which is available from the menu bar.

Exercises

2.1   A survey gathers the data for the weekly income of 20 people, and obtains the following results:

$0, $0, $250, $300, $360, $375, $400, $400, $400, $420, $425, $450, $462, $470, $475, $502, $520, $560, $700, $1020

Create an SPSS data file and enter these data, entering all the necessary labels. Save the file with an appropriate filename.

2.2   The following data represent time, in minutes, taken for subjects in a fitness trial to complete a certain exercise task.

31	39	45	26	23	56	45	80
35	37	25	42	32	58	80	71
19	16	56	21	34	36	10	38
12	48	38	37	39	42	27	39
17	31	56	28	40	82	27	37

The heart rate for each subject is also recorded in the same sequence as their time scores:

63	89	75	80	74	65	90	85
92	84	74	79	98	91	87	76
82	90	93	77	74	89	85	91
102	69	87	96	83	72	92	88
85	68	78	73	86	85	92	90

The first 20 of these scores (reading from left to right) are taken from males and the second 20 from females.

Create an SPSS data file and enter these data, entering all the necessary labels. Save the file with an appropriate filename.

2.3   A research project has collected information from 10 people on the following variables:

Television Watched Per Night (in minutes)	Main channel watched	Satisfaction with quality of programs
170	Commercial	Very satisfied
140	Public/government	Satisfied
280	Public/government	Satisfied
65	Commercial	Very satisfied
180	Commercial	Not satisfied
60	Commercial	Not satisfied
150	Public/government	Satisfied
160	Commercial	Not satisfied
200	Public/government	Satisfied
120	Commercial	Not satisfied

Prepare an SPSS data file for these data, creating variables and variable labels, values and value labels.

3

The Tabular Description of Data

Tolstoy's *War and Peace* is a very long book. It would not be possible to do such a book justice in any way other than to read it from cover to cover. However, this takes a lot of time and concentration, each of which may not be readily available. If we want simply to get a gist of the story, a shorter summary is adequate. A summary reduces the thousands of words that make up the original book down to a few hundred, while (hopefully) retaining some of the essence of the story. Of course, the summary will leave out a great deal of detail, and the way the book is summarized for one purpose will be different from the way it is summarized for another. Nevertheless, although much is lost, something is also gained when a book so large is summarized effectively.

The same holds true with social research. Most research projects will generate a wealth of information. Presenting the results of such research in their complete form may be too overwhelming for the reader so that an 'abridged version' is needed. This chapter, and the ones that immediately follow, will focus on the procedures used to provide this abridged version, which we call **descriptive statistics**.

Descriptive statistics are the numerical, graphical, and tabular techniques for organizing, presenting, and analyzing data.

The great advantage of descriptive statistics is that they make a mass of research material easier to 'read'. By *reducing* a large set of data into a few statistics, or into some picture such as a graph or table, the results of research can be clearly and concisely presented.

Assume we conduct a survey that gathers the data for the weekly income of 20 people, and obtain the following results:

$0, $0, $250, $300, $360, $375, $400, $400, $400, $420, $425, $450, $462, $470, $475, $502, $520, $560, $700, $1020

This arrangement of the measurements of a variable is called a **distribution**. I could present this distribution of the **raw data** as the results of the research, which, strictly speaking, they are. It is not difficult to see, however, that very little information is effectively communicated this way. It is evident that the raw data, when presented in this 'naked form', do not allow us to make any meaningful sense of the variable we are investigating. It is not easy to make any sense about the way income is distributed among this group of people.

We can, alternatively, take this set of 20 numbers and put them through a statistical 'grinder', which produces fewer numbers – **statistics** – that capture the relevant information contained in the raw data. Descriptive statistics tease out some important feature of the distribution that is not evident if we just present the raw scores. One such feature we will focus on in later chapters is the notion of average. For example, we might calculate a single figure for the 'average' income and present this single number as part of the results of the research. The measure of 'average' chosen will certainly not capture all the information contained in the primary data – no description ever does that – but hopefully it will give a general notion of what the 20 cases 'look like' and allow some meaningful interpretation to be made.

Types of descriptive statistics

We have just introduced the notion of 'average' as an important feature of a distribution of scores that we might be interested in. In more technical terms this is called a **measure of central tendency**. But there are descriptive statistics that capture other important features of a distribution. There are descriptive statistics that give an indication of the spread of cases around the average: these are called **measures of dispersion**. We call both these kinds of measures **numerical techniques** for describing data since they involve the use of mathematical formulas for making calculations from the raw data. Chapter 3 will look in detail at how measures of central tendency and measures of dispersion are calculated, and the appropriate instances in which they can be used to describe a distribution.

There is also a variety of ways in which data can be represented visually to make the information easier to read. One of these methods, which will be the subject of the rest of this chapter, is the construction of **tables** that describe the distribution of cases across the range of values for a variable. Chapter 5 will go on to discuss how various **graphs** can concisely present (and sometimes misrepresent) information.

In Chapters 7 to 11 we will also come across a more complicated set of descriptive statistics that summarize the relationship between two or more variables: the extent to which a change in the value of one variable is linked (if at all) to a change in the values of another variable. These are called **bivariate descriptive statistics**. Here too we have a range of tabular, graphical, and numerical methods for describing data, such as **bivariate tables**, **scatter plots**, and **measures of association**.

Chapters 24 and 25 will go on to extend these techniques to situations where more than two variables may be related to each other. These chapters provide a rudimentary introduction to **multivariate descriptive statistics**.

All of these various ways of describing data are summarized in Table 3.1.

Table 3.1 Types of descriptive statistics

Type	Function
Tables	Provide a frequency distribution for a variable
Graphs	Provide a visual representation of the distribution of a variable
Measures of central tendency	Calculate the average score for a distribution
Measures of dispersion	Calculate the spread or variety of scores for a distribution
Measures of association	Indicate the existence, direction, and strength of a relationship between two or more variables

Given the array of descriptive statistics available, how do we decide which to use in a specific research context? The considerations involved in choosing the appropriate descriptive statistics to generate are like those involved in drawing a map. Obviously, a map on the scale of 1 to 1 is of no use (and difficult to fold). A good map will be on a different scale, and identify only those landmarks that the person wanting to cover that piece of terrain needs to know. When driving we do not want a roadmap that describes every pothole and change of grade on the road. We instead desire something that will indicate only the major curves, turn-offs, and distances that will affect our driving. Alternatively a map designed for bushwalkers will concentrate on summarizing different terrain than one designed for automobile drivers, since certain ways of describing information may be ideal for one task but useless for another.

Similarly, the amount of detail to capture through the generation of descriptive statistics cannot be decided independently of the purpose and audience for the research. Descriptive statistics are meant to *simplify* – to capture the essential features of the terrain – but in so doing they also leave out information contained in the original data. In this respect, descriptive statistics might hide as much as they reveal. Reducing a set of 20 numbers that represent the weekly income for each of 20 subjects down to one number that reflects the average obviously misrepresents cases that are very different from the average (as we shall see).

In other words, just as a map loses some information when summarizing a piece of geography, some information is lost in describing data using a small set of descriptive statistics: it is a question of whether the information lost would help to address the research problem at hand. Sometimes it might be sufficient to summarize the data in a table at other times it might be important also to calculate some measure of average and/or dispersion. In other words, *the choice of descriptive statistics used to summarize research data depends on the research question we are investigating.*

Despite this general point, some specific factors guide the choice of descriptive statistics. For example, we will see that the level of measurement is very important. The rest of this chapter, and the ones that follow, will explore the choices in more detail, and the conditions under which each is relevant.

Frequency tables

The most common way of describing data so that we can make sense of research results is through the construction of **frequency tables**.

Frequency (*f*) refers to the number of times that a particular score appears in a set of data.

We will look at a variety of tables for presenting the frequency of scores in a distribution and the conclusions they allow us to reach about a variable. The tables we will cover are:

- listed data tables
- simple frequency tables
- relative frequency tables
- cumulative frequency tables

Listed data tables

Consider Table 3.2, which presents the results of a hypothetical survey of 20 people. I am interested in three separate variables: age, sex, and health level. Age is measured by asking people their age in whole years on their last birthday (interval/ratio). Survey respondents are also asked to rate their own health levels as 'very healthy', 'healthy', or 'unhealthy' (ordinal). Finally, sex is measured by classifying cases into male or female (nominal).

Table 3.2 Results of a survey of 20 people

Case number	Sex	Health rating	Age in years
1	Male	Very healthy	18
2	Male	Very healthy	21
3	Female	Healthy	20
4	Male	Unhealthy	18
5	Female	Very healthy	19
6	Male	Unhealthy	18
7	Female	Unhealthy	22
8	Male	Very healthy	19
9	Female	Healthy	18
10	Male	Healthy	20
11	Male	Unhealthy	18
12	Female	Very healthy	19
13	Male	Very healthy	22
14	Male	Very healthy	19
15	Female	Unhealthy	20
16	Female	Healthy	18
17	Male	Unhealthy	21
18	Female	Unhealthy	19
19	Male	Healthy	18
20	Male	Very healthy	20

A table like this is called a **listed data table**, since the score that each case has for each variable is *listed separately*. Such a table has as many rows as there are cases, and as many columns as there are variables for which observations have been taken. This form of presentation is not very informative, and, where we have a large number of cases, impractical. Imagine if the survey was of 2000 people rather than 20! Space would prohibit the construction of a listed data table. Its advantage is that having the raw data for each case separately, we can calculate a variety of other descriptive statistics, which we will encounter later.

Simple frequency tables

A more informative way of describing the data is to construct a **simple frequency table** (or just **frequency table** for short). This presents the frequency distribution for a variable by tallying the number of times (*f*) each value of the variable appears in a distribution.

A **simple frequency table** reports, for each value of a variable, the number of cases that have that value.

From the raw data presented in Table 3.2, a separate frequency table can be constructed for each variable (Tables 3.3–3.5).

Table 3.3 Sex of respondents

Sex	Frequency (*f*)
Male	12
Female	8
Total	20

Table 3.4 Health rating of respondents

Health rating	Frequency (*f*)
Unhealthy	7
Healthy	5
Very healthy	8
Total	20

Table 3.5 Age of respondents

Age in years	Frequency (*f*)
18	7
19	5
20	4
21	2
22	2
Total	20

Source: Hypothetical data

These tables indicate the bare minimum structure that all frequency tables must possess:

- a clear title explaining the variable whose distribution is displayed in the table;
- clearly labeled categories that are mutually exclusive;
- the total number of cases; and
- the source of data, as in Table 3.5 (although in most of the tables that follow in this book we will not follow this rule, since they are generally constructed from hypothetical data).

Notice also that in Table 3.3 we have placed males in the first row and females in the second. This may seem arbitrary given that as this is a nominal variable, we can order the categories (the rows of the table) in any way we choose. We have placed males first because it is commonplace *with nominal variables to arrange the rows so that the category with the highest frequency (what we will learn to call the mode) is the first row, the category with the second highest frequency is the second row, and so on.* This is because the modal category is often of specific interest when analyzing the distribution of a nominal variable.

With Tables 3.4 and 3.5, however, the ordering of the categories is restricted by the fact that we are using ordinal and interval/ratio scales. For these levels of measurement, we generally start with the lowest value in the distribution and then increase down the page. Thus 18 appears first in Table 3.5, which is the lowest value for age in the distribution, and then we gradually 'ascend' the scale as we move down the table row by row.

Example

The blood types of the 20 respondents in the previous example are recorded in the following listed data table (Table 3.6).

Table 3.6 Blood type of respondents

Case number	Blood type
1	O
2	O
3	AB
4	A
5	A
6	O
7	A
8	AB
9	A
10	A
11	O
12	A
13	B
14	O
15	O
16	A
17	O
18	A
19	A
20	B

To describe these raw data in the form of a simple frequency table we construct a table with the categories of the variable down the first column and the frequency with which each appears in the distribution down the second column (labeling each column appropriately) (Table 3.7). We then tally up the number of times each category appears in the distribution; we find that there are seven people with type O, two people with type AB, nine people with type A, and two people with type B.

Table 3.7 Blood type of respondents

Blood type	Frequency
A	9
O	7
B	2
AB	2
Total	20

Since blood type is a nominal variable, we have placed the category with the highest frequency (type A), which is called the **modal** category, in the first row.

Relative frequency tables: percentages and proportions

Some extra information can be calculated as part of a frequency table, if required. This is the **relative frequency distribution**.

Relative frequencies express the number of cases within each value of a variable as a percentage or proportion of the total number of cases.

In order to generate a relative frequency table for the data in the previous example, we need to acquaint ourselves with **percentages** and **proportions**.

According to one country's census data (Australian Bureau of Statistics (1991) *Census of Population and Housing*, cat. no. 2720.0) in 1986 there were 324,167 one-parent families, out of a total of 4,158,006 families. In 1991 there were 552,412 one-parent families out of a total of 4,298,710. What does this tell us about the changing nature of families? On the basis of this information we can say that there were more single-parent families in 1991 than in 1986. Absolute numbers, though, do not tell us much about the *relative* importance of single-parent families in each year. If, however, I said that such families accounted for 7.8 percent of all family types in 1986 and 12.85 percent in 1991, the pattern is immediately obvious: single-parent families have become a *relatively* larger group.

By calculating these percentages we have in effect compensated for the different total number of families present in each year.

Percentages are statistics that standardize the total number of cases to a base value of 100.

The formula for calculating a percentage is:

$$\% = \frac{f}{n} \times 100$$

where:
f is the frequency or number of cases in a category
n is the total number of cases in all categories.

We can see where the percentage figures came from in the example by putting ('substituting') the raw numbers into this formula:

$$1986: \quad \frac{324,167}{4,158,006} \times 100 = 7.8\%$$

$$1991: \quad \frac{552,412}{4,298,710} \times 100 = 12.85\%$$

It should be fairly clear that if I calculate the percentages for each family type in a given year and summed them, the total will be 100 percent. For example, if I add the percentage of single-parent families to the percentage of non-single-parent families in 1991, the total will be 100 percent. Thus knowing that 12.85 percent of all families in 1991 were headed by a single parent allows me to calculate quickly the percentage of families *not* headed by a single parent:

$$100 - 12.85 = 87.15\%$$

Proportions are close cousins of percentages. A proportion (p) does exactly the same job as a percentage, except that it uses a base of 1 rather than 100. In fact, it is calculated in exactly the same way as a percentage, except for the fact that we do not multiply by 100:

$$p = \frac{f}{n}$$

The result is that we get a number expressed as a decimal. In the example above the results expressed as proportions are:

$$1986: \quad \frac{324,167}{4,158,006} = 0.078$$

$$1991: \quad \frac{552,412}{4,298,710} = 0.1285$$

Generally, percentages are easier to work with – for some reason people are more comfortable with whole numbers than with decimals. But in later chapters we will use proportions extensively, so it is important to learn the simple relationship between proportions and the more familiar percentages.

To convert a proportion into its corresponding percentage value, move the decimal point two places to the right (this is the same as multiplying by 100).

To convert a percentage into its corresponding proportion, move the decimal point two places to the left (this is the same as dividing by 100).

This may all seem pretty straightforward. There are some words of caution that need to be borne in minds, though, when working with proportions and percentages, or when encountering them in other people's work. The first thing to look for when confronted with a percentage or proportion is the raw total from which they are calculated. This is because percentages and proportions are sometimes used to conceal dramatic differences in absolute size. An increase in unemployment rates from 10 percent to 10.5 percent does not seem dramatic in statistical terms. But if this 0.5 percent represents 35,000 people it is, in socioeconomic terms, a large increase.

Conversely, a large change in percentage figures may be trivial when working with small absolute numbers. The number of people attending a pro-capital-punishment meeting may be 150 percent greater than the number that attended the last meeting, but if this is actually due to five people attending the recent meeting rather than the two who attended the previous one, it is hardly a dramatic rise. When working with small absolute numbers, small additions to either the total or the categories that make up the total will greatly affect the percentage figure calculated.

Now that we have familiarized ourselves with percentages and proportions we can use them to construct **relative frequency tables** for the data we introduced earlier. We can add to the table for each variable a column that expresses the percentage (or proportion) of cases that fall in each category. Tables 3.8 and 3.9 show the calculations involved in producing relative frequencies. Of course, when actually reporting results these calculations are not included, as in Table 3.10.

Table 3.8 Sex of respondents

Sex	Frequency	Percentage (%)
Female	8	$\frac{8}{20} \times 100 = 40$
Male	12	$\frac{12}{20} \times 100 = 60$
Total	20	100

Table 3.9 Health rating of respondents

Health rating	Frequency	Percentage (%)
Unhealthy	7	$\frac{7}{20} \times 100 = 35$
Healthy	5	$\frac{5}{20} \times 100 = 25$
Very healthy	8	$\frac{8}{20} \times 100 = 40$
Total	20	100

Table 3.10 Age of respondents

Age in years	Frequency	Percentage (%)
18	7	35
19	5	25
20	4	20
21	2	10
22	2	10
Total	20	100

Notice that the column of percentages must add up to 100 percent, since all cases must fall into one classification or another. Sometimes tables do not strictly follow this rule when numbers have been 'rounded off'. For example, exact percentages to 1 decimal place may be 22.3%, 38.4%, and 39.3%. This may affect the readability of the table so the numbers are rounded off to the nearest whole number: 22%, 38%, 39%. These rounded numbers add up to only 99%. Where this occurs a footnote should be added to the table which states 'May not sum to 100 due to rounding', or words to that affect.

Cumulative frequency tables

With ordinal and interval/ratio data one further extension to the simple frequency table can be made. This is the addition of columns providing **cumulative frequencies** and **cumulative relative frequencies**. Since ordinal and interval/ratio data allow us to rank-order cases from lowest to highest, it is sometimes interesting to know the number, and/or percentage, of cases that fall above or below a certain point on the scale.

A **cumulative frequency table** shows, for each value in a distribution, the number of cases up to and including that value.

A **cumulative relative frequency table** shows, for each value in a distribution, the percentage or proportion of the total number of cases up to and including that value.

Sometimes all the absolute and relative frequencies and cumulative frequencies for a variable can be combined in the one table, as in Table 3.11 and Table 3.12.

Table 3.11 Health rating of respondents

Health rating	Frequency	Cumulative frequency	Percentage (%)	Cumulative percentage (%)
Unhealthy	7	7	35	$\frac{7}{20} \times 100 = 35$
Healthy	5	7+5 = 12	25	$\frac{7 + 5}{20} \times 100 = 60$
Very healthy	8	7+5+8 = 20	40	$\frac{7 + 5 + 8}{20} \times 100 = 100$
Total	20		100	

Table 3.12 Age (in years) of respondents

Age	Frequency	Cumulative frequency	Percentage (%)	Cumulative percentage (%)
18	7	7	35	35
19	5	12	25	60
20	4	16	20	80
21	2	18	10	90
22	2	20	10	100
Total	20		100	

With the distributions summarized in this way, I can now answer specific research questions that might be of interest. If I was interested in how many respondents are either 18 or 19 years of age I simply look at the sum of cases in the first two rows of Table 3.12. The cumulative frequency at this point is 12, which is 60% of all cases. Similarly, if I am interested in how many cases are over 19 years of age, I can see that since 60% are 19 or below, there must be 40% of cases (100 − 60 = 40%) above this age.

Class intervals

One additional point needs to be made about working with interval/ratio data, as we have been with the age distribution of respondents in our example. With interval/ratio data we often use **class intervals** rather than individual values to construct a frequency distribution.

A **class interval** groups together a range of values on a distribution for presentation and analysis.

The point of using class intervals is to collapse data into a few easy-to-work-with categories. But this increase in 'readability' comes at the cost of information, and therefore should not be undertaken if the data already come in a few, easily presented, individual values. In the example we have been working with, measuring age in whole years already provides a 'workable' number of values to organize the data into. It would not be useful to group these individual years into say 5 year class intervals, since this will only hide variation in the data that would otherwise help us answer our research question. *We only use class intervals if the range of values is so large that it makes presentation and analysis difficult.*

We will use the data we introduced above for the income of 20 people to illustrate the usefulness of class intervals, and the general rules that apply to the construction of class intervals. These data are represented in listed format in Table 3.13.

Table 3.13 Weekly income of 20 survey respondents: listed data

Case number	Income
1	$0
2	$0
3	$250
4	$300
5	$360
6	$375
7	$400
8	$400
9	$400
10	$420
11	$425
12	$450
13	$462
14	$470
15	$475
16	$502
17	$520
18	$560
19	$700
20	$1020

We can see that, even where we have rank-ordered the cases from lowest to highest, a listed data table is not a useful summary of the data: a table with 20 rows of individual numbers does not get us far.

We can instead produce a simple frequency table by indicating the total number of cases that have each value of the variable contained in the data (Table 3.14). This simple frequency table has condensed the data slightly, but overall it has not greatly simplified matters for us. We have so many individual values appearing in the distribution that when we use each one separately to group the cases, we still end up with a table with an impractical number of rows. To describe the data in a more meaningful way, we instead *cluster together ranges of values for people's income and indicate the total number of people that fall within each range* (Table 3.15).

Table 3.14 Weekly income of 20 survey respondents: simple frequency table

Weekly income	Frequency
$0	2
$250	1
$300	1
$360	1
$375	1
$400	3
$420	1
$425	1
$450	1
$462	1
$470	1
$475	1
$502	1
$520	1
$560	1
$700	1
$1020	1
Total	20

Table 3.15 Weekly income of 20 survey respondents: simple frequency table with class intervals

Weekly income	Frequency
$0–99	2
$100–199	0
$200–299	1
$300–399	3
$400–499	9
$500–599	3
$600 or more	2
Total	20

We can see that the 'compacted' version of the data distribution in Table 3.15 is easily interpreted. We can immediately observe the high frequency of cases within the $400–499 class interval. We can also see the spread of scores across the intervals.

Notice that in Table 3.15 we have not used the individual values that appear in the distribution to label each row. We have instead used **stated class limits**.

Stated class limits are the upper and lower bounds of a class interval that determine its **width**.

Generally, class intervals should have the same width, although at the lower and upper end of the data range we often have open-ended class intervals, such as the '$600 and more' interval in Table 3.15. The actual width of class intervals depends on the particular situation, especially the amount of information required. The wider the class intervals the easier it is to 'read' a distribution, but less information is communicated.

For example, if we used class intervals that are $200 wide (i.e. $0–199, $200–399, etc.) a great deal of information will be lost. Cases that are very different in terms of the variable of interest, such as the person who earned $400 and the person who received $560 in weekly income, will now be considered to be the same. Generally, when collecting values into class intervals we lose information about the variation contained in the data, and the wider the interval the greater the loss of information.

Conversely, if we have a very narrow width for the class intervals in a table we will be able to detect more variation in the data, but we will not simplify the data in a manageable and readable way. For example, if we used class intervals with a width of $50 for our income data (i.e. $0–49, $50–99, etc.) the number of rows in the table will not reduce down into the readable form we are after.

When constructing class intervals we need to ensure that the intervals are mutually exclusive. Thus in choosing $100 as the width of the class intervals in Table 3.13 the class intervals are $0–99, $100–199, $200–299, etc. Notice that the upper stated limit of each interval does not 'touch' the lower stated limit of the next interval: there appears to be a gap between 99 and 100, 199 and 200, 299 and 300, and so on. Won't some cases fall down this gap and not be included in any interval? *Provided that the unit with which the variable is measured is the same as that used to construct the class intervals, all cases will fall into one class or another.* We will be able to account for every case, in this example, because I have chosen to measure income in terms of dollars. Someone is in either the $0–99 group or the $100–199 group. A person cannot fall in between because of the units in which income is measured: no one can have an income of $99.63, simply because we have not measured income at that level of precision. If income is measured in a more precise unit, such as dollars and cents, the class intervals will have to be expressed in dollars *and cents* as well.

Another concept that will be used when working with class intervals in later chapters is the **mid-point (*m*)** of the interval. This is simply the sum of the lower and upper limits divided by 2:

$$\text{mid - point} = \frac{\text{lower limit} + \text{upper limit}}{2}$$

For example, the mid-point for the class interval $0–99 will be the sum of $0 and $99 divided by two:

$$m = \frac{0 + 99}{2}$$

$$= \$49.50$$

Thus the frequency table for the data in Table 3.15, with stated limits and mid-points, is as shown in Table 3.16.

Table 3.16 Weekly income of 20 survey respondents

Weekly income	Mid-point	Frequency
$0–99	$49.50	2
$100–199	$149.50	0
$200–299	$249.50	1
$300–399	$349.50	3
$400–499	$449.50	9
$500–599	$549.50	3
$600 or more	$649.50	2
Total		20

The reason for laboring through this process of calculating limits and mid-points for tables using class intervals may not be immediately obvious. However, it does affect the types of calculations we might want to generate on the basis of such tables, as we will see when we come to Chapter 4. So some familiarity with their construction now will help us down the track later.

Example

A drug is administered to a sample of 50 patients and the time elapsed (in seconds) before the drug has an effect is recorded for each patient. These times are:

78, 37, 99, 66, 90, 79, 80, 89, 68, 57, 71, 78, 53, 81, 77, 58, 93, 79, 98, 76, 60, 77, 49, 92, 83, 80, 74, 69, 90, 62, 84, 74, 73, 48, 75, 98, 32, 75, 84, 87, 65, 59, 63, 86, 95, 55, 70, 62, 85, 72

To construct class intervals for these data I have to define my intervals in the same unit of measurement as the raw data, which in this case is whole seconds. I also have to select interval widths that are neither too wide (which will conceal variation we are interested in) nor too small (which will not adequately condense the data into manageable groupings). This often takes a little trial and error; here I will choose 10 second intervals, which, as you will hopefully agree after inspecting Table 3.17, provide an appropriate summary of the data.

Table 3.17 Drug response times

Time intervals (seconds)	Frequency
30–39	2
40–49	2
50–59	5
60–69	8
70–79	15
80–89	10
90–99	8
Total	50

The concentration of scores within a narrow range of times is now clearly evident, as well as the spread of scores around this range.

Deciles

Another common way of grouping interval/ratio data into manageable and readable clusters is with the construction of **deciles**. Instead of using the values of the variable to group cases, deciles use particular **percentages of cases** to construct a table around. The set of cases is rank-ordered, and 'split' into 10 groups of equal size. This is commonly used to analyze data on the distribution of income. For example, we could order all families in a certain population in terms of income, from the poorest to the richest, and then split them into 10 equally sized groups. The first decile comprises the 10 percent of families that are the poorest, the second decile comprises the next 10 percent of families, right through to the tenth decile, which comprises the richest 10 percent of families. By looking at the percentage of total income held by each decile, we can get a sense of income distribution and the nature of changes that have occurred.

Table 3.18 Gross income by decile, Australia 1989

Decile	Share of gross income, 1989, %
Lowest	1.7
Second	2.8
Third	3.9
Fourth	5.2
Fifth	6.8
Sixth	8.6
Seventh	10.7
Eighth	13.4
Ninth	17.3
Highest	29.4

It is clear that the distribution of gross income is not equally spread across households (according to this measure).

Frequency tables using SPSS

In Chapter 2 we set up an SPSS data file with the data we have used to construct the frequency tables above. We will now use this file to generate the same tables with the aid of SPSS. Opening a data file that we have created in previous work sessions is much like saving the file. From the menu we select **File/Open** and then select the appropriate directory and filename in the dialog box (Figure 3.1). For example, the files that will be used in later chapters are all located on the CD that comes with this book. They can be selected by highlighting the appropriate file, or typing its name, once the CD has been selected as the location where the files reside.

Ideally, if you followed the procedures in the previous chapter you will have saved the file we are using below somewhere on your computer or network (I have stored it on my Desktop) with the filename **chapter2.sav**. SPSS adds the filename extension **.sav** to the end of a file so that it recognizes it as a data file, even though we did not specifically include it in the filename when we originally typed it (Figure 3.2).

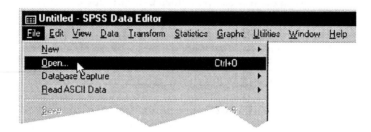

Figure 3.1 The **File/Open** command

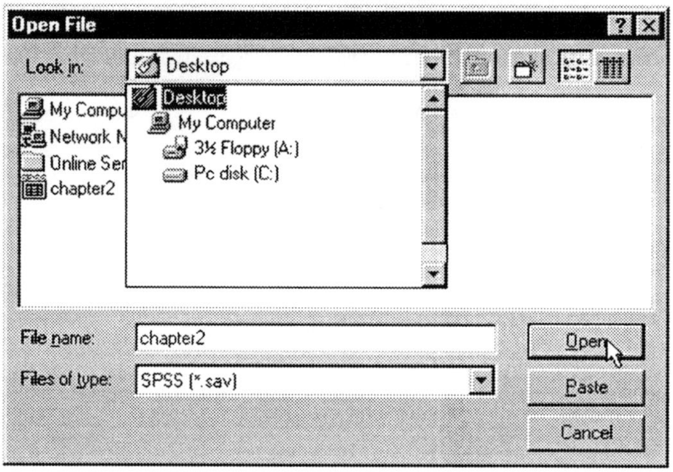

![Open File dialog box]

Figure 3.2 The **Open File** dialog box

It is important to note that, unlike most other computer programs you may be familiar with, SPSS will not allow more than one data file to be open at any one time. Thus when you choose to open another file, the currently active file will be closed. SPSS will prompt you to save your data before it closes a file, but this limitation should be borne in mind, especially when copying data to and from files.

Using the file we created in Chapter 2, we can generate frequency tables similar to those above (Table 3.19, Figure 3.3). Notice the appearance of the dialog box in Figure 3.3. It has some features in common with most of the dialog boxes we will encounter in later chapters so we will take a moment to note these. On the left of the box is an area with a list of the variables created in the **Data Editor**. This is called the **source variable list** which provides the

list of variables we can analyze using the particular command we have chosen
from the menu (in this instance the **Analyze/Descriptive Statistics/
Frequencies** command). On the right is another area which is initially blank,
but which eventually contains the variable(s) we have actually chosen to
analyze. This is called the **target variable list**. Variables can be moved back
and forth from one list to the other, as we have done here, by clicking on them
and then clicking on the ▶ button between the two lists.

Table 3.19 The **Frequencies** command on SPSS (file: **Ch03.sav**)

SPSS command/action	Comments
1 From the menu select **A̲nalyze/D̲escriptive Statistics/F̲requencies**	This will bring up a dialog box headed **Frequencies**. This will contain an area with a list of the variables for which data have been entered
2 Select the variable(s) to generate a frequency table for by clicking on their name(s)	A number of frequency tables can be generated simultaneously by pasting more than one variable into the **Variable(s):** box. Here we want all three variables, so we will paste all of them
3 Click on ▶	This will paste the selected variable(s) into the area below **Variable(s):**, which is the list of variables for which a frequency table will be generated
4 Click on **OK**	

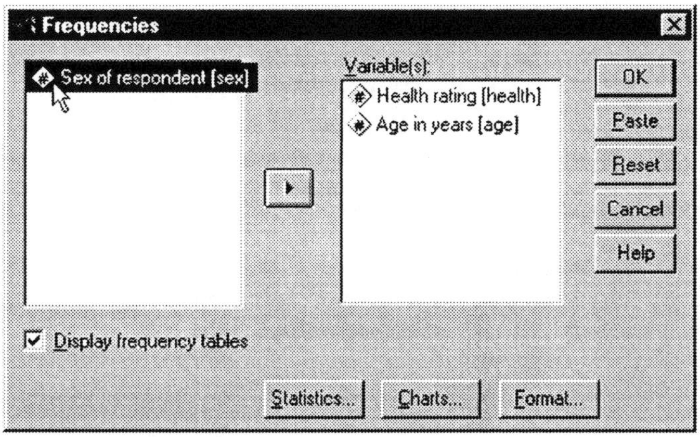

Figure 3.3 The **Frequencies** dialog box

Many of the dialog boxes we will encounter have **default** settings. These are
options that are preselected by SPSS; they will automatically be used when the
OK button is clicked. For example, in the **Frequencies** dialog box you will
notice a tick mark, ✓, in the tick-box next to **D̲isplay frequency tables**. This
indicates that a frequency table will automatically be generated for each of the
variables pasted into the target variable list. SPSS does not have to be

specifically asked to generate the tables. If we did not want a frequency table to be generated for each of the target variables, we would click on this box to remove the tick mark. If at any point you want to return to the default setting for any given dialog box so you can begin a procedure from scratch, click the **Reset** button on the right-hand side of the box.

The set of instructions shown in Table 3.19 will produce the minimum information available under the **Analyze/Descriptive Statistics/Frequencies** command: a table for each variable with raw, relative and cumulative frequencies (basically a computer-generated version of the tables above). In addition the output also contains at the top a summary **Statistics** table which indicates the total number of cases tabulated for each variable (Figure 3.4).

Frequencies

Statistics

		Age in years	Health rating	Sex of respondent
N	Valid	20	20	20
	Missing	0	0	0

Frequency Table

Age in years

		Frequency	Percent	Valid Percent	Cumulative Percent
Valid	18	7	35.0	35.0	35.0
	19	5	25.0	25.0	60.0
	20	4	20.0	20.0	80.0
	21	2	10.0	10.0	90.0
	22	2	10.0	10.0	100.0
	Total	20	100.0	100.0	

Health rating

		Frequency	Percent	Valid Percent	Cumulative Percent
Valid	Unhealthy	7	35.0	35.0	35.0
	Healthy	5	25.0	25.0	60.0
	Very healthy	8	40.0	40.0	100.0
	Total	20	100.0	100.0	

Sex of respondent

		Frequency	Percent	Valid Percent	Cumulative Percent
Valid	female	8	40.0	40.0	40.0
	male	12	60.0	60.0	100.0
	Total	20	100.0	100.0	

Figure 3.4 SPSS **Frequencies** output

We can immediately compare these tables with the ones we generated 'by hand' above to confirm that all the figures are the same. The usefulness of the value labels that we specified in Chapter 2 should now be obvious. If we had not specified that 1=female and 2=male, for example, then the last table would not have these value labels printed along the left. Thus we might be left scratching our heads or hunting back through our notes to remember which category the value 1 represented and which category 2 represented. Here we have all the information printed with the output.

Valid cases and missing values

If you look closely at each table in the SPSS output you will see that there are two identical columns, one headed **Percent** and another headed **Valid Percent**. This seems a little redundant; why print two identical columns of numbers?

The reason for printing these two columns in the frequency tables arises because sometimes the data include cases for which a variable has not been adequately measured. These are called, as we discussed in the previous chapter, **missing cases**, and the presence of missing cases will cause the values in the **Percent** and **Valid Percent** columns to diverge. The number of valid cases is equal to the total number of cases minus the number missing:

$$\text{valid cases} = \text{total cases} - \text{missing cases}$$

For example, suppose that in filling out the questionnaire, 2 of the 20 respondents neglected to fill in the question regarding their sex, and it is not feasible to go back and find out who they are and complete the information. Suppose that these 2 people are actually males, but the researcher cannot know this from the returned questionnaires. As far as the researcher is concerned, these are 2 missing cases out of the total of 20, leaving 18 'useable' responses (valid cases) for sex: 8 females and now only 10 males. The frequency table for this variable, *using only the valid cases*, will then be as shown in Table 3.20.

Table 3.20 Sex of respondents

Sex	Frequency (all cases)	Percentage (all cases)	Frequency (valid cases)	Valid percentage
Female	8	$\frac{8}{20} \times 100 = 40\%$	8	$\frac{8}{18} \times 100 = 44.4\%$
Male	10	$\frac{10}{20} \times 100 = 50\%$	10	$\frac{10}{18} \times 100 = 56.6\%$
Missing	2	$\frac{2}{20} \times 100 = 10\%$		
Total	20		18	100%

To do this in SPSS, we enter either the system missing value (a space which appears as a period in the relevant cell) or the user-defined missing value, which we defined in the previous chapter as 9 for this variable.

Assume that case numbers 19 and 20 are the two males who did not specify their sex. If 9 is now typed into the cells for these two males, rather than 2, the **Analyze/Descriptive Statistics/Frequencies** command for sex will produce the output in Figure 3.5.

Frequencies

Statistics

Sex of respondent

N	Valid	18
	Missing	2

Sex of respondent

		Frequency	Percent	Valid Percent	Cumulative Percent
Valid	female	8	40.0	44.4	44.4
	male	10	50.0	55.6	100.0
	Total	18	90.0	100.0	
Missing	9	2	10.0		
Total		20	100.0		

Figure 3.5 SPSS **Frequencies** output

In the summary **Statistics** table SPSS indicates that there are **18 Valid cases** with **2 Missing**. The actual frequency table is then printed. This breaks down the distribution according to the value labels and the missing value. Here the Valid Percent differs from the Percent column and it is the former we pay attention to since this excludes the missing data. The Cumulative Percent is then calculated on the basis of the 18 valid cases. (Before proceeding you may wish to go back to your **Data Editor** window and type 2 into the cells under sex for case numbers 19 and 20, so that we do not include the missing values we have just typed in later analyses.)

The SPSS Recode command

We will now introduce a very important SPSS command. This is the **Transform/Recode** command. *This command is used to create new values and value labels based on existing variable definitions.* This is particularly useful when we want to collapse the original values of a variable down into a smaller number of values. For example, assume that in the course of analyzing our data in Table 3.2 we decide that we are only interested in whether respondents rated themselves to be 'unhealthy' or 'not unhealthy': we are no longer interested in the finer distinction between healthy and very healthy. This new classification and its relationship to the original coding is represented in Figure 3.6.

Old values: *New values*:

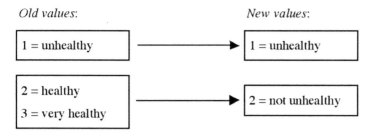

Figure 3.6 Recoding scheme

In other words, although we originally separated people according to the finer ordinal scale, we now want to regroup respondents and place healthy and very healthy respondents into the same basket. To generate a frequency table on SPSS with this new grouping of cases, we need to recode the data in a manner analogous to Figure 3.6 (Table 3.21, Figure 3.8). Although this procedure seems to involve a large number of steps, we are actually doing something very simple: 'repackaging' the values we originally entered into the data file. It helps to write out a recoding scheme by hand in a manner similar to Figure 3.6 before doing it on SPSS to keep the overall picture in mind.

When the recoding procedure in Table 3.21 is followed a fourth column of data will appear in the **Data Editor** window (Figure 3.9) containing the new variable we have created. (It will help, before employing this new variable in any further analysis, to use the procedures detailed in the previous chapter to give this new variable value labels, with 1=Unhealthy and 2=Not unhealthy.)

If we generate a frequency table on SPSS for this recoded variable, we will get the output in the **Viewer** window displayed in Figure 3.7.

Frequencies

Statistics

Recoded health rating

N	Valid	20
	Missing	0

Recoded health rating

		Frequency	Percent	Valid Percent	Cumulative Percent
Valid	Unhealthy	7	35.0	35.0	35.0
	Not unhealthy	13	65.0	65.0	100.0
	Total	20	100.0	100.0	

Figure 3.7 SPSS frequency table with recoded data

You can see that the five people who were originally coded as healthy and the eight people originally coded as very healthy are now all recoded together into the new 'not unhealthy' category, with a frequency of 13.

Table 3.21 The <u>R</u>ecode command using SPSS

SPSS command/action	Comments
1 Select <u>T</u>ransform/<u>R</u>ecode/Into <u>D</u>ifferent Variables	This brings up the **Recode into Different Variables** dialog box
2 Click on **Health rating**	This selects the variable whose existing values will be used as the basis for the new categories
3 Click on ▶	This pastes the selected variable name into the area headed **Numeric Variable**
4 Click in the box headed <u>N</u>ame:	This allows you to give the recoded variable a new variable name
5 Type **health2**	As with any variable name, you can use up to 8 letters for the new variable name. I have selected **health2** since it is as reasonable as any other option
6 Click on <u>C</u>hange	This pastes the new variable name into the area headed **Numeric <u>V</u>ariable**
7 Click on <u>O</u>ld and New Values	This brings up the **Old and New Values** dialog box
8 Type **1**	
9 Click on the circle next to **Co<u>p</u>y old value(s)**	
10 Click on **Add**	This instructs SPSS to use the old value **1** (Unhealthy) as the new value **1**
11 Click on the circle next to **Ra<u>n</u>ge** and type **2**	
12 Strike the **tab** key and type **3**	
13 Click on the small circle next to **Va<u>l</u>ue:** and Type **2**	
14 Click on <u>A</u>dd	This instructs SPSS to group together the old values 2 and 3 into a single value 2 for the new variable
15 Click on **Continue**	
16 Click on **OK**	

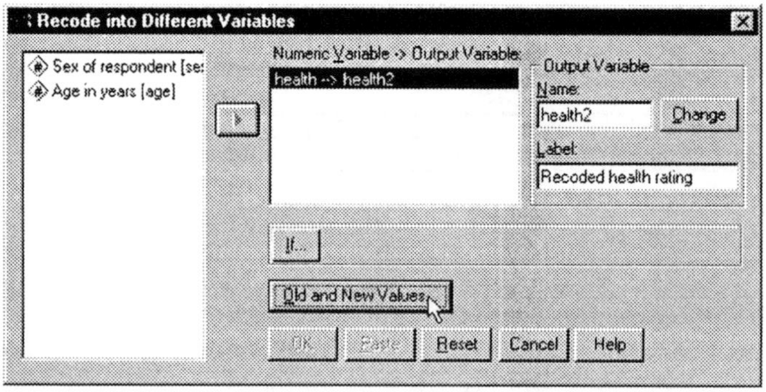

Figure 3.8(a) The **Recode into Different Variables** dialog box

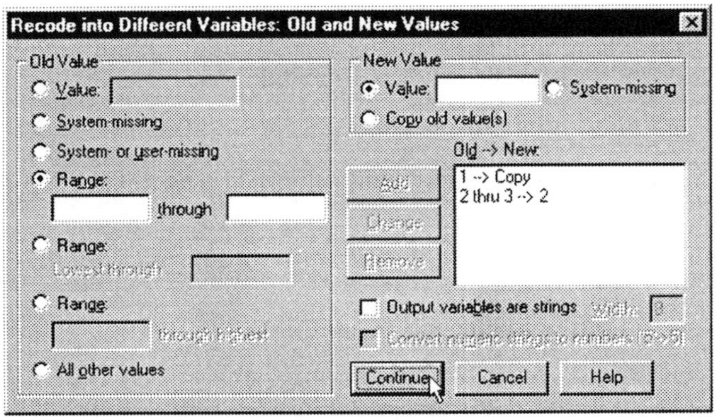

Figure 3.8(b) The **Old and New Values** dialog box

	sex	health	age	health2
1	2	3	18	2.00
2	2	3	21	2.00
3	1	2	20	2.00
4	2	1	18	1.00
5	1	3	19	2.00
6	2	1	18	1.00
7	1	1	22	1.00
8	2	3	19	2.00
9	1	2	18	2.00
10	2	2	20	2.00

Figure 3.9

Exercises

3.1 How does a proportion differ from a percentage?

3.2 Why will a proportion always be smaller than its equivalent percentage value?

3.3 Convert the following proportions into percentages:
(a) 0.01
(b) 0.13
(c) 1.24
(d) 0.0045

3.4 Convert the following percentages into proportions:

(a) 12%
(b) 13.4%
(c) 167%
(d) 3.5%

3.5   The following data represent time, in minutes, taken for subjects in a fitness trial to complete a certain exercise task.

31	39	45	26	23	56	45	80
35	37	25	42	32	58	80	71
19	16	56	21	34	36	10	38
12	48	38	37	39	42	27	39
17	31	56	28	40	82	27	37

The heart rate for each subject is also recorded in the same sequence as their time scores:

63	89	75	80	74	65	90	85
92	84	74	79	98	91	87	76
82	90	93	77	74	89	85	91
102	69	87	96	83	72	92	88
85	68	78	73	86	85	92	90

(a) Using the class intervals 1–9, 10–19, 20–29, and so on, organize the data for each of these variables into frequency tables, displaying both raw and cumulative frequencies and percentages. What are the mid-points of these class intervals?

(b) Open the file you created as part of Exercise 2.2 to store these data. Using the **R**ecode command, use SPSS to generate a frequency table with these class intervals.

3.6   The following data indicate attendance at selected cultural venues across eight regions:

Region	People attending public libraries	People attending popular music concerts
A	1409	1166
B	1142	870
C	713	604
D	423	280
E	497	332
F	130	99
G	90	32
H	38	74
Total	4442	3456

For each of these variables add columns and calculate the relative frequencies for each region.

3.7 From a recent newspaper or magazine find examples of the use of the techniques outlined in this chapter. Do these examples follow the rules of description outlined here?

3.8 In Exercise 2.1 you created an SPSS file to store the data for the example we used in the text for the weekly income of 20 survey respondents:

$0, $0, $250, $300, $360, $375, $400, $400, $400, $420, $425, $450, $462, $470, $475, $502, $520, $560, $700, $1020

(a) Open this file and generate a simple frequency table that corresponds to Table 3.14.
(b) Using the class intervals we employed in the text above, generate a frequency table that corresponds to Table 3.15.

3.9 In Exercise 2.3 you created an SPSS file for the following data:

Television watched per night (in minutes)	Main channel watched	Satisfaction with quality of programs
170	Commercial	Very satisfied
140	Public/government	Satisfied
280	Public/government	Satisfied
65	Commercial	Very satisfied
180	Commercial	Not satisfied
60	Commercial	Not satisfied
150	Public/government	Satisfied
160	Commercial	Not satisfied
200	Public/government	Satisfied
120	Commercial	Not satisfied

(a) Generate a frequency table for each of these variables.
(b) Recode minutes of TV watched into categories of less than 100 minutes, and 100 minutes or more. Generate a frequency table for this new variable. What is its level of measurement?

3.10 Using the **Employee data** file that comes with the SPSS program (usually located in the **C:\Program Files\SPSS** directory), and also on the CD that comes with this book, generate frequency tables that will allow you to determine:
(a) The number of employees that are from minority groups.
(b) The percentage of employees that are from a minority group.
(c) The percentage of employees with 15 years of education or less.
(d) The percentage of employees whose starting salary was greater than $17,100.

3.11 Using the **Employee data** file that comes with the SPSS program collapse the beginning salary data into appropriate class intervals using the **Recode** command. Justify your choice of interval width, and determine the class mid-points.

4

The Numerical Description of Data: Measures of Central Tendency and Measures of Dispersion

The previous chapter looked at the description of data in tabular form. Tables as a form of describing data give some sense of the overall distribution of cases. A quick glance at a frequency table will identify the value or values which seem to be the 'center' of the distribution, and also the spread of cases around that central point. However, we sometimes want to capture these characteristics of the data in more precise terms: what does the 'typical' or 'average' case look like, and how much variety or similarity is there among the cases?

Measures of central tendency

Descriptive statistics that represent the 'average' or 'typical' score are called measures of central tendency.

Measures of central tendency indicate the typical or average value for a distribution.

There are three common measures of central tendency: mode, median, and mean. Each of these embody a different notion of average, and, as Table 4.1 indicates, the choice of measures that can be calculated on any given set of data is restricted by the level at which a variable is measured.

Table 4.1 Measures of central tendency

Level of measurement	Measure of central tendency
Nominal	Mode
Ordinal	Mode, Median
Interval/ratio	Mode, Median, Mean

In this table we can see one of the basic rules of statistics: *techniques that can be applied to a particular level of measurement can also be applied to a higher level*. For example, the measure of central tendency that can be calculated for nominal data (mode) can also be calculated for ordinal and interval/ratio data. Similarly, the measures that can be calculated for ordinal data can also be calculated for interval/ratio. This should be borne in mind as you the read the rest of the book; when I refer to nominal-level statistical techniques I really mean 'nominal or above', and ordinal data techniques really refers to 'ordinal or above'. The converse, however, is not true: measures that can be calculated for a particular level of measurement cannot always be calculated for lower levels. The mean, for example, can only be calculated for the highest level of measurement (interval/ratio).

To see how each of these measures of central tendency is calculated we will use the tables from Chapter 2 containing the hypothetical survey results shown in Tables 4.2, 4.3, and 4.4.

Table 4.2 Sex of respondents

Sex	Frequency
Male	12
Female	8
Total	20

Table 4.3 Health rating of respondents

Health rating	Frequency
Unhealthy	7
Healthy	5
Very healthy	8
Total	20

Table 4.4 Age of respondents

Age in years	Frequency
18	7
19	5
20	4
21	2
22	2
Total	20

The mode

We will start with the **mode** (M_o), which is the simplest measure of central tendency, and which can be calculated for all levels of measurement.

The **mode** is the value in a distribution with the highest frequency.

The mode is the only measure of central tendency that can be calculated for nominal data, and even with ordinal and interval/ratio data its great advantage over other choices is that it is very easy to calculate. A simple inspection of a frequency table is enough to determine the modal value or category.

For example, the category for sex that has the highest frequency in Table 4.2 is male, with 12 responses; that is, the mode (M_o) = male. For health rating in Table 4.3 the mode is 'very healthy', and for Table 4.3 the mode is 18 years of age.

Although it is exceptionally easy to determine the mode, occasionally people make the mistake of specifying as the mode the frequency of the value that occurs the most, rather than the actual value. That is, 12 might be reported as the mode for Table 4.2 since this is the highest frequency. This is incorrect – the important point to remember is that the mode is the *value* of the variable that occurs most frequently, not the number of times that value appears in the distribution.

The mode has one feature that does not apply to the median or mean as measures of central tendency: there can be more than one mode for the same distribution. For example, assume we have the distribution for age shown in Table 4.5.

Table 4.5 Age of respondents

Age in years	Frequency
18	7
19	5
20	4
21	2
22	7
Total	25

We can see that two categories have the highest frequency: 18 years and 22 years. This is called a bimodal distribution. The median or the mean, on the other hand, will always produce only a single number as the average, regardless of the distribution.

The mode has one major limitation when it is used to describe listed data for interval/ratio variables. Take, for example, the following scores which represent the time in seconds for a drug to take effect on a sample of patients, arranged in rank order:

33, 36, 36, 81, 82, 84, 86, 89, 91, 95, 97, 98

It is clear to the naked eye that the data are 'centered' somewhere in the 80–90 seconds range. Yet the mode for this distribution of listed data is 36 seconds since this appears twice in the distribution, whereas every other score only appears once. Clearly, the mode is not really reflecting the central tendency of this distribution. In such cases, we should either use other measures of central tendency, such as those we are about to discuss, or else organize the data into suitable class intervals, and report the modal class interval, rather than the individual modal score.

The median

With ordinal and interval/ratio data we can also calculate the **median** (M_d) score, along with the mode. We cannot calculate the median for nominal data since the determination of the median requires that the cases be rank-ordered from lowest to highest in terms of the quantity of the variable each case possesses. If all the cases in a distribution are ranked from lowest to highest, *the median is the value that divides the data in half*. Half of all the cases have a value for the variable greater than the median and half of all cases have a value less than the median. In other words, if I randomly select a case from a rank-ordered series, there is exactly a 50 percent chance that it will fall above the median and exactly a 50 percent chance that it will fall below the median.

For an odd number of rank-ordered cases, the median is the middle score.

For an even number of rank-ordered cases, the median is the average of the two middle scores.

Thus if I lined up the 20 people in the survey, starting with the 7 that are unhealthy at one end, then the 5 that are healthy, and then the 8 that rated themselves as very healthy, we can see that the mid-point of the distribution (between the 10th and 11th cases in line) is in the healthy group (Figure 4.1).

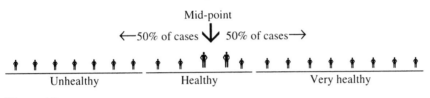

Figure 4.1

Interval/ratio data can also be rank-ordered so that the median can also be calculated for the age distribution of survey respondents, as shown in Figure 4.2.

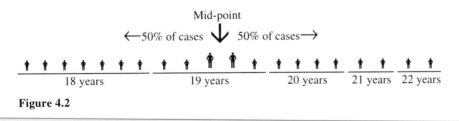

Figure 4.2

With an even number of cases, as we have here, the median is the average of the two middle scores, which are both 19 years, so the median will be:

$$\text{median} = \frac{19 + 19}{2}$$

$$= 19 \text{ years}$$

However, if the 10th student was 19 years of age, and the 11th was 20 years of age, the median will then be:

$$\text{median} = \frac{19 + 20}{2}$$

$$= 19.5 \text{ years}$$

If a cumulative relative frequency table has been generated (Table 4.6), an easier way to calculate the median is to identify the value at which the cumulative frequency passes 50 per cent.

Table 4.6 Age (in years) of respondents

Age	Frequency	Cumulative percentage
18	7	35%
19	5	60%
20	4	80%
21	2	90%
22	2	100%
Total	20	

Example

Consider the following data:

93, 25, 87, 3, 56, 64, 12

To find the median of these data we first rank-order them from lowest to highest:

Score:	3	12	25	**56**	64	87	93
Rank:	1st	2nd	3rd	**4th**	5th	6th	7th

Since there are seven cases (an odd number) the median value will be the 4th in line, which is 56.

If the same data set included one additional value of 98 the rank ordering will be:

Score:	3	12	25	**56**	**64**	87	93	98
Rank:	1st	2nd	3rd	**4th**	**5th**	6th	7th	8th

We now have eight cases (an even number). The median will therefore be the average of the 4th and 5th values:

$$\text{median} = \frac{56 + 64}{2}$$

$$= 60 \text{ years}$$

The mean

With interval/ratio data the (arithmetic) **mean** can be calculated in addition to the mode and the median. The mean is the notion of average that is most commonly used, and in fact is often (incorrectly) synonymous with the term average. Generating the mean involves a simple calculation.

The **arithmetic mean** is the sum of all scores in a distribution divided by the total number of cases.

When calculating the mean for an entire population we use the Greek symbol μ (pronounced 'mu'). When calculating the mean for a sample, we use the Roman symbol $\overline{X}$ (pronounced 'X-bar'). The actual formula we use to calculate the mean depends on whether we have the data in listed form, or in a frequency table, or arranged into class intervals.

Listed data If we have the raw data in listed form (with each individual datum listed separately) the equation for the mean of the population and the mean of a sample will respectively be:

$$\mu = \frac{\Sigma X_i}{N}$$

$$\overline{X} = \frac{\Sigma X_i}{n}$$

where:
N is the size of the population
n is the size of the sample
X_i is each score in a distribution.

The Σ (pronounced 'sigma') means 'the sum of' (or 'add up'), so we read these equations in the following way: 'the mean equals the sum of all scores divided by the number of cases'. Thus if I had the following listed distribution of sample scores:

12, 15, 19, 21

the mean will be:

$$\bar{X} = \frac{\Sigma X_i}{n} = \frac{12 + 15 + 19 + 21}{4}$$

$$= 16.75$$

Frequency data We sometimes do not have data presented in listed form, but instead have data grouped into a frequency table such as Table 4.5. In this table we do not have the age for each person listed individually. Instead we have a frequency distribution of data grouped by years. In this case we use the following formula to calculate the mean for a sample:

$$\bar{X} = \frac{\Sigma f X_i}{n}$$

This formula instructs us to:

1. multiply each value in the distribution by the frequency (*f*) with which it occurs;
2. sum these products; and
3. divide the sum by the number of cases.

Here we have seven respondents aged 18, five aged 19, four aged 20, two aged 21, and another two aged 22. The mean is:

$$\bar{X} = \frac{(18 \times 7) + (19 \times 5) + (20 \times 4) + (21 \times 2) + (22 \times 2)}{20}$$

$$= 19.35 \text{ years}$$

Frequency data using class intervals Sometimes frequency tables only specify the class intervals in which data fall, rather than the specific values and the frequency with which each value occurs. A slightly more complicated procedure is involved when the data are grouped into class intervals, rather than by specific values. For example, we may be reading a report that includes Table 4.7 with the following information about children's ages.

Table 4.7 Children's ages grouped by class intervals

Intervals	Frequency
1–5 years	7
6–10 years	10
11–15 years	6
Total	23

The report, however, does not calculate the average age, so if we want this extra bit of description we need to calculate it for ourselves. With data grouped into class intervals we need first to calculate the class mid-points (*m*) and then multiply the frequencies by these mid-points:

$$\overline{X} = \frac{\Sigma fm}{n}$$

The procedure involved in using this equation is:

1. calculate the mid-point of each class interval;
2. multiply each mid-point by the number of cases in that interval;
3. sum these products; and
4. divide the total by the number of cases.

Thus for data in Table 4.7, the mid-points and the mid-points multiplied by the frequency of each class are as given in Table 4.8.

Table 4.8 Calculations for the mean for class interval frequency data

Class intervals	Mid-point, (*m*)	Frequency, (*f*)	*fm*
1–5	3	7	$3 \times 7 = 21$
6–10	8	10	$8 \times 10 = 80$
11–15	13	6	$13 \times 6 = 78$
Total		*n* = 23	Σfm = 179

Substituting these data into the formula we get (rounding to 1 decimal place):

$$\overline{X} = \frac{\Sigma fm}{n} = \frac{179}{23}$$

$$= 7.8$$

Choosing a measure of central tendency

Let us summarize the calculations we have conducted on the three variables of age, sex, and health rating in our example of the 20 hypothetical survey respondents (Tables 4.9–4.11).

Table 4.9 Sex of respondents

Measure of central tendency	Value
Mode	Male

Table 4.10 Health rating of respondents

Measure of central tendency	Value
Mode	Very healthy
Median	Healthy

Table 4.11 Age of respondents

Measure of central tendency	Value
Mode	18 years
Median	19 years
Mean	19.3 years

It is clear from Tables 4.10 and 4.11 that where more than one measure of average can be calculated we will not always get the same answer, even when calculated on the same raw data. This is because each measure defines 'average' in a slightly different way. In fact, unless the distribution is perfectly **symmetrical**, that is if the distribution is **skewed**, there will always be some difference in the various measures of central tendency. We can see examples of symmetrical and skewed distributions in Figure 4.3.

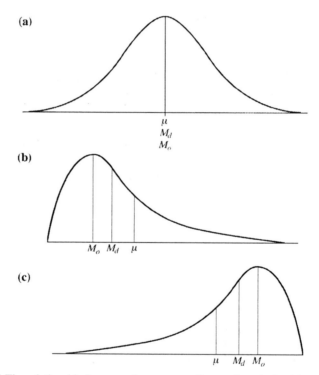

Figure 4.3 The relationship between the mean, median, and mode for (**a**) a symmetrical, (**b**) a right-skewed, and (**c**) a left-skewed distribution

The symmetrical curve has a nice bell-shape, and the measures of central tendency are all equal. With skewed distributions, though, the measures diverge. Notice also that in describing the direction to which a distribution is skewed we refer to the side of the curve that has the long tail, and not the side with the 'hump'.

Generally, when a distribution is heavily skewed the mean is a misleading notion of average. Since the mean is calculated from *every* value in the distribution it is influenced by extreme scores (called outliers). For example, we may have the following exam scores:

$$X_1 = 60, \quad X_2 = 62, \quad X_3 = 66, \quad X_4 = 67, \quad X_5 = 69$$

With each datum listed separately, the mean for this distribution is:

$$\bar{X} = \frac{\Sigma X_i}{n} = \frac{60 + 62 + 66 + 67 + 69}{5}$$

$$= 64.8$$

Consider the effect on the mean if the scores vary only slightly so that the fifth score is 95 instead of 69:

$$X_1 = 60, \quad X_2 = 62, \quad X_3 = 66, \quad X_4 = 67, \quad X_5 = 95$$

Even though only one score has changed, causing the distribution to skew to the right, the value of the mean has changed dramatically:

$$\bar{X} = \frac{\Sigma X_i}{n} = \frac{60 + 62 + 66 + 67 + 95}{5}$$

$$= 70$$

The 'average' student suddenly looks a lot smarter, because of this one change. The median for both distributions, though, remains 66. This is the score that the student in the middle of the distribution receives. Since the median depends solely on the value of this one score at the mid-point, it is not 'pulled' in one direction or another by scores at the extreme ends of the range, and is, for interval/ratio data, therefore best used with a skewed distribution.

Measures of dispersion

We have seen that there are various ways by which the average of a distribution can be conceptualized and calculated. But how average is average? Consider the two distributions of cases according to annual income shown in Table 4.12.

Table 4.12 Annual incomes

Group A ($)	Group B ($)
5000	20,000
6500	28,500
8000	35,000
55,000	36,000
85,000	40,000

The mean income for each of these groups is the same:

$$\overline{X}_A = \frac{5000 + 6500 + 8000 + 55,000 + 85,000}{5}$$

$$= \$31,900$$

$$\overline{X}_B = \frac{20,000 + 28,500 + 35,000 + 36,000 + 40,000}{5}$$

$$= \$31,900$$

These distributions have the same mean, yet it is clear that there is also a major difference between the two. Although the mean is the same, the spread or **dispersion** of scores is very different.

Measures of dispersion are descriptive statistics that indicate the spread or variety of scores in a distribution.

We will begin with measures of dispersion for interval/ratio data: the range, interquartile range, standard deviation, and coefficient of relative variation. We will then explore a measure of dispersion for categorical data: the index of qualitative variation.

The range

The simplest measure of dispersion is the **range**.

The **range** is the difference between the lowest score and highest score in a distribution.

This is a quickly and easily calculated measure of dispersion, because it involves a straightforward subtraction of one score from another. Thus for the two distributions of income the ranges in Table 4.12 will be:

$$R_A = 85,000 - 5000 = \$80,000$$

$$R_B = 40,000 - 20,000 = \$20,000$$

We can immediately see that even though the two distributions have the same mean, there is considerable difference in the spread of scores around this average. Group A has much more variation.

The advantage of the range as a measure of dispersion is that it is very easily calculated, since it is simply the subtraction of one number from another. However, this advantage of the range is also its major limitation: it only uses the extreme scores, and therefore changes with the values of the two extreme scores. Consider the distribution of income for group B: all the cases fall in a $20,000 range between $20,000 and $40,000. If we add a sixth person to this group, whose annual income is $150,000, the range is suddenly stretched out by this one score. It is now $130,000. To compensate for the effect of such outliers, a slight variation on the range, called the **interquartile range**, can be generated.

The interquartile range

The **interquartile range** (IQR) overcomes the problems that can arise with the simple range by ignoring the extreme scores of a distribution.

The **interquartile range** is the difference between the upper limits of the first quartile and the third quartile.

In other words, it is the range for the middle 50 percent of cases in a rank-ordered series (Figure 4.4).

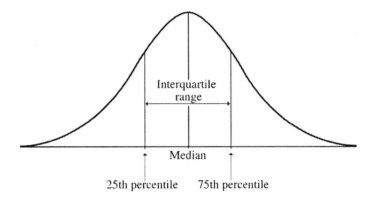

Figure 4.4 The interquartile range

To see how the IQR is calculated we will use the age data from the 20 survey respondents. There are 20 cases, so each quartile will consist of 20 ÷ 4 = 5 cases. The first quartile ends with a person who is 18 years of age. The third quartile ends with a person (the 15th) who is 20 years of age (Figure 4.5).

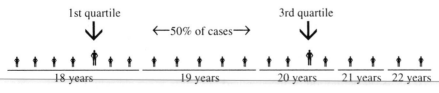

Figure 4.5

The interquartile range is:

$$IQR = 20 - 18 = 2 \text{ years}$$

Unlike the simple range, the interquartile range will not change dramatically if we add one or two people who are much older or much younger to either end of the distribution.

The standard deviation

Many readers will have had the experience of dining out with a large group of people where one or two people proceed to order expensive meals and lots of drinks, and when the bill arrives these same people suggest dividing it up evenly to make the calculation of everyone's share easier! Everyone at the dinner table will be aware of the difference between the value of their own dinner and the cost of the 'average' meal so that they can gauge whether paying the average will put them ahead or behind. In this situation everyone is aware of the difference between average and spread, and how the mean may be a misleading representation of a distribution when taken just on its own.

In a similar manner the standard deviation tries to capture the average distance each score is from the average. The standard deviation assesses spread by employing in its calculation the difference between each score and the mean. As with the calculation for the mean, the formulas we use vary slightly depending on whether we have the data in listed form or in grouped form. In either case we use the Roman symbol, s, to symbolize the standard deviation for a sample, and the Greek letter, σ, for the standard deviation for a population. With listed data the standard deviation for the sample and population are respectively given by:

$$s = \sqrt{\frac{\Sigma\left(X_i - \overline{X}\right)^2}{n-1}}$$

$$\sigma = \sqrt{\frac{\Sigma\left(X_i - \mu\right)^2}{N}}$$

A close look at each of these formulas indicates how they capture the notion that the standard deviation is the average distance that each score is from the average. The numerator is simply the difference between each score and the mean, and the denominator adjusts those differences by the number of observations. The formulas are slightly more complicated, since the differences are squared and the square root of the whole lot taken (for reasons that are not necessary to the present discussion), but the basic idea is still evident.

To focus on the notion of the standard deviation more sharply, consider again the distribution of ages for our 20 survey respondents. We have already calculated the mean age to be 19.3 years. All the scores deviate from the mean, either above or below it, to a greater or lesser degree. This is illustrated in Figure 4.6.

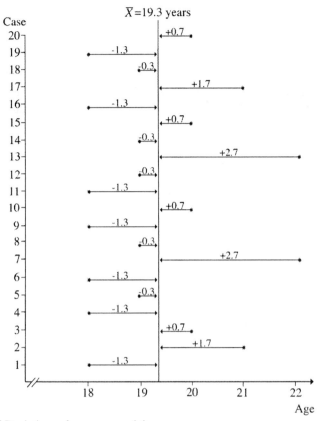

Figure 4.6 Deviations of scores around the mean

The age of each person is plotted on a graph, with the line for the mean age running down the middle. The distance from the mean to each person's age is then drawn in. Respondents 7 and 13 are relatively a long way above the mean, while respondents 5, 8, 12, 14, and 18 are only slightly below the mean. What is the average of these distances?

Unfortunately, we cannot simply add all the **positive deviations** (scores above the mean) with all the **negative deviations** (scores below the mean), since by definition, these will sum to zero. This is why the equation for the standard deviation squares the differences: it thereby turns all the deviations into positive numbers, so that the larger the differences, the greater the value of the standard deviation.

Let us actually calculate the standard deviation for this distribution. We can use the equation above to do this, but we have only introduced it because it captures the idea that the standard deviation is the average distance from the mean. In actually calculating the standard deviation for listed data we work with a slightly different equation that is easier to compute, but which will always give us the same answer as the equation above:

$$s = \sqrt{\frac{\Sigma X_i^2 - \frac{(\Sigma X_i)^2}{n}}{n-1}}$$

The term ΣX_i^2 reads 'the sum of all the squared scores', while the term $(\Sigma X_i)^2$ reads 'the sum of all the scores squared'. For the first term we square all the scores and then add them, while the second term reverses the procedure: we add up the scores and then square the sum. Table 4.13 goes through these steps.

Table 4.13 Calculations for the standard deviation of age

Case	Age in years, X_i	X_i^2
1	18	324
2	21	441
3	20	400
4	18	324
5	19	361
6	18	324
7	22	484
8	19	361
9	18	324
10	20	400
11	18	324
12	19	361
13	22	484
14	19	361
15	20	400
16	18	324
17	21	441
18	19	361
19	18	324
20	20	400
Total	$\Sigma X_i = 387$	$\Sigma X_i^2 = 7523$

Substituting these numbers into the equation, we get:

$$s = \sqrt{\frac{\Sigma X_i^2 - \frac{(\Sigma X_i)^2}{n}}{n-1}} = \sqrt{\frac{7523 - \frac{(387)^2}{20}}{20-1}}$$

$$= 1.35 \text{ years}$$

In Table 4.13 we listed each respondent's age separately. However, we may not have the individual values for each case, but rather have data grouped in a frequency table. With data organized in a frequency table we use the following formula to compute the standard deviation for a sample:

$$s = \sqrt{\frac{\Sigma f X_i^2 - \dfrac{(\Sigma f X_i)^2}{n}}{n-1}}$$

In other words, we multiply each value by the frequency with which it appears in a distribution. Thus if we have the data for age arranged in a frequency table, rather than as a complete list of all ages, the computations will be as shown in Table 4.14.

Table 4.14 Calculations for the standard deviation of frequency data

Age	Frequency (f)	X_i^2	$f X_i^2$	$f X_i$
18	7	$18 \times 18 = 324$	$7 \times 324 = 324$	$7 \times 18 = 126$
19	5	361	1805	95
20	4	400	1600	80
21	2	441	882	42
22	2	484	968	44
Total	$n=20$		$\Sigma f X_i^2 = 7523$	$(\Sigma f X_i) = 387$

$$s = \sqrt{\frac{\Sigma f X_i^2 - \dfrac{(\Sigma f X_i)^2}{n}}{n-1}} = \sqrt{\frac{7523 - \dfrac{(387)^2}{20}}{20-1}}$$

$$= 1.35 \text{ years}$$

We obtain the same answer as when we listed each case separately.

Before moving on to other measures of dispersion, we should note that as with the mean (which is part of the calculation) the standard deviation is not an appropriate measure of dispersion for data that are heavily skewed.

Coefficient of relative variation

The standard deviation is has some limitations which are overcome by the **coefficient of relative variation** (CRV). The coefficient of relative variation is used:

- for comparing distributions measured in the same units but which have very different means, and
- for comparing distributions measured with different units.

There is no absolute way of saying, in the previous example, whether 1.35 years is a large or small amount of dispersion around the mean. Moreover, the standard deviation for one set of observations cannot be compared with that for another set of scores in order to decide which distribution is the more disperse. For example, two distributions may have standard deviations of 1.35 years, but if the means of each are 5 years and 50 years respectively, it is clear that a standard deviation of 1.35 represents *relatively* more variation for the distribution with the smaller mean.

In other instances we may wish to compare the variation for two separate variables each measured in different units. For example, we might be interested in whether the age of a group of respondents, which has a standard deviation of 1.35 years, displays more variation than their weekly income, which has a standard deviation of $65. We cannot compare these two standard deviations and say one variable is more disperse than the other, because each is measured with different units. We are effectively comparing apples with oranges.

To provide a *standardized* measure of dispersion, we calculate the **coefficient of relative variation** (CRV) which expresses the standard deviation as a percentage of the mean:

$$CRV = \frac{s}{\bar{X}} \times 100$$

Using this formula with the distribution of ages for our 20 survey respondents we get:

$$CRV = \frac{s}{\bar{X}} \times 100 = \frac{1.35}{19.35} \times 100$$

$$= 7\%$$

If we had another group of people and their ages we can then calculate the CRV for that group and compare it with this one to see which has the greatest amount of dispersion. Thus if I found that a second group of respondents had a standard deviation for their ages of 5 years, and a mean of 21 years, the CRV will be:

$$CRV = \frac{s}{\bar{X}} \times 100 = \frac{5}{21} \times 100$$

$$= 24\%$$

This second set of people display more variation in their ages than the first. In fact we can actually say that they exhibit 17 percent more variation.

Index of qualitative variation

The measures of dispersion we have just considered all apply to the highest level of measurement of interval/ratio, since they require us to measure the distances between scores. Data, as we know from Chapter 1, do not always permit these operations. How can we express variation in a distribution where the data are only categorical? An often neglected measure of variation is available for such situations, called the **index of qualitative variation** (IQV).

The **index of qualitative variation** is the number of differences between scores in a distribution expressed as a proportion of the total number of possible differences.

The IQV allows us to measure the amount of variation contained in a distribution, even where we only have nominal data. For example, in our earlier example we had a nominal variable, sex of respondents, whose variation cannot be captured by any of the measures of dispersion we have previously looked at (Table 4.15).

Table 4.15 Sex of respondents

Sex	Frequency
Male	12
Female	8
Total	20

The IQV locates the actual amount of variation contained in our data as falling somewhere between two possible extremes. One extreme possibility is if there is no variation in the data. This occurs when all the cases fall into the same category; in this example, if all the cases were either male or female. By definition, if all the case have the same score for a variable, there is no variation. This then constitutes the *minimum* amount of variation that it is possible to observe.

The *maximum* amount of variation that we could possibly observe in a distribution is if the cases are evenly distributed across the categories of the variable, as would be the case if we obtained the results in Table 4.16.

Table 4.16 Sex of respondents: maximum possible variation

Sex	Frequency
Male	10
Female	10
Total	20

In this distribution we have 100 differences: each of the 10 females is different to each of the 10 males in terms of their sex.

There is a simple method for calculating the maximum possible number of differences that can be observed for any set of categorical data, using the following formula:

$$\text{maximum possible differences} = \frac{n^2(k-1)}{2k}$$

where k is the number of categories.

We can use this formula to arrive at the maximum number of differences for the number of cases and categories in our example for respondents' sex:

$$\text{maximum possible differences} = \frac{n^2(k-1)}{2k} = \frac{20^2(2-1)}{2(2)}$$

$$= 100$$

If we look at the actual distribution of responses in Table 4.15 it is evident that it more closely resembles the extreme of maximum variation (Table 4.16) than the situation of no variation. The IQV allows us to express this quantitatively. To do this we need to determine the number of observed differences in the distribution of scores we are analyzing. Take one of the 8 females. How many other people in the distribution are they different to in terms of sex? Clearly this is the 12 males in the distribution. For each of the 8 females there will be 12 other people in the distribution from whom they are different, producing a total of 96 observed differences.

The IQV for the sex of respondents will therefore be:

$$IQV = \frac{\text{observed differences}}{\text{maximum possible differences}} = \frac{96}{100}$$

$$= 0.96$$

An IQV of 0.96 indicates that we have a very high amount of variation in the data for this variable. If, on the other hand, we did have all females or all males, so that there are no observed differences in the data, it is relatively easy to see that the IQV will equal 0, indicating no variation.

Let us now calculate the amount of variation, using this measure, evident in the distribution of responses according to health rating (Table 4.17).

Table 4.17 Health rating of respondents

Health rating	Frequency
Unhealthy	7
Healthy	5
Very healthy	8
Total	20

How many times do cases in this distribution differ from other cases? Starting with the 8 very healthy people, each of these are different in their health rating to the 5 healthy and 7 unhealthy people, producing 96 differences. To this can be added the 35 difference between the 5 healthy people and the 7 unhealthy people. The total number of observed differences is:

$$\text{observed differences} = (8 \times 5) + (8 \times 7) + (5 \times 7)$$

$$= 131$$

The maximum number of differences we could observe (if the cases were evenly spread across the three categories) is:

$$\text{maximum possible differences} = \frac{n^2(k-1)}{2k} = \frac{20^2(3-1)}{2(3)}$$

$$= 133.3$$

The IQV will therefore be:

$$IQV = \frac{\text{observed differences}}{\text{maximum possible differences}} = \frac{131}{133.3}$$

$$= 0.98$$

This indicates that there is almost the maximum possible variation between these cases in terms of their health ratings. We can also say that there is about the same amount of variation between these cases in terms of their health rating as there is in terms of their sex.

Example

To see how all these measures apply in a given instance, let us go back to the data we introduced in previous chapters for the weekly income of 20 people in a sample:

$0, $0, $250, $300, $360, $375, $400, $400, $400, $420, $425, $450, $462, $470, $475, $502, $520, $560, $700, $1020

Notice that we have the data individually listed so that we will use the appropriate formulas, where relevant. Notice also that the data are interval/ratio, which opens up a wide choice in selecting measures of central tendency and measures of dispersion.

Starting with measures of central tendency, we begin with the mode. We can see without too much effort that the value that occurs the most is $400:

$$M_o = \$400$$

The data are also rank-ordered, from lowest to highest, so we can also calculate the median with relative ease. With 20 cases to work with (an even number) the median will be the average of the two middle scores; that is, the average of the incomes for the 10th and 11th people in line. These scores are $420 and $425:

$$M_d = \frac{420 + 425}{2} = \$422.50$$

The mean for this set of data is:

$$\overline{X} = \frac{X_i}{n} = \frac{8489}{20}$$

$$= \$424.45$$

We can see that the mean is only slightly higher than the median, which is higher than the mode, indicating that the data are skewed slightly to the right. This is obviously due to the one very high income earner who receives a weekly income of $1020 (not an uncommon feature of income distribution data). However, the fact that these differences are not too large indicates that the distribution is only slightly skewed.

We will now calculate the measures of dispersion appropriate to this set of data to see the extent to which this average is a fair representation of the distribution. The range is the largest score ($1020) minus the lowest score ($0):

$$R = 1020 - 0 = \$1020$$

The one high score of $1020, though, renders the simple range inaccurate as a measure of dispersion, so we will calculate the interquartile range as well. The first quartile ends with the income for the 5th person in the rank order ($360), and the third quartile ends with the income for the 15th person in the rank order ($475):

$$IQR = 475 - 360 = \$115$$

We can see that this is a 'truer' reflection of the spread of scores around the mean, which even an 'eyeball' inspection of the listed data tells us is not very large.

We will now calculate the standard deviation. To help calculate the relevant numbers to put into the equation I construct the following table (Table 4.18):

Table 4.18 Calculations for the standard deviation of income

Case	Income ($), X_i	X_i^2
1	0	0
2	0	0
3	250	62,500
4	300	90,000
5	360	129,600
6	375	140,625
7	400	160,000
8	400	160,000
9	400	160,000
10	420	176,400
11	425	180,625
12	450	202,500
13	462	213,444
14	470	220,900
15	475	225,625
16	502	252,004
17	520	270,400
18	560	313,600
19	700	490,000
20	1020	1,040,400
Total	$\Sigma X_i = 8489$	$\Sigma X_i^2 = 4,488,623$

$$ s = \sqrt{\frac{\Sigma X_i^2 - \frac{(\Sigma X_i)^2}{n}}{n-1}} = \sqrt{\frac{4,488,623 - \frac{(8489)^2}{20}}{20-1}} $$

$$ = \$216 $$

The standard deviation falls somewhere between the range and the interquartile range. It does not completely ignore the extreme cases, such as $1020, which the IQR leaves aside, but it also does not give them as great a weight in the measurement of dispersion, as is the case with the simple range.

Assume that I am now presented with another set of cases that have a mean income of $510 and a standard deviation of $300. Which of these two distributions displays the greatest variation? It might be tempting to compare the standard deviations, but we know this is not an appropriate comparison given the differences in the means around which the scores deviate. Instead we need to calculate the CRV for each set of scores.

For the first set of data the CRV will be:

$$ CRV = \frac{s}{\bar{X}} \times 100 = \frac{216}{424.45} \times 100 $$

$$ = 51 $$

For the second set of scores the CRV will be:

$$CRV = \frac{s}{\overline{X}} \times 100 = \frac{300}{510} \times 100$$

$$= 59$$

Thus I can say that the second distribution possess 8 percent more variation in incomes than the first set of cases. It not only has a higher average, but is relatively more dispersed.

Measures of central tendency and dispersion using SPSS

The measures of central tendency that we calculated above for these data can also be generated on SPSS as part of the **Analyze/Descriptive Statistics/ Frequencies** command. We will begin by generating the relevant measure of central tendency for age. Once the file is open we follow the procedure in Table 4.19 and Figure 4.7.

Notice that we have many options to select from in choosing which descriptive statistics will be generated to accompany the frequency table. The computer does not discriminate between levels of measurement and will calculate anything we ask for. We need to be careful to select only the measures that are appropriate to the data we are analyzing and the question we want to answer. If we were analyzing the sex of respondents, for example, we would not select the mean or median option for measures of central tendency; SPSS will calculate them but the numbers are meaningless for nominal data. It is up to us to choose only the appropriate measures so that the output is not cluttered with unnecessary statistics.

Table 4.19 Measures of central tendency and dispersion using SPSS (file: **Ch04.sav**)

SPSS command/action	Comments
1 Select **Analyze/Descriptive Statistics/ Frequencies** from the menu	This brings up the **Frequencies** dialog box
2 Select from the source list the variable to be analyzed (in this case **age**)	The selected variable will be highlighted
3 Click ▶	This pastes **age** into the **Variable(s):** target list
4 Click on **Statistics**	This brings up a new box headed **Frequencies: Statistics**
5 In the area headed **Central Tendency** click on the square to the left of **Mean, Median**, and **Mode**	This places a ✔ in the tick-boxes to indicate which measures will be calculated
6 In the area headed **Dispersion** click on the square to the left of **Std. deviation** and **Range**	
7 In the area headed **Percentile Values** click on the square to the left of **Quartiles**	
8 Click on **Continue**	
9 Click on **OK**	

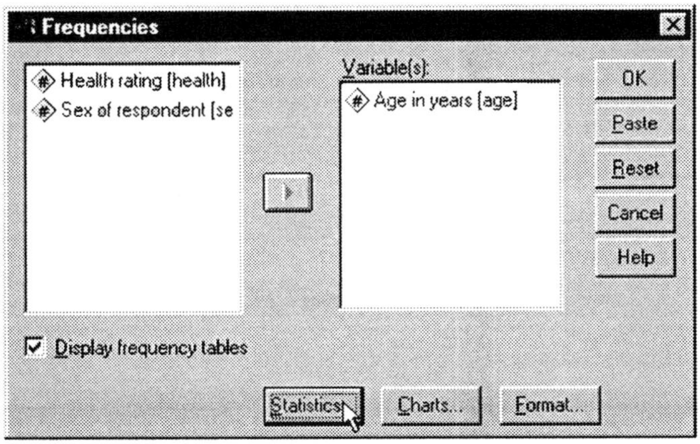

Figure 4.7(a) The **Frequencies** dialog box

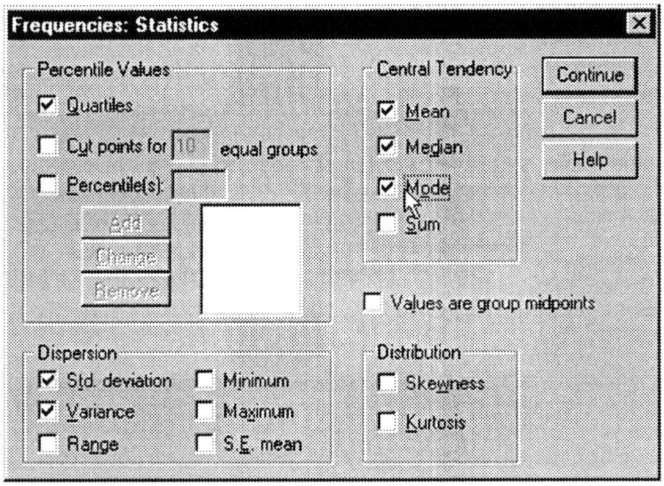

Figure 4.7(b) The **Statistics** dialog box

The result (Figure 4.8) is almost identical to the output we received in Chapter 3 when we first asked for a frequency table for age. This time, however, in the summary **Statistics** table we have the values for the descriptive statistics we asked to be generated. All of these figures correspond to the statistics we generated by hand in the previous chapter. The interquartile range (IQR) is not actually calculated, but we have all the information to do it ourselves. The first (25 percent) quartile has an upper value of 18. The third (75 percent) quartile has an upper limit of 20. The difference of 2 years is the IQR.

Statistics

Age in years

N	Valid	20
	Missing	0
Mean		19.35
Median		19.00
Mode		18
Std. Deviation		1.35
Range		4
Percentiles	25	18.00
	50	19.00
	75	20.00

Figure 4.8 SPSS descriptive statistics output

I leave it to you to use SPSS to calculate the appropriate descriptive statistics for sex and health rating of respondents and to compare these to the values we calculated by hand above.

Summary

In this and the previous chapter we have worked through a number of ways of summarizing data and displaying a distribution. Many formulas and rules have been encountered and the options may seem a little overwhelming. Fortunately, computers have made life easy for us, and all the measures we have introduced, as we have seen, can be generated with the click of a button. However, life should not get too easy. There is a level of understanding that can only be obtained by working through the hand calculations, especially an understanding of the limits to many of the techniques we have introduced.

Exercises

4.1   Can we calculate the mean on ordinal data? Why or why not?

4.2   What are the advantages and disadvantages of the range as a measure of dispersion?

4.3   What do the symbols μ, s, σ, $\bar{X}$ represent?

4.4   In a set of eight scores the mean is 5. If seven of these scores are 9, 3, 4, 5, 6, 4, 7 what must the remaining score be?

4.5   Calculate the mean and median, and the range and standard deviation for each of the following distributions:

(a) 5,   9,   13,   15,   26,   72
(b) 121, 134, 145,   212,   289,   306,   367,   380,   453
(c) 1.2, 1.4, 1.9,   2.0,   2.4,   3.5,   3.9,   4.3,   5.2

4.6   A student switched from one class to another. This student's 'friends' commented that such a move raised the average IQ of each class. What does this comment suggest about the relationship of this student's IQ to the average in each class?

4.7   Consider the following data set:

43, 22, 56, 39, 59, 73, 60, 75, 80, 11, 36, 66, 45, 57, 20, 36, 68, 87, 50, 68, 9.

(a) Rank-order these values and determine the median.
(b) Calculate the mean.
(c) By comparing the value for the mean and the median, determine whether the distribution is symmetric, skewed to the left, or skewed to the right.
(d) If a score of 194 is added to this data set, how will it affect the median and the mean? Explain the changes to the previous calculation for these measures.

4.8   Consider the following data regarding the annual income (in $'000) for people employed in a particular agency:

12	40	22	30	18	36	45	19
22	22	37	35	72	28	36	29
42	56	52	35	16	23	37	26
22	29	35	62				

(a) Calculate the mean, median, and mode for these data.
(b) Calculate the range, interquartile range, and standard deviation for these data.

4.9   The following data represent time, in minutes, taken for subjects in a fitness trial to complete a certain exercise task.

31	39	45	26	23	56	45	80
35	37	25	42	32	58	80	71
19	16	56	21	34	36	10	38
12	48	38	37	39	42	27	39
17	31	56	28	40	82	27	37

In Exercise 3.5 you were asked to generate a frequency table by grouping these data into class intervals of 1–9, 10–19, 20–29, etc.

(a) Calculate the mean and median, using both the raw data and the grouped data. Are these values different from your calculations for the ungrouped data? Explain.

(b) If you created an SPSS data file for these data in Exercise 2.2 use SPSS to generate the relevant descriptive statistics for this variable.

4.10   Consider the following data sets:

Course of enrollment

Course	Frequency
Social science	32
Arts	45
Economics	21
Law	13
Other	8

Time spent studying for exams

Time	Frequency
1 hour	12
2 hours	25
3 hours	27
4 hours	30
5 hours	26

Satisfaction with employment

Satisfaction	Frequency
Very dissatisfied	12
Not satisfied	25
Satisfied	92
Very satisfied	38

For each of the data sets:

(a) Indicate the level of measurement.

(b) Calculate all possible measures of central tendency. Explain any differences between the measures and discuss which is most appropriate.

4.11   Consider the following data from a survey of employees of a factory:

School years completed

Years	Number of employees
1–4	127
5–8	500
9–12	784
13–16	59
17–20	8

(a) Calculate the mean, median, and mode of this distribution.

(b) If they differ, explain why.

4.12   Is 2100 the mode for the following distribution?

Migrants in local area, place of origin

Place	Number
Asia	900
Africa	1200
Europe	2100
South America	1500
Other	300
Total	6000

4.13   Using the **Employee data** file that comes with the SPSS program, calculate the appropriate descriptive statistics that will allow you to answer the following questions.

(a) What is the difference between mean starting salary and mean current salary?

(b) Which of these two variables displays the most variation?

(c) What is the interquartile range for the amount of previous experience of employees, expressed in years?

5

The Graphical Description of Data

Chapter 3 looked at ways of summarizing data by producing frequency tables. However, often the most striking way of summarizing information is with a **graph**. A graph (sometimes called a **chart**) provides a quick visual sense of the main features of the data. The particular graphs that can be constructed in any given context are determined largely by the level of measurement, as indicated in Table 5.1.

Table 5.1 Graphs by level of measurement

Level of measurement	Graph
Nominal and ordinal	Pie graph
	Bar graph
Interval/ratio	Pie graph
	Bar graph (discrete variables)
	Histogram (continuous variables)
	Polygon

Some general principles

In this chapter, to illustrate the procedures and principles involved in constructing graphs, we will use the hypothetical data for 20 people that we introduced in Chapter 2 and which are contained in the SPSS file **Ch05.sav** on the CD that comes with this book (Table 5.2–5.4).

Table 5.2 Sex of respondents

Sex	Frequency
Male	12
Female	8
Total	20

Table 5.3 Health rating of respondents

Health rating	Frequency
Unhealthy	7
Healthy	5
Very healthy	8
Total	20

Table 5.4 Age of respondents

Age in years	Frequency
18	7
19	5
20	4
21	2
22	2
Total	20

The same general rules that apply to the construction of these tables also apply to the construction of graphs. Most importantly a graph should be a *self-contained* bundle of information. A reader should not have to search through the text in order to understand a graph (if one does have to search the text this may be a sign that the graph is concealing information rather than illuminating it). In order for a graph to be a self-contained description of the data we need to:

- give the graph an **appropriate title**;
- clearly identify the **categories or values** of the variable;
- indicate, for interval/ratio data, the **units of measurement**;
- indicate the **total number of cases**;
- indicate the **source of the data**.

We will now look at the construction of different types of graphs. Unlike previous chapters where we separated the SPSS procedures from the hand calculations, here we will only use SPSS to generate the relevant graphs. The superiority of computer graphics has made the hand-drawing of graphs redundant; unlike calculating the mean, where some knowledge of the procedure for doing things by hand can be helpful, we almost invariably go directly to a computer to generate a graph.

Pie graphs

A pie graph can be constructed for all levels of measurement.

A **pie graph** presents the distribution of cases in the form of a circle. The relative size of each slice of the circle is equal to the proportion of cases within the category represented by the slice.

To generate a pie graph on SPSS we select **Graphs/Pie** from the menu (Figure 5.1). The **Pie Charts** dialog box will appear, which provides some options for how the pie graph is to be defined. We are using the default setting, which is to group cases according to their values for the same variable. This is the appropriate choice for the data we are using so we click on the **Define** button. This brings up the dialog box shown in Figure 5.2.

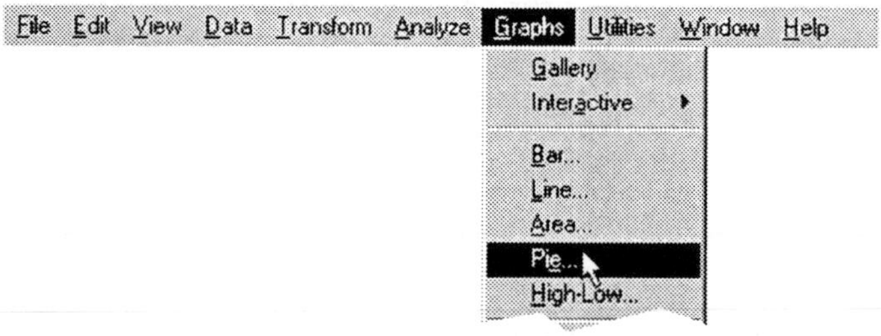

Figure 5.1 The **Pie Graph** command

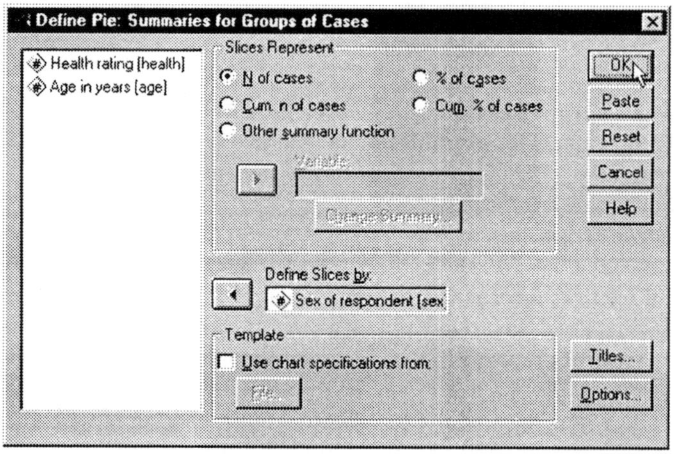

Figure 5.2 The **Define Pie** dialog box

In this dialog box we select the variable we want to analyze and what the slices of the pie will represent. The default setting is for the slices to represent the *number* of cases in each category, which is what we want here. The output shown in Figure 5.3 will be generated when we click on the **OK** button.

The pie chart describes the data in the same way as the frequency table above, but in a more visually striking form. However, the basic SPSS procedure produces a bare minimum amount of information. We do not get a title, nor the number or proportion of cases in each slice. Some of this information could have been generated if we had clicked on the **Titles** button in the **Define Pie** dialog box.

A more complete set of options for improving the presentation of graphs in SPSS is available if we simply double-click on the graph in the **Viewer** window. This brings up the graph in a new SPSS window called the SPSS **Chart Editor** (Figure 5.4).

Graph

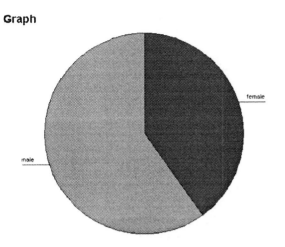

Figure 5.3 SPSS **Pie Graph** output

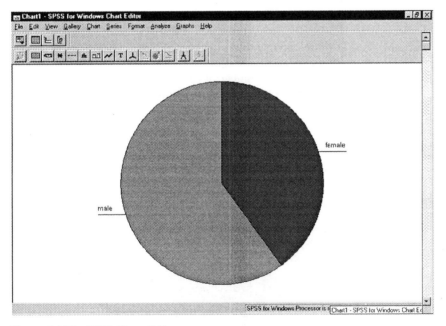

Figure 5.4 The SPSS **Chart Editor**

From the menu bar at the top (or the tool bar below it) we have a range of options for improving the quality of our graph. Here we simply want to attach a title to the pie graph, and to provide appropriate labels to the slices. I leave it to you to explore the full range of options available under the **Chart Editor**. To attach a title and labels to the graph we use the **Chart/Title**, **Chart/Options**, and **Chart/Footnotes** commands.

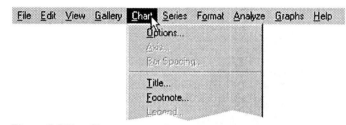

Figure 5.5 The **Chart** command

- The **Title** command allows us to type in various levels of titles. Here our needs are simple so we type in 'Sex of respondents' as Title 1.
- The **Options** command allows us to change the information that is 'attached' to each slice of the pie. We can see in Figure 5.3 that the default setting is for the text labels (in this example 'male' and 'female') represented by each slice to be included. If we click on the boxes next to **Values** and **Percents** we will also generate the absolute and relative frequencies for each slice displayed, along with the text label. You may also wish to click on the **Format** button and set the number of decimal places to 0.
- Using the **Footnote** command we can type 'Source: Hypothetical survey' for Footnote 1 and 'n=20' for Footnote 2 to indicate respectively the source of data and the total number of cases represented by the graph. We can also right-justify these footnotes under **Footnote Justification**.

If we follow these commands Figure 5.6 will appear.

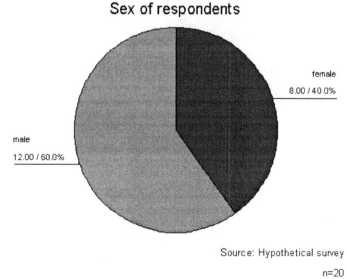

Figure 5.6 SPSS pie chart

We can see that the basic chart is still the same, but now we have all the relevant information as well. Female respondents represent 8 out of 20 students, so the slice representing the frequency of female respondents is 8/20ths of the circle (40%). Male respondents represent 12 out of 20 cases (60%).

Now that we have the pie chart in front of us with all the necessary information what does it tell us about the distribution of the variable we are investigating? *Pie graphs emphasize the relative importance of a particular category to the total.* They are therefore mainly used to highlight distributions where cases are concentrated in only one or two categories. For example, Figure 5.7 illustrates the distribution of students by age, and clearly reflects the large proportion of total cases that are 18 years of age.

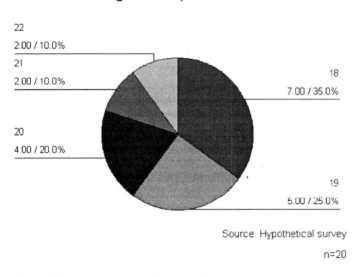

Age of respondents

22	
2.00 / 10.0%	
21	18
2.00 / 10.0%	7.00 / 35.0%
20	
4.00 / 20.0%	
	19
	5.00 / 25.0%

Source: Hypothetical survey

n=20

Figure 5.7 SPSS pie chart with relative frequencies

Pie graphs begin to look a bit clumsy when there are too many categories for the variable (about six or more categories, as a rule of thumb, is usually too many for a pie graph). If we look at the pie graph for the age distribution of students, we can see that if there were any more slices to the pie the chart will begin to look a little cluttered.

A pie chart is actually a specific case of a more general type of graph. Any shape can be used to represent the total number of cases, and the area within it divided to show the relative number of cases in various categories. For example, the United Nations has used a champagne glass to illustrate the distribution of world income (Figure 5.8). Rather than using a simple circle, the metaphor of the champagne glass, a symbol of wealth, makes this graph a powerful illustrative device for showing the inequality of world income.

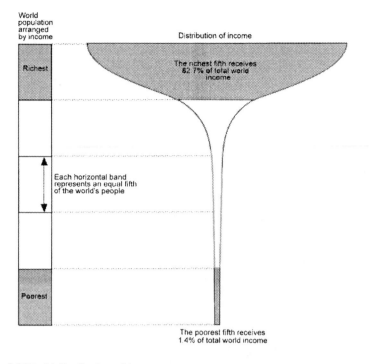

Figure 5.8 World distribution of income
Source: United Nations Development Program (1992) *Human Development Report 1992*, Oxford: Oxford University Press.

Bar graphs

Another type of graph that can be produced from the same set of data as that used to generate a pie chart is a **bar graph**. While these two types of graph can be generated from exactly the same set of data, they describe different aspects of the distribution of that data. We have noted that a pie graph emphasizes the relative contribution of the number of cases in each category to the total. On the other hand, *bar graphs emphasize the frequency of cases in each category relative to each other*.

A bar graph has two sides or axes:

- Along one side, usually the horizontal base, of the graph are the values of the variable. This axis of the bar graph is called the **abscissa**.
- Along the left vertical side of the graph are the frequencies, expressed either as the raw count or as percentages of the total number of cases. This vertical axis is known as the **ordinate**.

To generate a bar graph on SPSS we choose the **Graphs/Bar** command from the menu bar. This brings up the **Bar Charts** dialog box (Figure 5.9).

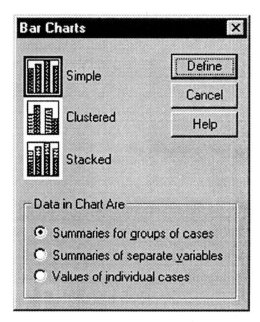

Figure 5.9 The **Bar Charts** dialog box

From this box we choose one of three types of bar charts, each of which we will explore separately:

- Simple bar graphs
- Clustered bar graphs
- Stacked bar graphs

Simple bar graphs

The default setting in the SPSS **Bar Charts** dialog box (Figure 5.9) is for a simple bar chart to be generated. This is evident from the dark border around the **Simple** button.

If we click on **Define** the **Define Simple Bar:** dialog box appears, which is almost identical to the **Pie Graph** dialog box we came across in the previous section. In this dialog box we select the variable we are investigating from the source variable list, which in this instance is 'Sex of respondents', and click on **OK**. This will generate a bar graph in the **Viewer** window.

As with the pie graph we generated earlier we can 'tidy' up this basic graph by going into the **Chart Editor** (double-click on the graph). I have generated a bar chart and edited to add information about the source of data and the sample size, and to improve its appearance (Figure 5. 10).

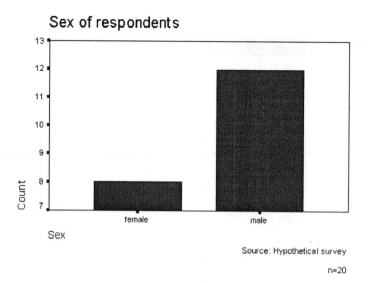

Figure 5.10 An SPSS bar chart

Again I emphasize that SPSS provides many options for improving the layout and appearance of a graph and the amount of information it contains. Often these choices (such as the wording and placement of titles) are matters of aesthetic judgment so you need not follow my preferences exactly. Play around with the options so that you produce something that you like, but always keep in mind the general rules of graph construction that we discussed above.

Stacked bar graphs

An alternative way of presenting information is to stack the categories on top of each other, rather than side by side.

A **stacked bar graph** (sometimes called a **component bar graph**) layers in a single bar the number (or proportion) of cases in each category of a distribution.

Each bar is divided into layers, with the area of each layer proportional to the frequency of the category it represents. It is very similar in this respect to a pie chart, but using a rectangle rather than a circle.

One advantage of a stacked bar graph is that a number of distributions can be combined into a single chart. Such a graph is especially helpful in comparing cases broken down by the categories of another variable, such as distributions over time. For example, a health assessor may want to compare the current health rating of respondents with their ratings for the previous 2 years, the data for which are given in Table 5.5.

Table 5.5 Health ratings of respondents, 1997–1999

Health rating	1997	1998	1999
Very healthy	3	6	8
Healthy	9	6	5
Unhealthy	15	11	7
Total	27	23	20

To generate a stacked bar graph in SPSS we click on the **Stacked** button from the **Bar Charts** dialog box (Figure 5.9). I have entered the data from Table 5.5 in a separate SPSS file, with the year of the survey as a separate **category axis** variable. This generates the stacked bar graph in Figure 5.11.

Health rating of respondents 1997-99

Figure 5.11 SPSS stacked bar chart output

We can immediately see that, relatively speaking, these people regard themselves as getting healthier. Notice that we are using percentages in this graph to standardize the distributions, since the totals for each year vary.

Stacked bar graphs have the same limitations as pie graphs, especially when there are too many values stacked on top of each other. Figure 5.11 contains only three values stacked on top of each other to form each bar, but when there are more than five categories, and some of the layers are very small, the extra detail hinders the comparison of distributions that we want to make, rather than illuminating it.

Clustered bar graphs

An alternative to a stacked bar chart is to place the bars for each category side by side along the horizontal. This is called a **clustered bar graph**.

A **clustered bar graph** displays, for each category of one variable, the distribution of cases across the categories of another variable.

Figure 5.12 presents a clustered bar graph for health rating across years.

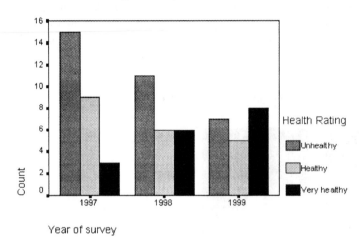

Figure 5.12 An SPSS clustered bar chart

Again I can see the relative decrease in the proportion of unhealthy respondents and the gradual increase in the proportion of very healthy respondents.

Histograms

Bar graphs constructed for discrete variables always have gaps between each of the bars: there is no gradation between male and female, for example. A person's age, on the other hand, is a continuous variable, in the sense that it progressively increases. Even though we have chosen discrete values (whole years) for age to organize the data, the variable itself actually increases in a continuous way (as we discussed in Chapter 1). As a result, the bars on a **histogram**, unlike a bar graph, are 'pushed together' so they touch. The individual values (or class mid-points if we are working with class intervals) are displayed along the horizontal, and a rectangle is erected over each point. The width of each rectangle extends half the distance to the values on either side. *The area of each rectangle is proportional to the frequency of the class in the overall distribution.*

Using the example of the age distribution of students we can construct the following histogram. We select **Graphs/Histogram** from the SPSS menu which brings up the **Histogram** dialog box (Figure 5.13).

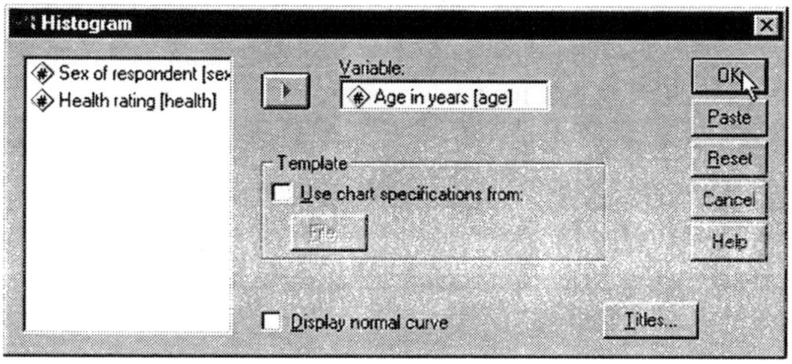

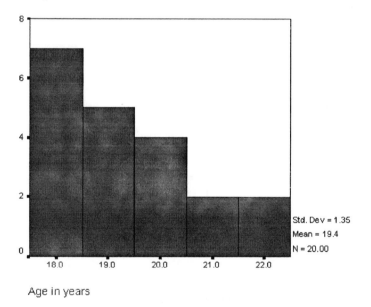

Figure 5.13 The **Histogram** dialog box

This dialog box is one of the more straightforward ones that appear in SPSS. We basically select the relevant variable from the source list and transfer it to the target list. (Note for the next chapter, though, the option to **Display normal curve**.) Selecting **Age in years** and clicking on **OK** will produce the histogram in Figure 5.14.

Std. Dev = 1.35
Mean = 19.4
N = 20.00

Age in years

Figure 5.14 SPSS **Histogram** output

We can see that the area for the rectangle over 18 years of age, as a proportion of the total area under the histogram, is equal to the proportion of all cases having this age. The histogram indicates that we are working with a continuous variable whereby we have clustered cases to the nearest whole year, so that a score of 18 years of age gathers together cases that are actually between 17.5 and 18.5 years, a score of 19 years of age gathers together cases that are actually 18.5–19.5 years, and so on. SPSS has also generated some other descriptive statistics: the standard deviation, mean, and total number of cases, which conform to our calculations in Chapter 4.

Frequency polygons

When working with continuous interval/ratio data, we can also represent the distribution in the form of a **frequency polygon.**

> A **frequency polygon** is a continuous line formed by plotting the values or class mid-points in a distribution against the frequency for each value or class.

If we place a dot on the top and center of each bar in a histogram, and connect the dots, we produce a frequency polygon (Figure 5.15). To illustrate this point I have not used SPSS to generate a polygon (which SPSS calls a line graph) for the age distribution of respondents, since we cannot superimpose a polygon onto the equivalent histogram in SPSS.

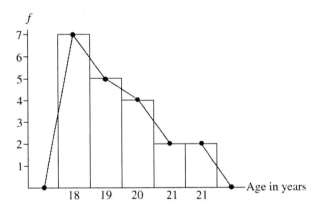

Figure 5.15 A frequency polygon

Notice that the polygon begins and ends on a frequency of zero. To explain why we 'close' the polygon in this way we can think of this distribution as having seven values for age, rather than five, by including the ages 17 and 23. Since there are no such respondents with either of these ages the dot at these values is on the abscissa, indicating a frequency of zero.

There are certain common shapes to polygons that appear in research. For example, Figure 5.16 illustrates the bell-shaped (symmetric) curve, the J-shaped curve, and the U-shaped curve. The bell-shaped curve is one we will explore in much greater length in later chapters.

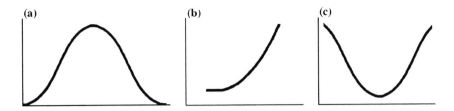

Figure 5.16 Three polygon shapes: **(a)** a bell-shaped curve; **(b)** a J-shaped curve; and **(c)** a U-shaped curve

For polygons that have a 'bell shape' such as that in Figure 5.16(a) we usually describe two aspects of it. The first is the **skewness** of the distribution, an issue we raised in Chapter 4. If the curve has a long tail to the left, it is negatively skewed, whereas if it has a long tail to the right it is said to be positively skewed. The second important aspect of a 'bell-shaped' curve is **kurtosis**. Kurtosis refers to the degree of 'peakedness' or 'flatness' of the curve. We can see in Figure 5.17(a) a curve with most cases clustered closed together. Such a curve is referred to as **leptokurtic**, while curve (b) that has a wide distribution of scores which 'fatten' the tails is referred to as **platykurtic**. Curve (b) lies somewhere in between, and is called **mesokurtic**.

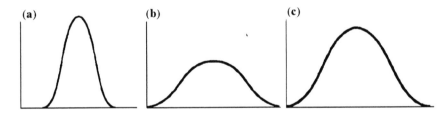

Figure 5.17 A **(a)** leptokurtic, **(b)** platykurtic, and **(c)** mesokurtic curve

There are precise numerical techniques for measuring the skewness and kurtosis of a distribution, but these are beyond the scope of this book. Wherever necessary we will simply rely on a visual inspection of a polygon to describe these aspects of the distribution.

One aspect of frequency polygons (and histograms) that will be of utmost importance in later chapters needs to be pointed out, even though its relevance may not be immediately obvious. A polygon is constructed in such a way that *the area under the curve between any two points on the horizontal, as a proportion of the total area, is equal to the proportion of cases in the distribution that have that range of values.* Thus the shaded area in Figure 5.18, as a proportion of the total area under the curve, is equal to the proportion of cases that are aged 21 or above. This is 4/20, or 0.2 of all cases.

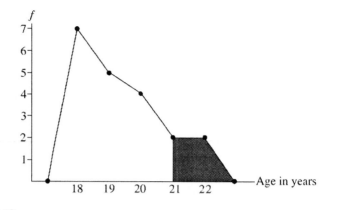

Figure 5.18

Another way of looking at this is to say that the **probability** of randomly selecting a respondent aged 21 years or more from this group is equal to the proportion of the total area under the curve that is shaded. This probability is 0.2, or a 1-in-5 chance of selecting a respondent in this age group.

Common problems and misuses of graphs

Unfortunately graphs lend themselves to considerable misuse. Practically every day in a newspaper we can find one (if not all) of the following 'tricks', which can give a misleading impression of the data. For those wishing to look at this issue further the starting point is Darrell Huff's cheap, readable, and entertaining classic, *How to Lie with Statistics* (New York: W.W. Norton, various printings).

Relative size of axes

The same data can give different graphical 'pictures' depending on the relative sizes of the two axes. By stretching either the abscissa or the ordinate the graph can be 'flattened' or 'peaked' depending on the impression that we might desire to convey. Consider for example the data represented in Figure 5.19.

This provides two alternative ways of presenting the same data. The data are for a hypothetical example of the percentage of respondents who gave a certain answer to a survey item over a number of years. Graph (a) has the ordinate (the vertical) 'compressed' relative to graph (b); similarly graph (b) has the abscissa (the horizontal) relatively more 'compressed'. The effect is to make the data seem much smoother in graph (a) – the rise and fall in responses is not so dramatic. In graph (b) on the other hand, there is a very sharp rise and then fall, making the change appear dramatic. Yet the two pictures describe the same data!

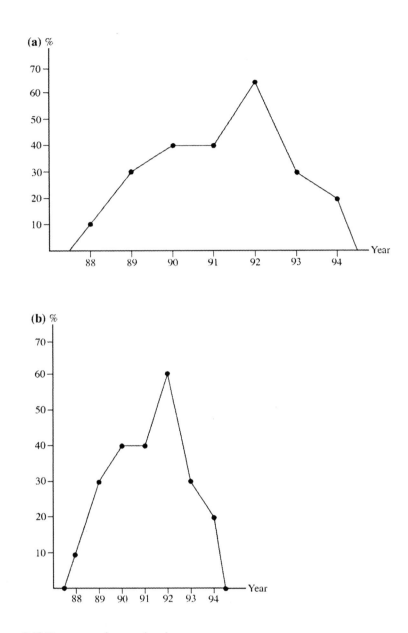

Figure 5.19 Two ways of presenting data

In order to avoid such distortions the convention in research is to construct graphs, wherever possible, such that *the vertical axis is around two-thirds to three-quarters the length of the horizontal.*

Truncation of the ordinate

A similar effect to the one just described can be achieved by cutting out a
section of the ordinate. Consider the data on the relative pay of women to men
in Australia between 1950 and 1975, shown in Figure 5.20.

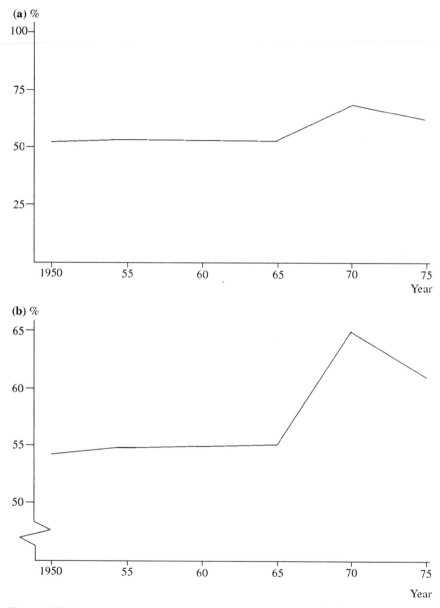

Figure 5.20 Women's income as a percentage of men's income, 1950–1975 presented in
two different ways

Graph (a) is complete in the sense that the vertical axis goes from 0 through to 100 percent. The vertical axis in graph (b) though has been truncated: a large section of the scale between 0 percent and 50 percent has been removed and replaced by a squiggly line to indicate the truncation. The effect is obvious: the improvement in women's relative pay after 1965 seems very dramatic, as opposed to the slight increase reflected in graph (a).

Selection of the start and end points of the abscissa

This is especially relevant with data that describe a pattern of change over time. Varying the date at which to begin the data series and to end it can give different impressions. For example, we may begin in a year in which the results were unusually low, thereby giving the impression of increase over subsequent years, and vice versa if we choose to begin with a year in which results 'peaked'. Consider, for example, the time series of data over a 15 year period shown in Figure 5.21.

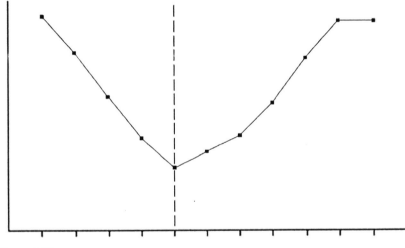

Figure 5.21

If we wanted to emphasize steady growth we could begin the graph where the dashed line is displayed, which would completely transform the image presented by the graph.

Exercises

5.1   Which aspects of a distribution do pie graphs emphasize and which aspects do bar graphs emphasize?

5.2   Explain the difference between a bar graph and a histogram.

5.3   Survey your own statistics class in terms of the variables age, sex, and health rating. Use the graphing techniques outlined in this chapter to describe your results.

5.4   In Exercise 2.2 the following data were entered into SPSS (time, in minutes, taken for subjects in a fitness trial to complete a certain exercise task):

31	39	45	26	23	56	45	80
35	37	25	42	32	58	80	71
19	16	56	21	34	36	10	38
12	48	38	37	39	42	27	39
17	31	56	28	40	82	27	37

Using SPSS select an appropriate graphing technique to illustrate the distribution. Justify your choice of technique against the other available options.

5.5   Consider the following list of prices, in whole dollars, for 20 used cars:

8600	9200	8200	11,300	10,600
7980	11,100	12,900	10,750	9200
13,630	9400	11,800	10,200	12,240
11,670	10,000	11,250	12,750	12,990

From these data:
(a)   Construct a frequency table using class intervals:

       7000–8499, 8500–9999, 10000–11499, 11500–12999, 13000–14499.

(b)   Construct a histogram using these class intervals.
(c)   Construct a frequency polygon using these class intervals.

5.6   Construct a pie graph to describe the following data:

Migrants in local area, place of origin

Place	Number
Asia	900
Africa	1200
Europe	2100
South America	1500
Other	300
Total	6000

What feature of this distribution does your pie graph mainly illustrate?

5.7   From a recent newspaper or magazine find examples of the use of graphs. Do these examples follow the rules outlined in this chapter?

5.8   Use the **Employee data** file to answer the following problems with the aid of SPSS.

(a)   I want to emphasize the high proportion of all cases that have clerical positions. Which graph should I generate and why? Generate this graph using SPSS, and add necessary titles and notes.

(b)   Use a stacked bar graph to show the number of women and the number of men employed in each employment category. What does this indicate about the sexual division of labor in this company?

(c)   Generate a histogram to display the distribution of scores for current salary. How would you describe this distribution in terms of skewness?

6

The Normal Curve

Chapter 5 looked at the options available for displaying a distribution in the form of a graph. A researcher will encounter many distributions when collecting data on different variables, and each will have a unique shape when graphed. For example, the distribution of people's income will have a particular shape that is different from the distribution of their height, and different again from the distribution of their ages, satisfaction with life, or any other variable we could conceive of measuring.

This chapter will detail the properties of one particular distribution, called the **normal curve**. The term 'normal' is not meant to signify 'usual' or 'common'. In fact, it might seem like a very artificial construct that is anything but normal. However, it does play a central role in statistical analysis and is the basis for many of the procedures that follow in later chapters. So while the reasons for studying this particular curve (among the multitude on which we can focus) may not be immediately apparent, hopefully they will become evident later.

The normal distribution

This chapter will try to 'circle in' on the nature of the normal distribution. We will begin with a very simple and approximate definition, gradually expanding on this definition as we become more familiar with it.

The **normal curve** is a smooth, unimodal curve that is perfectly symmetrical. It has 68.3 percent of the area under the curve within one standard deviation of the mean.

These features of the normal curve are illustrated in Figure 6.1. We can use the properties of the normal curve illustrated in Figure 6.1 to derive specific conclusions about the frequency distribution of scores that we think is normally distributed.

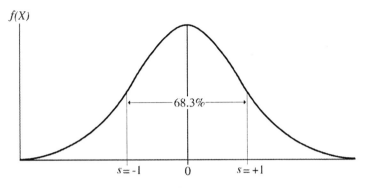

Figure 6.1 Areas under the standard normal curve

For example, we might be interested in people's ages and have the following descriptive statistics for the average and spread of ages for a population of 400 people:

$$\mu = 35 \text{ years}$$

$$\sigma = 13 \text{ years}$$

If age is normally distributed, 68.3 percent of people in this population will fall within 1 standard deviation of the mean. In other words, 272 people (68.3 percent of 400) will have ages somewhere between 22 years (35 – 13) and 48 years (35 + 3).

This property of the normal curve holds true regardless of the particular values for the standard deviation and mean for the collection of cases we are dealing with. For example, we may have three different groups of 400 people with ages described by the following statistics (Table 6.1, Figure 6.2).

Table 6.1 Average age and spread for three populations

Group	Mean age (years)	Standard deviation (years)	Age range of middle 68.3% of cases (years)
1	35	13	22 to 48
2	35	7	28 to 42
3	35	20	15 to 56

All three distributions have the same average age, but are different in terms of the *spread* of ages around the mean. If we can assume that they are each normal distributions we can derive the age ranges for the middle 68.3 percent of people in each group. If these are normal distributions, it follows that 272 people in group 1 will have ages between 22 and 48 years; 272 people in group 2 will have ages ranging from 28 to 42 years; and for group 3 the range is 15 to 56 years.

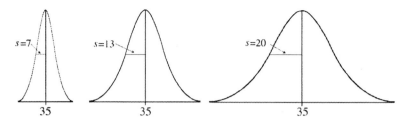

Figure 6.2 Three normal distributions with different standard deviations

This process of stating the spread of cases in terms of the number of standard deviations from the mean is called **standardizing the distribution**, and produces the **standard normal distribution** (Figure 6.3). The standard normal distribution has a mean of zero and a standard deviation of one (by definition, the mean is zero standard deviation units from the mean, and one standard deviation is one standard deviation unit away from the mean).

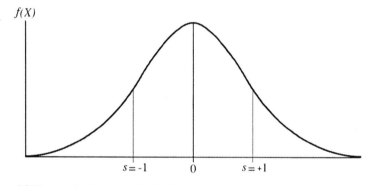

Figure 6.3 The standard normal distribution

This standardization procedure allows us to measure all normal distributions in terms of common units – standard deviation units – regardless of the units in which the variable is initially measured. It is analogous to expressing the price of various goods from different countries in terms of a common currency. We may have a whole list of prices, some of which are expressed in US dollars, some in British pounds, others in Euros. But if we convert all the prices into a common unit such as the amount of gold each unit of currency will purchase, a comparison can be made. Similarly, a distribution may be expressed in terms of years, or crime rates, or births per thousand. But expressing these various distributions according to standard deviation units gives a common scale of measurement.

We noted that the normal curve is symmetrical. Since the curve is symmetrical the same percentage of cases that falls within a certain range above the mean also falls within the same range below the mean (Figure 6.4). In other words, if 68.3 percent of all cases fall within one standard deviation unit *either side* of the mean, half of this (34.15 percent) will fall *above* the mean, and the other half (34.15 percent) *below* the mean. For group 1 in Table 6.1, this will imply that 136 people will be between 22 and 35 years of age, and another 136 will be between 35 and 48 years of age.

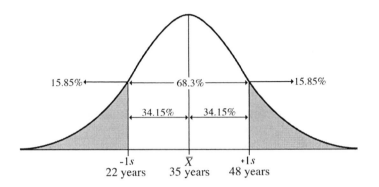

Figure 6.4 Distribution of age for group 1

The other thing to notice about the spread of cases under a normal curve in Figure 6.4 is that the percentage of cases falling *further* than one standard deviation from the mean is equal to the total number of cases (100%) minus the percentage that fall within the range (68.3 percent):

$$100 - 68.3 = 31.7\%$$

Again we can divide this region in two so that 15.85 percent of cases have ages above one standard deviation from the mean (i.e. for group 1 this is older than 48 years), and another 15.85 percent of cases are at the other end (or tail) of the curve. Thus if a woman from this group informs me that she is 52 years of age I will also know that she is in the oldest 16 percent of the population.

This simple exercise hopefully illustrates the usefulness of the normal curve. If we know, or can assume, that a distribution is normal we can then make a conclusion about the range of values into which a certain percentage of cases falls, given the mean and standard deviation. This makes the use of the normal curve important for two reasons, as follows.

The normal curve as an aid to data description

There are some *empirical* distributions (i.e. they exist in the 'real world') that are *fairly close to being normal*, which allows us to determine that a certain percentage of cases falls a specific distance above and/or below the mean. This is similar to the way in which we apply the equation for the area of the circle. A circle is defined as a shape where every point along the circumference is equidistant from the center, or, to put it another way, the radius is constant. A figure defined in this way has an area equal to πr^2, but there are very few shapes that we encounter that *exactly* conform to this definition. This does not limit the applicability of the exact formula for a circle because there are many shapes in ordinary life that are close enough to a circle (they 'approximate' a circle) such that using this formula to calculate their areas is not unreasonable.

Just as with figures that are 'close enough' to being a circle, there are instances when it is not unrealistic to assume that a distribution is 'close enough' to being normal, even though, strictly speaking, it isn't. In other words, just as we never encounter perfect circles, yet still use the formula for the area of a circle in everyday life, we can make statements describing any empirical distribution that (we think) is **approximately** normal. Sometimes near enough is good enough. Many physical characteristics of people, such as height, are approximately normal. If we took a random sample of people and measured their height we would actually find that about 68 percent of cases fall within one standard deviation of the mean.

The normal curve as a tool for inferential statistics

The second reason for understanding the properties of a normal curve, and probably the most important, is that it forms the basis of the procedures that allow us to make inferences from a random sample to a population. The role of the normal curve in inferential statistics will be covered in Part 3, where the convenience of knowing the percentage of cases that fall above and below a certain distance from the mean will become very apparent.

Using normal curves to describe a distribution

The rest of this chapter will employ the normal curve as a descriptive tool, leaving its use as a tool for making an inference from a sample to a population for Part 3. We proceed by expanding slightly the definition of the normal curve, by defining the percentage of the total area under the normal curve within two standard deviation units from the mean, and within three standard deviation units (Figure 6.5).

Between ±1 standard deviations from the mean of a normal distribution lies 68.3 percent of the area under the curve.

Between ±2 standard deviations from the mean of a normal distribution lies 95.4 percent of the area under the curve.

Between ±3 standard deviations from the mean of a normal distribution lies 99.7 percent of the area under the curve.

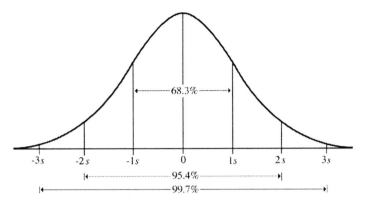

Figure 6.5 Areas under the standard normal curve

This information can be presented in a simple table (Table 6.2).

Table 6.2 Areas under the standard normal curve

Standard deviations from the mean	Area under curve between both points	Area under curve beyond both points (two tails)	Area under curve beyond one point (one tail)
±1	0.683	0.317	0.1585
±2	0.954	0.046	0.0230
±3	0.997	0.003	0.0015

There are a two aspects to Table 6.2 worth noticing:

- Instead of expressing the area under the curve as a percentage, it is expressed as a proportion: 68.3 percent is converted to 0.683, and so on.
- The values in the first two columns will always sum to one (e.g. 0.683 + 0.317 = 1). This is because the two areas together must equal the total area under the curve, which is 100 percent.

The normal curve is a very specifically defined polygon, a type of graph we introduced in Chapter 5. This allows us to interpret the proportions in the table as **probabilities**. A probability in this context is simply the chance that any given case will have a certain value, or fall within a certain range of values. For example, assume that someone is chosen at random from group 1 and you have to guess what their age is. We can use the table to conclude that the probability that this person's age is somewhere between 22 years and 48 years (i.e. it is within one standard deviation either side of the mean) is 0.683, or around 68 in

100. The probability that the person has an age of less than 22 years is 0.1585, or around 16 in 100. This is common sense: there is usually a high probability that someone chosen at random from a set of cases will reflect the average. It is more likely that someone will be 'typical' rather than 'unusual'. This way of interpreting the area under the normal curve as a probability will be especially useful in the following chapters on inference.

z-scores

Instead of using the expression 'number of standard deviations from the mean' we will instead speak of **z-scores**. A z-score of +1 indicates one standard deviation above the mean. A z-score of −1.5 indicates 1.5 standard deviations below the mean. For a normal population or normal sample, we can work out the z-score associated with any actual value using the respective formulas:

$$Z = \frac{X_i - \mu}{\sigma}$$

$$z = \frac{X_i - \overline{X}}{s}$$

where:
X_i is the actual value measured in original units
μ is the mean of the population
σ is the standard deviation of the population
$\overline{X}$ is the mean of the sample
s is the standard deviation of the sample.

For example, consider the population of 400 people in group 1 above, with a mean age of 35 years and standard deviation of 13 years. A member of this group tells me he is 61 years of age. Even before we complicate the matter with equations and z-scores, it is fairly clear that this person is much older than the average, so intuitively we can conclude that very few people will be this old or older. In fact, I can, at this point, use a verbal description and say that given the mean and standard deviation for this group only a 'handful' of people will be 61 years of age or more. We can, however, be more precise than this, and actually calculate what this 'handful' of people is as a proportion of the total. To do this I put the information into the formula for calculating Z-scores for a population and calculate the Z-score associated with this age:

$$Z = \frac{X_i - \mu}{\sigma} = \frac{61 - 35}{13}$$

$$= 2$$

This immediately tells me that 61 is two standard deviations above the average. By referring to the last column in Table 6.2, we conclude that the proportion of people that are 61 years of age or more is only 0.023, or 2.3 percent of the total.

In fact, statisticians have worked out the area under the standard normal curve between the mean and *every* point along the horizontal axis of the normal curve. This information is summarized in a table that appears in the back of every statistics textbook (including this one, see Table A1 in the Appendix). Since we are going to work with this table frequently throughout this chapter, and to familiarize ourselves with it, it is reproduced in Table 6.3.

Table 6.3 Areas under the standard normal curve

z	Area under curve between both points	Area under curve beyond both points	Area under curve beyond one point
±0.1	0.080	0.920	0.4600
±0.2	0.159	0.841	0.4205
±0.3	0.236	0.764	0.3820
±0.4	0.311	0.689	0.3445
±0.5	0.383	0.617	0.3085
±0.6	0.451	0.549	0.2745
±0.7	0.516	0.484	0.2420
±0.8	0.576	0.424	0.2120
±0.9	0.632	0.368	0.1840
±1	0.683	0.317	0.1585
±1.1	0.729	0.271	0.1355
±1.2	0.770	0.230	0.1150
±1.3	0.806	0.194	0.0970
±1.4	0.838	0.162	0.0810
±1.5	0.866	0.134	0.0670
±1.6	0.890	0.110	0.0550
±1.645	0.900	0.100	0.0500
±1.7	0.911	0.089	0.0445
±1.8	0.928	0.072	0.0360
±1.9	0.943	0.057	0.0290
±1.96	0.950	0.050	0.0250
±2	0.954	0.046	0.0230
±2.1	0.964	0.036	0.0180
±2.2	0.972	0.028	0.0140
±2.3	0.979	0.021	0.0105
±2.33	0.980	0.020	0.0100
±2.4	0.984	0.016	0.0080
±2.5	0.988	0.012	0.0060
±2.58	0.990	0.010	0.0050
±2.6	0.991	0.009	0.0045
±2.7	0.993	0.007	0.0035
±2.8	0.995	0.005	0.0025
±2.9	0.996	0.004	0.0020
±3	>0.996	<0.004	<0.0020

It may help at this point to reiterate why we bother defining the normal curve in such minute detail. Why have statisticians gone to such lengths as to actually work out and have printed a table that indicates the number of cases that fall within defined regions of a normal distribution? After all, there are an infinite number of possible frequency distributions we could come across – the distribution of families according to total income will be different from the distribution of cities according to crime rates, and neither will be remotely like a normal distribution. Why don't we construct tables that define the areas under these curves?   First, there are many empirical distributions that are approximately normal so that this table will provide an aid in describing such distributions, and, second, because there is a distribution at the heart of inferential statistics that is normal, and which we will see in later chapters renders the normal curve exceptionally useful in making an inference from a sample to a population.

The rest of this chapter will work through a series of examples. The objective is to familiarize ourselves with the use of the normal curve as a descriptive tool. In the process we will also familiarize ourselves with the procedures for looking up values in the area under the standard normal curve table, which will be useful for later chapters.

For example, assume that I have exam grades out of 100 for a sample of 100 students and obtain the following results:

$$\overline{X} = 60$$
$$s = 10$$

I graph these data on a frequency polygon and observe that the distribution looks approximately normal. There are a number of statistical measures for assessing the extent to which a distribution is normal, one of which we will explore in Chapter 12.   A more detailed examination of these measures is beyond the scope of this book.   Here I have simply relied on an 'eyeball' examination of a histogram to decide whether the distribution is approximately normal.   Knowing that this group of students is normally distributed (or close to it) according to exam scores allows me to answer various questions about this variable.

The area between the mean and a point on the distribution

I might want to know how many students are between the mean of 60 and a score of 65, which I consider to be a reasonable range of scores for students to achieve. The first thing to do is convert 65 into a z-score:

$$z = \frac{X_i - \overline{X}}{s} = \frac{65 - 60}{10}$$

$$= 0.5$$

The next step is to refer to the table for the area under the standard normal curve and find the area between this point and the mean. A condensed version

of the table is presented in Table 6.4 to show its use. For a *z*-score of 0.5 we get
the result shown.

Table 6.4 Areas under the standard normal curve

z	Area under curve between both points	Area under curve beyond both points	Area under curve beyond one point
±0.1	0.080	0.920	0.4600
±0.2	0.159	0.841	0.4205
±0.3	0.236	0.764	0.3820
±0.4	0.311	0.689	0.3445
±0.5	**0.383**	0.617	0.3085
±0.6	0.451	0.549	0.2745
±0.7	0.516	0.484	0.2420
±0.8	0.576	0.424	0.2120
±0.9	0.632	0.368	0.1840
±1	0.683	0.317	0.1585
⋮	⋮	⋮	⋮
±3	>0.996	<0.004	<0.0020

In other words, 0.383 of all cases will have a grade of 5 marks *above or below*
the mean. Since we are interested in only those students that are 5 marks *above*
the mean, we divide 0.383 in half:

$$\text{proportion of students with grades between 60 and 65} = \frac{0.383}{2}$$

$$= 0.1915$$

This is illustrated in Figure 6.6.

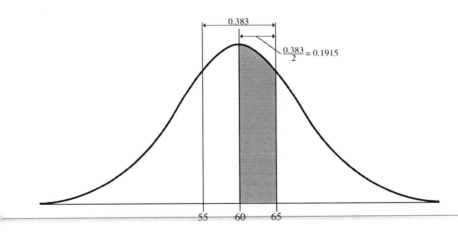

Figure 6.6

Thus, I can say that just over 0.19 (19 percent) of the students received grades between 60 and 65 (remember that a proportion can be transformed into a percentage by moving the decimal point two places to the right).

The area beyond a point on the distribution

A very similar logic applies to finding the percentage of cases that fall *beyond* a certain point on the distribution. For example, I might be interested in the percentage of students who did exceptionally well, which I regard to be a score over 65.

From the previous exercise we know that the z-score associated with a grade of 65 is:

$$z = \frac{X_i - \overline{X}}{s} = \frac{65 - 60}{10}$$

$$= 0.5$$

This time, when referring to the table for the standard normal curve, we refer to the column for the area *beyond* the point defined by a z-score of 0.5. In other words, we are only interested in the area under **one tail** of the distribution (Table 6.5).

Table 6.5 Areas under the standard normal curve

z	Area under curve between both points	Area under curve beyond both points	Area under curve beyond one point
±0.1	0.080	0.920	0.4600
±0.2	0.159	0.841	0.4205
±0.3	0.236	0.764	0.3820
±0.4	0.311	0.689	0.3445
±0.5	0.383	0.617	0.3085
±0.6	0.451	0.549	0.2745
±0.7	0.516	0.484	0.2420
±0.8	0.576	0.424	0.2120
±0.9	0.632	0.368	0.1840
±1	0.683	0.317	0.1585
⋮	⋮	⋮	⋮
±3	>0.996	<0.004	<0.0020

This indicates that 0.3085 (30.85%) of students scored 65 or above.

If we look at the answers to these two problems we can see that the percentages sum to 50 (Table 6.6). This is because the two areas we have defined together make up exactly half the curve (Figure 6.7).

Table 6.6 Areas under the curve

Range of exam scores	Percentage of cases (%)
Between 60 and 65	19
65 or over	31
Total	50

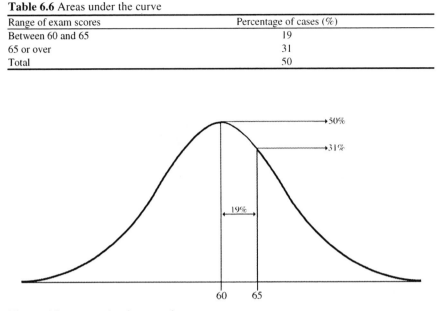

Figure 6.7 Areas under the normal curve

In a similar fashion I may be interested in the proportion of students that have failed the exam. I calculate the z-score associated with a grade of less than 50:

$$z = \frac{X_i - \overline{X}}{s} = \frac{50 - 60}{10}$$

$$= -1$$

Looking at Table 6.5 I can see that there is 0.1586 of the curve beyond a z-score of –1, which indicates that nearly 16 percent of students failed.

The area between two points on a normal distribution

Another question I might be interested in is the percentage of cases that fall within a range not bounded on one side by the mean. For example, I might be interested in the proportion of students that received a credit grade, which is a grade between 65 and 75.

The solution to this puzzle is apparent by looking at Figure 6.8. The area between 65 and 75 is the area left over if we subtract the area between 65 and the mean from the area between 75 and the mean. In other words we need to calculate two proportions, that bounded by the mean and 65 and that bounded by the mean and 75.

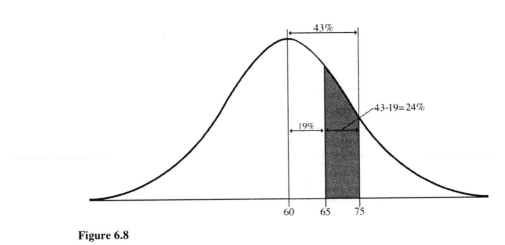

Figure 6.8

We know from our earlier example that 19 percent of cases will have grades between 60 and 65. To determine the percentage of cases that will have a grade between 60 and 75, I first calculate the z-score for this range of scores:

$$z = \frac{X_i - \overline{X}}{s} = \frac{75 - 60}{10}$$

$$= 1.5$$

From the table for the area under the standard normal curve (Table 6.3) 0.866 (86.6 percent) of cases will fall 1.5 z-scores above and below the mean, so that half of this (43.3 percent) will fall above the mean, with grades between 60 and 75. The result is 24 percent of students received a credit grade.

Calculating values from z-scores

In the above examples we wanted to identify the percentage of cases that have a certain range of grades. However, the problem we want to address might be slightly different. We might already have a predefined proportion of cases we are interested in, and want to derive the grade range within which this percentage falls. For example, we might be interested in the range of scores that identify the middle 50 percent of students. Another way of posing this problem is to ask which scores mark the upper and lower bounds of the interquartile range.

We begin by looking at Table 6.7 which presents the areas under the standard normal curve to find the z-scores that will mark off the 0.5 (50 percent) region. We look down the column for the area under the curve between points and find the cell that has a probability of 0.5 (or the closest to it).

Table 6.7 Areas under the standard normal curve

z	Area under curve between both points	Area under curve beyond both points	Area under curve beyond one point
±0.1	0.080	0.920	0.4600
±0.2	0.159	0.841	0.4205
±0.3	0.236	0.764	0.3820
±0.4	0.311	0.689	0.3445
±0.5	0.383	0.617	0.3085
±0.6	0.451	0.549	0.2745
±0.7	0.516	0.484	0.2420
±0.8	0.576	0.424	0.2120
±0.9	0.632	0.368	0.1840
±1	0.683	0.317	0.1585
⋮	⋮	⋮	⋮
±3	>0.996	<0.004	<0.0020

The closest value to 0.5 is 0.516, which is associated with z-scores of +0.7 and −0.7.

To convert these z-scores of −7 and +7 into the actual units (exam grades) in which we are measuring the variable, we rearrange the basic formula slightly:

$$z = \frac{X_i - \overline{X}}{s} \quad \rightarrow \quad X_i = \overline{X} \pm z(s)$$

If we put the two z-scores that define the region into this equation we obtain:

$$X_i = \overline{X} \pm z(s)$$

$$X_i = 60 + 0.7(10) = 67$$

$$X_i = 60 - 0.7(10) = 53$$

Therefore the 'middle' 50 percent of students scored between 53 and 67 in the exam. This also means that 25 percent of students are below 53 and 25 percent of students are above 67.

Normal curves on SPSS

We introduced the concept of the normal curve using a hypothetical survey of all 400 people in a community, with mean and standard deviation for age of:

$$\mu = 35 \text{ years}$$

$$\sigma = 13 \text{ years}$$

The data for this hypothetical survey have been entered into SPSS which will allow us to use SPSS to confirm the results we obtain from hand calculations. First, we can use SPSS to assess the extent to which the spread of scores can be described by a normal distribution. To do this we simply extend the procedure we learnt in Chapter 5 for generating a histogram. We can ask SPSS to generate a histogram, and also to 'fit' a normal curve onto this histogram. By looking at the results we can see the extent to which the distribution of data approximates a normal distribution. To generate a frequency table, a histogram, and a normal curve centered on the mean superimposed on the histogram, we use the procedure shown in Table 6.8 and Figure 6.9.

Table 6.8 Generating a histogram with a normal curve on SPSS (file: **Ch06.sav**)

SPSS command/action	Comments
1 From the menu select **Graphs/Histogram**	This brings up the **Histogram** dialog box
2 Select a variable from the source list by clicking on it, in this case select **Age of respondent**	
3 Click on ▶	This pastes the selected variable into the target **Variable(s):** list for which a frequency table will be generated
4 Click on the small square next to **With normal curve**	A ✓ will appear in the check-box to indicate that a normal curve will be 'fitted' to the histogram
5 Click on **OK**	

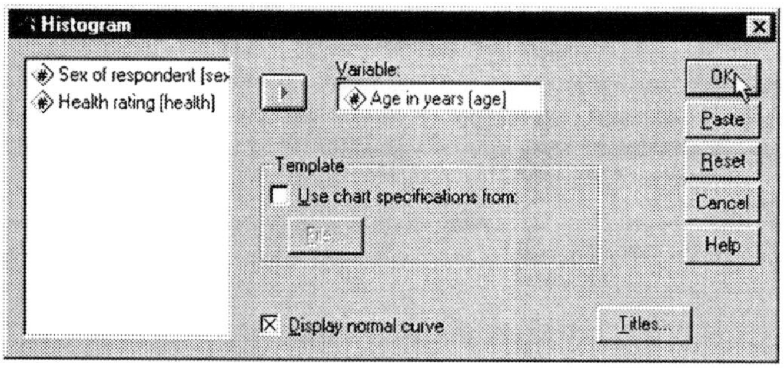

Figure 6.9 Generating a histogram with a normal curve

These procedures will generate the output shown in Figure 6.10. Looking at the histogram with the normal curve superimposed on it in Figure 6.10, we can see that even though the original data comprise age measured in years, SPSS will group cases together into more manageable class intervals. Here the class intervals are 5 year periods, with the mid-points for each class interval being 0, 5, 10, 15, and so on. We can also see that the histogram 'sort of' has the bell-shaped, symmetric features of the normal curve; it is **approximately** normal. A normal curve is a smooth continuous distribution – there are no 'jumps' from one value to another. We, on the other hand, are using a histogram with data arranged according to discrete units of measurement (age in whole years). Since histograms will always have jagged edges brought about by the use of discrete units of measurement, they will never perfectly fit the smoothly rising and falling normal curve. There are also some bars in which the normal curve does not pass exactly through the mid-point. For example, the bar for the middle group in the distribution, with a mid-point of 35 years, has more people in it than would be the case if the distribution was perfectly normal. Despite this variation, the distribution appears to the eye to be approximately normal.

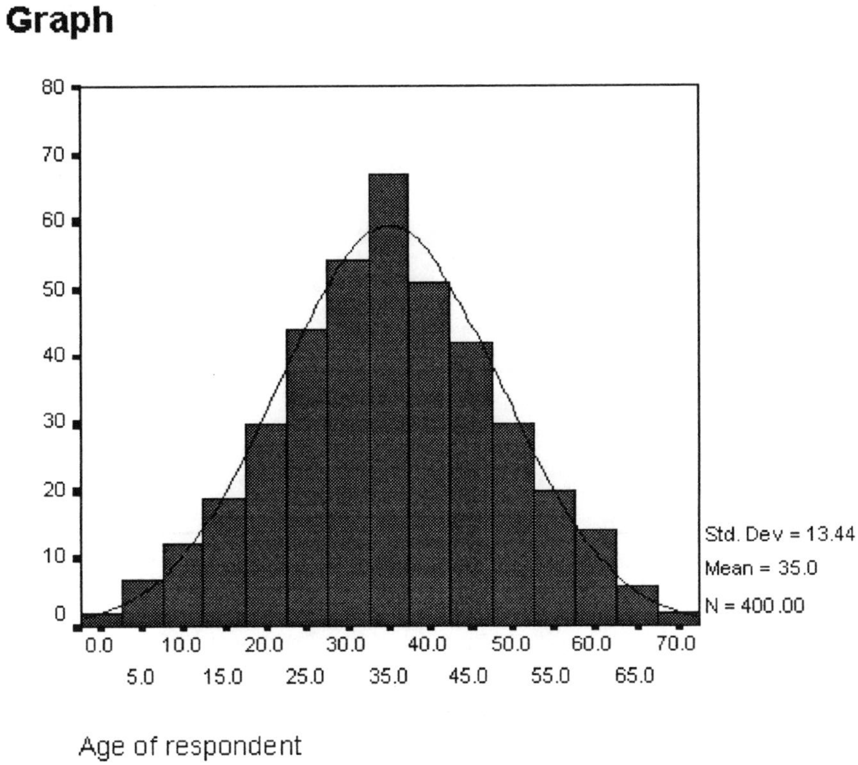

Graph

Figure 6.10 SPSS histogram with normal curve

Since the distribution is approximately normal, we can use z-scores to analyze it. For example, we might be interested in the proportion of people who are not eligible to vote because of their age. This means finding the proportion of people who are less than 18 years of age. The first step is to determine how many z-scores 18 is from the mean of 35 years. Since we are working with a population distribution the appropriate formula is:

$$Z = \frac{X_i - \mu}{\sigma} = \frac{18 - 35}{13}$$

$$= -1.3$$

Since we are only interested in the area in one tail of the distribution, we refer to the column for the area under the curve *beyond one point* when referring to Table 6.9 for the standard normal curve.

Table 6.9 Areas under the standard normal curve

z	Area under curve between both points	Area under curve beyond both points	Area under curve beyond one point
±0.1	0.080	0.920	0.4600
±0.2	0.159	0.841	0.4205
±0.3	0.236	0.764	0.3820
±0.4	0.311	0.689	0.3445
±0.5	0.383	0.617	0.3085
⋮	⋮	⋮	⋮
±1.1	0.729	0.271	0.1355
±1.2	0.770	0.230	0.1150
±1.3	0.806	0.194	0.0970
±1.4	0.838	0.162	0.0810
±1.5	0.866	0.134	0.0670
±1.6	0.890	0.110	0.0550
±1.645	0.900	0.100	0.0500
±1.7	0.911	0.089	0.0445
±1.8	0.928	0.072	0.0360
±1.9	0.943	0.057	0.0290
±1.96	0.950	0.050	0.0250
±2	0.954	0.046	0.0230
⋮	⋮	⋮	⋮
±3	>0.996	<0.004	<0.0020

Only 0.097, or 9.7 percent, of the curve lies beyond a z-score of -1.3, as shown in Figure 6.11.

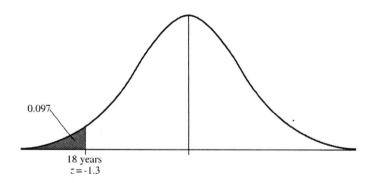

0.097

18 years
$z = -1.3$

Figure 6.11

If you went into the data file you would find that the *actual* percentage of cases whose age is less than 18 years is 10 percent. Thus by using the normal curve to describe the distribution we are very close to the actual results. We can confirm this by looking at the proportion of cases that fall within certain ranges around the mean. As we discussed above, for a normal curve we know that 68 percent of cases will fall within 1 z-score from the mean, and for this population this was bounded by 22 and 48 years of age. If we generate a frequency table and add the percentage of cases that have ages between 22 and 48 (inclusive) the sum will be 68 percent, which is consistent with the percentage of cases we expect to find in this range based on the normal curve.

This little exercise indicates that when a distribution is approximately normal, the calculation of z-scores can be a quick way of determining the proportion of cases within any range of values that may interest us. Of course, because any distribution is only approximately normal, the proportions obtained by using z-scores will not always be exactly equal to the actual proportion of cases within the range of values we are interested in.

Exercises

6.1 From the table for the area under the standard normal curve find the probability that a normally distributed variable will have a z-score:
(a) above 1.3
(b) below 1.3
(c) between 0.5 and 3.4
(d) between –2.3 and 2
(e) greater than 2.3 and less than –1.4
(f) less than –1.6 and greater than 1.6
(g) less than –1.96 and greater than 1.96.
For each of these regions draw a sketch of the normal curve and shade in the appropriate area.

6.2 If a set of cases is normally distributed, using the table for the area under the standard normal curve, find the z-score(s) that define the following proportions of cases:
(a) the middle 0.683 of cases
(b) the 0.018 cases with the highest scores
(c) the 0.05 cases with the lowest scores
(d) the 0.134 cases which together form the extremes of the distribution.
For each of these regions draw a sketch of the normal curve with the appropriate area shaded.

6.3 If X is a variable with a normal distribution, a mean of 60, and a standard deviation of 10, how many standard deviations from the mean are the following values for X_i?

(a) 60
(b) 52
(c) 85
(d) 43
(e) 73

6.4   A (hypothetical) study has discovered that the income of families headed by a single mother is normally distributed, with an average annual income of $17,500, and standard deviation of $3000. If the poverty line is considered to be $15,000, how many families headed by a single mother are living in poverty? Sketch the normal curve to illustrate your answer.

6.5   If the mean life of a certain brand of light bulb is 510 hours and the standard deviation is 30 hours, what percentage of bulbs lasts no more than 462 hours? (Assume a normal distribution.)

6.6   The average selling price of a new car is $19,800 and the standard deviation is $2300.
(a) What proportion of new cars will sell for less than $16,000?
(b) Within what limits will the middle 95 percent fall? (Assume a normal distribution.)

6.7   The reaction time of a motorist is such that when traveling at 60 km/h his average breaking distance is 40 meters with a standard deviation of 5 meters.
(a) If the motorist is traveling at 60 km/h and suddenly sees a dog crossing his path 47 meters away, what is the probability he will hit it?
(b) How far away will the dog have to be to have a 95 percent chance of not being hit? (Assume a normal distribution.)

6.8   (a) In the example used in this chapter for the distribution of the ages of 400 community residents, calculate, using z-scores, the proportion of cases that are of working age, that is between 18 and 65 years old.
(b) Calculate the range of ages that determine the middle 50 percent of cases. Confirm your calculations by referring to the frequency table generated by SPSS for this distribution.

6.9   Based on past results, a charity organization expects that donations for the forthcoming year can be modeled using a normal curve. It expects to receive donations of $1.5 million in the following year, with a standard deviation of $200,000. Its target is $1.7 million in donations.
(a) What is the expected probability of meeting this target?
(b) If the charity considers $1.2 million to be the minimum amount it requires to cover costs and meet the basic needs of the poor in its

area, what is the expected probability that it will receive enough to meet this minimum?

6.10 A local energy-generating program is proposed using wind power. This form of energy generation is only viable if wind speed in a certain area is over 15 km/h for at least 25 percent of the time. The average wind speed is 12 km/h with a standard deviation of 6 km/h. Is there sufficient evidence to suggest that the project will be viable?

PART 2

Bivariate Descriptive Statistics

7

Investigating the Relationship Between Two Variables: The Tabular Description of Nominal and Ordinal Data

The chapters in the first part of this book deal with methods for analyzing one variable at a time; hence the term **univariate descriptive statistics**. We may have data for a single variable, such as income, and we describe it in the appropriate way given the research problem being addressed and the level of measurement for the variable. For example, we may describe weekly income, measured in dollars, in any or all of the following three ways:

- **tabular description** by generating a relative frequency table;
- **graphical description** by generating a frequency polygon;
- **numerical description** by calculating the mean and standard deviation to gage the central tendency and dispersion of this distribution.

Each of these procedures focuses solely on the *one* variable with which we are interested.

The relationship between variables

Of course, in the process of doing research we may, and usually do, collect data on many variables. We may not only have collected data on people's weekly income, but also gather information on their age, health levels, how much TV they watch, and a myriad number of other variables that may be of interest. We can analyze each of these variables separately, or we may, instead, be interested in examining whether there is a **relationship** between two or more variables. Everyone probably has a common-sense notion of what it means for two variables to be 'related to', or 'dependent on', each other. We know that as children grow older they also get taller: age and height are related. We also know that as our income increases the amount we spend also increases: income and consumption are related. These examples express a general concept that we have an intuitive feel for. This is the idea that as the value of one variable changes from one case to another, the value of the other variable also changes.

Usually we choose to investigate two variables because we think they are related in some systematic way. For example, we may believe that a person's income is somehow related to where they live. To investigate this we collect data from a sample of people and find that people living in one town tend to have a certain income level, people in a different town have a higher level of income, and people in a third town tend to have an even higher income. These results suggest that place of residence and income level are somehow related or dependent. If these two variables are indeed related, then when we compare two people and find that they live in different districts, we will expect them to have different income levels as well.

Thus we do not treat income as a wholly distinct variable, but see it as somehow 'connected' to a person's place of residence. To draw out such a relationship in the data we collect, we use descriptive statistics that do not just summarize the distribution of each variable separately, but rather *describe the way in which changes in the value of one variable are related to changes in the value of the other variable.*

Let's consider the opposite situation where two variables are not related, or in other words they are **independent**.

Two variables are **independent** if the pattern of variation in the scores for one variable is not related to the pattern of variation in the scores for the other variable.

The level of education in Ecuador is probably independent of the rate of infant mortality in Mali. The two variables will change over time, but these changes will not be related to each other in any systematic way. A change in Ecuador's education level will not be connected in any regular way to Mali's infant mortality rate.

There are several techniques, collectively called **bivariate descriptive statistics**, which can be used to analyze whether a relationship exists between two variables (Table 7.1).

Table 7.1 Bivariate descriptive statistics

Method	Examples
Tabular and graphical methods These present data in a way that reveals a possible relationship between two variables	Bivariate table for categorical data (nominal and ordinal) Scatter plot for continuous data (interval/ratio)
Numerical methods These are the mathematical operations used to quantify, in a single number, the strength of a relationship. They are called measures of association. When both variables are measured at least at the ordinal level they also indicate the direction of the relationship	Lambda, Cramer's V (nominal) Gamma, Somers' d, Kendall's tau-b and tau-c (ordinal scales with few values) Spearman's rank-order correlation coefficient (ordinal scales with many values) Pearson's product moment correlation coefficient (interval/ratio)

These methods are complementary and reinforce each other. The aim of each is to provide evidence of any dependence that may exist between two variables.

Modeling relationships between variables

We will learn in this and subsequent chapters the specific techniques for investigating the relationship between two variables, but first we need to look, at a conceptual level, at what it means for two variables to be related. Suppose we have collected data for two variables: income and place of residence. We conduct research because we believe there is a relationship between these two variables, and we hope to discover the characteristics of that relationship in the data we gather. We can characterize, or **model**, the possible relationship between these (or any) two variables in many different ways. The simplest way in which two variables can be causally related is through a **direct relationship**, which has three possible forms, as follows.

One-way direct relationship with income as dependent This models the relationship as a one-way street running from place of residence to income (Figure 7.1). We may have a theory which argues that job and career opportunities vary across towns and this affects the income levels of people living in those towns. In this case we argue that there is a pattern of dependence with income as the dependent variable and place of residence as the independent variable.

Figure 7.1 One-way direct relationship with income as dependent

One-way direct relationship with place of residence as dependent Another group of social researchers may disagree with the previous model; they come from another theoretical perspective that agrees there is a pattern of dependence between the two variables, but it runs in the other direction. People with high incomes can choose where they live and will move to the town with the most desirable environment. Thus place of residence is the dependent variable and income is the independent variable (Figure 7.2).

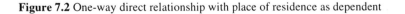

Figure 7.2 One-way direct relationship with place of residence as dependent

Two-way direct relationship with place of residence and income mutually dependent A third group of social scientists may agree that the two variables are related, but believe that both types of causality are operating so that the two variables affect each other. In this model, it is not appropriate to characterize one variable as the independent and the other as the dependent. Instead they are **mutually dependent** (Figure 7.3).

Figure 7.3 Two-way direct relationship with place of residence and income mutually dependent

Thus it is important not to confuse the identification of a dependent relationship with the closely related but distinct problem of specifying dependent and independent variables. It is only in the case of a one-way relationship that it is appropriate to specify one of the variables as independent and the other variable as dependent.

The important point to remember is that we choose a model based on particular theoretical views about the nature of the world and people's behavior. These models may or may not be correct. Statistical analysis cannot prove any of the types of causality illustrated above. All they can show is some statistical relationship between observed variables based on the data collected. The way we organize data and the interpretation we place on the results are contingent upon these theoretical presuppositions. The same data can tell many different stories depending on the theoretical preconceptions of the story-teller. For instance, we have presented the three simplest models for characterizing a relationship between two variables. There are more complex models which involve the relationship between three or more variables. To explore more complex relationships would take us into the realm of **multivariate analysis** – the investigation of relationships between more than two variables. We defer the investigation of multivariate models until later chapters. However, it is important to keep in mind when interpreting bivariate results the fact that any observed relationship between two variables may be more complicated than the simple cause-and-effect models we described above.

We will now turn to the techniques for describing bivariate relationships. In the rest of this chapter we concentrate on the simplest, and most commonly used of these, the **bivariate table**.

Describing categorical data with crosstabulations

Let us assume that we are conducting a study to investigate whether there is a relationship between people's place of residence and their income level. We suspect that there is a relationship between these two variables, and moreover we believe it to be a one-way causal relationship running from income level to place of residence. In other words, we argue that income level is the independent variable and place of residence is the dependent variable. Remember though that this is only a supposition for what we expect to find. The 'real world', or at least the data we gather from it, may not agree with this expectation. The two variables may not be related; instead they may be independent of each other. How can we organize the data we collect to inform us whether our model is correct or whether the two variables are in fact independent?

Place of residence is operationalized by asking 720 people whether they live in a rural of urban area (nominal). Income for these 720 people is measured on an ordinal scale by determining whether a person earns above or below the national median weekly income; those who earn below the national average are classified into 'low income' and those who earn above the national average are classified into 'high income'.

The research will yield 720 pairs of numbers: each person will have a value assigned to them indicating where they live and another value indicating their income group. How can we organize these 1440 numbers in such a way as to reveal any relationship that exists between income and place of residence? We could use the univariate methods we learnt in earlier chapters to construct a separate frequency distribution for each variable (Tables 7.2 and 7.3).

Table 7.2 Frequency distribution for place of residence

Place of residence	Frequency
Urban	397
Rural	323
Total	720

Table 7.3 Frequency distribution for income level

Income	Frequency
Low income	372
High income	348
Total	720

It is clear that these *separate* univariate frequency tables do not help us much. It is hard to see if there is a relationship between the two variables, which is the aim of our research. To capture any possible relationship that may exist between variables measured with categorical data we use a **bivariate table** which is also known as a **contingency table** or **crosstabulation** (or 'crosstab' for short).

A **bivariate table** displays the joint frequency distribution for two variables.

The crosstabulation for the data we have (hypothetically) collected is presented in Table 7.4.

Table 7.4 Place of residence by income level

Place of residence	Income		
	Low	High	Total
Urban	167	230	397
Rural	205	118	323
Total	372	348	720

Source: Hypothetical survey responses.

A crosstab shows the **joint distribution** for two variables, since we can 'read off' the score any given case has for each of the variables simultaneously. Looking at Table 7.4, for example, we can see that there are 205 cases who are both residents of rural areas *and* have a low income. Since bivariate tables describe data in a way that reveals this joint distribution, it allows us to investigate whether two variables are related.

There are certain rules we follow in the construction of a bivariate table:

• *Give the table an appropriate title* A crosstab should always have a title with clear labeling for both variables.
• *Indicate the source of data* This is usually done in the text immediately before or after the table, or as a footnote attached to the table (as in the example shown in Table 7.4).
• *Place the appropriate variables in the rows and columns* If there is reason to believe that the two variables are not only related to each other, but that one of the variables is dependent on the other (a one-way relationship), the *independent variable should be arranged across the columns* and the *dependent variable down the rows*. In this example we have specified that income is the independent (column) variable and place of residence is the dependent (row) variable. We do this because we believe, on the basis of our model of the world, that people's income is determined by a range of other factors and this then affects where a person lives. However, we could just as validly argue the reverse: income is the dependent and place of residence the independent variable. If we believe in this model of the world, then we will construct the bivariate table with income down the rows and residence across the columns. Alternatively we could argue that the dependence is mutual and therefore it does not matter which variable is down the rows and which is across the columns.

In discussing the use of crosstabs as a means of describing data, we need to become familiar with some terminology:

• *The size and dimensions of the table* The size of the table is defined as the number of categories for the row variable times the number of categories for the column variable. In this example there are two categories for place of residence (rural and urban) and two categories for income ('low' and 'high'), producing a 2 by 2 table. If income level was measured on a four-point scale, on the other hand, such as 'very low', 'low', 'high', and 'very high', the dimensions of the table will be 2 by 4.

- *The cells of the table* Each square in the table, which contains the number of cases that have a particular combination of values for the two variables, is called a table cell.
- *The marginals of the table* The entries in the Total column are called column marginals. Similarly, the entries in the Total row are called row marginals.

Crosstabulations with relative frequencies

We can improve our ability to draw out any possible relationship contained in the data by calculating the **relative frequencies**, rather than just the absolute number of cases in each joint category. In each cell of the table we present the information in terms of percentages of either the column totals or the row totals. The relative frequencies based on **column totals** (with calculations) are as given in Table 7.5.

Table 7.5 Place of residence by income level ($n = 720$)

Place of residence	Income		
	Low	High	Total
Urban	$\frac{167}{372} \times 100 = 45\%$	$\frac{230}{348} \times 100 = 66\%$	$\frac{397}{720} \times 100 = 55\%$
Rural	$\frac{205}{372} \times 100 = 55\%$	$\frac{118}{348} \times 100 = 34\%$	$\frac{323}{720} \times 100 = 45\%$
Total	$\frac{372}{372} \times 100 = 100\%$	$\frac{348}{348} \times 100 = 100\%$	$\frac{720}{720} \times 100 = 100\%$

The value of 55 percent is the number of people who live in rural areas *and* have a low income *as a percentage of the total number of low income earners*:

$$\frac{205}{372} \times 100 = 55\%$$

The crosstab can, alternatively, provide the relative frequencies in terms of the **row totals**, as shown in Table 7.6, including the calculations for the urban residents. We can immediately see from this that 42 percent of people, *as a percentage only of the total number of people living in urban areas*, have a low income.

Table 7.6 Place of residence by income ($n = 720$)

Place of residence	Income		
	Low	High	Total
Urban	$\frac{167}{397} \times 100 = 42\%$	$\frac{230}{397} \times 100 = 58\%$	100%
Rural	63%	37%	100%
Total	52%	48%	100%

Sometimes the different frequency tables can be combined to give the raw data and the relevant percentages by adding extra columns or rows. The appropriate structure depends on the context in which the data are being used and the intended audience. In any case, regardless of the totals from which the relative frequencies are calculated, it is important to include the actual sample size so that percentages can be converted back into absolute numbers if required by the reader.

Crosstabulations using SPSS

The data from the previous example have been entered in SPSS, so we can see how to generate crosstabs (Table 7.7, Figure 7.4).

Table 7.7 Generating crosstabs on SPSS (file: **Ch07.sav**)

SPSS command/action	Comments
1 From the menu select **Analyze/Descriptive Statistics/Crosstabs**	This brings up the **Crosstabs** dialog box
2 Click on the variable in the source list that will form the rows of the table, which in this case **Place of residence**	This highlights **Place of residence**
3 Click on ▶ that points to the target list headed **Row(s):**	This pastes **Place of residence** into the **Row(s):** target list
4 Click on the variable in the source list that will form the columns of the table, which in this case **Income level**	This highlights **Income level**
5 Click on ▶ that points to the target list headed **Column(s):**	This pastes **Income level** into the **Column(s):** target list
6 Click on **OK**	

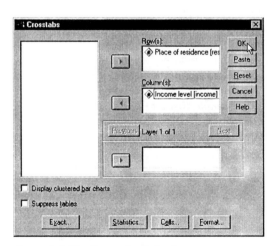

Figure 7.4 The **Crosstabs** dialog box

The following crosstab (Figure 7.5) will appear in the **Editor** window.

Place of residence * Income level Crosstabulation

Count

		Income level		Total
		Low	High	
Place of residence	Urban	167	230	397
	Rural	205	118	323
Total		372	348	720

Figure 7.5 SPSS **Crosstabs** output

The crosstabs command can be extended to provide relative as well as absolute frequencies. This option is selected by clicking on the **Cells** button at the bottom of the **Crosstabs** window. This will bring up another dialog box headed **Crosstabs: Cell Display** (Figure 7.6).

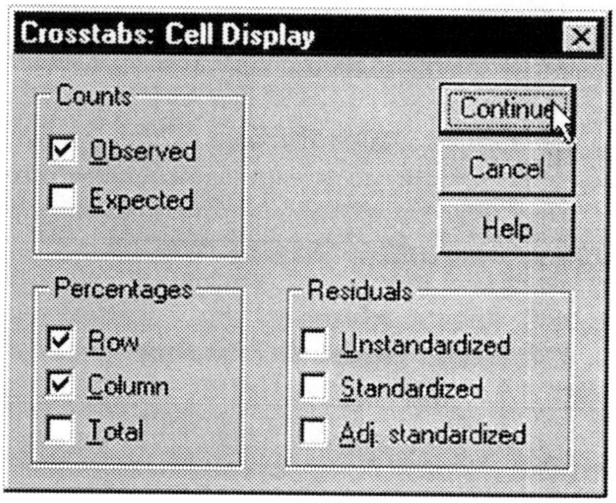

Figure 7.6 The **Cell Display** dialog box

This window provides the options for deciding how much information each cell will contain. The default setting, which we just used, is for the cells to contain the raw count only. If we want the row percentages in addition to the raw count we click on the small square next to **Row**. This will place a ✓ in the check-box to show that it is selected. Similarly, if we want column percentages we click on the check-box next to **Column**.

Figure 7.7 illustrates the output if we select both types of relative frequencies at the same time.

Place of residence * Income level Crosstabulation

			Income level		Total
			Low	High	
Place of residence	Urban	Count	167	230	397
		% within Place of residence	42.1%	57.9%	100.0%
		% within Income level	44.9%	66.1%	55.1%
	Rural	Count	205	118	323
		% within Place of residence	63.5%	36.5%	100.0%
		% within Income level	55.1%	33.9%	44.9%
Total		Count	372	348	720
		% within Place of residence	51.7%	48.3%	100.0%
		% within Income level	100.0%	100.0%	100.0%

Figure 7.7 SPSS crosstab output with relative frequencies

In one table we are provided with all the information we generated separately above in Tables 7.4, 7.5, and 7.6.

Interpreting a crosstabulation: the pattern and strength of a relationship

We have introduced the construction of a very important descriptive tool in social and health research: a crosstabulation. Its importance rests in the fact that so much data collected in social research are discrete, categorical data on nominal or ordinal scales. Having transformed a set of raw data into a crosstab, the task is then to interpret it – to assess whether it reveals that a relationship exists between the two variables. When interpreting a relationship evident in a crosstab we generally look for two features:

- pattern
- strength

To draw out these features of a relationship it is helpful to highlight the modal cell for each column (Table 7.8).

Table 7.8 Place of residence by income level

Place of residence	Income		Total
	Low	High	
Urban	167	230	397
	45%	66%	
Rural	205	118	323
	55%	34%	
Total	372	348	720

By highlighting the modal cell for each column we can see that there is a relationship. Looking at the relative frequencies it is evident that 55 percent of low income earners live in rural areas, whereas 66 percent of high income earners live in urban areas. Thus we can interpret the table as suggesting a relationship exists between income and place of residence, and the **pattern** of this relationship is that low income earners are concentrated in the country while high income earners are concentrated in the cities.

We can also asses the **strength** of this relationship by looking at the proportion of cases in each column 'captured' by the modal cell in each column. We can see that while the modal category for low income earners in terms of where they live is rural, there is still a very high percentage of low income earners that live elsewhere. Similarly, while the majority of high income earners live in urban, a large percentage of them do not. This result indicates to us that the relationship between income and place of residence is not very strong.

Interpreting a crosstabulation when both variables are ordinal

The previous sections discussed the construction of a crosstab, and how we go about interpreting any relationship revealed by such a crosstab. We looked at an example where we had one nominal variable (place of residence) and one ordinal variable (income). The rules and procedures we learnt in this instance apply generally to the construction of a crosstab with variables measured at any combination of levels.

When *both* variables are measured at the ordinal level, however, the interpretation of the pattern of a relationship found in a crosstab can be taken one step further to incorporate a discussion of the **direction** and the **consistency** of the relationship.

Direction of the relationship

Notice that in the previous discussion of the relationship between place of residence and income we concluded that income is related to place of residence such that low income earners tend to be concentrated more in rural areas, whereas high income earners tend to be concentrated in urban areas. Because we are working with a variable (place of residence) that is measured on a nominal scale we can't talk about an increase or decrease in income being associated with an increase or decrease in place of residence. It makes no sense to talk about place of residence getting greater or smaller; place of residence varies across cases but it does not increase or decrease quantitatively.

When both variables are measured at least at the ordinal level, however, we can talk about the relationship having either a **positive** or **negative** direction.

A **positive relationship** exists where movement along the scale of one variable in one direction is associated with a movement in the same direction along the scale of the other variable.

A **negative relationship** exists where movement along the scale of one variable is associated with a movement in the opposite direction along the scale of the other variable.

For example, we might be interested in the relationship between income and the amount of TV someone watches, rather than income and place of residence. The amount of TV a person watches is measured by asking each person whether they watch TV 'never', 'some nights', or 'most nights', which is an ordinal scale. With *both* variables now measured at an ordinal level we can, if we find that a relationship does indeed exist, also talk about the direction of the relationship.

Assume that we have gathered data from 300 people measuring their respective incomes (this time on a three-point scale of 'low', 'medium', or 'high'), and the amount of TV they watch. We can initially collapse these 600 numbers that are the raw data of the research into a bivariate table. We suspect that if there is a pattern of dependence between these two variables it will run from income to TV watching. Thus we will arrange the table with income (independent variable) across the columns and TV watching (dependent variable) down the rows.

All the rules we learnt earlier with respect to the construction of a crosstab still apply. But with both variables measured on an ordinal scale there is one important additional rule.

When crosstabulating two ordinal-level variables arrange the table so that the values of the independent variable increase across the page from left to right, and the values of the dependent variable increase down the page.

The application of this rule is illustrated in Table 7.9.

Table 7.9 Frequency of TV watching by income

TV watching	Income			
	Low	Medium	High	Total
Never	75 / 71.5%	15 / 15%	10 / 10.5%	100
Some nights	20 / 19.0%	70 / 70%	10 / 10.5%	100
Most nights	10 / 9.5%	15 / 15%	75 / 79.0%	100
Total	105	100	95	300

To help with the interpretation of the table, as in our earlier example, we highlight the modal cell for each column. We can immediately see that there is a relationship between these two variables, in that as income increases so too does the amount of TV watched. Thus we have a *positive* relationship. If the modal cells were all lined up along the other diagonal, from High/Never to Low/Most nights, the table will describe a negative relationship.

Consistency of the relationship

In addition to discussing the direction of the relationship, when working with two ordinal variables, we can also look at whether the relationship is **consistent**. Notice that *all* the modal cells in Table 7.8 are arranged along the positive diagonal, so that there is smooth progression in the relationship across the whole range of values. Such a pattern of dependence is called a consistent relationship. If on the other hand we observe the results contained in Table 7.10, we will still conclude that there is a relationship between the two variables, but we describe it as a **non-consistent relationship**.

Table 7.10 Frequency of TV watching by income: a non-consistent relationship

TV watching	Income			
	Low	Medium	High	Total
Never	75	10	15	100
	71.5%	10.5%	15%	
Some nights	20	10	70	100
	19.0%	10.0%	70%	
Most nights	10	75	15	100
	9.5%	79.0%	15%	
Total	105	95	100	300

We can see that at the low end of the income scale, as income rises TV watching also increases, but that the relationship reverses as we move further up the income scale.

Example

Research is conducted to see whether the English proficiency of migrants from non-English-speaking backgrounds improves over time. English proficiency is rated by a standard verbal assessment test as 'very poor', 'poor', 'average', or 'above average'. Length of time since migration is measured by classifying migrants as being resident for 'less than 1 year', 'between 1 and 2 years', '2–5 years', or 'over 5 years'. In total, 690 migrants of non-English-speaking background are surveyed.

The raw data from this research are the 1380 numbers indicating for each person their English proficiency and their length of time since migration. These raw data are described in the contingency Table 7.11, which provides the frequencies and relative frequencies.

The first point to note is the construction of Table 7.11. It is clear that if these two variables are related, the appropriate model for this relationship will be one-way dependence with time since migration as the independent variable and English proficiency as the dependent variable. There is no sense in which we could argue that the reverse is true: it is not reasonable to argue that English proficiency somehow determines how long someone has lived in a country. Thus we have placed time since migration along the columns, and English proficiency down the rows.

Table 7.11 English proficiency by time since migration

English proficiency	Time since migration				
	1 year or less	1–2 years	2–5 years	Over 5 years	Total
Very poor	105	63	8	8	184
	70%	35%	5%	4%	
Poor	30	90	16	18	154
	20%	50%	10%	9%	
Average	12	20	128	162	322
	8%	11%	80%	81%	
Above average	3	7	8	12	30
	2%	4%	5%	6%	
Total	150	180	160	200	690

The other aspect of the table's construction worth noting is that the quantity of each of these variables increases as we move across the columns or down the rows. We have two ordinal-level variables, so that we need to ensure the values of the variables move in the appropriate direction. That is, people with the least time since migration are in the first column, and time increases across the page. Similarly, the people with the lowest English proficiency are in the first row, and the strength of this variable increases as we move down the page.

In order to interpret the table in terms of a possible relationship between these variables, we have calculated the relative frequencies in terms of column totals, and also highlighted the modal cell for each column.

The relationship can now be assessed in terms of its pattern and its strength. We can see that there is a general improvement in English proficiency reflecting a positive association between the two variables. The relationship is not perfectly consistent, as the effect of time since migration begins to peter out after 5 years of residency, and migrants' English skills reach the average level of the rest of the population. *After a point* there is clearly no association between these two variables.

In terms of the strength of the relationship we could argue that it is quite strong. For each column the modal cell seems to capture a very large proportion of cases in that column, indicating that for a vast majority of cases the pattern of association we have noted seems to hold.

Summary

We have investigated extensively the construction and interpretation of bivariate tables. We have seen that these tables are a useful way of describing categorical data in such a way as to reveal whether a relationship exists between two variables under investigation. We discussed the specific rules and procedures for transforming a collection of raw data into a compact crosstab, and the means for interpreting any relationship that a crosstab may reveal. With all tables we saw that this involved an assessment of the pattern and strength of the relationship. We have also seen that where both variables are measured at the ordinal level some additional aspects to a relationship can be gleaned from a crosstab, namely the direction of the relationship, and whether it is consistent.

Exercises

7.1 A study finds that the number of injured people at an accident is related to the number of ambulance officers attending the accident. Should ambulance officers stay away from accidents in order to reduce the injury rate?

7.2 For each of the following tables, calculate the column percentages.

(a)

Dependent	Independent		
	1	2	Total
1	30	60	90
2	45	50	95
Total	75	110	185

(b)

Dependent	Independent			
	1	2	3	Total
1	56	40	10	106
2	15	30	50	95
Total	71	70	60	201

7.3 For each of the following tables, calculate the row percentages.

(a)

Dependent	Independent		
	1	2	Total
1	30	60	90
2	45	50	95
Total	75	110	185

(b)

Dependent	Independent			
	1	2	3	Total
1	56	40	10	106
2	15	30	50	95
Total	71	70	60	201

7.4 Stratified samples of 30 people who voted for the Conservative Party at the last election and 30 people who voted for the Progressive Party at the last election are drawn to assess whether political preference is related to father's political preference. The results for each person are:

Case	Voting preference	Father's voting preference	Case	Voting preference	Father's voting preference
1	Progressive	Progressive	31	Conservative	Conservative
2	Progressive	Progressive	32	Conservative	Other
3	Progressive	Progressive	33	Conservative	Conservative
4	Progressive	Conservative	34	Conservative	Conservative
5	Progressive	Progressive	35	Conservative	Conservative
6	Progressive	Progressive	36	Conservative	Progressive
7	Progressive	Progressive	37	Conservative	Conservative
8	Progressive	Progressive	38	Conservative	Conservative
9	Progressive	Conservative	39	Conservative	Progressive
10	Progressive	Conservative	40	Conservative	Other
11	Progressive	Progressive	41	Conservative	Conservative
12	Progressive	Progressive	42	Conservative	Conservative
13	Progressive	Other	43	Conservative	Conservative
14	Progressive	Progressive	44	Conservative	Conservative
15	Progressive	Progressive	45	Conservative	Conservative
16	Progressive	Progressive	46	Conservative	Other
17	Progressive	Other	47	Conservative	Conservative
18	Progressive	Progressive	48	Conservative	Other
19	Progressive	Progressive	49	Conservative	Progressive
20	Progressive	Progressive	50	Conservative	Conservative
21	Progressive	Progressive	51	Conservative	Conservative
22	Progressive	Progressive	52	Conservative	Conservative
23	Progressive	Other	53	Conservative	Progressive
24	Progressive	Other	54	Conservative	Progressive
25	Progressive	Progressive	55	Conservative	Conservative
26	Progressive	Progressive	56	Conservative	Conservative
27	Progressive	Conservative	57	Conservative	Other
28	Progressive	Progressive	58	Conservative	Conservative
29	Progressive	Progressive	59	Conservative	Conservative
30	Progressive	Progressive	60	Conservative	Other

(a) Which of these variables would you consider to be independent and which dependent? What are their respective levels of measurement?

(b) Construct a bivariate table to describe this result, either by hand or on SPSS, or both.

(c) Looking at these raw figures, do you suspect a dependence between these variables? If so, how would you describe it in plain English?

7.5 Hypothetical samples of children from Australia, Canada, Singapore, and Britain are compared, in terms of the amount of TV they watch:

Amount of TV	Country				
	Canada	Australia	Britain	Singapore	Total
Low	23	25	28	28	104
Medium	32	34	39	33	138
High	28	30	40	35	133
Total	83	89	107	96	375

Can we say that the amount of TV watched is independent of country of residence?

7.6   A sample of 162 men between the ages of 40 and 65 years is taken and the state of health of each man is recorded. Each man is also asked whether he smokes cigarettes on a regular basis. The results are crosstabulated using SPSS:

Health Level * Smoking Habit Crosstabulation

Count

		Smoking Habit		Total
		Doesn't Smoke	Does Smoke	
Health Level	Poor	13	34	47
	Fair	22	19	41
	Good	35	9	44
	Very Good	27	3	30
Total		97	65	162

(a)   What are the variables and what are their respective levels of measurement?

(b)   Should we characterize any possible relationship in terms of one variable being dependent and the other independent? Justify your answer.

(c)   From this table calculate the column percentages.

7.7   Use the **Employee data** file to answer the following questions:

(a)   The total number of managers in the sample.

(b)   The total number of males in the sample.

(c)   The total number of male managers.

(d)   The total number of male managers as a percentage of all managers.

(e)   The percentage of female employees in custodial positions as a percentage of all females.

8

Numerical Description of Nominal Data: Measures of Association

The previous chapter looked at the construction of crosstabulations. Crosstabs are a means of organizing categorical data in such a way as to reveal whether a relationship exists between two variables. We used as an illustrative example the results contained in Table 8.1.

Table 8.1 Place of residence by income level

Place of residence	Income		
	Low	High	Total
Urban	167	230	397
	45%	66%	55%
Rural	205	118	323
	55%	34%	45%
Total	372	348	720
	100%	100%	100%

When analyzing a crosstab to see if a relationship exists we tend to ask two related questions:

- What is the pattern of the relationship?
- How strong is the relationship?

We can see that in this crosstab the **pattern** of the relationship is such that relatively more low income earners live in rural areas whereas relatively more high income earners live in urban areas. Put another way, an increase in income tends to be related to a change in residence from rural to urban areas.

We can also describe, in verbal terms, the **strength** of the relationship. The variation in income from low to high is related to a certain amount of variation in place of residence, from rural to urban, but it is not a great amount of change. My impression from the table leads me to use words like 'mild' or 'slight' to describe the strength of the relationship I observe. Notice, though, how subjective is this choice of words. You may be reading this and thinking that you would use words more like 'strong' or 'considerable' to describe the strength of the relationship that emerges out of the crosstab.

It would be more objective to have a way of *measuring* the strength of the relationship evident in a crosstab. Rather than leave it to an eyeball judgment that might vary from person to person, it would be better to have a way of measuring the strength of a relationship that will give the same answer, regardless of the person making the judgment. This is precisely the function of **measures of association**. An analogy may aid this discussion. I may regard today as being a 'fairly warm' day, while another person may judge it to be 'very warm', while another person may feel that the temperature is 'pretty cool'. We are all experiencing – 'observing' – the same thing, which is today's temperature, but our subjective interpretations of this experience are different. If, however, we all refer to a standard thermometer and see that the temperature is 20°C, this is something we can all agree about. The thermometer shows the same number regardless of who looks at it. The thermometer is an objective quantification of temperature since it is based on a common standard. Similarly, while different people may look at a crosstab and verbally assess the strength of a relationship in different ways, measures of association can provide an unequivocal index of the strength of a relationship that will give the same answer for everyone.

Measures of association as descriptive statistics

Measures of association are descriptive statistics that quantify a relationship between variables.

Measures of association indicate, in quantitative terms, the extent to which a change in the value of one variable is related to a change in the value of the other variable.

Effectively, association is another word for 'relationship' or 'dependence': when age increases does height also increase (or decrease)? Is a change in religious beliefs associated with a change in attitude to capital punishment?

As we have discussed, graphs and tables are some ways of identifying a relationship that may be present between two variables. We can, in addition to these simple methods of description, calculate measures of association to actually quantify the impressions gained from these tools. The most important thing to remember about measures of association is that they are meant to help us *describe* data. Rather than just relying on a visual impression of a crosstab or graph, they can, *in the appropriate circumstances*, provide a single figure for the strength and pattern of association.

The problem with these measures is determining the appropriate circumstances in which they can provide this information. If the right circumstances do not apply then these numerical measures may be misleading, and we should just rely on the graphs and tables accompanied by appropriate verbal descriptions to describe a relationship.

Unfortunately, putting the concept of association into practice is a slippery problem. Working with measures of association can be a very frustrating experience because there are a large number to choose from, each with its own peculiarities and limitations, and often they do not lead to the same result. For example, many measures of association are sensitive to the decision as to which variable is designated as independent and which is dependent. Such measures are **asymmetric**. Asymmetric measures are useful where we believe that the relationship is such that one variable is dependent on the other. If, on the other hand, we suspect that the relationship is one of mutual dependence, we use **symmetric** measures that take on the same value regardless of the variable that is specified to be the independent variable and that which is specified to be the dependent variable.

Table 8.2 provides some guide for choosing between the more common measures detailed in the following chapters. The starting point for selecting a measure is the level at which each variable is measured. (Those wanting a more complete treatment of measures of association that covers the full range of measures available should consult either of the two following texts, which provide an excellent, although sometimes very technical, discussion: H.T. Reynolds (1977) *The Analysis of Cross-Classifications*, New York: The Free Press; A.L. Liebetrau (1983) *Measures of Association*, Beverly Hills, CA: Sage Publications.)

Table 8.2 Measures of association

Lowest level of measurement	Measure of association
Nominal	Lambda
	Goodman and Kruskal tau
	Cramer's *V*
Ordinal	Somer's *d*
	Gamma
	Kendall's tau-*b*
	Kendall's tau-*c*
	Spearman's rank-order correlation coefficient
Interval/ratio	Pearson's product moment correlation coefficient

When two variables are measured at different levels, as a general rule, the choice of a measure depends on the *lowest* of the two levels of measurement. For example, in investigating whether there is an association between sex (nominal) and job satisfaction (ordinal) the lowest level of measurement of these two variables is nominal, and this will restrict the range of measures that can be calculated to those in Table 8.2 listed next to Nominal.

In constructing a measure of association it is desirable for it to have the following properties:

- It is ideal for measures of association to take on the value of 1 (or −1 where appropriate) in situations of perfect association. Unfortunately this is not always the case, and the cause of much of the frustration tied up with using measures of association. Some measures can take on values larger than 1, while others (such as gamma) can take on the value of 1 where perfect association does not exist.

- It is ideal for measures of association to take on the value of 0 in situations of no association. Unfortunately not all measures meet this ideal quality. Some measures can take on a value of 0 even where an association is evident to the naked eye.
- Where both variables are measured at least at the ordinal level, a + or – sign should indicate the direction of association: whether an increase in the value of one variable is associated with an increase (positive association) or decrease (negative association) in the value of the other variable.

The rest of this chapter discusses measures of association for two variables when one or both of the variables is measured at the nominal level. Before doing so, it is important to remember that all that these measures do is detect association. They do not necessarily show whether one variable *causes* a change in another. We may suspect theoretically that one variable causes a change in the other, but the statistics we will learn here cannot prove causation, only provide supporting evidence for a theoretical presupposition. For example, we may observe a relationship between the number of storks in an area and the birth rate in that area, and we may calculate a measure which quantifies this statistical relationship. However, we cannot go from this statistical regularity to the conclusion that the storks cause the birth rate!

Measures of association for nominal variables

A measure of association, as we discussed above, can be thought of as a numerical index that indicates the strength of a relationship. These measures range between two extremes. One extreme is the case of **perfect association**. In the case of perfect association, all cases with a particular value for one variable have a certain value for the other variable. Using the example of income and place of residence, Table 8.3 illustrates what we will get in a crosstab if these two variables are perfectly associated.

Table 8.3 Perfect association

Place of residence	Income		
	Low	High	Total
Urban	0	397	397
Rural	323	0	323
Total	323	397	720

We can see that knowing if someone has a low income allows us to state with perfect certainty that they are also a resident of a rural area. Income is, for this group of cases, a **perfect predictor** of place of residence: knowing the income level of a person allows us to predict perfectly where this person lives. Put another way, a change from low to high income will always be associated with a change in residence from rural to urban. With perfect association we can say that all the variation in the dependent variable (place of residence) is *explained* by the variation in the independent variable (income): *the difference between two cases in terms of where they live can be explained just by referring to the difference in their incomes.*

The opposite extreme, displayed in Table 8.4, is the case of **no association**: knowing the value of a case for one variable gives no indication as to its likely value for the other variable.

Table 8.4 No association

Place of residence	Income		
	Low	High	Total
Urban	178	219	397
	55%	55%	
Rural	145	178	323
	45%	45%	
Total	323	397	720

Variation in income, in this instance, has no relationship to the variation in place of residence. The same percentage of low income earners live in the city as do high income earners. *For each of the categories of the independent variable, exactly the same pattern of responses exists for the dependent variable.*

The two cases of no association and perfect association form the two opposite ends of the scale. The case of no association is given a value of 0 and perfect association a value of 1 (Figure 8.1).

No association   Perfect association

0   1

Figure 8.1 Scale for nominal measures of association

We never actually gather data that fit either of these two extremes. They simply act as reference points. Data normally fall somewhere in between, such as the example we have been working with (Table 8.5).

Table 8.5 Place of residence by income level: observed frequencies

Place of residence	Income		
	Low	High	Total
Urban	167	230	397
Rural	205	118	323
Total	372	348	720

A visual inspection of this crosstab tells us that there is some relationship between these variables, but it is also clear that this is not a case of perfect association. If you had to give the strength of the relationship in this table a number between 0 and 1, with 0 representing no association and 1 representing perfect association, what would you give it? Is it closer to the data in Table 8.3 or Table 8.4, or somewhere in the middle?

The calculation of **lambda** gives us this number. Lambda gives us an exact numerical location for where our actual result falls along the continuum in Figure 8.1. It does this by measuring the 'statistical distance' between the table containing the actual data we observe and each of the two possible extreme situations of no association and perfect association.

Lambda is one of a class of measures called **proportional reduction in error** (PRE) measures. The logic behind PRE measures is that if two variables are associated, then we should be able to predict the score that a case has on one variable on the basis of the score it has for the other variable. If income and place of residence are indeed related, then we should be able to predict where a person lives by knowing their income level, and the stronger the relationship the more accurate will be our prediction.

All PRE measures follow a similar procedure. We try to predict how the cases will be distributed in a bivariate table under two conditions:

- we predict the distribution of cases along the dependent variable *without* any knowledge of their scores for the independent variable;
- we predict the distribution of cases along the dependent variable *with* knowledge of their scores for the independent variable.

To see how we make these predictions assume that the 720 people in our survey are lined up outside a room, and they will be marched in one by one. Before each person enters we have to guess – predict – whether they live in a rural or urban area (i.e. predict their scores on the dependent variable). In making these predictions you are given only one piece of information, which is that the majority of *all* 720 people live in an urban area.

What guess will you make before each person walks in the room? Knowing only that the majority of people live in urban areas the best guess is to predict that all 720 people live in urban areas. In other words, with no other information, guess the average! This is in effect using the no-association model in Table 8.4 as your prediction rule.

Now if there was not much of a relationship between these two variables this prediction rule would generate very few errors. The closer that the actual pattern of cases resembles the no-association model the fewer errors that will be made when using this prediction rule to guess where someone lives. In our example, if we guess all 720 people live in urban areas we will make a prediction error of 323. This is the number of people from a rural area that we have incorrectly guessed as living in an urban area. We call this E_1:

$$E_1 = 323$$

Now let us assume that the same 720 people are taken back out, and then asked to re-enter the room randomly one by one. This time, though, before each person enters you are told whether they have a low income or high income. Suspecting that there is an association between income and place of residence such that low income people live in rural areas and high income people live in urban areas, you predict that *every* low income person lives in the country and *every* high income person lives in the city. This is effectively using the perfect association model from Table 8.3 as the prediction rule.

Following this prediction rule you make 285 mistakes. This is made up of the 167 low income earners from urban areas who were misclassified as living in the country, plus the 118 high income earners from rural areas who were wrongly predicted as living in cities. We call this E_2:

$$E_2 = 167 + 118 = 285$$

The question is whether I have made fewer mistakes when given the extra information about the score each case has on the independent variable. Did my suspicion about a possible association between these two variables reduce the error rate when making these predictions? The reduction in errors is $323 - 285 = 38$. We have made 38 fewer errors by using the perfect association prediction rule than when we used the no-association prediction rule, indicating that there is some relationship in the data.

Lambda calculates this reduction in errors as a proportion of E_1:

$$\lambda = \frac{E_1 - E_2}{E_1}$$

where:
E_1 is the number of errors without information for the independent variable
E_2 is the number of errors with information for the independent variable.

As a proportion, the error rate has been reduced by:

$$\lambda = \frac{E_1 - E_2}{E_1} = \frac{323 - 285}{323}$$

$$= 0.12$$

Therefore, by having information about a person's income level (the independent variable) we are able to minimize errors when predicting where someone lives by 12 percent. This is the great advantage of PRE measures: they measure something meaningful, which is changes in prediction error rates, and thus have a specific interpretation.

We can see in Figure 8.2 that the result places the observed distribution of data much closer to the no-association extreme than to the perfect association extreme.

Figure 8.2

Lambda shows, in a clear-cut way, that although there is some relationship between these two variables, it is not very strong. Generally, we speak of association between variables as being weak, moderate, or strong (or some combination of these words, such as 'very weak' or 'moderately strong'). There is no sharp dividing line that determines when PRE values are to be called weak and when they are called strong, but to give a guide, one author suggests the terminology shown in Table 8.6. (See T.H. Black (1993) *Evaluating Social Science Research*, London: Sage Publications, 137.)

Table 8.6 Interpreting values of lambda

Range (±)	Relative strength
0.0–0.2	Very weak, negligible relationship
0.2–0.4	Weak, low association
0.4–0.7	Moderate association
0.7–0.9	Strong, high, marked association
0.9–1.0	Very high, very strong relationship

We can see that for the data we are investigating the relationship is in the very weak range.

Properties of lambda

As a measure of association lambda has certain properties, some of which are desirable, but others (unfortunately) limit its applicability. We will briefly describe the main properties in turn.

Lambda will always equal 1 where data exhibit perfect association   If we look at the way lambda is constructed it will have the desirable property that in the case of perfect association it will equal 1.   If there is perfect association between two variables, the data will correspond exactly to the second of our prediction rules, producing no errors. If I make no errors with information about the independent variable ($E_2 = 0$) then the equation for lambda will simply be:

$$\lambda = \frac{E_1}{E_1} = 1$$

Lambda will always equal 0 where data exhibit no association   If there is absolutely no association in the data, the observed results will conform exactly to the model of no association, and making predictions using the no-association model will yield no errors ($E_1 = 0$). This will generate a value for lambda of 0.

Lambda will sometimes equal 0 where data exhibit some association Although lambda will always equal 0 when there is no association, the converse is not necessarily true: sometimes when lambda equals 0 there may indeed be association. This is a major limitation to the use of lambda and will be explored further at the end of the chapter.

Lambda is an asymmetric measure of association This means that the value for lambda will be different depending on which of the two variables is considered to be independent and which is considered to be dependent. In other words, if in the example above we try to predict income levels based on where someone lives, rather than the other way around, the value for lambda will change. Thus when using lambda we need to be explicit about the nature of the relationship we think ties the two variables together. This makes lambda especially useful when we have strong reasons to believe that there is a one-way relationship between the two variables running in a certain direction.

To see this let us 'flip' the variables in our example around, and treat place of residence as the independent variable and income level as the dependent variable. This will require us to construct the crosstab with place of residence across the columns and income down the rows (Table 8.7).

Table 8.7 Place of residence by income level

Income	Place of residence		
	Urban	Rural	Total
Low	167	205	372
High	230	118	348
Total	397	323	720

Without any knowledge of the distribution of the independent variable (place of residence) we predict that all cases fall into the modal group of low income earners, thereby misclassifying the 348 people who actually have a high income:

$$E_1 = 348$$

If we try to predict people's income levels, but with knowledge of whether they live in rural or urban areas, we will predict that all the people from urban areas have a high income, thereby making 167 errors, and all the people from rural areas have a low income, thereby making 118 errors. Our total error rate therefore, when using the perfect-association model, is:

$$E_2 = 167 + 118 = 285$$

The value of lambda using this model of the relationship will be:

$$\lambda = \frac{E_1 - E_2}{E_1} = \frac{348 - 285}{348}$$

$$= 0.18$$

In other words there is a fairly weak association, in the sense of being able to predict someone's income level on the basis of where they live. The association between these two variables is slightly stronger when income level is regarded as dependent rather than place of residence.

Lambda using SPSS

Lambda can be generated as part of the **Crosstabs** command in SPSS, which we introduced in Chapter 7. It is an option, along with other measures of association, in the **Crosstabs** command. Using the data we used in the previous chapter for income and place of residence, we follow the procedure given in Table 8.8 and Figure 8.3.

Table 8.8 Generating lambda on SPSS (file: **Ch08.sav**)

SPSS command/action	Comments
1 From the menu select **Analyze/Descriptive Statistics/ Crosstabs**	This brings up a window headed **Crosstabs**
2 Click on the variable that will form the rows of the table, which in this case **Place of residence**	This highlights **Place of residence**
3 Click on ▶ that points to the area headed **Row(s):**	This pastes **Place of residence** into the **Row(s):** target variable list
4 Click on **Income level**	This highlights **Income level**
5 Click on ▶ that points to the area headed **Column(s):**	This pastes **Income level** into the **Column(s):** target variable list
6 Click on the **Statistics** button	This brings up the **Crosstabs: Statistics** box. In the top-left corner you will see an area headed **Nominal Data**. These are the measures of association available when at least one variable is measured at the nominal level. In this instance **Place of residence** is measured at the nominal level
7 Select **Lambda** by clicking on the tick-box next to it	This places ✓ in the tick-box to show that lambda has been selected
8 Click on **Continue**	
9 Click on **OK**	

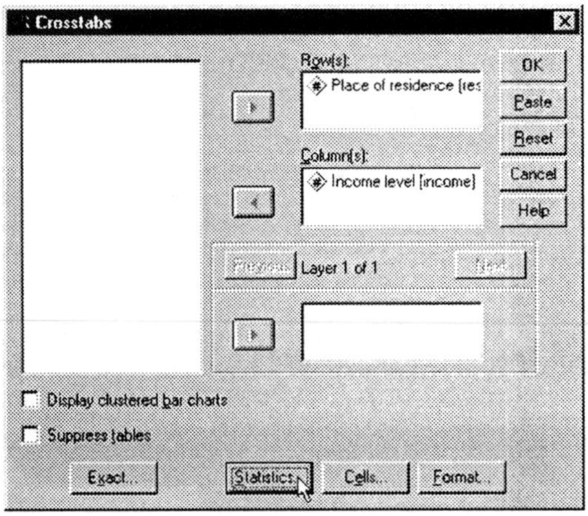

Figure 8.3(a) The **Crosstabs** dialog box

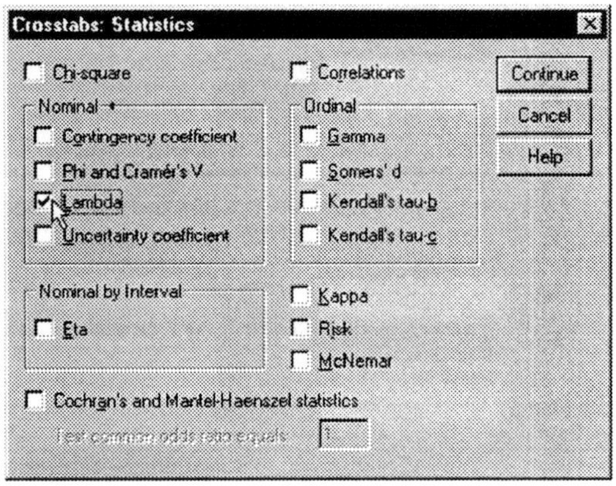

Figure 8.3(b) The **Crosstabs: Statistics** dialog box

Notice that in the **Statistics** dialog box we have the range of measures that we noted in Table 8.1 (plus others), broken down in a similar way by level of measurement. Thus we will be coming back to this dialog box frequently over the next two chapters as we work through the various measures of association.

If we follow the procedure in Table 8.10 we will obtain, along with the crosstab we generated in Chapter 7, the following table (Figure 8.4) labeled **Directional Measures** (which is SPSS's term for measures of association whose value depends on the specification of independent and dependent variables). Since lambda depends in this specification the table produces three versions of lambda: symmetric, asymmetric with place of residence as dependent, and asymmetric with income level as dependent, from which we choose the one appropriate to our preconceived model of the relationship.

Directional Measures

			Value	Asymp. Std. Error[a]	Approx. T[b]	Approx. Sig.
Nominal by Nominal	Lambda	Symmetric	.151	.047	3.061	.002
		Place of residence Dependent	.118	.056	1.976	.048
		Income level Dependent	.181	.052	3.184	.001
	Goodman and Kruskal tau	Place of residence Dependent	.045	.015		.000[c]
		Income level Dependent	.045	.015		.000[c]

a. Not assuming the null hypothesis.

b. Using the asymptotic standard error assuming the null hypothesis.

c. Based on chi-square approximation

Figure 8.4 SPSS **Crosstabs: Statistics** output

The symmetric version is used when there is no reason to suspect that one of the variables is dependent on the other, but rather that they are mutually dependent on each other. It is actually calculated as a weighted average of the two asymmetric versions: in this example the symmetric value of 0.151 falls somewhere in between the two asymmetric values of 0.118 and 0.181. The asymmetric version has two possible values, based on which of the two variables we believe is dependent.

For each of the two possible asymmetric versions, the values calculated by SPSS are the same as those we calculated by hand above, although it does so to 3 decimal places, rather than the 2 decimal places which we used in our hand calculations.

The table also produces the value of another nominal measure of association called Goodman and Kruskal *tau*, which has a much smaller value for the association than lambda. This indicates a 'problem' we will encounter a number of times in this and the next chapter, which is that different measures of association calculated on the *same* data will produce *different* values. This is because each measure conceptualizes the notion of association in slightly different ways and therefore will not always be in agreement.

The other columns in the **Directional Measures** table contain information that is not relevant at this point, but deals with issues that arise in later sections of this book. They deal with the problem of making an inference from a sample to a population.

Example

I suspect that there is a relationship between people's political orientation and their attitudes to equal rights legislation that has been proposed. I believe that political orientation is the independent variable and attitude to equal rights legislation is the dependent variable. One hundred people are selected and each person is asked to walk into a room. Before each person enters I have to guess whether that person favors or opposes equal rights legislation. However, I am given no information about each person's political orientation before they enter: I have to make a blind guess about each person's political beliefs (conservative or progressive). The only information I am given is that for the sample as a whole the modal response (the one with most cases) for the dependent variable is the 'support' category. Limited to this information, the best strategy is to guess that all 100 people support equal rights legislation. Since the modal category by definition is the category with the most observations we make the fewest errors, when we have no other information to inform our prediction, by predicting that all cases fall into it (Table 8.9).

Table 8.9 Prediction with no information about the independent variable

Attitude to equal rights	Political orientation		
	Progressive	Conservative	Total
Oppose	0	0	0
Support	50	50	100
Total	50	50	100

I again have to predict the attitude of each person, but this time I am told the political orientation of each person. I use the perfect association model as the basis for prediction and guess that *all* conservative people oppose the legislation and *all* progressive people support it (Table 8.10).

Table 8.10 Prediction with information about the independent variable

Attitude to equal rights	Political orientation		
	Progressive	Conservative	Total
Oppose	0	50	50
Support	50	0	50
Total	50	50	100

The question is whether I have made fewer mistakes when given the extra information about each person's political leanings. To which one of these extremes does the actual data most closely conform? If there is little association between the two variables, the actual data will more closely resemble those in Table 8.9, whereas the stronger the association, the more closely the observed distribution will conform to that in Table 8.10. The extent to which the observed data are closer to one extreme or the other, or somewhere in between, will be expressed by the difference in error rates we make under each prediction rule.

Assume that the observed data are those contained in Table 8.11.

Table 8.11 Observed frequency distribution

Attitude to equal rights	Political orientation		
	Progressive	Conservative	Total
Oppose	6	42	48
Support	44	8	52
Total	50	50	100

Even before we do any calculations an eyeball inspection of the crosstab will tell us that there is a strong association between these two variables, with a very high proportion of conservatives opposing and a high proportion of progressives supporting the legislation. We would place this table much closer to Table 8.10, which represents the case of perfect association, than to Table 8.9, which represents the case of no association. Thus the second prediction rule (perfect association) will dramatically reduce our errors when compared to the errors we make under the first prediction rule (no association). Before we proceed to actually calculate these error rates and lambda, can you guess what lambda will be as a quantity between 0 (no association) and 1 (perfect association)?

Without any knowledge of the independent variable (i.e. whether a person is conservative or progressive), 42 conservatives who oppose the legislation are incorrectly classified as supporting it, and 6 progressives who oppose the legislation are incorrectly classified as supporting it. Therefore total errors made are:

$$E_1 = 42 + 6 = 48$$

With knowledge of a person's political orientation, however, 6 progressives are incorrectly classified as supporting the legislation, and 8 conservatives are incorrectly classified as opposing it. Therefore total errors made in this situation are:

$$E_2 = 8 + 6 = 14$$

Lambda calculates the difference in the two error rates as a proportion of the initial situation where I had no knowledge of the independent variable – hence the term 'proportional reduction in error':

$$\lambda = \frac{E_1 - E_2}{E_1} = \frac{48 - 14}{48}$$

$$= 0.71$$

Therefore, by having information about political leaning we are able to minimize errors when predicting whether a person will support the proposed legislation by 71 percent. This indicates a strong relationship between the two variables. Did this figure correspond with the value you thought expressed the strength of the relationship based on just your visual inspection of the crosstab?

Limitations on the use of lambda

Despite its intuitive appeal and ease of calculation, a problem is all too frequently encountered when using lambda. The problem is one we have already noted above when discussing the properties of lambda. Lambda can have a value of 0 even though a relationship does exist between the two variables (which is evident just by looking at the crosstab).

The cause of the problem is data that are highly skewed along the dependent variable.

Lambda will equal 0 when the modal category for the dependent variable is the same for all categories of the independent variable.

To see what this means in practice, we will analyze the following data (Table 8.12). In this hypothetical example respondents are asked whether the government is doing enough to alleviate poverty.

Table 8.12 Should the government do more to alleviate poverty?

Agree	Age group		
	Under 45	45 or over	Total
No	110	168	278
	18%	42%	
Yes	490	232	722
	82%	58%	
Total	600	400	1000

Looking at the crosstab we can see that there is some relationship. A much higher percentage of under 45s agree with the statement about government policy than people who are 45 or older. Clearly, there is some dependence between the two variables, and we might even describe it in verbal terms by saying that it appears to be fair to moderate in strength.

However, if we try to quantify this relationship with lambda we get a *measured* association of zero. Notice that the modal response for the dependent variable for all 1000 cases is 'yes', which is also the modal response for each of the two categories of the independent variable: the majority of people under 45 stated yes, and the majority of people aged 45 or over also stated yes. This skewed distribution in terms of the dependent variable will produce a lambda of zero, even when it is clear to the naked eye that some association does exist between the variables.

To see how, I need first to calculate the number of errors when predicting without knowledge of the independent variable (age group). I predict that all 1000 cases will fall in the 'yes' category, since this will minimize my error rate. I therefore make 278 mistakes:

$$E_1 = 278$$

With information about the independent variable, I will still make the same number of mistakes. Considering first the respondents aged under 45, I predict that all 600 respond 'yes' (110 mistakes). Second, I predict all 400 people aged

45 or over respond 'yes' (168 mistakes). This sums to 278 total errors, which is the same as predicting without knowledge of the respondents' sex.

$$E_2 = 278$$

The value for lambda will be:

$$\lambda = \frac{E_1 - E_2}{E_1} = \frac{278 - 278}{278}$$

$$= 0$$

Lambda has failed to pick up the observable relationship, which is evident to the naked eye. This highlights one important rule:

Whenever lambda equals 0 inspect the relative frequency distribution to decide whether this actually reflects no association or whether it is due to a skewed distribution for the dependent variable.

If an inspection of the column percentages leads you to conclude that a value of 0 for lambda is due to a skewed distribution (as in this case), there are three options:

Don't bother with measures of association Stick to the crosstab and the relative frequencies it contains, and base your conclusion regarding the relationship on this alone. This requires the researcher to make some subjective judgments, but as long as the crosstab is there for readers to assess for themselves, there is no problem with structuring an argument using only the relative frequencies as evidence. These frequencies sometimes 'speak for themselves': calculating more advanced statistics on top (and all the problems that sometimes come with them) may only serve to bury important information in an avalanche of suspect numbers.

Calculate other measures of association There are other measures of association for nominal data that can be used if there are problems with lambda. Another PRE measure, which appeared in the SPSS output above, is the Goodman-Kruskal tau. Like lambda this is an asymmetric measure of association that ranges between 0 and 1. Unlike lambda it does not use the modal response for the independent variable in making predictions, but rather the frequency distribution of cases across all the categories of the independent variable. Since it is less sensitive to skewed marginal distributions than lambda it is a convenient alternative when skewness causes lambda to equal zero.

Another measure of association is Cramer's *V*. This is available in SPSS and will always produce a value greater than 0 where an association exists between two variables. However, it does not have a simple interpretation in terms of PRE, and therefore cannot be used to assess the strength of a relationship for any given crosstab. It can be useful though when *comparing the strength of bivariate relationships across different tables.* The formula for Cramer's *V* is given by:

$$V = \sqrt{\frac{\chi^2}{n(k-1)}}$$

where:

χ^2 is the chi-square statistic for the crosstab (see Chapter 20)
k is the number of rows or the number of columns, whichever is smaller.

Cramer's *V* is one of the options, along with lambda, for nominal data when choosing statistics in the SPSS **Crosstabs** command.

Standardize the table so that the row totals are all equal   This is a slightly more complicated procedure, and one not often suggested by texts on statistics. (For a more complete discussion of standardization procedures and their use with measures of association see Y.M.M. Bishop, S.E. Feinberg, and P.W. Holland (1975) *Discrete Multivariate Analysis: Theory and Practice,* Cambridge: MIT Press, 392–93; and H.T. Reynolds (1977) *The Analysis of Cross-Classifications,* London: Macmillan, 31–33.)

(This next section is optional.) The process of standardizing a table involves trying to eliminate the variation in the data brought about by the skewed distribution for the dependent variable, while still retaining the variation across the categories of the independent variable. In a report that uses this procedure it should be made clear that lambda is not calculated on the raw data, by adding a comment (maybe as a footnote) such as: 'In calculating lambda, row marginals are standardized to sum to 100.' When working with lambda we standardize the row marginals so that each row sums to 100. This involves the calculation of the row percentages, which are then treated as if they are real numbers of cases. That is, we calculate the percentage of the total 'yes' respondents that are under 45 and the percentage that are 45 or over. We do the same for the 'no' responses (Table 8.13).

Table 8.13 Should the government do more to alleviate poverty?

Agree	Age group		Total
	Under 45	45 or over	
No	$\frac{110}{278} \times 100 = 40\%$	$\frac{168}{278} \times 100 = 60\%$	100%
Yes	$\frac{490}{722} \times 100 = 68\%$	$\frac{232}{722} \times 100 = 32\%$	100%

We then use these percentage figures *as if* they are counts of actual cases, as in Table 8.14.

Table 8.14 Should the government do more to alleviate poverty?

Agree	Age group		Total
	Under 45	45 or over	
No	40	60	100
Yes	68	32	100

Remember that these are percentages: 40 represents 40 percent of 278 total no responses, and so on. But we treat them *as if* they are individual cases. This means that the total sample size 'is' 200 rather than 1000: the 100 yes 'respondents' and the 100 no 'respondents'.

Using the data from the standardized table (Table 8.14), I recalculate lambda. Without knowledge of the independent variable, I classify all 200 'respondents' in either yes or no, and therefore make 100 errors:

$$E_1 = 100$$

With knowledge of the independent variable I make the following predictions. Starting with the under 45s, I predict that all said yes, since this gives me the lowest error rate (40 mistakes). For 45 or over I predict that all said no, and therefore make 32 mistakes:

$$E_2 = 40 + 32 = 72$$

Lambda will therefore equal:

$$\lambda = \frac{E_1 - E_2}{E_1} = \frac{100 - 72}{100}$$

$$= 0.28$$

After standardization, there turns out to be a weak to moderate association between these variables that lambda calculated on the original data could not extract.

Exercises

8.1   What is the difference between asymmetric and symmetric measures of association? Which is the appropriate measure to use in situations in which two variables are thought to be mutually dependent?

8.2   Why is it important, when calculating lambda, to decide whether one variable is likely to be dependent on the other, and if so to specify which is dependent and which is independent?

8.3   Calculate lambda for the following tables, and interpret the strength of any relationship:

(a)

Dependent	Independent		
	1	2	Total
1	30	60	90
2	45	50	95
Total	75	110	185

(b)

Dependent	Independent			
	1	2	3	Total
1	56	40	10	106
2	15	30	50	95
Total	71	70	60	201

(c)

Dependent	Independent			
	1	2	3	Total
1	70	40	10	106
2	50	45	38	133
3	43	30	14	87
Total	163	165	172	500

(d)   (optional) If any of these tables produce a lambda equal to zero, standardize the distribution and recalculate lambda.

8.4   A researcher is interested in the relationship between gun ownership and attitude toward capital punishment. The researcher surveyed 3000 people and obtained the following results:

Capital punishment	Gun owners	Non-owners
For	849	367
Against	191	1593

Calculate lambda for these data and interpret the result.

8.5   A survey of 50 'blue-collar' and 50 'white-collar' workers asked respondents if they could sing their National Anthem from start to finish.

Blue–collar: Yes = 29, No = 21
White–collar: Yes = 22, No = 28

Arrange these data into a crosstabulation. What should be the dependent and independent variables? Calculate lambda for these data.

8.6   (optional) A study finds that the association between two variables, using Cramer's V as the measure, is 0.34. In the past, studies have measured association between the same variables using V as ranging from 0.15 to 0.21. How should the researchers report their result?

8.7   (optional) Calculate Cramer's V for the following sets of data:
(a) $\chi^2 = 3.5$, $n = 20$, rows = 4, columns = 2
(b) $\chi^2 = 9.8$, $n = 90$, rows = 2, columns = 4
(c) $\chi^2 = 12$, $n = 800$, rows = 3, columns = 3

8.8   Open the **Employee data** file. Recode current salary into class intervals based on $10,000 income brackets. Use this recoded variable to:
(a)   assess the strength of any association between current income and gender;
(b)   assess the strength of any association between current income and employment category.
In your answers you should be careful to specify how you are modeling the relationships and choose the measure accordingly.

9

Numerical Description of Ordinal Data

In Chapter 7 we saw that data measured at the ordinal level can be described in the form of a crosstabulation. It is important to begin with a visual inspection of a crosstab – to 'eyeball' the table – in order to observe directly whether the two variables are independent or whether they exhibit some kind of relationship. A visual inspection of the table tries to identify the variation in the data, and based on this we interpret the nature of any relationship that the crosstab reveals. In Chapter 8 we also noted that this visual inspection of a crosstab allows us to determine whether it is worth calculating measures of association in conjunction with the table to give quantitative precision to the conclusions we draw from this inspection.

This chapter concentrates on measures of association for variables measured at the ordinal level. These are PRE measures of association that are similar to lambda in their basic logic and how we interpret them. With lambda, we try to predict the value an *individual* case takes for the dependent variable. We do this by assuming first that there is no association between the variables, and then second by assuming that there is perfect association between the two variables. By comparing the error rates under each prediction rule we can assess the relationship actually contained in the set of data we collect.

We undertake a similar procedure with ordinal data, but we make use of the extra information about the variables given to us by the ordinal level of measurement. With ordinal data, unlike nominal data, we know the ranking of cases. We therefore try to predict the rank order of *pairs* of cases, and base the measures of association on the success in predicting these rankings.

For relationships, such as that in the example described in Table 9.1, we can proceed to quantify the strong, positive relationship we observe by calculating the relevant ordinal measures of association. There are a number of PRE measures of association that can be calculated for such a table, varying slightly in their respective methods. All of the measures for ordinal data we will discuss have the common characteristic of being based on the distinction between **concordant** and **discordant pairs**.

Table 9.1 Frequency of TV watching by income

TV watching	Income			
	Low	Medium	High	Total
Never	75	15	10	100
	71.5%	15%	10.5%	
Some nights	20	70	10	100
	19.0%	70%	10.5%	
Most nights	10	15	75	100
	9.5%	15%	79.0%	
Total	105	100	95	300

Concordant pairs

Assume that one of the 75 high income people in Table 9.1 who watches TV most nights is named Alex, and one of the 70 medium income people who watch TV some nights is called Andrea. These two people can be ranked against each other for each of the two variables (Figure 9.1):

- In terms of income Alex is ranked above (has a higher income than) Andrea.
- In terms of TV watching Alex is also ranked above Andrea, since she watches TV most nights whereas Andrea watches only some nights.

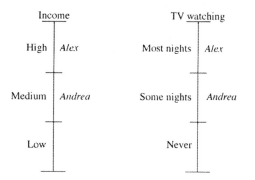

Figure 9.1: Ranking of a concordant pair

The ranking of this pair of cases is summarized Table 9.2.

Table 9.2 A concordant pair of cases

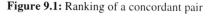

Independent variable: income	Dependent variable: TV watching
Alex ranked above Andrea	Alex ranked above Andrea
(has a higher income)	(watches more TV)

Therefore these two cases *are ranked the same for each variable*. This might sound like a strange use of language: how can they be the same if they have different values? The point is that they are *ranked* the same: Alex is ranked above Andrea for each variable. We describe such a pair of cases as a **concordant pair** (N_c).

> A **concordant pair** is formed by two cases in a joint distribution that are ranked the same on both variables.

We have picked out two cases from the whole set of 300 cases that form a concordant pair. How do we calculate the *total* number of concordant pairs contained in the table? To see this look at the shaded cells in the crosstab from which we drew Andrea and Alex (Table 9.3).

Table 9.3 Frequency of TV watching by income

TV watching	Income		
	Low	Medium	High
Never	75	15	10
Some nights	20	70	10
Most nights	10	15	75

In the discussion above I formed a concordant pair by matching Alex, who is one of the 75 cases who have a high income and also watches TV most nights, with Andrea, who is one of the 70 medium income earners who watches TV some nights. In fact I can pair Alex up with *each and every* one of the 70 people in the 'medium/some nights' cell, producing 70 concordant pairs: Alex plus each of the 70 people in the middle cell of the table (including Andrea). I can then do the same for each of the other 74 people who are high income earners and watch TV most nights and watch TV every day. This will produce, in total, 75 lots of 70 concordant pairs:

$$75 \times 70 = 5250$$

Looking at Table 9.4, though, we see that there are still more combinations that will form concordant pairs.

Table 9.4 Frequency of TV watching by income

TV watching	Income		
	Low	Medium	High
Never	75	15	10
Some nights	20	70	10
Most nights	10	15	75

Each of the 75 cases in the bottom-right cell is also ranked above each of the 15 cases in the 'never/medium' cell: they both have a higher income and watch TV more. So this will add the following number of concordant pairs:

$$75 \times 15 = 1125$$

In fact, any case will form a concordant pair with any other case in a cell *above and to the left* of it in the table (provided the table has been constructed with the values increasing down the rows and across the columns). The total number of concordant pairs, therefore, will be as shown in Table 9.5.

Table 9.5 Calculating concordant pairs

75	15	10
20	70	10
10	15	**75**

$(75\times70)+(75\times15)+(75\times20)+(75\times75) = 13{,}500$

+

75	15	10
20	70	**10**
10	15	75

$(10\times15)+(10\times75) = 900$

+

75	15	10
20	70	10
10	**15**	75

$(15\times20)+(15\times75) = 1425$

+

75	15	10
20	**70**	10
10	15	75

$(70\times75) = 5250$

$$N_c = 13{,}500 + 900 + 1425 + 5250 = 21{,}075$$

Discordant pairs

Now if I take one of the 10 people who have a low income and watch TV most nights, named Chris, and compare him with Andrea (one of the 70 people with medium income and watches TV some nights), the ranking will not be the same for both variables. Chris is ranked *below* Andrea in terms of income, but ranked *above* Andrea in terms of TV watching (Figure 9.2).
Such cases are called **discordant pairs** (N_d).

A **discordant pair** is formed by two cases in a joint distribution whose ranking on one variable is different to their ranking for the other variable.

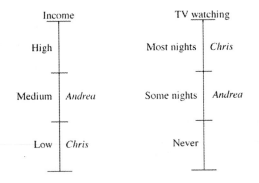

Figure 9.2: Ranking of a discordant pair

A case will form a discordant pair with any other case in the table that is in any cell *above and to the right.* To calculate the total number of discordant pairs we begin with the bottom-left cell in Table 9.6 and match it with all cells above and to the right of it.

Table 9.6 Calculating discordant pairs

75	**15**	**10**	
20	**70**	**10**	$(10 \times 70)+(10 \times 15)+(10 \times 10)+(10 \times 10) = 1050$
10	15	75	
			+
75	**15**	**10**	
20	70	10	$(20 \times 15)+ (20 \times 10) = 500$
10	15	75	
			+
75	15	**10**	
20	70	**10**	$(15 \times 10)+ (15 \times 10) = 300$
10	**15**	75	
			+
75	15	**10**	
20	**70**	10	$(70 \times 10) = 700$
10	15	75	

$$N_d = 1050 + 500 + 300 + 700 = 2550$$

Measures of association for ordinal variables

All PRE measures of association use the difference between concordant and discordant pairs as the basis for assessing whether an association exists and determining its direction. The reason why we look at these concordant and discordant pairs is that they give us information that we can use in prediction. If two variables are positively associated then the crosstab will contain more concordant pairs than discordant pairs, and vice versa for negative association.

Positive association between variables The data will contain a lot of concordant pairs and few discordant pairs. If this is this situation, and I am told a person ranks above another in terms of income, I will also predict that that person ranks above the other in terms of frequency of TV watching as well.

$$\text{Positive association: } N_c - N_d > 0$$

Negative association between variables The data will contain a lot of discordant pairs, so I will make the opposite prediction: knowing that a person ranks above another in terms of income will lead me to guess that that person ranks below the other in terms of frequency of TV watching.

$$\text{Negative association: } N_c - N_d < 0$$

No association between variables   The data will contain just as many concordant pairs as discordant pairs, and I will not increase my ability to predict the category of the dependent variable a case falls into by knowing the category of the independent variable that case falls into.

$$\text{No association: } N_c - N_d = 0$$

There are four principal PRE measures of association for ordinal data: Somers' *d*, Gamma, Kendal's tau-*b*, and Kendal's tau-*c*. These are all similar in that they have a PRE interpretation, and they all use the difference between N_c and N_d as the basis for assessing the strength of a relationship. The difference between them is in terms of how they standardize this difference. We will begin by exploring the simplest of these, which is gamma.

Gamma

Gamma is a common PRE measure of association for two variables measured at least at the ordinal level and arranged in a bivariate table. Gamma is a **symmetric measure of association** so that the value calculated will be the same regardless of which of the variables is specified as independent and which is specified as dependent. In other words, if we flipped the rows and columns around in our table, so that income is down the rows and TV watching is across the columns, the calculation of gamma will not be affected. Thus it is not sensitive to the particular model we believe characterizes the relationship between the two variables.

The formula for gamma expresses the difference between the number of concordant pairs and the number of discordant pairs *as a proportion of the total number of concordant and discordant pairs.* Using the data from our example, gamma will be:

$$G = \frac{N_c - N_d}{N_c + N_d} = \frac{21{,}075 - 2550}{21{,}075 + 2550}$$

$$= 0.78$$

This indicates that we have a strong positive association between these two variables, which reinforces the conclusion we drew based just on the visual inspection of the crosstab.

It is evident that the range of possible values for gamma is between −1 and 1. A gamma of −1 indicates perfect negative association: knowing that a case ranks above another along one variable indicates that it must rank below for the other variable. Such a result would be obtained if there were *only discordant pairs*, as in Table 9.7.

Table 9.7 Frequency of TV watching by income: perfect negative association

TV watching	Income		
	Low	Medium	High
Never	0	0	100%
Some nights	0	100%	0
Most nights	100%	0	0

If, on the other hand, there are *only concordant pairs* the value of gamma will be +1, indicating perfect positive association: knowing a case ranks above another for the independent variable indicates that it must also rank above for the dependent variable. Such a situation is reflected in Table 9.8.

Table 9.8 Frequency of TV watching by income: perfect positive association

TV watching	Income		
	Low	Medium	High
Never	100%	0	0
Some nights	0	100%	0
Most nights	0	0	100%

A gamma of zero indicates no association. If there are *just as many concordant pairs as there are discordant pairs*, then knowing the ranking along one variable gives no guide as to the ranking on the other variable. This situation is illustrated in Table 9.9.

Table 9.9 Frequency of TV watching by income: no association

TV watching	Income		
	Low	Medium	High
Never	50%	0	50%
Some nights	0	100%	0
Most nights	50%	0	50%

These three tables illustrate the three extreme points on a standardized scale measuring the strength of association between two ordinal variables (Figure 9.3).

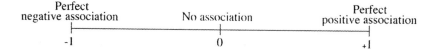

Figure 9.3 The range of gamma

Clearly the data for the example we are actually working with does not conform to any of these three extreme situations. It is a question of which prediction rule will be closest to the results we actually obtain. It is clear that the perfect positive association table is the one that the actual data most closely resemble, and gamma captures this quantitatively with a value of 0.78. It is not quite +1, but closer to it than to 0 or −1.

Gamma is very popular in the literature because of its relative ease of calculation, although this advantage is now vitiated by the use of computer programs such as SPSS, which makes the calculation of all measures as easy as clicking buttons. I suspect that another element to its popularity is that compared to other ordinal measures of association, it generates the highest value for the strength of association.

Gamma does have some important limitations though, which we need to be mindful of. The first is that it is only a symmetric measure, and therefore does not take advantage of information provided by the data where we believe the most appropriate model for describing a relationship is one-way dependence (as we presumed in our example). The other main limitation is that, while perfect association will produce a value of +1 or −1, the converse is not always true: a gamma of +1 or −1 will not always indicate perfect association. It is possible to generate a value of −1 or +1 for a crosstab even where there is clearly less than perfect association evident in the data. This occurs where the relationship is not consistent. We should follow the rule, therefore, that *before using gamma a bivariate table should be inspected to assess whether the relationship is consistent.*

Both these limitations in fact stem from the same feature in the calculation of gamma. This is the failure of gamma to include **tied cases** in its formula. There are three types of tied cases.

Cases tied on the independent variable (T_x) These are pairs of cases that have the same value for the independent variable but have different values for the dependent variable. These are usually any two cases in the same column of a crosstab but in different rows. In our example these are pairs of cases that have the same income but watch different amounts of TV.

Cases tied on the dependent variable (T_y) These are pairs of cases that have the same value for the dependent variable but which have different values for the independent variable. In practical terms, these are any two cases in the same row of a crosstab but in different columns. In our example these are pairs of cases that watch the same amount of TV but have different income.

Cases tied on both variables (T_{yx}) These are cases that have the same value for both the variables. These are pairs of cases drawn from the same cell in the table. In our example these are pairs of cases that have the same income and watch the same amount of TV.

The other PRE measures of association for ordinal data seek to redress the limitations with gamma by including some or all of these tied cases in their calculation.

Somers' *d*

Somers' *d* is an **asymmetric measure of association**, in that it is sensitive to which variable is characterized as the independent variable and which is characterized as the dependent. Thus it is especially useful where we feel the relationship between two variables is best described by a one-way dependence model. The logic behind Somers' *d* is based on the idea that two cases which vary in terms of the independent variable but do not vary in terms of the dependent variable (they are *tied* on the dependent variable) reflect no association. In the example we have been working with, pairs tied on the dependent variable but not on the independent variable are those pairs of cases that are different in terms of income but watch exactly the same amount of TV. Somers' *d* calculates the association as a proportion of all concordant and discordant pairs *plus pairs tied on the dependent variable*:

$$d = \frac{N_s - N_d}{N_s + N_d + T_y}$$

To calculate the number of tied cases we take each cell, starting at top left, and multiply the number of cases it contains by the total number of cases in the cells to its right (Table 9.10). Substituting these calculations into the equation for Somers' *d* we get the following value:

$$d = \frac{N_c - N_d}{N_c + N_d + T_Y} = \frac{21,075 - 2550}{21,075 + 2550 + 6350}$$

$$= 0.62$$

A value of 0.62 indicates a moderate, positive association between these variables: an increase in income is associated with an increase in TV watching.

Table 9.10 Calculations for tied cases on the dependent variable

75	15	10	
20	70	10	$(75 \times 15)+(75 \times 10) = 1875$
10	15	75	

$+$

75	15	10	
20	70	10	$(15 \times 10) = 150$
10	15	75	

$+$

75	15	10	
20	70	10	$(20 \times 70)+(20 \times 10) = 1600$
10	15	75	

$+$

75	15	10	
20	70	10	$(70 \times 10) = 700$
10	15	75	

$+$

75	15	10	
20	70	10	$(10 \times 15)+(10 \times 75) = 900$
10	15	75	

$+$

75	15	10	
20	70	10	$(15 \times 75) = 1125$
10	15	75	

$$T_y = 1875 + 150 + 1600 + 700 + 900 + 1125 = 6350$$

Notice that the equation for Somers' d is almost the identical equation to that for gamma, except for the term in the denominator for the number of dependent variable ties. As a result, whenever there are such tied cases, d will always have a lower value than gamma. In other words, by ignoring tied cases, gamma may overstate the strength of association between two variables in an asymmetric relationship, especially when there are many tied cases.

Since Somers' d is an asymmetric measure of association we can actually calculate two alternative versions of it, for any given crosstab. In other words, we can calculate Somers' d with one variable as independent and the other as dependent, and we can then flip the variables around and calculate Somers' d again. In our example we have calculated d with income as the independent and TV watching as the dependent variable, since our theoretical model of this relationship depicts the causation as running in that direction. Someone with a different theory that postulated that somehow TV watching determines income would alternatively calculate d with income as dependent, and this will produce a different value.

Kendall's tau-*b*

Kendall's tau-*b* is a symmetric, PRE measure of association for ordinal data arranged in a bivariate table. Its main feature is that it makes use of the information provided by cases tied on the dependent and on the independent variables:

$$\text{tau-}b = \frac{N_c - N_d}{\sqrt{\left(N_c + N_d + T_y\right)\left(N_c + N_d + T_x\right)}}$$

For the mathematically minded we note that tau-b is the geometric mean of the two alternative values for Somers' d. It is sometimes therefore referred to as the **symmetric version of Somers' d**, even though this terminology is slightly confusing since d by definition is asymmetric. Since tau-b is the geometric mean of Somers' d it will have a value somewhere between the two values for d that can be calculated for any given crosstab.

Unfortunately, tau-b will only range between -1 and $+1$ where the number of rows in the crosstab is equal to the number of columns (a square table), and is therefore generally only used in this special case.

Kendall's tau-*c*

Kendall's tau-c is a symmetric, PRE measure of association much like tau-b. It is used in situations where a symmetric measure is desired for a table with an unequal number of rows and columns (which limits tau-b), and which has many tied cases (which limits gamma). The exact formula for tau-c is:

$$\text{tau-}c = \frac{2k\left(N_c - N_d\right)}{N^2(k-1)}$$

where:
k is the number of rows or the number of columns or the number of rows, whichever is smaller; and
N is the total number of cases.

In our example, we have the same number of rows as we have columns (three), so $k = 3$. The value for tau-c will be:

$$\text{tau-}c = \frac{2k\left(N_c - N_d\right)}{N^2(k-1)} = \frac{2(3)(21075 - 2550)}{300^2(3-1)}$$

$$= 0.62$$

This turns out to be the same as the value for Somers' d that we calculated above, so that the two alternative measures are in agreement with each other.

Measures of association using SPSS

We can obtain these results using SPSS. These measures of association are available as part of the **Crosstabs** command which we explored in Chapter 7 (Table 9.11, Figure 9.4).

Table 9.11 Ordinal measures of association on SPSS (file: **Ch09-1.sav**)

SPSS command/action	Comments
1 From the menu select **A**nalyze/**D**escriptive **Statistics**/**C**rosstabs	This brings up the **Crosstabs** dialog box
2 Click on the variable in the source list that will form the rows of the table, which in this case **Frequency of TV watching**	This highlights **Frequency of TV watching**
3 Click on ▶ that points to the **R**ow(s): target variables list	This pastes **Frequency of TV watching** into the **R**ow(s): target variables list
4 Click on the variable in the source list that will form the columns of the table, which in this case **Income level**	This highlights **Income level**
5 Click on ▶ that points to the **C**olumn(s): target variables list	This pastes **Income level** into the **C**olumn(s): target variables list
6 Click on the **S**tatistics button	This brings up the **Crosstabs: Statistics** box. You will see an area headed **Ordinal**, which provides a list of the measures of association available for this level of measurement
7 Select **G**amma and **S**omers' d by clicking the boxes next to them	This places ✓ in the tick-boxes to indicate the statistics selected
8 Click on **Continue**	
9 Click on **OK**	

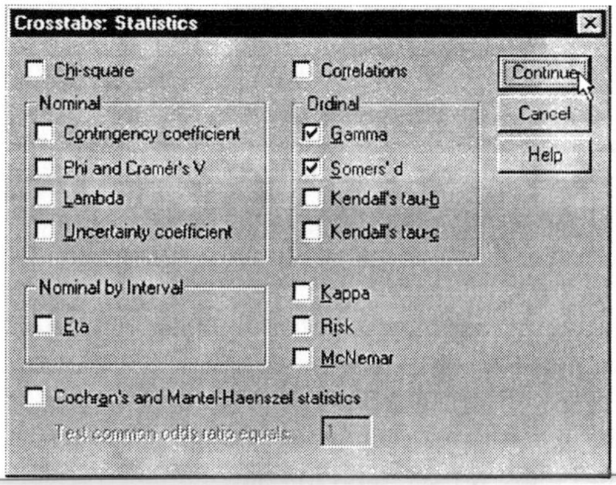

Figure 9.4 The Crosstabs: Statistics dialog box

Figure 9.5 illustrates the results of this set of instructions.

Directional Measures

			Value	Asymp. Std. Error[a]	Approx. T[b]	Approx. Sig.
Ordinal by Ordinal	Somers' d	Symmetric	.618	.043	14.192	.000
		Frequency of TV watching Dependent	.618	.043	14.192	.000
		Income level Dependent	.618	.043	14.192	.000

a. Not assuming the null hypothesis.

b. Using the asymptotic standard error assuming the null hypothesis.

Symmetric Measures

		Value	Asymp. Std. Error[a]	Approx. T[b]	Approx. Sig.
Ordinal by Ordinal	Gamma	.784	.043	14.192	.000
N of Valid Cases		300			

a. Not assuming the null hypothesis.

b. Using the asymptotic standard error assuming the null hypothesis.

Figure 9.5 SPSS **Crosstabs: Statistics** output

SPSS has produced the values for gamma and Somers' *d* in separate tables, since one is a symmetric measure and the other is asymmetric (which SPSS calls 'directional'). In either case we see that the values generated by SPSS, in the column headed Value in each table, are the same as those we calculated by hand above. These reflect the moderate to strong association that exists between these two variables for this group of cases. If there was a negative association, a negative sign will be printed in front of the value, provided that the data are arranged in the table in the correct format, that is with values increasing across the columns and down the rows.

Example of an asymmetric relationship

A public health researcher investigates whether a new drug improves rehabilitation for stroke victims. The researcher compares a group of 1013 stroke victims who do not take the drug with 588 stroke victims who do. Based on their ability to complete certain basic tasks the researcher classifies each person as showing 'no improvement', 'some improvement', 'moderate improvement', or 'strong improvement'. The researcher initially describes the data in the crosstab in Table 9.12.

It is very important to remember in constructing a bivariate table for ordinal data that the values increase when going down the rows and across the columns. That is, the table begins with the lowest value for the row variable (which is normally the dependent variable) and moves down to the highest value. Similarly the first column should be the lowest value for the column variable (usually the independent variable) and increase across the page. This ensures that our procedures for calculating concordant and discordant pairs are appropriate.

Table 9.12 Effect of drug on health condition

Condition	Take drug?		
	No	Yes	Total
No improvement	42	15	57
	4%	3%	
Some improvement	86	31	117
	9%	5%	
Moderate improvement	316	123	439
	31%	21%	
Strong improvement	569	419	988
	56%	71%	
Total	1013	588	1601

Looking at the column percentages in this table it is evident that there is a relationship. For example, a higher percentage (71 percent) of people who have taken the drug showed strong improvement in their health condition than people who did not (56 percent). There is clearly a pattern of positive association: as drug taking increases (effectively from zero to one) health condition also increases. We can also see, however, that the modal category for each group is 'strong improvement' indicating that there is not a very strong relationship evident in the data. In summary, our visual inspection of the table suggests a weak, positive association. By calculating the measures of association we get an exact quantitative measure of this impression.

The calculations needed to determine the number of concordant pairs for these data are presented in Table 9.13.

Table 9.13 Calculating concordant pairs

42	15	
86	31	
316	123	$(419\times316)+(419\times86)+(419\times42) = 186,036$
569	**419**	

+

42	15	
86	31	
316	**123**	$(123\times86)+(123\times42) = 15,744$
569	419	

+

42	15	
86	**31**	
316	123	$(31\times42) = 1302$
569	419	

$$N_c = 186,036 + 15,744 + 1302 = 203,082$$

The number of discordant pairs is calculated in Table 9.14.

Table 9.14 Calculating discordant pairs

42	**15**
86	**31**
316	**123**
569	419

$(569 \times 123) + (569 \times 31) + (569 \times 15) = 96,161$

+

42	**15**
86	**31**
316	123
569	419

$(316 \times 31) + (316 \times 15) = 14,536$

+

42	**15**
86	31
316	123
569	419

$(86 \times 15) = 1290$

$$N_c = 96161 + 14536 + 1290 = 111987$$

Putting all this into the formula for calculating gamma, we obtain:

$$G = \frac{N_c - N_d}{N_c + N_d} = \frac{203,082 - 111,987}{203,082 + 111,987}$$

$$= 0.29$$

To calculate Somers' *d* we need to work out the number of pairs tied on the dependent variable, which is done in Table 9.15.

Table 9.15 Calculating tied cases on the dependent variable

42	15
86	31
316	123
569	**419**

$(569 \times 419) = 238,411$

+

42	15
86	31
316	**123**
569	419

$(316 \times 123) = 38,868$

+

42	15
86	**31**
316	123
569	419

$(86 \times 31) = 2666$

+

42	**15**
86	31
316	123
569	419

$(42 \times 15) = 630$

The total number of pairs tied on the dependent variable will be:

$$T_y = 238,411+38,868+2666+630 = 280,575$$

This will yield a value for Somers' *d* of:

$$d = \frac{N_c - N_d}{N_c + N_d + T_y} = \frac{203,082 - 111,987}{203,082 + 111,987 + 280,575}$$

$$= 0.15$$

This is considerably weaker than the value for gamma, indicating the high number of tied cases. *Given that this is clearly a case of one-way dependence, Somers' d, as an asymmetric measure of association, is preferred.* In terms of the research question it would seem relevant to include in our calculations all those pairs of people who differed in terms of whether they took the drug yet showed no difference in health improvement.

Example of a symmetric relationship

A survey is conducted to assess whether the presence of union officials in the workplace is related to the accident rate for that workplace. The researcher thinks there is a relationship of mutual dependence between these variables: the level of unionization is affected by the accident rate, but also in turn affects the accident rate by raising consciousness and policing of safety regulations. The researcher will therefore use gamma, since it is a symmetric measure of association.

One hundred and seventy-seven workplaces are included in the survey and these are classified as having a low, moderate, or high level of union presence. These workplaces are also classified as having either a high or low accident rate. The results of the survey are presented in Table 9.16.

Table 9.16 Accident rates at the workplace by union presence

Accident rate	Union presence			
	Low	Moderate	High	Total
Low	17	32	35	84
High	43	27	23	93
Total	60	59	58	177

Can we detect an association between these variables?

To calculate gamma we begin with concordant pairs. For a 2-by-3 table such as this the combination of concordant pairs can be determined by following the calculations in Table 9.17.

Table 9.17 Calculating concordant pairs

17	32	35
43	27	23

$(23 \times 17) + (23 \times 32) = 1127$

+

17	32	35
43	27	23

$(27 \times 17) = 459$

$$N_c = 1127 + 459 = 1586$$

To calculate the number of discordant pairs we work in the opposite direction (Table 9.18).

Table 9.18 Calculating discordant pairs

17	32	35
43	27	23

$(43 \times 32) + (43 \times 35) = 3311$

+

17	32	35
43	27	23

$(27 \times 35) = 945$

$$N_d = 3311 + 945 = 4256$$

Putting this information into the equation for gamma we get:

$$G = \frac{N_c - N_d}{N_c + N_d} = \frac{1586 - 4256}{1586 + 4256}$$

$$= -0.46$$

This indicates that in predicting the order of pairs on one variable, we will make 41 percent fewer errors if we take into account the way that the pairs are ordered on the other variable (level of unionization). There is a moderate, negative association between these two variables. Higher unionization is associated with a lower accident rate.

The other symmetric measure available to us is tau-*c* (tau-*b* is not appropriate since this is a table with a different number of rows and columns):

$$\text{tau-}c = \frac{2k(N_c - N_d)}{N^2(k-1)} = \frac{2(2)(1586 - 4256)}{177^2(2-1)}$$

$$= -0.34$$

This is slightly lower than gamma, which is due to the presence of tied cases, but it still points to the existence of a moderate, negative relationship between these two variables.

Spearman's rank-order correlation coefficient

The PRE measures we have investigated so far apply in situations where the ordinal scales do not have too many categories. With only a few categories these data can be displayed in a crosstabulation. Five or less categories is a good rule of thumb for the appropriate range of scores. There are situations, though, where the ordinal scales have a wide range of possible scores and we are reluctant to collapse them down to a few categories just to be able to describe the data with a crosstab. This is especially the case where the underlying variable is continuous. An example is an attitude scale. People's attitude to the quality of health care services, for example, is essentially a continuous variable – attitude will be different from person to person, but it may be a gradual smooth change. We may try to capture this intrinsic characteristic of the variable by ensuring that there are a wide number of categories to express the variation that exists in people's attitude to health care services, from one extreme of 'very unfavorable' to the other extreme of 'very favorable'. We may in fact have a 10 point scale with these two extremes at either end. If we collapse these categories into a smaller number we will lose the scale's sensitivity to small differences in people's attitudes.

Where we have two ordinal scales with a large number of values (or one ordinal and one interval/ratio) another PRE measure is available other than those we discussed above. This is **Spearman's rank-order correlation coefficient**, which is also known as **Spearman's rho**. The basic logic underlying rho is the same as that for the other measures, in so far as it tries to predict the ranking of pairs of cases on the dependent variable given their ranking on the independent variable. However, it makes use of the longer scale.

To illustrate the calculation of rho, we will work through the following hypothetical example. A physiotherapist uses a new treatment on a group of patients and is interested in whether their age affects their ability to respond to the treatment. After taking into account a number of other variables, such as the severity of the injury, each patient is given a mobility score out of 15, according to his or her ability to perform a number of tasks. The results of the study are shown in Table 9.19, along with the ranking of each person in terms of each variable.

Notice in Table 9.19 that Jordan and Alana had the same mobility score so they each are assigned the average rank of 7.5. To calculate the value of rho we calculate the difference in rank for each person, D, and then square these differences (Table 9.20).

Having made these calculations we can enter the information into the equation for Spearman's rho:

$$r_s = 1 - \frac{6\Sigma D^2}{n(n^2 - 1)} = 1 - \frac{6(1225.5)}{16(16^2 - 1)}$$

$$= -0.8$$

Table 9.19 Age and mobility scores with rankings

Patient	Age	Ranking on age	Mobility	Ranking on mobility
Danielle	23	1	14	15
Christine	25	2	15	16
Leanne	28	3	12	13
Marie	30	4	8	5
Erin	35	5	13	14
Ben	37	6	10	10
Luke	38	7	11	12
Sophie	39	8	8	5
Elli	40	9	10	10
Jordan	41	10	9	7.5
Timothy	45	11	10	10
Alana	50	12	9	7.5
Amanda	52	13	7	3
Lisa	55	14	8	5
Stacey	60	15	4	1
Chloe	62	16	6	2

Table 9.20 Calculating rank differences

Patient	Ranking on age	Ranking on score	Rank difference, D	D^2
Danielle	1	15	$1-15 = -14$	196
Christine	2	16	$2-16 = -14$	196
Leanne	3	13	$3-13 = -10$	100
Marie	4	5	-1	1
Erin	5	14	-9	81
Ben	6	10	-4	16
Luke	7	12	-5	25
Sophie	8	5	3	9
Elli	9	10	-1	1
Jordan	10	7.5	2.5	6.25
Timothy	11	10	1	1
Alana	12	7.5	4.5	20.25
Amanda	13	3	10	100
Lisa	14	5	9	81
Stacey	15	1	14	196
Chloe	16	2	14	196
				$\Sigma D^2 = 1225.5$

Spearman's rho is a PRE measure, and therefore has a concrete interpretation. A value of 0.8 indicates a strong correlation between these two variables, and the negative sign indicates that this is a negative correlation. In other words, increase in age strongly reduces the effect of the treatment. The older the patient, the less benefit received from the program.

Spearman's rho using SPSS

The commands needed to calculate rho for these data are shown in Table 9.21 and Figure 9.6.

Table 9.21 Generating Spearman's rho on SPSS (file: **Ch09-2.sav**)

SPSS command/action	Comments
1 From the menu select **A**nalyze/**C**orrelate/ **B**ivariate	This brings up the **Bivariate Correlations** dialog box. You will notice an area called **Correlation Coefficients**, with the box next to **Pearso**n selected. This is the default setting. Pearson's coefficient is applicable to interval/ratio data, so is not appropriate here when one variable is ordinal
2 Click on **age** in the source variable list	This highlights **age**
3 Click on ▶	This pastes **age** into the **Variables:** target list
4 Click on **Score on mobility test** in the source variable list	This highlights **Score on mobility test**
5 Click on ▶	This pastes **Score on mobility test** into the **Variables:** target list
6 Click on the box next to **Pearso**n	This removes ✓ from the tick-box so that this measure of correlation is no longer selected
7 Click on the box next to **Spearman**	This replaces ✓ in the tick-box so that this measure of correlation is selected
8 Click on **OK**	

Figure 9.6(a) The **C**orrelate/**B**ivariate command

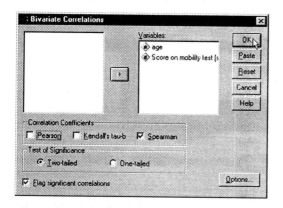

Figure 9.6(b) The **Bivariate Correlations** dialog box

The output from this command is illustrated in Figure 9.7.

Correlations

			AGE	Score on mobility test
Spearman's rho	AGE	Correlation Coefficient	1.000	-.814**
		Sig. (2-tailed)	.	.000
		N	16	16
	Score on mobility test	Correlation Coefficient	-.814**	1.000
		Sig. (2-tailed)	.000	.
		N	16	16

**. Correlation is significant at the .01 level (2-tailed).

Figure 9.7 SPSS **Bivariate Correlations** output

What does all this mean? SPSS calculates the correlation coefficient for each variable with itself and all the other variables we pasted into the target variable list in the dialog box. Looking at the first row of the **Correlations** table we see that age has a correlation coefficient with itself of 1.000; any variable by definition is perfectly correlated with itself. Age has a correlation coefficient with Score on mobility test of –0.814, which is the same as our hand calculation. Note the minus sign indicating a negative correlation: as age increases mobility scores decrease.

The second row of the **Correlations** table does the same thing in reverse. It gives the correlation coefficient for Score on mobility test correlated with age which is –0.814. In other words, since rho is a symmetric measure of association it does not matter which way we view the direction of causality (age to mobility or vice versa) since the value calculated will be the same. Age is also correlated with itself, which produces a perfect correlation of 1.

The table also provides a row of information titled Sig. (2-tailed). This deals with issues we will discuss in Chapter 23, where we will refer to this output. For those who are already familiar with the logic of statistical inference, or have read ahead and are coming back to this chapter, I will quickly explain this portion of the output. Although we have significance of .000 this does not mean a zero significance. The exact probability is less than 5 in 10,000 (i.e. $p < 0.0005$), which SPSS has rounded off to .000. Thus this probability should be read as 'less than 1 in 50,000', which is clearly a significant result. The strong relationship we have detected in the sample is due to such a relationship holding in the population, and not just due to sampling error.

Example

An instructor is interested in whether the heavy use of formal exams as a form of assessment is biased against students who might perform better under different exam conditions, such as verbal presentations. A group of 15 students is selected and each student is assessed in terms of their verbal presentation skills and in terms of their formal examination skills. These 15 students are rank-ordered on each of these variables as indicated in Table 9.22, along with the calculations we need to generate rho.

Table 9.22 Calculating rank differences

Student	Rank on exam	Rank on presentation	Rank difference D	D^2
1	4	15	−11	121
2	6	3	3	9
3	9	14	−5	25
4	12	9	3	9
5	3	10	−7	49
6	13	11	2	4
7	5	6	−1	1
8	1	4	−3	9
9	14	8	6	36
10	2	1	1	1
11	10	2	8	64
12	7	5	2	4
13	15	7	8	64
14	8	12	−4	16
15	11	13	−2	4
				$\Sigma D^2 = 416$

Substituting these data into the equation for rho:

$$r_s = 1 - \frac{6\Sigma D^2}{n(n^2-1)} = 1 - \frac{6(416)}{15(15^2-1)}$$

$$= -0.26$$

This indicates a weak, negative association between the two types of skills. The instructor might therefore conclude that exams are not a good indicator of other forms of learning skills: students who perform poorly in exams might perform well in verbal presentations. Similarly, students who do well in exams might not relatively do all that well when other skills are required. A mixed form of assessment methods might give a better indication of students' learning.

Summary

We have investigated the calculation of a variety of PRE measures of association where both variables are measured at least at the ordinal level. Unfortunately, there is no easy rule for deciding which is the 'best' measure to use. Part of the problem lies with the notion of association itself, and the fact that this concept is operationalized in slightly different ways. For example, gamma, the tau measures, and rho are symmetric measures, whereas the Somers' d is asymmetric, so the choice should be guided by the model of the

relationship we believe in. In practice, these measures usually 'point' in the
same direction, in so far as they will generally give similar answers.

Exercises

9.1   If decreases in the value of a variable are associated with increases in
the value of another variable, what is the direction of association?

9.2   Why do we not speak of association between two variables as being
either positive or negative, when at least one variable is measured at
the nominal level?

9.3   For the **emboldened** cells in each of the following tables, calculate the
number of concordant pairs, assuming that the numbers on the edge of
each table indicate the values of an ordinal scale:

(a)

	1	2	3
1	60	24	12
2	32	**14**	8

(b)

	1	2	3
1	60	**24**	12
2	32	14	8

(c)

	1	2	3	4
1	12	17	25	42
2	10	14	**19**	24
3	6	11	16	20

(d)

	1	2	3	4
1	12	17	25	42
2	10	14	19	24
3	6	11	**16**	20
4	3	9	14	22

9.4   For the **emboldened** cells in each of the following tables, calculate the
number of discordant pairs, assuming that the numbers on the edge of
each table indicate the values of an ordinal scale:

(a)

	1	2	3
1	60	24	12
2	32	**14**	8

(b)

	1	2	3
1	60	24	12
2	**32**	14	8

(c)

	1	2	3
1	60	**24**	12
2	32	14	8

(d)

	1	2	3	4
1	12	17	25	42
2	10	14	19	24
3	6	**11**	16	20

9.5   For the **emboldened** cells in each of the following tables, calculate the number of pairs of cases tied on the dependent variable but varying on the independent variable, assuming that the numbers on the edge of each table indicate the values of an ordinal variable:

(a)

	1	2	3
1	60	24	12
2	32	**14**	8

(b)

	1	2	3
1	60	24	12
2	**32**	14	8

(c)

	1	2	3
1	60	**24**	12
2	32	14	8

(d)

	1	2	3	4
1	12	17	25	42
2	10	14	19	24
3	6	**11**	16	20

9.6   For the example in Table 9.16, which looks at the relationship between accident rates and unionization in the workplace, calculate Somers' *d* and compare it to the value for gamma we calculated in the text.

9.7   Calculate gamma and Somers' *d* for the following table:

Mother working	Child achievement level			
	Poor	Good	High	Total
No	20	58	22	100
Part-time	15	62	23	100
Full-time	12	62	26	100
Total	47	182	71	300

Interpret your result.

9.8 Consider the following crosstabulation. The table displays the distribution of 162 patients whose health was assessed on a four-point scale, and who were also coded as smokers or non-smokers. This latter variable is considered ordinal for the purposes of this study since it indicates level of smoking.

Health level	Smoking level		
	Doesn't smoke	Does smoke	Total
Poor	13	34	47
Fair	22	19	41
Good	35	9	44
Very good	27	3	30
Total	97	65	162

(a) Looking at the raw distribution can you detect an association between these two variables? What is the direction of association? How will this direction manifest when calculating a measure of association?

(b) Calculate gamma and Somers' *d* and draw a conclusion about the relationship between health and smoking.

9.9 Eleven countries are rank-ordered in terms of two variables: infant mortality rate and expenditure on the military as a proportion of national income. These ranks are:

Country	Rank on infant mortality	Rank on military spending
A	9	8
B	4	5
C	6	6
D	2	2
E	7	11
F	3	4
G	10	7
H	5	3
I	8	9
J	1	1
K	11	10

(a) Calculate Spearman's rank-order correlation coefficient for these data. What can you conclude about the relationship between these variables?

(b) Enter the data for these 11 countries on SPSS and calculate rho to confirm your results.

9.10 Does price reflect quality? When people pay more for something are they actually getting something better? To assess this, a number of expert judges are asked to taste and rank 15 wines whose identity and price are not disclosed to them. The wine rated 15 is considered the highest quality, while the wine scoring 1 is considered the most inferior. The rank of each wine according to the judges and its retail price is listed below:

Quality	Price
1	3.00
2	4.00
3	5.50
4	5.90
5	11.99
6	6.80
7	7.50
8	9.00
9	18.00
10	3.50
11	11.50
12	12.00
13	9.00
14	4.50
15	13.00

Calculate Spearman's rank-order correlation coefficient to assess the nature of any relationship between quality and price. Check your answer by calculating rho through SPSS

9.11 A group of ten runners is interested in whether running ability is associated with age. These nine runners record their ages in years and also their order in finishing a run. The results are:

Name	Age	Place
Kenny	54	4
Schuey	46	1
Scotty	29	6
Pat	28	2
Garth	25	3
Ian	36	9
Michael	15	10
Mat	26	5
Todd	38	8
George	34	7

Calculate Spearman's correlation coefficient to assess whether there is any relationship between age and running ability. Enter these data on SPSS to assess your answer.

9.12   Open the **Employee data** file. Recode current salary into class
intervals based on $10,000 income brackets. Use this recoded variable
to assess the strength of the relationship between current income and
employment category, treating the latter variable as ordinal variable
indicating employment status. Why is tau-*b* not a useful measure in
this instance?

10

Graphical and Numerical Description of Interval/Ratio Data: Scatter Plots and Linear Regression

In the previous two chapters we explored methods for describing data when at least one of the variables is measured at the nominal or ordinal level. With only a few categories to express the range of variation, our initial means of describing such data is in the form of a crosstabulation. The crosstab shows the joint distribution for two variables and allows us visually to gage whether there is an association between the two variables. If inspection of the relative frequency distribution in the table leads us to suspect that these two variables are related, the next step is to calculate measures of association that give a precise numerical value to any such suspicion.

However, if the data for the two variables under investigation have been collected at the interval/ratio level, which usually means a large number of values, crosstabulations are not a convenient means of describing the distribution. The equivalent descriptive technique to a crosstabulation for interval/ratio data is a **scatter plot**.

Scatter plots

It is difficult to arrange interval/ratio data into a crosstabulation. Interval/ratio data do not usually fall into a small number of discrete categories such as large or small, old or young, etc. Such data can of course be collapsed into a few values, but this is at the cost of information. Since there are usually many values for variables measured at the interval/ratio level, a contingency table will have to have as many rows or columns as there are values in the data. If we are looking at the distribution of age in years for a country's population we will need over 100 rows of data to take account of the fact that age spreads out over a wide range. A scatter plot, which allows for the greater range of values that we usually have with interval/ratio scales, is the best way to organize such data to get an initial impression as to whether any correlation exists. A scatter plot (just like a crosstab) shows the combination of values that each case 'scores' on two variables simultaneously.

A **scatter plot** displays the joint distribution for two continuous variables. **Coordinates** on a scatter plot indicate the values each case takes for each of the two variables.

For example, we might be interested in the relationship between unemployment rates and the level of civil unrest across cities. From official statistics we obtain the information in Table 10.1 about the rate of unemployment (which we think is the independent variable, X) and the number of civil disturbances (which we think is the dependent variable, Y) for five cities.

Table 10.1 Unemployment and civil unrest in five cities

City	Unemployment rate, X	Civil disturbances, Y
A	25	17
B	13	15
C	5	10
D	10	5
E	2	4

Arranging this information in a scatter plot (Figure 10.1) makes these data easier to 'read' in order to determine whether an association exists.

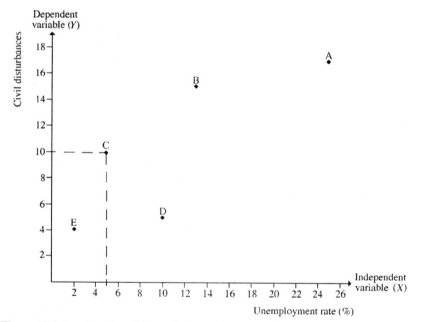

Figure 10.1 A scatter plot of data points

It is the convention to put the dependent variable (*Y*) on the vertical axis and the independent variable (*X*) on the horizontal axis when constructing a scatter plot. If we look at any one of these points (A–E) and draw a straight line down to the horizontal axis, we can find the unemployment rate in that town. Similarly, by drawing a straight line across to the vertical axis we can 'read off' the number of civil disturbances. Grid lines for city C have been drawn to illustrate this procedure. For this town the unemployment rate is 5 percent and there are also 10 incidents of civil unrest.

Looking at Figure 10.1, it can intuitively be seen that an association exists; because we can imagine a sloping line running through these five points. The direction of association is indicated by whether this imaginary line slopes up (positive) or down (negative). In this case the slope is positive, indicating that an increase in unemployment rate is associated with an increase in the number of civil disturbances.

Linear regression

Regression analysis is simply the task of fitting a line through a scatter plot of cases that 'best fits' the data. Any line can be expressed in a mathematical formula. The general formula for a straight line is:

$$Y = a \pm bX$$

where:
Y is the dependent variable
X is the independent variable
a is the *Y*-intercept (the value of *Y* when *X* is zero)
b is the slope of the line
+ indicates positive association
− indicates negative association.

This formula says that a line is defined by two factors. One is its starting point along the vertical axis, *a*, and the second is the slope of the line from this point, ±*b*. It is the value of *b* that we are most interested in since any slope, either positive or negative, indicates some correlation between the two variables. In Figure 10.2 we see three different lines reflecting the value of *b* in the three alternative situations of positive correlation, negative correlation, and no correlation.

Each and every straight line that can drawn in the area defined by the scatter plot has a unique equation that distinguishes it from every other line. Deriving this equation for any particular line is like giving a person a unique combination of first and last names so that this person can be differentiated from everybody else. The general formula for the equation of a line is much like a form that has a space entitled Firstname and another space entitled Lastname.

$$Y = \text{Firstname} \pm \text{Lastname}$$

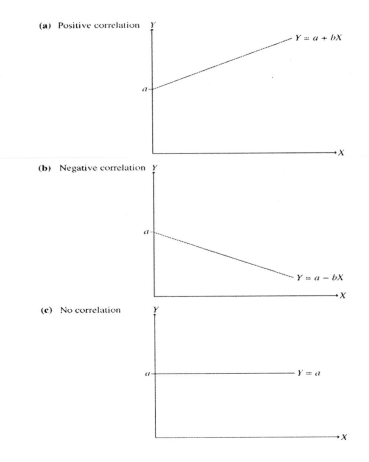

Figure 10.2 Three lines exhibiting **(a)** positive, **(b)** negative, and **(c)** no correlation

We write in the specific combination of names that identifies the relevant individual. If I try to identify somebody using just their first name, say Pablo, this will not differentiate that person from all the other people with the same first name. Similarly, if I identify someone just by their last name, say Picasso, this will not differentiate this person from all other people with the same last name. But writing both names *together* will identify a unique individual. Similarly with identifying a line. Thousands of straight lines can be drawn through the space marked out by the vertical and horizontal axes of a scatter plot. But to identify the individual line that we think best fits the scatter plot we need to provide it with a unique first and last name. The line's first name is its point of origin along the *Y*-axis. But obviously this is not enough to distinguish it from the multitude of lines that can start from the same point. This is illustrated in Figure 10.3, which shows only some of the lines that will share the same value for *a* in their equation.

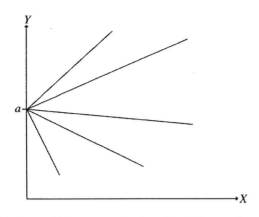

Figure 10.3 Straight lines with the same value for *a* but different values for *b*

Specifying the slope of a straight line on its own is also insufficient to distinguish it from all the others that could occupy the space. This is illustrated in Figure 10.4, which presents lines that will all have the same value for *b*.

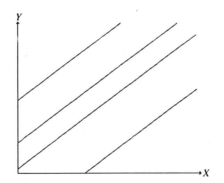

Figure 10.4 Straight lines with the same value for *b* but different values for *a*

However, if we specify *both* the point of origin on the *Y*-axis *and* the slope of the line from that point, then we are able to identify uniquely any line within the space. The trick to linear regression is to come up with the unique combination of values for *a* and *b* that identify the **line of best fit**.

Looking at the data for the five cities, we can draw many straight lines through this scatter plot, and each of these lines will have its own unique formula. For example, in Figure 10.5 I have drawn a line that looks to me to fit the data pretty well. I could call this 'line 1' or 'line A' or 'my line'. Instead, I have called it by its mathematical name:

$$Y = 5 + 0.6X$$

Where did this equation come from?

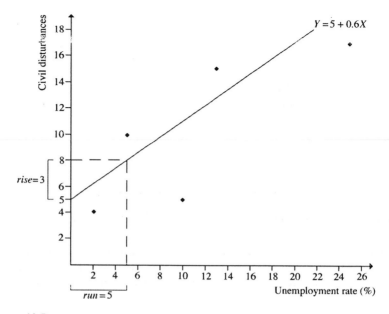

Figure 10.5

- The value for a (5) is the point on the Y-axis where the line 'begins'. This is the number of civil disturbances we expect to find in a city with an unemployment rate of zero.
- The + sign means that the line has a positive slope, which indicates a positive correlation between these two variables.
- The value of 0.6 for b is the slope, or **coefficient**, of the regression line. The regression coefficient indicates by how much civil disturbances will increase if unemployment increases by 1 percent. Since the slope of any straight line is 'rise over run', to actually calculate this value I take any 'rise' in civil disturbances, such as the increase of 3 between 5 and 8. I then 'read off' the corresponding increase in the unemployment rate, which gives a 'run' of 5. Dividing rise over run, the slope will be:

$$b = \frac{\text{rise}}{\text{run}} = \frac{3}{5}$$

$$= 0.6$$

The line we have just identified gives us a range of **expected values** for civil disturbance, depending on the value of the unemployment rate. The difference between the expected value and the actual value for civil disturbance at a particular unemployment rate is called the **residual** or **error term**.

The **residual** or **error term** is the difference between the observed value of the dependent variable and the value of the dependent variable predicted by a regression line.

Notice that no straight line will pass through all the points in a scatter plot. In fact, a 'good' line might not touch *any* of the points: there will usually be a gap between each plot and the regression line. Unless a point falls exactly on the line there will be a residual value. For example, my line predicts that, for city D with unemployment of 10 per cent, the number of civil disturbances will be:

$$Y = 5 + 0.6X = 5 + 0.6(10)$$

$$= 11$$

Instead, there were five civil disturbances for city D with an unemployment rate of 10 percent. The error (e) term at this point is –6:

$$e = Y_{actual} - Y_{expected} = 5 - 11$$

$$= -6$$

This is illustrated in Figure 10.6.

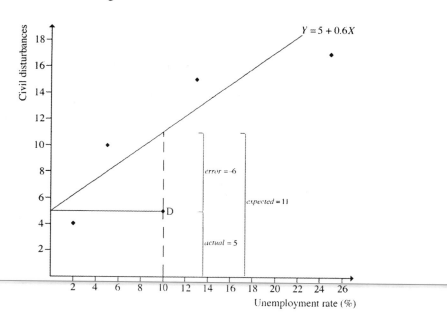

Figure 10.6 Observed and expected scores

I drew the particular line in Figure 10.6 on the basis of what looked to me, with the naked eye, to be the line that best fits these data. Someone else might think that they could draw a better line through these points, and this new line would have its own equation to define it, and the residuals between the expected values and actual values will be different to the ones I derived. It might be hard to determine which of these lines is the 'best' one just on the basis of our eyeball impression. We obviously need an objective principle for determining which line is the 'best'. Of all the possible lines that could run through the points, it seems plausible to suggest that the *best* line is the one that makes the residuals as small as possible: the one that *minimizes* the residuals.

Regression analysis uses this idea (although in a slightly more complicated form). The logic is called **ordinary least squares regression** (OLS): we want a line such that the gaps between the estimated values of Y and the actual values of Y (squared) are as small as possible. (We *square* the residuals, rather than just *sum* them, because the sum of residuals for *any* line that passes through the point that is the mean for both the dependent and independent variables will equal zero. To eliminate the effect of the positive and negative signs, the residuals are squared so that we are only dealing with positive numbers.)

Ordinary least squares regression is a rule that tells us to draw a line through a scatter plot that minimizes the sum of the squared residuals.

We could find the OLS regression line through a process of trial and error. We could keep drawing lines through the scatter plot, working out their respective equations and residuals, until we finally hit on the one that minimizes these residuals.

Fortunately there is an alternative. If we use the following two rules, we can derive the OLS regression line directly.

The OLS regression line must pass through a point whose coordinates are the averages of the dependent and independent variables ($\overline{Y}$, $\overline{X}$) The average number of civil disturbances, $\overline{Y}$ (pronounced 'Y-bar'), is:

$$\overline{Y} = \frac{\Sigma Y_i}{n} = \frac{55}{5}$$

$$= 11$$

The average unemployment rate, $\overline{X}$ (pronounced 'X-bar'), is:

$$\overline{X} = \frac{\Sigma X_i}{n} = \frac{51}{5}$$

$$= 10.2$$

Thus the OLS regression line will pass through the coordinate point (10.2, 11).

The slope of the regression line, b, is defined by the formula:

$$b = \frac{\Sigma\left(X_i - \overline{X}\right)\left(Y_i - \overline{Y}\right)}{\Sigma\left(X_i - \overline{X}\right)^2}$$

While this equation captures the essential idea that the line needs to minimize the squared differences between actual and expected values, the value of b is easier to calculate using the following formula:

$$b = \frac{n\Sigma\left(X_iY_i\right) - \left(\Sigma X_i\right)\left(\Sigma Y_i\right)}{n\Sigma X_i^2 - \left(\Sigma X_i\right)^2}$$

Although this formula still looks scary, if we work through it step by step we will see that it is a rather straightforward calculation. The calculations for city A are included in Table 10.2 to show how the numbers are derived.

Table 10.2 Calculations for the slope of the OLS regression line

City	Unemployment rate, X	Civil unrest, Y	X_i^2	Y_i^2	X_iY_i
A	25	17	25×25 = 625	17×17 = 289	25×17 = 425
B	13	15	169	225	195
C	5	10	25	100	50
D	10	5	100	25	50
E	2	4	4	16	8
	$\Sigma X_i = 55$	$\Sigma Y_i = 51$	$\Sigma X_i^2 = 923$	$\Sigma Y_i^2 = 655$	$\Sigma X_iY_i = 728$

Putting all these data into the equation for the slope of the regression line, we get:

$$b = \frac{n\Sigma\left(X_iY_i\right) - \left(\Sigma X_i\right)\left(\Sigma Y_i\right)}{n\Sigma X_i^2 - \left(\Sigma X_i\right)^2} = \frac{5(728) - (55)(51)}{5(923) - (55)^2}$$

$$= \frac{3640 - 2805}{4615 - 3025}$$

$$= +0.53$$

The value of b, called the **regression coefficient**, is very important because it quantifies any correlation between two variables.

The **regression coefficient** indicates by how many units the dependent variable will change, given a one-unit change in the independent variable.

Now that we have fixed the regression line through a specific point (the averages of *X* and *Y*) and also given it a 'last name' by calculating the slope of the line through this point, we can give it a complete label by deriving the value for *a*. We use the following formula, which uses both of the features of the regression line we have identified (it passes through the average of *X* and *Y*, and has a slope equal to *b*):

$$a = \bar{Y} - b\bar{X}$$

Therefore the value of *a* will be:

$$a = \bar{Y} - b\bar{X} = 10.2 - 0.53(11)$$

$$= 4.4$$

Thus we can define the line of best fit, for this set of cases, with the following equation:

$$Y = 4.4 + 0.53X$$

In Figure 10.7 this regression line is drawn through the scatter plot.

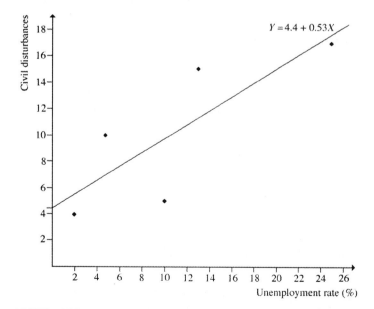

Figure 10.7 The OLS regression line

What does this tell us about the relationship between unemployment rates and civil disturbances, for this set of cases?

- There is a positive relationship between the two variables: an increase (decrease) in the unemployment rate is correlated with an increase (decrease) in the number of civil disturbances.
- We can quantify this positive correlation: an increase in the unemployment rate of 1 percent is correlated with an increase of 0.53 civil disturbances.

I can now use this formula for the purpose of prediction: I can predict the number of civil disturbances a city is likely to have, given a certain rate of unemployment. For example, if I was told that another city has an unemployment rate of 18 percent, my best guess will be to say that it experiences 13.9 civil disturbances:

$$Y = 4.4 + 0.53(18)$$

$$= 13.9$$

If you are still a little confused about what this all means, imagine that you are arranging for a serviceman to come and fix an appliance in your home. The charge is a flat fee of $50 for the visit plus $20 for each hour spent working in your home. We can summarize what we are required to pay the serviceman using the following equation:

$$\$payment = 50 + 20(number\ of\ hours)$$

For *any* given amount of time spent in the home we can calculate the total cost. For example, if the serviceman comes and finds nothing wrong and therefore does not charge for time, we will still be obligated to pay $50 (the constant fixed amount) for the visit. If it takes 2 hours to fix a problem, on the other hand, we are up for $90. The regression line does essentially the same thing: it tells us what we predict will be the value of the dependent variable, given a certain value for the independent variable. The only difference is that we will never get the exact amount, since the data points do not all fall exactly on the regression line, so we have to allow for error.

Pearson's product moment correlation coefficient

We have seen that the value of b is an indicator of whether a correlation exists between two variables measured at the interval/ratio level, and also the direction of such correlation. But does it also indicate the *strength* of the relationship? Does a value of $b = 0.53$ indicate a strong, moderate, or weak association? Unfortunately it does not.

The problem is that the units of measurement vary from one situation to another. For example, if I use proportions rather than percentage points to measure unemployment rates, so that instead of using in my calculations 22, 20, 15, 10, 9, I use 0.22, 0.20, 0.15, 0.1, 0.09, the estimated value of b will be 53 rather than 0.53. The actual relationship I am looking at has not changed, only the units of measurement. In other words, the value of b is affected not only by the strength of the correlation, but also *by the units of measurement*. Therefore there is no way of knowing whether any particular value for b indicates a weak, moderate, or strong correlation.

To overcome this problem, we convert the value of b into a standardized measure of correlation called the **product moment correlation coefficient, Pearson's** r. Pearson's r will always range between -1 and $+1$, regardless of the actual units in which the variables are measured. The formula for r is:

$$r = \frac{\Sigma\left(X_i - \bar{X}\right)\left(Y_i - \bar{Y}\right)}{\sqrt{\left[\left(X_i - \bar{X}\right)^2\right]\left[\left(Y_i - \bar{Y}\right)^2\right]}}$$

or

$$r = \frac{n\Sigma\left(X_i Y_i\right) - \left(\Sigma X_i\right)\left(\Sigma Y_i\right)}{\sqrt{\left[n\Sigma X_i^2 - \left(\Sigma X_i\right)^2\right]\left[n\Sigma Y_i^2 - \left(\Sigma Y_i\right)^2\right]}}$$

Fortunately, we have already calculated the elements of this equation in the table we used above for calculating b (Table 10.2). If we substitute the statistics from this table into this second formula we get:

$$r = \frac{n\Sigma\left(X_i Y_i\right) - \left(\Sigma X_i\right)\left(\Sigma Y_i\right)}{\sqrt{\left[n\Sigma X_i^2 - \left(\Sigma X_i\right)^2\right]\left[n\Sigma Y_i^2 - \left(\Sigma Y_i\right)^2\right]}}$$

$$= \frac{5(728) - 55(51)}{\sqrt{\left[5(923) - (55)^2\right]\left[5(655) - (51)^2\right]}}$$

$$= \frac{3640 - 2805}{\sqrt{[4615 - 3025][3275 - 2601]}}$$

$$= 0.81$$

The value of r tells us the strength as well as the direction of association. A value of 0.81 indicates that the correlation between these two variables for this set of cases is a strong positive one.

Explaining variance: the coefficient of determination

We have already used the regression line to predict the number of civil disturbances in a city, given a particular rate of unemployment. But we also saw that there will usually be a margin of error in this prediction, depending on how closely the plots are clustered around the line. We can use the regression line to say that a certain increase in X will produce so much increase in Y, but if there are large error terms between the regression line and the actual data points the likelihood that our predictions will be wrong will be greater than in a situation where the scores are tightly packed around the regression line.

We can see in Figure 10.8 that even though the same regression line best fits both sets of plots, we will have a greater confidence in our predictive ability in (a) than in (b). This is because the regression line in (a) explains a greater proportion of the variance of Y than the line in (b). We therefore need some measure of how much of the variation in the dependent variable is explained by a regression line.

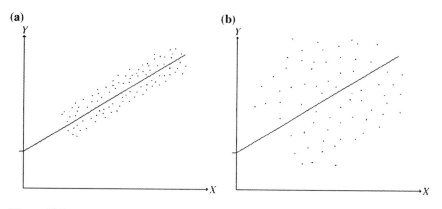

Figure 10.8

Fortunately we can do this by simply squaring r and obtaining the **coefficient of determination**, r^2, the variance explained by the regression line relative to the variance explained in the case of no association:

$$r^2 = (0.81)^2$$

$$= 0.65$$

The coefficient of determination can be interpreted as an asymmetric PRE measure of association, much like the PRE measures we encountered in the previous two chapters. In fact, it has a logic very similar to lambda, but applied to interval/ratio data. We make predictions about the expected value of the dependent variable *without* any information about the independent variable. We then make predictions *with* knowledge of the independent variable and compare the error rates.

For example, if we have to guess the number of civil disturbances in each city, and all we know is that the average number of disturbances *for all* five cities is 10.2, the best guess we can make is to say that the number of civil disturbances in *each* city is 10.2, regardless of the actual unemployment rate. In other words, we draw a straight horizontal line at this value as the regression line through the scatter plot (Figure 10.10).

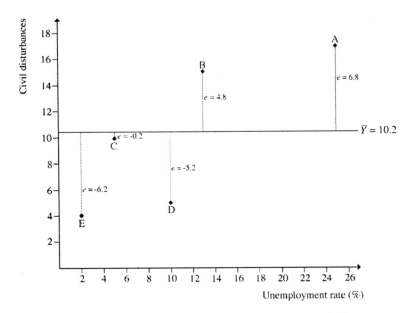

Figure 10.9 Regression line without knowledge of the independent variable

This horizontal line is the line we draw if there is no correlation between these two variables; knowing whether the unemployment rate is high or low will not cause me to change my expected number of civil disturbances from the average. Sometimes this line comes very close to the mark. For city C we see that this line predicted, at an unemployment rate of 5 percent, that there will be 10.2 civil disturbances. There were in fact 10 civil disturbances producing an error (e) for this city of only –0.2. However, in other instances we make a large error using this line. For city A, at an unemployment rate of 25 percent we again predict 10.2 civil disturbances, but in fact there were 17, producing an error of 6.8.

Now we compare these errors with the errors we make when predicting on the basis of the least squares regression line (Figure 10.10). Does this line substantially improve our guesswork?

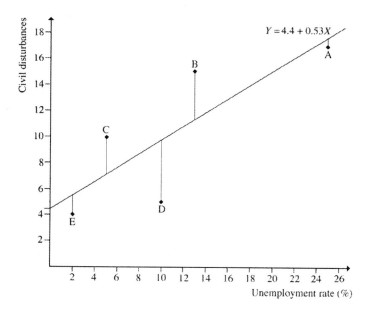

Figure 10.10 Regression line with knowledge of the independent variable

We can see that if there is a close correlation between these two variables, the least squares regression line will reduce the error rate. The gaps between the data points and the line will be much smaller when using the least squares regression line than when using the horizontal line based on the assumption of no correlation. It is precisely this aspect of the regression line that the coefficient of determination captures. A value for r^2 of 0.65 indicates that the least squares regression line explains 65 percent of the variance of the dependent variable relative to the variance explained by the horizontal line. This is a substantial reduction in the error rate.

It may pay to stop at this point and discuss the difference between r and r^2 since they are very closely related. The correlation coefficient is a standardized measure of the relationship between two variables; that is, it indicates the extent to which a change in one variable will be associated with a change in another variable. Thus r (like b) is primarily a tool for prediction. The coefficient of determination, on the other hand, is a PRE measure of the amount of variation explained by a regression line, and therefore gives a sense of how much *confidence* we should place in the accuracy of our predictions.

Plots, correlation, and regression using SPSS

The data from this example have been entered into SPSS. To generate the results we obtained above on SPSS, we use one set of commands to get the graphical description of the data in the form of scatter plot (with a regression line), and another command to get the numerical descriptions in the form of the regression equations and correlation coefficients.

Generating a scatter plot with a regression line

To obtain a simple scatter plot of the data, we use the following procedures given in Table 10.3 and Figure 10.11.

Table 10.3 Scatter plots using SPSS (file: **Ch10.sav**)

SPSS command/action	Comments
1 From the menu select **Graphs/Scatter**	This brings up the **Scatterplot** dialog box. You will notice that there is a heavy border around the option **Simple** which is the default setting. Since we are only after a simple scatter plot we will not change this setting
2 Click on **Define**	This brings up the **Simple Scatterplot** box
3 Click on **Number of civil disturbances**	
4 Click on the ▶ that points to the **Y Axis:** target variable list	This pastes **Number of civil disturbances** as the variable to be displayed on the *Y*-axis (dependent)
5 Click on **Unemployment rate**	This highlights **Unemployment rate**
6 Click on the ▶ that points to the **X Axis:** target variable list	This pastes **Unemployment rate** as variable to be displayed on the *X*-axis (independent)
7 Click on **OK**	

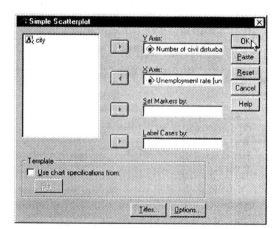

Figure 10.11 The **Simple Scatterplot** dialog box

This will produce the scatter plot in Figure 10.12.

Graph

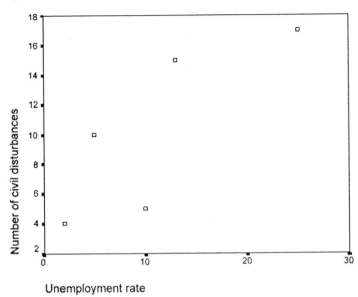

Figure caption axes: Number of civil disturbances (y-axis), Unemployment rate (x-axis)

Figure 10.12 An SPSS scatter plot

If we want a regression line to be included with this scatter plot we then proceed with the instructions in Table 10.4 (Figure 10.13).
This will redraw the scatter plot with the OLS regression line through it (Figure 10.14).

Table 10.4 Adding a regression line to a scatter plot using SPSS

	SPSS command/action	Comments
1	Double click on the scatter plot in the **Viewer** window	This brings up the scatter plot in the **Chart Editor** window
2	From the menu select **Chart/Options**	This brings up the **Scatterplot Options** box. You will see an area headed **Fit Line**, which has an option labeled **Total** with a tick-box next to it
3	Click on the tick-box next to **Total**	This places ✓ in the tick-box to show that it has been selected
4	Click on **OK**	

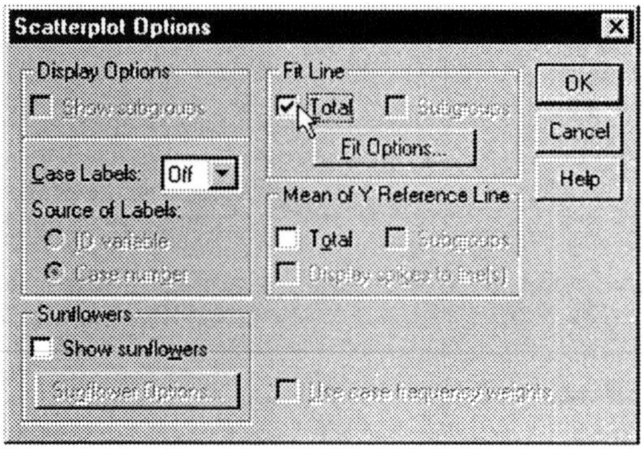

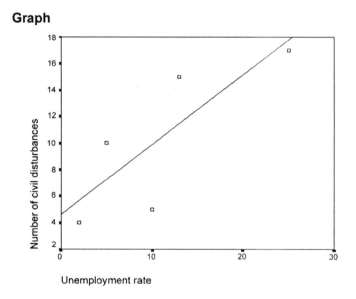

Figure 10.13 The **Scatterplot Options** dialog box

Graph

Figure 10.14 An SPSS scatter plot with a regression line

Regression statistics

To generate the statistics behind this regression line we follow the procedure in Table 10.5 (Figure 10.15).

A wealth of output is generated as a result of this command (Figure 10.16), much of which is beyond the scope of this book. The two parts of the output that concern us now are the tables headed **Model Summary** and **Coefficients**.

Table 10.5 Regression with curve estimation using SPSS

SPSS command/action	Comments
1 From the menu select **Analyze/Regression/ Linear**	This brings up the **Linear Regression** dialog box
2 Click on **Number of civil disturbances**	
3 Click on ▸ that points to the **Dependent:** target variable list	This pastes **Number of civil disturbances** as the dependent variable
4 Click on **Unemployment rate**	This highlights **Unemployment rate3**
5 Click on ▸ that points to the **Independent(s):** target variables list	This pastes **Unemployment rate** as the independent variable
6 Click on **OK**	

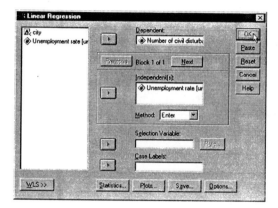

Figure 10.15 The **Linear Regression** dialog box

In the **Model Summary** table we see that Pearson's product moment correlation coefficient, R, is .807, and the coefficient of determination, R Square, is .651, which are the same as our hand calculations. The important part of the **Coefficients** table is the column headed B under Unstandardized Coefficients. This tells us that:

- the value for the *Y*-intercept (which we called *a* in the analysis above but SPSS calls the Constant) is **4.423**, and
- the slope of the regression line, which is the coefficient for Unemployment rate, is **.525**.

Again these are the same values we calculated by hand. The figure under Standardized Coefficients, .807, should look familiar: this is the value for Pearson's *r*, which was also given to us in the other table.

Regression

Variables Entered/Removed[b]

Model	Variables Entered	Variables Removed	Method
1	Unemploy ment rate[a]		Enter

a. All requested variables entered.

b. Dependent Variable: Number of civil disturbances

Model Summary

Model	R	R Square	Adjusted R Square	Std. Error of the Estimate
1	.807[a]	.651	.534	3.96

a. Predictors: (Constant), Unemployment rate

ANOVA[b]

Model		Sum of Squares	df	Mean Square	F	Sig.
1	Regression	87.701	1	87.701	5.586	.099[a]
	Residual	47.099	3	15.700		
	Total	134.800	4			

a. Predictors: (Constant), Unemployment rate

b. Dependent Variable: Number of civil disturbances

Coefficients[a]

Model		Unstandardized Coefficients		Standardized Coefficients	t	Sig.
		B	Std. Error	Beta		
1	(Constant)	4.423	3.019		1.465	.239
	Unemployment rate	.525	.222	.807	2.364	.099

a. Dependent Variable: Number of civil disturbances

Figure 10.16 SPSS **Regression** command output

Example

A museum keeps track of the number of visitors on randomly selected days across the year, in order to help it plan for crowds. It suspects that the daily temperature is a good predictor of the number of people who will pass through on any given day. The data on the daily temperature, measured in degrees Celsius, and the number of people attending, together with the calculations needed to construct a regression line, are included in Table 10.6.

Table 10.6 Calculations for the slope of the regression line

Temperature, X_i	People, Y_i	X_i^2	Y_i^2	X_iY_i
13	501	169	251,001	6513
28	175	784	30,625	4900
32	390	1024	152,100	12,480
20	452	400	204,304	9040
11	550	121	302,500	6050
15	734	225	538,756	11,010
9	620	81	384,400	5580
33	199	1089	39,601	6567
16	390	256	152,100	6240
29	223	841	49,729	6467
12	768	144	589,824	9216
15	679	225	461,041	10,185
18	410	324	168,100	7380
26	320	676	102,400	8320
18	590	324	348,100	10,620
17	650	289	422,500	11,050
27	258	729	66,564	6966
32	201	1024	40,401	6432
28	458	784	209,764	12,824
23	534	529	285,156	12,282
$\Sigma X_i = 422$	$\Sigma Y_i = 9102$	$\Sigma X_i^2 = 10,038$	$\Sigma Y_i^2 = 4,798,966$	$\Sigma(X_iY_i) = 170,122$

We can use this information to calculate the mean for each variable:

$$\bar{X} = \frac{\Sigma X_i}{n} = \frac{422}{20}$$

$$= 21.1$$

$$\bar{Y} = \frac{\Sigma Y_i}{n} = \frac{9102}{20}$$

$$= 455.1$$

These figures produce the equation for the slope of the regression line:

$$b = \frac{n\Sigma(X_iY_i) - (\Sigma X_i)(\Sigma Y_i)}{n\Sigma X_i^2 - (\Sigma X_i)^2} = \frac{20(170,122) - 422(9102)}{20(10,038) - (422)^2}$$

$$= -19$$

The value for a will be:

$$a = \overline{Y} - b\overline{X} = 455.1 - (-19.34)(21.1)$$

$$= 863$$

The OLS regression line therefore is defined by the following equation:

$$Y = 863 - 19X$$

If we wanted to use less mathematics and use plain words rather than symbols, this equation is:

$$\text{estimated number of patrons} = 863 - 19(\text{daily temperature})$$

A negative correlation exists between the temperature and the number of people attending the museum. We predict that for every degree that the temperature increases, 19 fewer people will attend the museum. The value for a indicates that when the temperature falls to zero the museum should expect 863 visitors.

To assess the strength of this relationship, and the confidence we can place in the predictions based on it, we also calculate the correlation coefficient and then the coefficient of determination.

$$r = \frac{n\Sigma(X_i Y_i) - (\Sigma X_i)(\Sigma Y_i)}{\sqrt{\left[n\Sigma X_i^2 - (\Sigma X_i)^2\right]\left[n\Sigma Y_i^2 - (\Sigma Y_i)^2\right]}}$$

$$= \frac{20(170,122) - 422(9102)}{\sqrt{\left[20(10,038) - (422)^2\right]\left[20(4,798,966) - (9102)^2\right]}}$$

$$= -0.8$$

$$r^2 = (-0.8)^2$$

$$= 0.64$$

These indicate that there is a strong negative relationship and that the OLS regression line explains a high proportion of the variance in the data, allowing the museum to make confident predictions.

The assumptions behind regression analysis

We have used the concept of least squares regression to derive a measure of correlation between two interval/ratio-level variables. However, implicit in the use of OLS are certain assumptions, which, if violated, will mean that this will not be the best rule for fitting a line through a scatter plot. It is worth noting these assumptions, although a more detailed discussion would take us too far from the needs of this book.

Linear relationships

Least squares regression assumes that the line of best fit is a straight one, or in more technical terms that there is a **linear relationship**. However, this is not always the case (Figure 10.17).

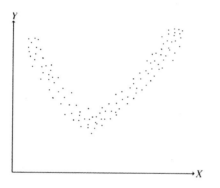

Figure 10.17 A non-linear relationship

It is clear that the line of best fit for this scatter plot will be curvilinear. We can ask SPSS to fit a regression line through these data points, and it will give us the best straight line, but clearly a straight line is not the best line!

Stability

Looking back at the example regarding the relationship between unemployment and civil unrest, the range of values for the independent variable was 9–22 percent. It might be tempting to use the regression line fitted for these data to predict the number of civil disturbances in a city with an unemployment rate of 30 percent. In other words, we might try to project the regression line out past the right-edge of the scatter plot when employing it as a tool for prediction. To do this we have to assume that the relationship is **stable**: that the correlation coefficient will be the same for the whole range of values over which we want to make predictions. This is analogous to the concept of consistency when looking at a crosstab.

This can sometimes be a very dangerous assumption. The statistics we have generated apply just to the cases for which we have information, and to extend their domain to cases for which we don't have information requires some justification. It may be, for example, that when unemployment rates hit a certain threshold level, such as 25 percent, the crime rate jumps up dramatically.

The other aspect of stability relates to time. Unlike the physical sciences, a relationship between two variables in the social sciences is not always the same over time. The relationship between force and mass seems relatively permanent, but the relationship between unemployment and civil disturbance may not be, because history brings about changes to social institutions that may alter the character of the relationship. For example, governments may respond to a strong relationship between unemployment and civil disturbance by creating new social institutions such as income support schemes and community programs that could soften the effect of unemployment. Using the information from one historical period for another historical period may therefore be inaccurate.

Homoscedasticity

The strict definition of homoscedasticity is that the variance of the error terms (residuals) of a regression line is constant. The best way to explain this is through an illustration (Figure 10.18).

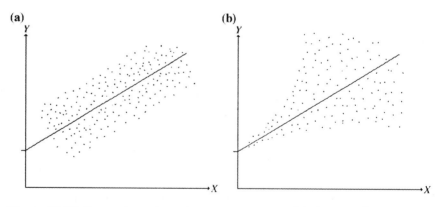

Figure 10.18 Regression where the error terms are **(a)** homoscedastic and **(b)** heteroscedastic

In Figure 10.18(a) we can see that the spread of the data points around the regression line is fairly constant over the length of the regression line. The data points form a 'cigar shape' around the line. In Figure 10.15(b), though, the data points lie far away from the line at one end, and gradually get closer as the value of the independent variable decreases. Graph (a) is the case of homoscedasticity, whereas graph (b) shows heteroscedasticity. The presence of heteroscedasticity causes any significance test on the value of r to be invalid, so that we are not able to generalize from a sample result to the population. Usually a simple inspection of a scatter plot will be sufficient to detect whether this assumption is valid.

Reversibility

This is not so much an assumption regarding the construction of a regression line but rather an assumption in its use. A positive correlation, for example, implies that when the value of an independent variable increases, the value of the dependent variable increases as well, and that when it decreases the dependent variable decreases as well. However, it is not always the case that the same relationship holds for increases as it does for decreases. We all know that there is a positive correlation between income levels and consumption levels: when we have more to spend we spend more! A researcher may look at a period of rising income levels and calculate a value for the regression coefficient (b) of 0.8: when income increases by $100, consumption will go up by $80. Can this researcher then argue that if income decreases by the same amount, consumption levels will go back to where they were before the initial increase? The answer is no. Most people adjust their spending patterns to the higher income level, and do not tend to give it up very easily, even if income falls again. People go into debt or sell off assets in order to maintain the higher spending patterns they have become accustomed to, so that the correlation observed in one direction may not be the same as that observed in the other direction.

Summary

This chapter has introduced the concepts of correlation and regression. But we have only just skimmed the surface. We could spend a whole course discussing this topic alone, and still not give it adequate treatment. Moreover, you will have noticed that there were many options within SPSS that we did not explore, sticking only to the bare minimum needed to get the results we were after. It is not within the scope of this book to pursue these issues in more detail – we only want to introduce the key concepts and methods. There are many other books that delve into regression analysis in far more depth. Nevertheless, the key ideas hopefully have emerged by sticking to the basics and not elaborating further on more advanced topics. Having digested this much, the task of absorbing the more advanced material may prove a little easier.

Exercises

10.1   Why should we draw a scatter plot of data before undertaking regression analysis?

10.2   What does the *Y*-intercept of a regression line indicate?

10.3   What is the principle used for drawing the line of best fit through a scatter plot?

10.4   For each of the following regression equations, state the direction of the relationship:
(a) $Y = 30 + 42X$
(b) $Y = 30 - 0.38X$
(c) $Y = -0.5 + 0.38X$
(d) $Y = -0.5$
(e) $Y = -0.5X$

10.5   Graph each of the following equations on graph paper. On your graph indicate the *Y*-intercept and the slope:
(a) $Y = 30 + 42X$
(b) $Y = 30 - 0.38X$
(c) $Y = -0.5 + 0.38X$
(d) $Y = -0.5$
(e) $Y = -0.5X$

10.6   Explain the difference between the correlation coefficient, *r*, and the coefficient of the regression line, *b*.

10.7   (a) Using graph paper draw a scatter plot for the following data:

X	5	6	9	10	10	13	15	18	22	27
Y	35	28	30	22	28	28	20	21	15	18

(b)   Looking at the data, what do you expect the sign in front of the coefficient to be (i.e. is there a positive or negative correlation)?
(c)   Draw a regression line through these data using the naked eye. Determine the equation for your line, and predict *Y* for $X = 12$.
(d)   Calculate the least squares regression line through these data. What is the least squares estimate for *Y* when $X = 12$?
(e)   What is the sum of the squared errors for your freehand line and the OLS line? Which of these sums is smallest?
(f)   Enter these data on SPSS and run the regression command to confirm your results.

10.8 A regression line is plotted through data on life expectancy in years and government expenditure on health care per head of population (in $'000) for a group of developing nations. Life expectancy is considered the dependent variable and expenditure the independent variable. The equation for the regression line is:

$$Y = 40 + 0.7X$$

(a) What will life expectancy be if the government spends no money on health care?

(b) What will life expectancy be if the government spends $30,000 per head on health care?

(c) Can you say that there is a strong relationship between the two variables?

10.9 A university lecturer in statistics wants to emphasize to her students the value of study to exam performance. The lecturer monitors the amount of time in minutes that all 11 students in the class spend in the library per week, and the final grades for each student. The figures are recorded in the following table:

Library time (minutes)	Exam score
41	52
30	44
39	48
48	65
55	62
58	60
65	74
80	79
94	80
100	90
120	86

The lecturer analyzes these data using the regression command in SPSS. Enter these data yourself into SPSS and from the output answer the following questions:

(a) From this information write down the equation for the OLS regression line for these data.

(b) What is the strength and direction of the relationship between these variables?

(c) Will a student who spends no time in the library fail?

(d) A student wants to use this information to work out the minimum amount of time the student needs to spend in the library in order to get a bare pass grade (50). What is the minimum amount of time he needs to spend in the library? Can the student be very confident in this prediction? What is the problem with using the regression line for such a purpose?

(e)   Draw a scatter plot of these data to check that it was appropriate for the lecturer to use linear regression.

(f)   Use the raw data to calculate by hand the same values presented in the SPSS output.

10.10   A real-estate agent wants to explore the factors affecting the selling price of a house. The agent believes that the main factor explaining differences in selling prices is house size. In this model which variable is cast as the independent and which is the dependent?

The agent collects data on these two variables, with the following results:

Selling price ($,000)	House size (squares)
260	20
240	15
245	20
210	13
230	18
242	14
295	28
235	16
287	24
252	20
270	23
275	25

(a)   Calculate all the relevant statistics needed to assess the agent's model, both by hand and by SPSS.

(b)   In SPSS create another column to enter the data for the selling price of houses, but this time enter the data without rounding to the nearest $,000, i.e. enter 250,000, 240,000, 243,000, etc. Recalculate your regression statistics. What, if anything, is different. Interpret any changes.

10.11   Enter into SPSS the data we used in the example above relating visitors to a museum with the daily temperature, and generate all the relevant descriptive statistics.

10.12   A study investigates the factors that may lead to a reduction in the number of working days lost due to illness at a certain factory. Ten people are studied and the following information about their respective number of hours of exercise per week and the number of working days they were absent due to illness is recorded in the table on the following the page.

(a)   What is the correlation between these two variables?

(b)   If someone exercises 8 hours a week, how many days do you predict that they will be absent from work due to illness over the course of the year?

Hours of exercise	Days lost
3	12
8	10
1	10
0	15
0	18
4	7
7	7
2	14
5	9
0	16
9	8
3	10

10.13 Using the **Employee data** file can we say that beginning salary is a good predictor of current salary?

10.14 From the **World95** data file that comes with SPSS, a social worker finds the correlation between female life expectancy and birth rate per 1000 people to be −0.862. What does this mean? Use SPSS to determine the full regression equation for this relationship and interpret the results.

PART 3

Inferential Statistics: The One-sample Case

11

Sampling Distributions

So far, we have looked at ways of summarizing information; we collect measurements from a set of cases and then reduce these hundreds (sometimes thousands) of numbers into descriptive statistics such as the mean or standard deviation. We have seen how such descriptive statistics provide a useful summary of the overall distribution, drawing out those features of a distribution that will help us answer our research question.

If the set of cases from which we take a measurement includes all the possible cases of interest – the **population** – the research process would end with the calculation of these descriptive measures. An investigation that includes every member of the population is a **census** and the descriptive statistics for a population are **parameters**.

A **parameter** is a statistic that describes some feature of a population.

When using mathematical notation, parameters are denoted with Greek symbols, such as μ and σ for the population mean and standard deviation respectively.

Sometimes we actually have information about the whole population of interest, such as when a government agency conducts a census of people and can tell us the age distribution of the entire population at a certain date. Other times we don't have information about the population – it is out there but we just can't get our hands on it. Therefore, in research we often work with a smaller sub-set; a **sample** of the population. The descriptive measures used to summarize a sample are **sample statistics**. These sample statistics are denoted, in mathematical shorthand, with Roman letters: $\overline{X}$ for the sample mean, and s for the sample standard deviation.

There are several reasons why we may draw a sample from a population, rather than conduct a complete census:

- Samples are usually cheaper and quicker.
- It is sometimes impossible to locate all the members of a population, either because a complete list of the population is unavailable, or because some of its members are difficult to get to or unwilling to participate in the study.

- Research sometimes destroys the units of analysis so that a census would destroy the population. For example, a factory might be interested in a quality control check of the batteries it produces. Testing that the products have sufficient battery life may involve running the units down until they have run out of power, a process that will cause bankruptcy if it is applied to all the batteries that the firm produced.
- Sometimes sampling is more accurate. If there is reason to believe that the survey process generates errors, then a full-scale census may amplify these errors. For example, assembling the research team required to undertake a census may lead to inexperienced survey staff being used to collect data, whereas a smaller team might be better trained and more experienced.

For whatever reason sampling is undertaken, a central problem arises. Are the descriptive statistics we get from a *sample* the same as the corresponding statistics we would get if a complete and accurate census was undertaken? Are the sample statistics in some sense 'representative' of the population from which the sample is drawn? Even though we may do everything in our power to draw a 'representative' sample from a population, the operation of **random variation** may cause the sample to be 'off'. On what basis then can we make a valid generalization from the sample to the population?

For example, we might sample a group of 120 people from a certain area and ask each their age in years. Here the variable of interest (age) is measured at the interval/ratio level. We can describe the information contained in the data by calculating a measure of central tendency to give a sense of the spread of scores; by calculating a measure of dispersion to give a sense of the spread of scores around the average; and by drawing a graph to give us an overall impression of the distribution. These are not the only ways of describing a distribution (as we have seen) but will often satisfy many of our research questions.

This information might be interesting in itself, but usually we compile information about a sample because we have another issue to address: what is the average age of *all* people in this area? If the average age for this sample is 36 years, can I generalize from this to the whole population? This is where the operation of random variation may cause us to feel uneasy about making such generalizations from the sample statistics. How can we be sure that our sample did not happen by chance to include a few disproportionately old or disproportionately young people, in relation to the population?

We address this problem by using **inferential statistics**.

Inferential statistics are the numerical techniques for making conclusions about a population based on the information obtained from a random sample drawn from that population.

To undertake statistical inference we generate three separate sets of numbers:

1. *Raw data* These are the measurements taken from each case for a variable (e.g. the age of each person, measured in years). This will often be a very large set of numbers, depending on the actual sample size.
2. *Sample statistics* These are the descriptive statistics that summarize the raw data obtained from the sample (e.g. the mean, standard deviation, or frequency distribution).
3. *Inferential statistics* These help us to make a decision about the characteristics of the population based on the sample statistics.

Although the detailed steps involved in making an inference vary from situation to situation, we use the same general procedure, which involves generating these three sets of numbers. This procedure is illustrated in Figure 11.1.

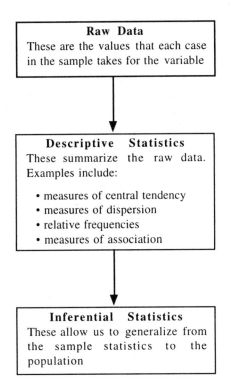

Figure 11.1 The process of inferential analysis

Random samples

The most important condition that must apply if we are to use inferential statistics to generalize from a sample to a population is that the sample must be **randomly selected** from the population.

Random selection is a sampling method where each member of the population has the same chance of being selected in the sample.

A telephone survey of the population is not perfectly random. Only people in a household with a telephone at the time of the survey have a chance of being included. This excludes the homeless and households without a phone. Similarly, it gives households with more than one telephone number a greater chance of being included. In fact, very few surveys will be perfectly random in terms of the strict definition. The important consideration is whether the deviation from random selection is likely systematically to over-represent or under-represent cases of interest such that the results will have a **bias**. A biased sample favors the selection of some members of the population over others.

Sometimes there are good reasons to deviate from simple random selection by using **stratified random sampling**. A stratified random sample is used on a population that has easily discernible strata. Each stratum is a segment of the population that we suspect is uniform in terms of the variable we want to measure. We first predetermine the proportion of the total sample that will come from each stratum. We then randomly select cases from *within* each stratum. For example, we might feel that men are similar to each other in terms of a particular variable and that women are also similar to each other in terms of this variable, but there is a difference between men and women. Thus we might stratify a sample to ensure that 50 percent of the sample are women and 50per cent men. Having divided the sample into two segments we then randomly select the required number of women and the required number of men.

Random sampling is often called **probability sampling**. But there is a whole range of non-probability (non-random) sampling techniques, such as **snow-ball sampling**. Snow-ball sampling involves selecting cases on the basis of information provided by previously studied cases. Such a sampling method is particularly useful when conducting research on close-knit populations that are difficult to get to, or whose exact size and composition cannot be known in advance.

There is no inherent reason why probability sampling should be considered 'better' than non-probability sampling. Each method is appropriate for different research questions, and sometimes a research question will be better addressed by choosing a non-probability sampling method. One of the implications of using a non-probability sampling method, though, is that we cannot use the inferential statistics we are about to learn. This is not necessarily a bad thing, and other ways of interpreting information are as valid as statistical inference, and sometimes more so.

Unfortunately, the professional and academic worlds do not always see it this way. Research seems to acquire a 'scientific' look when dressed in terms of inferential statistics, and often research is forced into this framework just to suit the fashion. Inferential statistics are sometimes calculated on samples that are not randomly selected. In other instances, the research project is structured in such a way as to make inferential statistics applicable, even though other methods may have been more insightful. This is a problem with the practice of research that raises broader issues than can be dealt with here. All we will do now is issue a word of caution: the choice of research methods should never be undertaken on the basis of the technique to be used for analyzing data. It should be chosen on the basis of best addressing the research problem at hand, and if that happens to involve the kind of statistical analyses we will be learning below, then we will know how to deal with it. If not, then the project is not lost. It simply means other avenues should be pursued.

The sampling distribution of a sample statistic

Inferential statistics only apply to random samples, because the central tool used to make inferences is based on the assumption of random sampling. This tool is the **sampling distribution of a sample statistic**. Before defining the sampling distribution, we will illustrate the idea behind its construction through a very simple experiment. Assume that we have a board that consists of rows of nails that are evenly spaced and protrude from the board (Figure 11.2).

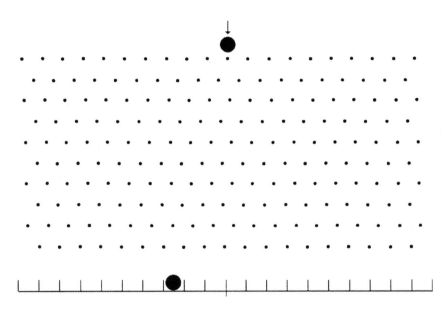

Figure 11.2

A ball is dropped directly above the middle nail in the top row and allowed to find its way down to the bottom. The path the ball takes will depend on a whole host of factors, but eventually the ball will bounce around and emerge somewhere at the bottom. The point at which any *individual* ball will fall is a random event.

However, if I dropped 100 identical balls from the same position and let each find its way down the rows of nails to pile up at the bottom, we might get a distribution that looks like Figure 11.3.

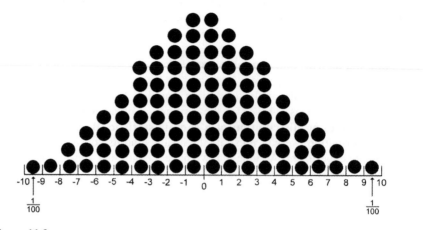

Figure 11.3

Most balls will bounce around, but since they are dropped from the same point plenty of balls will pile up in the center. But not all the balls will travel this path. Some will just happen to bounce to the left of each nail more often than they bounce to the right, and therefore emerge over to one side, and some will happen to keep bouncing to the right more often and come out on the other side. In fact the occasional odd ball will land way out to the left (position –9) or way out to the right (position 9). But we can see that the chances of a ball landing way out to the left, if allowed to fall freely, is only 1 in 100. In other words, although the location of any individual ball is a random event, the shape of the overall distribution of repeated drops is not random – it has a definite shape.

What has all this got to do with research statistics and inference? To see how the same logic applies in the 'real' world rather than just with balls and nails, let's go back to the example where people from a small community are surveyed and their age in years recorded. The parameters for this population of 400 are:

$$\mu = 35 \text{ years}$$

$$\sigma = 13 \text{ years}$$

Let us assume, however, that we do not survey all 400 members of this community. Instead we carry out the following experiment. We randomly select 120 people and ask only these 120 their respective ages and calculate their average age. We then put these people back into the community and randomly select another 120 residents (which may include members of the first sample). We proceed to draw a third sample of 120 residents. We keep doing this over and over again taking a random sample of 120 community members and calculating the average age for each *sample*.

This should sound a little like the experiment of dropping 100 balls down the board and seeing where they land, except instead of balls we are taking samples and seeing where the sample means 'fall'. I have actually performed this hypothetical experiment (not with real people but using SPSS, as will be illustrated below), and the results of these 20 repeated random samples are displayed in Table 11.1, in the order in which they were generated, rounding to the nearest decimal point.

Table 11.1 Distribution of 20 random sample means (*n* = 120)

Sample number	Sample mean
1	34.7
2	35.9
3	35.5
4	34.7
5	34.5
6	35.4
7	35.7
8	34.6
9	37.4
10	35.3
11	34.1
12	35.5
13	34.9
14	36.2
15	35.6
16	35.0
17	35.1
18	36.4
19	35.6
20	33.6

These results are plotted in Figure 11.4.

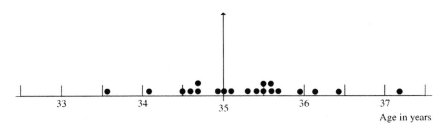

Age in years

Figure 11.4 Distribution of 20 random sample means (*n* = 20)

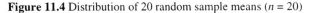

We can see that most of the results are clustered around the population value of 35 years, with a few scores a bit further out and one 'extreme' score of 37.4 years. This is obviously a sample that just happened by chance, through the operation of random variation, to include a few relatively older members of the community. Even so it is interesting that despite the fact that the individual ages of the 400 people in the community range from 2 years to 69 years of age, the *means of the samples* have a very narrow range of values. Nearly half of the 20 samples I took produced mean ages within half a year of the 'true' population average. This gives us some sense of the value and reliability of random samples.

Let us push this hypothetical example a little further, and imagine that we theoretically take an *infinite* number of random samples of equal size from this population and observe the distribution of all of these sample means. The pattern we have already observed with just 20 random samples will be reinforced. Most of the samples will cluster around the population parameter, with the occasional sample result falling relatively further to one side or the other of the distribution. Such a distribution is a **sampling distribution**.

> A **sampling distribution** is the theoretical probability distribution of an infinite number of sample outcomes for a statistic, using random samples of equal size.

A sampling distribution is a *theoretical distribution* in that it is a construct derived on the basis of a logical exercise – the result that will follow *if* we could take an infinite number of random samples of equal size. The distribution of a sample and the distribution of a population, on the other hand, are *empirical distributions* in the sense that they exist in the 'real world'.

Here we are dealing with the **sampling distribution of sample *means*** since it is the distribution of all the means obtained from repeated random samples. This sampling distribution of sample means will have three very important properties:

The mean of the sampling distribution is equal to the population mean In other words, the average of the averages ($\mu_{\bar{X}}$) will be the same as the population mean. This is written formally in the following way:

$$\mu_{\bar{X}} = \mu$$

The standard error will be related to the standard deviation for the population The standard deviation of the sampling distribution is known as the **standard error** ($\sigma_{\bar{X}}$), and its value is affected by the sample size and the amount of variation in the population. If we are only taking a sample of five people, and one of the people in this small sample happens to be 60 years of age, the average for this sample will be greatly affected by this one score. In other words, we expect small samples to be less reliable than large samples, since they have a higher probability of producing a very wide dispersion of results. If our sample size is 200 the effect of one large score will be diluted by a greater number of cases that are closer to the population mean. So repeated large samples will be clustered closer to the population value; they will be more reliable. Similarly, if we were drawing samples from a population where age spreads from 2 years of age to 102 years of age, the range of scores we would get from these samples will be much greater than if we were sampling from a population where age only ranged between 20 and 30 years. *The more homogeneous the population, the more tightly clustered will be random samples drawn from that population.* These two factors are captured by the following formula for the standard error:

$$\sigma_{\bar{X}} = \frac{\sigma}{\sqrt{n}}$$

The sampling distribution will be normally distributed The proportion of samples that will fall within a certain range of values will be given by the standard normal distribution.

These three features of the sampling distribution of sample means are illustrated in Figure 11.5.

(a) Population

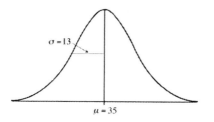

$\sigma = 13$

$\mu = 35$

(b) Sampling distribution, $n = 20$

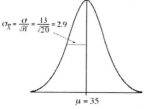

$\sigma_{\bar{X}} = \frac{\sigma}{\sqrt{n}} = \frac{13}{\sqrt{20}} = 2.9$

$\mu = 35$

(c) Sampling distribution, $n = 100$

$\sigma_{\bar{X}} = \frac{\sigma}{\sqrt{n}} = \frac{13}{\sqrt{100}} = 1.3$

$\mu = 35$

Figure 11.5 Sampling distributions with different sample sizes

Figure 11.5(a) displays the distribution of all 400 people which is the population of the community. Figure 11.5(b) is the sampling distribution of sample means for samples of size $n = 20$. In other words, it is the distribution of means we will get if we repeatedly sample 20 people from this community. Figure 11.5(c) is the sampling distribution of sample means for samples of size $n=100$. We can see that both sampling distributions will be centered on the population mean of 35 years. Both will also be normally distributed. However, the standard error for each sampling distribution will vary. With repeated samples of size $n = 20$ there is a greater spread of sample means, with a standard error of 2.9 years, whereas with the larger samples the sample results are clustered more tightly around the population value. Both sampling distributions are normal, in that 68 percent of all cases fall within one standard deviation from the mean. But for the sampling distribution where $n = 20$ this range will be between 32.1 years and 37.9 years:

$$35 \pm 2.9 = 32.1 \text{ and } 37.9 \text{ years}$$

whereas for the second sampling distribution this range will be much narrower, having a lower limit of 33.7 years and an upper limit of 36.3 years:

$$35 \pm 1.3 = 33.7 \text{ and } 36.3 \text{ years}$$

The central limit theorem

We have looked at the properties of a sampling distribution derived from a population that is normally distributed. In particular, the sampling distribution will also be normal. However, there are few populations in the social world that are even approximately normal. What if the ages of the 400 people in our small community are distributed in the way shown in Figure 11.6?

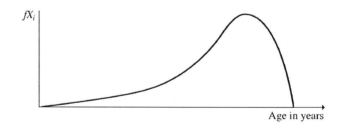

Figure 11.6 A skewed distribution

The distribution is skewed to the left, indicating that there are relatively more older people than younger people in this community. It would seem that repeated random samples from this skewed distribution will produce a skewed sampling distribution as well. However, this is not so. According to one of the key principles in statistics, the **central limit theorem** states that under certain conditions the sampling distribution will be normal, even though the population distribution from which the samples are drawn is not normal.

> The **central limit theorem** states that if an infinite number of random samples of equal size are selected from a population, the sampling distribution of the sample means will approach a normal distribution as sample size approaches infinity.

The population may be non-normal, yet repeated sampling will (theoretically) generate a normal sampling distribution. In fact, the sample size does not have to be as large as suggested in the formal statement of the theorem: once the sample size is greater than 100, the sampling distribution of sample means will be approximately normal.

Generating random samples using SPSS

We can generate repeated random samples on SPSS to see the spread of sample means. In fact this is how I got the results presented in Table 11.1. This is a fairly repetitive procedure, since we need to generate a large number of random sample means. There are two steps repeated in sequence over and over. The first is to select a random sample, and the second is to calculate the mean for the sample.

Selecting a random sample

Using the data that have been entered on the ages of the 400 residents of our hypothetical community, the first step is to ask SPSS to randomly select a certain number of cases, which in this instance will be 120 (Table 11.2, Figure 11.7).

When you have completed the commands listed in Table 11.2 and refer to the **Data Editor** window you will see that SPSS has placed a slash through most of the numbers in the shaded column on the left of the page. These cases are the ones that are not included in the calculation of the mean – the ones that have not been randomly selected. Similarly, you will notice that SPSS has created a new 'variable', which it calls **filter_$**. We do not actually use the filter ourselves, even though it will appear in variable lists. SPSS uses this variable to choose some cases in the sample and ignore others, by assigning a value of 1 to cases without a slash through their case number and 0 to those that have been 'slashed'.

Table 11.2 Generating repeated random samples on SPSS (file: **Ch11.sav**)

SPSS command/action	Comments
1 From the menu select **Data/Select Cases**	This brings up the **Select Cases** dialog box. The SPSS default setting is to use all cases, indicated by • in the radio button next to **All cases**
2 Select **Random sample of cases** by clicking on the small circle next to this option	A • will appear in the radio button next to **Random sample of cases** and the text below it will darken
3 Click on the **Sample** button	This brings up the **Select Cases: Random Sample** dialog box. This gives us the option of selecting a certain percentage of cases, or a certain number of cases. Here we want a certain number of cases (120)
4 Click on the small circle next to **Exactly**	The cursor will jump to the box next to **Exactly**
5 Type 120	This is the size of the sample we wish to draw
6 Type 400 in the box next to **from the first**	This is the total number of cases from which we want to draw the sample
7 Click on **Continue**	
8 Click on **OK**	

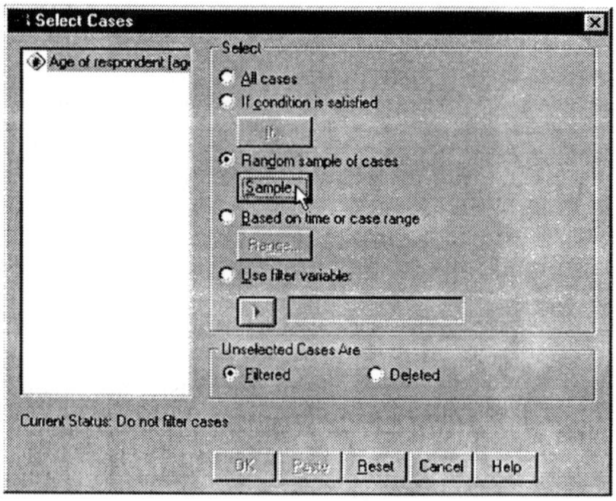

Figure 11.7(a) The **Select Cases** dialog box

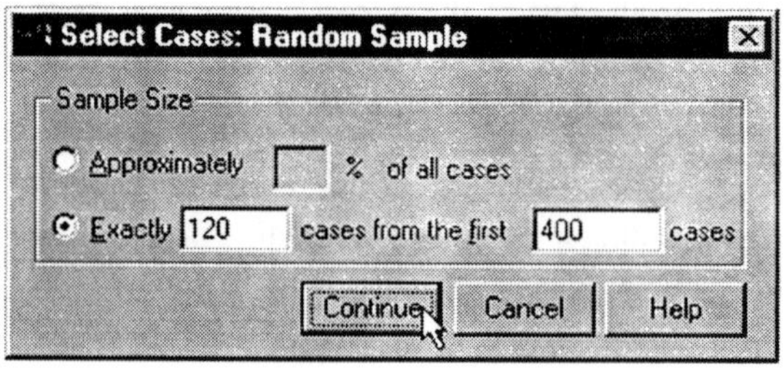

Figure 11.7(b) The **Random Sample** dialog box

Calculating the sample mean

The next step is to ask SPSS to calculate the mean for this sample using the **Analyze/Descriptive Statistics/Frequencies** command we learnt in Chapter 4. It might be helpful to select *only* the mean in this option, so that we do not get a frequency table and other descriptive statistics for each repeated sample, since this will generate more output than is necessary for our purpose here.

Repeating the sampling procedure

Running these two commands in sequence will generate a mean for the randomly selected sample of 120 cases. To draw another random sample all that is required is that we select the **Data/Select Cases** command and then click directly on **OK**. It is not necessary to again tell SPSS to randomly select 120 cases – it will automatically repeat the previous set of instructions and choose a new sample of 120. Similarly, by selecting **Analyze/Descriptive Statistics/Frequencies** and then clicking on **OK** a mean will be calculated without having to reselect all the options within this command. You will get 20 tables that each look like the one in Figure 11.8.

Frequencies

Statistics

Age of respondent

N	Valid	120
	Missing	0
Mean		35.76

Figure 11.8 SPSS mean for a random sample

Your own set of 20 results will have different values for each mean, since we are working with random samples. These results do not constitute a true sampling distribution, since there are only 20 samples, whereas a sampling distribution is theoretically the distribution of an *infinite* number of random samples. Despite this a general pattern should emerge from your repeated sampling procedure:

- Most of the sample results will be very close to the population value of 35 years. There will be some variation around this, but most sample results will be clustered around the population parameter.
- You should get one or two sample means that are relatively a great distance from the population parameter of 35. There is always a possibility that an individual sample may produce an 'odd' result, but most samples will tend to be 'true' to the population value.

Summary

We have spent a great deal of time in this chapter dealing with abstract theoretical concepts. In particular we have played around with a thought experiment: what if we could take an infinite number of samples of equal size from a certain population, and calculate the mean for each of these samples? At some point the critical reader will have thought 'but who gets to take an infinite number of samples?' Usually a social or health researcher only gets to take one sample from a population and has to determine what the population looks like from that one sample. What use is the sampling distribution then? In the next chapters we will see that it is the foundation stone on which inferences can be made from a single random sample to a population.

Exercises

11.1   What is the difference between a parameter and a sample statistic?

11.2   What is the difference between descriptive statistics and inferential statistics?

11.3   What is random variation? How does it affect our ability to make a generalization from a sample to a population?

11.4   State whether each of the following statements is true or false:

    (a)   The reliability of random sample means depends on the size of the sample, the variance of the population, and the size of the population.

    (b)   The means of random samples will cluster around the population mean.

    (c)   The standard deviation of random sample means will be greater than the standard deviation of the population from which they are drawn.

    (d)   The sampling distribution of sample means will be normal only if they are drawn from a normal population.

11.5   If the mean of a normal population is 40, what will the mean of the sampling distribution be with $n = 30$; with $n = 120$?

11.6   What is meant by the standard error? Will it be equal to, greater than, or less than the standard deviation for the population? Why?

11.7   Sketch the sampling distribution of sample means when $n = 30$ and when $n = 200$. In what way are these two distributions different, and in what way are they similar?

11.8   A teacher wants to evaluate a course by surveying registered
             students. The teacher writes the letters in the alphabet on separate
             pieces of paper and selects the one with G written on it out of a hat.
             The teacher therefore selects all students in class whose last names
             begins with G. In what ways, if any, is this sampling method non-
             random?

11.9   A library wants to assess the condition of the books in its possession.
             It randomly selects Thursday, and examines the condition of all
             books returned to the library on the following Thursday. In what
             ways, if any, is this sampling method non-random?

11.10   Describe a research project that might use the process of stratified
             random sampling.

11.11   Why is the central limit theorem so important to research?

11.12   Using the data for the age distribution of the community of 400
             people, draw another 20 random samples, this time using sample
             sizes of 30. How does the spread of results differ from that in the
             text, where sample size was 120?

12

Estimation and Confidence Intervals

In Chapter 11 we looked at the properties of a sampling distribution of sample means. This sampling distribution has three very important properties:

The mean of the sampling distribution is equal to the population mean Although the mean of any individual sample may differ from that of the population from which it is drawn, repeated random sample means will cluster around the 'true' population value.

$$\mu_{\bar{X}} = \mu$$

In other words, although individual results will vary from sample to sample, on average the sample means will be equal to that of the population. This property of a sample mean makes it an **unbiased estimator** of the population value.

A sample statistic is **unbiased** if its sampling distribution has a mean equal to the population parameter it is estimating.

The spread of sample results around the population value is affected by the sample size The standard deviation of the sampling distribution, called the standard error, is defined by the following equation:

$$\sigma_{\bar{X}} = \frac{\sigma}{\sqrt{n}}$$

As sample size increases the standard error of the sampling distribution gets smaller, so that sample results are more *tightly* clustered around the population value. In other words, large samples provide **efficient estimators** of the population values.

The sampling distribution of sample means is normal The proportion of sample means that will fall within a certain range of values will be given by the standard normal distribution. Given this fact, we can use the techniques we introduced in Chapter 6, whereby we use z-scores to describe the distribution of cases across a range of values. (In fact, it might help the following discussion if the reader returned to Chapter 6 for a quick refresher before proceeding.)

These three properties of the sampling distribution of sample means allow us to refer to the table for the area under the standard normal curve (Appendix A1) in order to gage the probability that any given sample mean will be within a certain range of values around the population mean. For example, we know that around 95 percent of repeated samples will have a mean within 1.96 standard errors of the population mean (Figure 12.1).

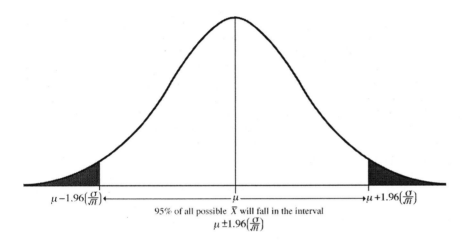

$$\mu - 1.96\left(\frac{\sigma}{\sqrt{n}}\right) \longleftarrow \qquad \mu \qquad \longrightarrow \mu + 1.96\left(\frac{\sigma}{\sqrt{n}}\right)$$

95% of all possible $\bar{X}$ will fall in the interval
$$\mu \pm 1.96\left(\frac{\sigma}{\sqrt{n}}\right)$$

Figure 12.1 The sampling distribution of sample means

This allows us to specify a range or **interval** of scores within which 95 percent of all possible sample means will fall, defined by the formula:

$$\mu \pm 1.96\left(\frac{\sigma}{\sqrt{n}}\right)$$

Estimation

In Figure 12.1 we posed the problem in a certain way. We have a population parameter, and estimate the range of values that 95 percent of all random samples drawn from that population will take. However, in research the problem usually poses itself in a different way. We have a single sample result, and we need to estimate the population value from the sample. This problem is illustrated in Figure 12.2.

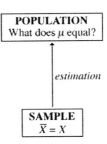

Figure 12.2 The process of estimating a population mean

For example, in the previous chapter we analyzed a population of 400 residents of a hypothetical community. The average age for this population was 35 years. We took random samples of size $n = 120$ from this population, and we saw that the averages for each of these samples were not equal to the population parameter, but most of them clustered around the population value. But what if we did not know that the mean age of the population was 35 years, and all we had to work with was *one* of these samples of 120 residents? Let us assume that this one and only sample is the one that produced an average age of 34.5 years and our task is to estimate the population parameter (which for the moment we are pretending we do not know) from this one sample result.

In estimating the population parameter we start with an assumption. We assume that the sample actually falls within a certain region of the sampling distribution. We assume that the sample mean is not one of those few, very unlikely and extreme results that are very different from the population value. For example, we might feel comfortable with the assumption that this one sample of 120 residents is one of the 95 percent of all *possible* samples that will fall within ±1.96 standard errors from the population mean.

Remember that this is only an assumption: we may have actually drawn one of those freakish samples that has a mean very different from the population parameter. We can never know if this is the case, but given the very low probability of this being the case (less than 5 in 100), the assumption seems reasonable. In other words we can be confident that this assumption is correct. In fact, we call this assumed probability the **confidence level**; in this instance we choose a 95 percent confidence level.

Given this assumption – that the sample result is within the range that 95 percent of all possible sample results will fall – we can make an **estimate** of the population value. We know that the sampling distribution will have a standard deviation, called the standard error, of:

$$\sigma_{\bar{X}} = \frac{\sigma}{\sqrt{n}}$$

Here, though, we do not know the standard deviation for the population, σ, so we use the sample standard deviation instead, which for this sample is equal to 13 years.

$$\sigma_{\bar{X}} = \frac{s}{\sqrt{n}} = \frac{13}{\sqrt{120}}$$

$$= 1.2 \text{ years}$$

Given this value for the standard error the furthest the population parameter can be *below* the sample value such that the sample value remains within the 95 percent region is −1.96 standard errors. This is called the **lower limit** of the estimate. It sets the maximum distance that the population value will be below the sample (Figure 12.3):

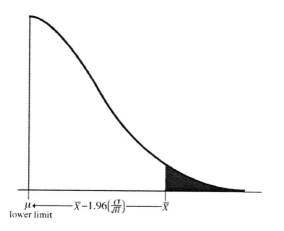

Figure 12.3

$$\text{lower limit} = \bar{X} - z\left(\frac{s}{\sqrt{n}}\right)$$

Using similar reasoning, the furthest the population parameter can be *above* the sample value so that the sample value is within the 95 percent region is +1.96 standard errors. This is called the **upper limit** and is illustrated in Figure 12.4.

Putting these two pieces of logic together allows us to define a range of values, called a **confidence interval** (*ci*), within which we estimate lies the population parameter.

A **confidence interval** is the range of values that, it is estimated, includes a population statistic, at a specific level of confidence.

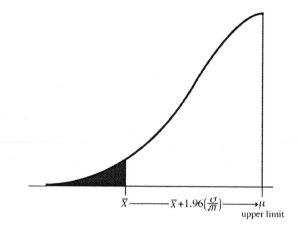

$$\overline{X} \underline{\hspace{2cm}} \overline{X}+1.96\left(\frac{\sigma}{\sqrt{n}}\right) \underline{\hspace{1cm}} \rightarrow \mu$$
upper limit

Figure 12.4

$$\text{upper limit} = \overline{X} + z\left(\frac{s}{\sqrt{n}}\right)$$

The steps involved in determining the lower limit and the upper limit of a confidence interval (Figure 12.5) can be combined in the following equation:

$$ci = \overline{X} \pm z\left(\frac{s}{\sqrt{n}}\right)$$

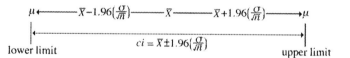

$$\mu \leftarrow \underline{\hspace{1cm}} \overline{X}-1.96\left(\frac{\sigma}{\sqrt{n}}\right) \underline{\hspace{1cm}} \overline{X} \underline{\hspace{1cm}} \overline{X}+1.96\left(\frac{\sigma}{\sqrt{n}}\right) \underline{\hspace{1cm}} \rightarrow \mu$$

lower limit $ci = \overline{X} \pm 1.96\left(\frac{\sigma}{\sqrt{n}}\right)$ upper limit

Figure 12.5 The 95 percent confidence interval

This equation simply states that we add and subtract from the sample result a distance defined by the maximum number of z-scores we assume the sample result can be from the population parameter. We have been working with a z-score of 1.96, because we assumed that the sample was one of the 95 percent of all possible samples that fall closest to the population mean. In the example of the age of our residents, the lower and upper limits are:

$$\text{lower limit} = \overline{X} - z\left(\frac{s}{\sqrt{n}}\right) = 34.5 - 1.96\left(\frac{13}{\sqrt{120}}\right)$$

$$= 32.2 \text{ years}$$

$$\text{upper limit} = \overline{X} + z\left(\frac{s}{\sqrt{n}}\right) = 34.5 + 1.96\left(\frac{13}{\sqrt{120}}\right)$$

$$= 36.8 \text{ years}$$

We write such an estimate in the following way: 34.5 [32.2, 36.8].

We have constructed a confidence *interval* because in estimating the average age of the population from a single sample we need to allow for the effects of sampling variation. Looking at the estimate we have constructed from this sample, we can see that it includes the actual population average of 35 years, which we pretended we did not know. The confidence interval is accurate in that the range of values between 32.2 and 36.8 years includes this actual population mean. Normally we do not know whether the estimate is accurate, but the confidence level indicates the probability of being accurate.

In fact I have constructed a confidence interval around all the 20 random samples drawn in Chapter 11 from this population. The sample averages have been graphed and the confidence intervals around them drawn in Figure 12.6.

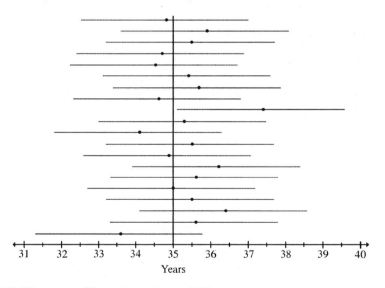

Figure 12.6 Twenty confidence intervals ($\alpha = 0.05$)

Looking at Figure 12.6 we can see the potential problem with making an estimate using sample results. If the one sample we drew happened to be the one that produced an average age of 37.4 years, our estimate will be inaccurate. The assumption that this is one of the 95 percent of samples that will fall within 1.96 standard errors from the population value is invalid: it is one of those 5 in 100 samples that fall a relatively long distance from the population mean.

Therefore the interval constructed on the basis of a 95 percent confidence level will not include the parameter of 35 years. We can never know whether this is the case – whether the one sample we do undertake just happens to be 'freakish'. However, we can see from Figure 12.7 that such an event is highly unlikely. In fact, 19 out of the 20 intervals do include the true population value of 35 years, which is in accord with the confidence level of 95 percent.

Another way to think of this is that with a confidence level of 95 percent we are prepared to be wrong only five times in every 100 samples (i.e. 1 in 20). This is the risk we take of not including the population parameter in our interval estimate, given that we have to make an estimate based on a sample that is affected by random variation. This probability of error is known as the **alpha level** (α), which is simply one minus the confidence level (expressed as a proportion). Thus the 95 percent (0.95) confidence level is the same as an alpha level of $\alpha = 0.05$. A 90 percent confidence level is the same as an alpha level of $\alpha = 0.10$, or a risk of being wrong 1 time in 10.

Changing the confidence level

In this discussion, we chose a confidence level of 95 percent. This is why we multiplied the standard error by a z-score of 1.96, since this defines the region under the sampling distribution that includes 95 percent of repeated sample results. This is the commonly used confidence level, but we can choose either larger or smaller levels, depending on how accurate we want to be. The larger the confidence level the more likely that the interval derived from it will include the population mean. If we choose a 99 percent confidence interval, for example, then we are assuming that a given sample mean is one of the 99 in 100 that falls *2.58* standard errors either side of the true mean:

$$ci = \overline{X} \pm 2.58\left(\frac{s}{\sqrt{n}}\right)$$

Making the starting assumption safer, however, by choosing a larger confidence level comes at a cost. In order for us to argue that the sample is one of the 99 percent that fall within a certain region around the true value, that region has to be widened. Rather than multiplying the standard error by $z = 1.96$, we multiply by $z = 2.58$. It is like firing an arrow at a target. Making an assumption that an arrow is likely to fall within 1 meter of the bullseye is safer than making the assumption that it will fall within 10 centimeters of the bullseye, but it has come at the cost of some accuracy. Making the target 'bigger' by widening the confidence interval means we are more likely to 'hit it' (i.e. make sure that the interval includes the population value), but we are no longer as precise in our shooting.

To see the effect of choosing different confidence levels we will work through the following example. A random sample of 200 nurses is taken and each nurse asked his or her annual income in whole dollars. These 200 nurses have an average income of $35,000, with a standard deviation of $5000.

$$\overline{X} = \$35,000$$
$$s = \$5000$$
$$n = 200$$

What is our estimate for the average annual income of all nurses? With a 95 percent confidence interval the range (rounded to the nearest whole dollar) is:

$$ci = \overline{X} \pm z\left(\frac{s}{\sqrt{n}}\right) = 35,000 \pm 1.96\left(\frac{5000}{\sqrt{200}}\right)$$

$$= \$35,000 \pm 695$$

The lower and upper limits will be:

lower limit: $35,000 - 695 = \$34,305$

upper limit: $35,000 + 695 = \$35,695$

We therefore estimate that the average income of all nurses, *with a 95 percent level of confidence*, will lie within the following range:

$$\$34,305 \leq \mu \leq \$35,695$$

The interval width is:

interval width $= 35,695 - 34,305 = \$1390$

With a 99 percent confidence interval, the z-score we use in the calculation is 2.58. The calculation will thereby be:

$$ci = \overline{X} \pm z\left(\frac{s}{\sqrt{n}}\right) = 35,000 \pm 2.58\left(\frac{5000}{\sqrt{200}}\right)$$

$$= 35,000 \pm 915$$

$$= \$35,000 \; [34,085, \; 35,915]$$

To be more confident that the interval will actually contain the true population value, it has become much wider; it now ranges from $34,085 to $35,915. The width of this interval is $1830.

If, on the other hand, I want to be more precise in my estimate I will choose a 90 percent confidence level, but this will be at the higher risk of being wrong. The confidence interval for this level will be, with $z = 1.645$:

$$ci = 35,000 \pm 1.645\left(\frac{5000}{\sqrt{200}}\right)$$

$$= \$35,000 \, [34,415, \, 35,585]$$

The effect of these changes to the confidence level on our estimates is summarized in Table 12.1 and Figure 12.7.

Table 12.1 Effect of confidence levels on intervals

Confidence level (%)	z-score	Confidence interval	Interval width
90	1.65	$\$35,000 \pm 585$	$1170
95	1.96	$\$35,000 \pm 695$	$1390
99	2.58	$\$35,000 \pm 915$	$1830

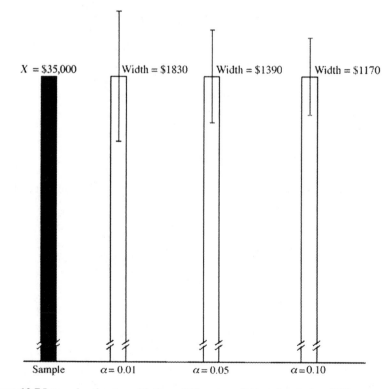

Figure 12.7 Interval estimates with three different confidence levels ($n = 200$)

Using a smaller confidence level reduces the interval width in which we estimate the population value lies. However, because this interval width is smaller the chances of being wrong (which is equal to the alpha level) have also increased. Having a narrower range of values increases the chance that it will not include the mean of the population. Making the bullseye on a target smaller allows us to say that we are better archers if we hit it, but it also increases the chances of not hitting it. On the other hand, choosing a confidence level of 99 percent widens the interval estimate so that it is more likely to include the population value, but it may as a result make the estimate meaningless from a theoretical or practical point of view. Knowing that the mean annual income of nurses can be anywhere between $34,085 and $35,915 may actually be saying nothing of practical importance.

Changing the sample size

Apart from the alpha level, the other factor that will determine the width of the confidence interval is the sample size. If we stick with a confidence level of 95 percent, and only vary the sample size, we will see that the width gets smaller (we increase our accuracy) as sample size increases.

Table 12.2 The effect of sample size on interval width ($\alpha = 0.05$)

Sample size	Interval width
100	$1970
200	$1390
500	$877
1000	$620
10,000	$196

One thing to notice about the effect of sample size is that enlarging the sample has its greatest effect on the interval width with small samples. Increasing the sample size from 100 to 200 reduces the interval width by $580, which is more than the $424 reduction in interval width when sample size is expanded from 1000 to 10,000.

This is why many social surveys and public opinion polls, even when generalizing to a population of millions, will have sample sizes of only 1200-1400. Samples of this size narrow the confidence interval to a relatively small width, and to increase sample size any further would increase research costs without obtaining much greater accuracy.

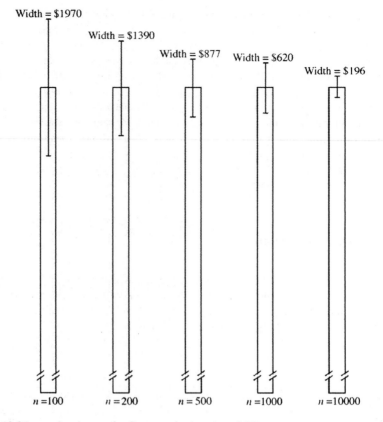

Figure 12.8 Interval estimates for five sample sizes ($\alpha = 0.05$)

Example

We want to estimate the mean age of all children in preschool. A random sample of 140 preschool children has a mean of 3.75 years and a standard deviation of 0.8 years. What do we estimate the average age of all preschool children to be?

$$\overline{X} = 3.75$$
$$s = 0.8$$
$$n = 140$$
$$z = 1.96 \ (\alpha = 0.05)$$

$$ci = \overline{X} \pm z\left(\frac{s}{\sqrt{n}}\right) = 3.75 \pm 1.96\left(\frac{0.8}{\sqrt{140}}\right)$$

$$= 3.75 \pm 0.13$$

We therefore expect the average age of all preschool children to be between 3.62 years and 3.88 years of age. We would write this estimate as 3.75 years [3.62, 3.88].

Example

A random sample of 300 people watches, on average, 150 minutes of TV nightly, with a standard deviation of 50 minutes. What can we estimate the population average to be?

If we choose a confidence level of 95 percent the lower limit will be:

$$\text{lower limit} = \overline{X} - z\left(\frac{s}{\sqrt{n}}\right) = 150 - 1.96\left(\frac{50}{\sqrt{300}}\right)$$

$$= 144.3 \text{ minutes}$$

The upper limit will be:

$$\text{upper limit} = \overline{X} + z\left(\frac{s}{\sqrt{n}}\right) = 150 + 1.96\left(\frac{50}{\sqrt{300}}\right)$$

$$= 155.7 \text{ minutes}$$

Thus the estimated average amount of TV watched nightly, with a 95 percent confidence level, is 150 minutes [144.3, 155.7].

Estimation using SPSS

We can use SPSS to calculate confidence intervals (Table 12.3, Figure 12.9). As we shall see in later chapters, confidence intervals are often generated by SPSS in the course of conducting other types of analyses. But we can also specifically request SPSS to generate a confidence interval for the mean of interval/ratio data. For example, we have the data for the number of minutes of TV watched per night for a sample of 20 children. What do we estimate the 95 percent confidence interval to be?

This command will generate a number of pieces of output. This is because the **Explore** command is an alternative method for generating many of the descriptive statistics we looked at in Part 1 of this book. The relevant part of the output for our purposes here is the table headed **Descriptives** (Figure 12.10).

Table 12.3 Confidence intervals using SPSS (file: **Ch12.sav**)

SPSS command/action	Comments
1 From the menu select **A̲nalyze/De̲scriptive Statistics/E̲xplore**	This brings up the **Explore** dialog box
2 Select **TV watched per night** from the source list of variables	
3 Click on ▶ pointing to the target list headed **Dependent List:**	This pastes **TV watched per night** into the target list headed **Dependent List:**
4 Click on **OK**	

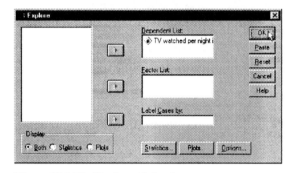

Figure 12.9 The **Explore** dialog box

Descriptives

			Statistic	Std. Error
TV watched per night in minutes	Mean		165.85	6.55
	95% Confidence Interval for Mean	Lower Bound	152.14	
		Upper Bound	179.56	
	5% Trimmed Mean		166.94	
	Median		165.00	
	Variance		857.924	
	Std. Deviation		29.29	
	Minimum		102	
	Maximum		210	
	Range		108	
	Interquartile Range		42.50	
	Skewness		-.450	.512
	Kurtosis		-.303	.992

Figure 12.10 SPSS **Explore** command output

The first three rows of the table provide in turn the mean, the lower bound and upper bound of the 95 percent confidence interval, which is the default confidence level. We can see that the estimate is 165.85 minutes [152.14, 179.56]. If we wanted a confidence interval based on a different confidence level, such 90 percent or 99 percent, we would click on the **Statistics** button in the **Explore** dialog box, and type over 95 with the desired level.

Choosing the sample size

In designing a research project a number of factors enter into the decision making. Sampling can be a very expensive procedure, if we account for the training, travel, and time that may be involved in conducting a large survey. Thus we want to ensure that we have a sufficiently large sample that will give us the accuracy we seek, but not larger than is necessary. We can use the logic of estimation to determine the 'right' size sample we need, given the level of accuracy we are after. For example, we might already have in mind a certain interval width; in the example we used above for the income of nurses, we might want to estimate within $1000 the average annual income of this group of people. Thus the interval width is pre-specified by the research problem, and now we work 'backwards' to determine the appropriate sample size that will yield a confidence interval of this size. Without going through the proof, we can derive the formula for selecting the appropriate sample size from the formula we used above:

$$ n = \frac{z^2 \times \sigma^2}{\left(\dfrac{\text{width}}{2} \right)^2} $$

Here we have pre-specified the width we want: $1000. If we choose a 95 percent confidence level, $z = 1.96$.

The last remaining bit of information needed to derive the sample size is the standard deviation for the population, and this is what limits the use of this technique. Since it is a procedure for designing a research project, rather than a procedure for analyzing data that we have already gathered, we obviously cannot use the sample standard deviation as a substitute for σ. The sample hasn't been taken yet! Thus this procedure is restricted to situations where the population standard deviation is known. Let's assume for the sake of exposition that the population standard deviation is known to be $5000. We can substitute the relevant information into the equation and determine the appropriate sample size:

$$ n = \frac{z^2 \times \sigma^2}{\left(\dfrac{\text{width}}{2} \right)^2} = \frac{1.96^2 \times 5000^2}{\left(\dfrac{1000}{2} \right)^2} $$

$$ = 384 $$

We need a sample size of at least 384 if we are to derive a confidence interval with a width no greater than $1000.

To illustrate the procedure again, let us now assume that we want to be much more accurate: we want our estimate to be no wider than $500, at a 95 percent level of confidence. For some reason we need to be much closer to the mark. What size sample should we be prepared to take?

$$n = \frac{z^2 \times \sigma^2}{\left(\dfrac{\text{width}}{2}\right)^2} = \frac{1.96^2 \times 5000^2}{\left(\dfrac{500}{2}\right)^2}$$

$$= 1537$$

We can see the same idea as that discussed above: to be more accurate in our estimate we need to take a much larger sample, since larger samples have a smaller standard error around the true population parameter. To narrow the estimate of nurses' annual income to a smaller band of $500 we have to use a sample of 1537.

Exercises

12.1 What is meant by interval estimation?

12.2 Explain what is meant by a confidence level. How do changes in the confidence level affect the width of the interval estimate?

12.3 How does sample size affect the confidence interval?

12.4 How does the standard deviation of the population affect the width of a confidence interval?

12.5 For each of the examples in the text regarding the age of preschool children and the amount of TV watched construct interval estimates for 90 percent and 99 percent confidence levels.

12.6 A survey is conducted to measure the length of time, in months, taken for university graduates to gain their first job. Assuming that this is a normally distributed variable, derive the interval estimates for the following sets of graduates, using a 95 percent confidence level:

Degree	Sample size	Mean	Standard deviation
Economics	45	6	2.5
Sociology	35	4	2.0
History	40	4.5	3.0
Statistics	60	3	1.5

12.7 To gage the effect of wage bargaining agreements, union officials select a sample of 120 workers from randomly selected enterprises across an industry. The average wage rise in the previous year for these

120 workers was $1018, with a standard deviation of $614. Estimate the increase for all workers within this industry (use both 95 percent and 99 percent confidence levels).

12.8 A hospital checks the records of 340 randomly selected patients from the previous year. The average length of stay in the hospital for these patients was 4.3 days, with a standard deviation of 3.1 days.
(a) What would be the estimated average length of stay of all patients in the previous year (at a 99 percent confidence level)?
(b) How would this compare with the average length of stay for all patients in another hospital of 4 days?
(c) What could the hospital do to improve the accuracy of the estimate?

12.9 A study of 120 divorced couples who had been married in the same year found an average length of marriage of 8.5 years, with a standard deviation of 1.2 years. What is the estimate for the average length of marriage for all divorced couples, using a confidence level of 95 percent?

12.10 Open the **Employee data** file and calculate the (a) 90 percent, (b) 95 percent, and (c) 99 percent confidence intervals for employees' current salary.

13

Introduction to Hypothesis Testing: The One-sample *z*-test for a Mean

Hypothesis testing: the general idea

The previous chapter analyzed the process of estimating an unknown population parameter from a sample result. The general problem addressed in Chapter 12 is illustrated in Figure 13.1.

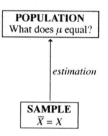

Figure 13.1 Estimating the population mean

   In estimation, that is, we try to find the value of the population mean, whatever that happens to be, given the value of the sample mean. However, in social and health research we are often confronted with a slightly different problem, one that involves the process of **hypothesis testing**. We are often interested in whether a population parameter, such as the mean, has a *specific* value, rather than just try to determine the range of values that will include the parameter (Figure 13.2).
   Before turning to a detailed description of hypothesis testing procedures, we will pose this problem in a slightly different way: as a problem of betting on a two-horse race.
   Assume you are at a racetrack and about to place a bet on an upcoming race that only has two horses running. From the form guide you know that one of these horses will win one race in every 100: will you put your money on it?

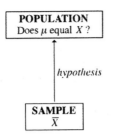

Figure 13.2 Making an hypothesis about the population mean

Probably not. If the odds of this horse winning are 1-in-20 races, will you bet on it? Maybe. Essentially, inferential statistics involve the same mental exercise – two 'runners' are lined up against each other, and the odds of one of these runners 'winning' are calculated. We then decide which one we will bet on.

The reason we have to gamble is that, as we have seen in previous chapters, information from a random sample is not always an accurate reflection of the population from which the sample is drawn. To see this we will work with the 400 people and their ages in years that we have introduced in earlier chapters. We know that this population has an average age of 35 years and standard deviation of 13 years.

We are also told that a sample of 150 people has an average age of 32 years:

$$\overline{X} = 32 \text{ years}$$

We want to know whether this sample did or did not come from the population of 400. There is a difference of 3 years between the sample and this population. Does this difference of 3 years suggest that this sample came from another population or did it come from this population with a mean age of 35 and the difference of 3 years is due to random variation when sampling? In other words, there are two possible explanations as to why a sample result may differ from a population that we suspect it may have been drawn from.

The first explanation is that *the sample did come from the population but the sample just happened to select, by chance, a lot of younger people*. We will call this explanation of our sample result the 'null hypothesis of no difference'. Mathematically we write this as:

$$H_0: \mu = 35 \text{ years}$$

An alternative explanation is that *the sample came from another population whose average age is not equal to 35 years*. We call this the 'alternative hypothesis'. Symbolically, we write:

$$H_a: \mu \neq 35 \text{ years}$$

These two hypotheses are mutually exclusive: if one is right the other is wrong. Either the sample came from the population whose average age is 35 or it did not. This is like the two-horse race where only one can win. We do not know which is correct: each statement is just an hypothesis that may or may not be right. If I now said the chances that the null hypothesis of no difference is correct are 100 to 1, will you bet on it? What about if the odds were 10 to 1? Inferential statistics provide us with these odds.

The whole hypothesis testing procedure proceeds on the assumption that the null hypothesis of no difference is correct. This may at first seem strange, since usually we undertake research in the hope of discovering a difference. Why then assume no difference? It is because we think this assumption is incorrect that we make it. The logical exercise involved in hypothesis testing is to show that the assumption of no difference is 'inconsistent' with our research findings, thereby leading us to argue that this is an unjustified hypothesis. We try to prove that there is a difference by disproving its opposite – the assumption of no difference. This may seem like the long way to go about reaching a conclusion, but if we work through enough examples in the following chapters we will see that we are *testing an assumption* by seeing whether our research data are 'plausibly' consistent with it.

In the context of the example we have been working with, I may strongly believe that the sample with a mean age of 32 years did not come from the population of 400 people whose mean age is 35 years. Despite how strongly I believe this to be true, I actually begin by assuming the opposite, what I believe to be untrue. If I can show that it is highly unlikely for a sample with a mean of 32 to be drawn from a population with a mean age of 35, then this starting assumption will not be plausible and I am justified in rejecting it. This is why we talk of 'hypothesis testing' – we put the null hypothesis to the test by comparing our actual sample result to it. And often we want it to fail the test!

Let us then *assume* for the sake of argument that the null hypothesis of no difference is true. We are assuming that the sample has come, despite the difference of 3 years, from the population whose average age is 35. Is the sample result of 32 inconsistent with the assumption that the population average is 35? What is the *probability* of getting a sample that differs from the population value of 35 by 3 years or more?

This is where the sampling distribution of sample means enters the picture. Remember that the sampling distribution is the distribution of means for repeated random samples of equal size. We can therefore refer to the sampling distribution, whose properties we know in detail, to determine the probability of getting a sample mean of 32, if the population value is 35. This will give us the odds to allow us to place our bet on either the null hypothesis or alternative hypothesis. Deriving these probabilities is a fairly straightforward (although somewhat tedious) procedure, which we are now familiar with: convert the sample statistic – the mean age – into a z-score and look up the associated probability from the table for the area under the standard normal curve in Table A1:

$$\text{sample result} \rightarrow \text{calculate } z \rightarrow \text{look up probability}$$

So the first step is to calculate the z-score that is associated with our sample result. When calculating z-scores for this case we use the following formula:

$$z = \frac{\overline{X} - \mu}{\sigma / \sqrt{n}}$$

For the sample of 150 people whose mean age is 32 years, the z-score is:

$$z = \frac{\overline{X} - \mu}{\sigma / \sqrt{n}} = \frac{32 - 35}{13 / \sqrt{150}}$$

$$= -2.8$$

This equation in effect has standardized the observed difference of 3 years between the sample score and the hypothesized population value by converting it into a z-score. The advantage of 'washing out' the natural units in which the difference is initially measured (in this instance years) is that we can now refer to the table for the area under the standard normal curve (Table 13.1) which is printed in every statistics textbook to determine the probability of getting a z-score of –2.8 or more.

Table 13.1 Areas under the standard normal curve

z	Area under curve between both points	Area under curve beyond both points	Area under curve beyond one point
±0.1	0.080	0.920	0.4600
±0.2	0.159	0.841	0.4205
±0.3	0.236	0.764	0.3820
±0.4	0.311	0.689	0.3445
±0.5	0.383	0.617	0.3085
±0.6	0.451	0.549	0.2745
±0.7	0.516	0.484	0.2420
±0.8	0.576	0.424	0.2120
±0.9	0.632	0.368	0.1840
±1	0.683	0.317	0.1585
⋮	⋮	⋮	⋮
±2.1	0.964	0.036	0.0180
±2.2	0.972	0.028	0.0140
±2.3	0.979	0.021	0.0105
±2.33	0.980	0.020	0.0100
±2.4	0.984	0.016	0.0080
±2.5	0.988	0.012	0.0060
±2.58	0.990	0.010	0.0050
±2.6	0.991	0.009	0.0045
±2.7	0.993	0.007	0.0035
±2.8	0.995	0.005	0.0025
±2.9	0.996	0.004	0.0020
±3	>0.996	<0.004	<0.0020

You might be wondering why I referred to the column headed *Area under curve beyond both points*, rather than the column headed *Area under curve beyond one point*. It relates to the way in which I have framed the problem. I am interested in the probability of randomly drawing a sample that differs from the hypothesized population mean of 32 years *by 3 years or more*, since this is the amount of difference we actually have between our sample (with a mean of 32) and the population (with a mean of 35) from which it may have been drawn. Since sampling variation may cause the means of random samples to be either higher or lower than the underlying population mean, a sample may differ by 3 years or more from the hypothesized value either by being 3 years *above it* (a mean of 38 years), or by being 3 years *below it*. We therefore refer to the middle column to determine the probability of drawing, through sampling variation alone, a sample that differs from the hypothesized population value by 3 years or more.

The area under the curve beyond the z-scores of +2.8 or –2.8 is 0.005. This is the probability of drawing, from a population with an average age of 35 years, a sample with an average age that is 3 years or more above or below this mean. In other words, only 5-in-1,000 samples will differ from a population mean of 35 years by 3 years or more. We are left with a choice. Either:

- we can still hold that the assumption that this sample came from a population with a mean age of 35 is correct, and explain the sample result as one of those freak 5 in 1000 events;

or

- we can reject the assumption that this sample came from a population with a mean age of 35; the sample statistic is not a 'freak', but instead reflects that the sample is drawn from an underlying population with an average age other than 35 years.

Given the long odds that the first choice is correct, it might be a safer bet to reject the assumption that the sample came from a population with an average age of 35. The difference of 3 years between the sample result and the hypothesized population value is so great that it is most unlikely that it came about by random variation when sampling. It instead reflects that we are not sampling from a population with an average age of 35 years.

To illustrate this procedure again, let's suppose that the sample of 150 people yielded the result:

$$\overline{X} = 36 \text{ years}$$

Again we will *assume* that this sample came from a population with a mean age of 35 years. Clearly there is again a difference between the sample statistic and the population parameter, this time of 1 year ($36 - 35 = 1$). There seems to be an apparent conflict between our *assumption* that the sample came from a population with a mean age of 35 and our *observation* that the sample result is not exactly equal to the population value. Should this cause us to reject the assumption and instead argue that the sample came from a different population?

To answer this we need to derive the probability of randomly selecting a sample that differs from a population with an average age of 35 by 1 year or more. We need first to convert the sample result into a z-score:

$$ z = \frac{\overline{X} - \mu}{\sigma / \sqrt{n}} = \frac{36 - 35}{13 / \sqrt{150}} $$

$$ = 0.9 $$

The table for areas under the standard normal curve (Table 13.2) indicates that the probability of obtaining this z-score or greater either side of the mean is 0.368.

Table 13.2 Areas under the standard normal curve

z	Area under curve between both points	Area under curve beyond both points	Area under curve beyond one point
±0.1	0.080	0.920	0.4600
±0.2	0.159	0.841	0.4205
±0.3	0.236	0.764	0.3820
±0.4	0.311	0.689	0.3445
±0.5	0.383	0.617	0.3085
±0.6	0.451	0.549	0.2745
±0.7	0.516	0.484	0.2420
±0.8	0.576	0.424	0.2120
±0.9	0.632	0.368	0.1840
±1	0.683	0.317	0.1585
⋮	⋮	⋮	⋮
±3	>0.996	<0.004	<0.0020

We assumed (hypothesized) that the population had an average age of 35. The sample, though, produced an average of 36 years. From a population with an average age of 35 nearly 37-in-100 samples will have a mean age that differs from 35 by 1 year or more. Random variation will cause roughly one-third of all samples to vary this much from a population with a mean value of 35. Given such a high probability, we can say that the sample result is simply due to random variation when sampling from a population with a mean age of 35 years.

The material to be presented in later chapters is simply a variation on this theme. The variation is due to the different amount of information that we encounter in doing research. These differences, however, do not change the basic method of approach. In fact, we can approach just about any problem of inference using the following five-step procedure:

Step 1: State the null and alternative hypotheses.
Step 2: Choose the test of significance.
Step 3: Calculate the sample score.
Step 4: Establish the critical score(s) and critical region(s).
Step 5: Make a decision.

We will go through each of these steps in more detail before turning to a couple of examples that illustrate this procedure.

Step 1: State the null and alternative hypotheses

We normally begin our investigations with a specific research question that we wish to answer. We begin with a very clear, precisely stated research question that will guide the way we conduct research and ensure that we do not just end up with a jumble of information that does not create any real knowledge. It is absolutely crucial to stress the importance of having a clear research question (or questions) in mind before undertaking statistical analysis. This will avoid the situation where huge amounts of data are gathered unnecessarily, and which do not lead to any meaningful results. I suspect that a great deal of the confusion associated with statistical analysis actually arises from imprecision in the research question which is meant to guide it. It is very difficult to home in on the *relevant* type of analysis to undertake, given the many *possible* analyses we could employ on a given set of data, if we are uncertain of our objectives. If we don't know why we are undertaking research in the first place, then it follows we will not know what to do with research data once we have gathered it. Conversely, if we are clear about the research question(s) we are addressing then the statistical techniques that should be applied follow almost as a matter of course. The following are examples of such precise research questions:

'Are men from Sweden on average taller than men from Russia?'

'Is the proportion of cigarette smokers who suffer from lung cancer higher than the proportion of non-smokers who suffer from lung cancer?'

'Do students from private schools have higher drop-out rates at university than students from state schools?'

These research questions have three crucial elements:

- they identify the population(s) we want to make a statement about;
- they identify the variable(s) for which we will gather data;
- they identify the relevant descriptive statistic for describing the data.

In the first of these research questions, for example, it is evident that we are interested in two populations: the population of males in Sweden and the population of males in Russia. It is also evident that of all the ways in which these two populations can vary, the particular variable we are interested in is height. Lastly, we are interested in the *average* height, as opposed to some other descriptive statistic such as its frequency distribution.

Once we have a clear research question it is then broken down into two, mutually exclusive hypotheses: the **null hypothesis** and the **alternative hypothesis**.

The null hypothesis of no difference (H_0)

This is a statement that the statistic we are using to describe the population under investigation will equal a specified, predefined value. The null must be clearly capable of being rejected or not rejected; that is, it can be shown to be false. There should be no ambiguity: either the population statistic we are investigating has a certain value, in terms of the operationalization of the variable, or it does not.

An abbreviated way of writing the null is in mathematical shorthand, depending on the particular descriptive statistic we are making an hypothesis about. If we are making an hypothesis about the population mean, for example, the general form of the null hypothesis is:

$$H_0: \mu = X$$

where X is the pre-specified 'test' value. For instance, in the example above we were testing whether $\mu = 35$ years.

Where does this test value stated in the null hypothesis come from? There are usually two different kinds of research questions that will prompt us to investigate whether a population parameter takes on a specific value. The first is where a particular value is chosen for *practical or policy reasons*. For example, a company may decide that anything more than a 5 percent reject rate for its product is commercially unacceptable. It therefore instructs its quality control department to sample 300 randomly selected products and determine whether the reject rate is 5 percent or more. Thus the company is not simply interested in finding whatever the value of the population parameter happens to be; it wants to know whether this population parameter is specifically 5 percent or more. Similarly, the government may have decided that it will devote extra health resources to any area where the average age is greater than 40 years. It will therefore want to test specifically whether a sample taken from a particular region indicates whether the whole population of that region is on average 40 years of age or more.

The other situation in which we will have a specified test value is where we want *to compare the population under investigation with another population whose parameter value is known*. For example, we want to compare two populations in terms of their respective average amounts of TV watched per day: the population of Australian children between 5 and 12 years of age and the population of British children between the ages of 5 and 12 years. We know from census data that British children watch on average 162 minutes of TV each day, but we only have a sample of children from Australia. We have to make an inference (which is basically a fancy way of saying an educated guess) whether the unknown average amount of TV watched by Australian children is equal to the known average for British children.

The alternative hypothesis (H_a)

This is a statement that the population parameter *does not* equal the pre-specified value; there is a difference:

$$H_a: \mu \neq X$$

The alternative hypothesis can actually take another, more precise, form. Instead of arguing that there is a difference, we might also suspect that the difference will have a direction. For example, we might suspect that the population of Australian children on average does not only watch a different amount of TV per day to the population of British children, but that they watch less. Alternatively, we may argue that on average they watch more TV per day. In either case, there is not only a difference, but also a direction of difference, and in mathematical notation we write each of these in the following ways:

$$H_a: \mu < X$$

or

$$H_a: \mu > X$$

Step 2: Choose the test of significance

There are many tests available to help us decide between the null and alternative hypotheses. All of these tests require random samples (or at least reasonably random samples), but they vary according to the information available to the researcher. In this chapter we have introduced the most basic test, called the one-sample z-test for a mean. Often these tests of significance are given a shorthand name based on the statistician who first devised them, such as the Wilcoxon test. Generally, the most important factors that determine the choice of a test are:

- the number of populations (and therefore samples) for which inferences are being made;
- the descriptive statistic that we are using to summarize the raw data, which is dependent upon the level of measurement;
- whether we have independent or dependent samples.

Each test, in other words, applies in very specific circumstances. Tables 13.3 to 13.6 provide a quick guide for selecting the appropriate test of significance, based on these main factors. These do not exhaust all the possible hypothesis tests available; they present only those that will be covered in this and following chapters.

Table 13.3 Tests of significance: the one-sample case

Level of measurement	Test of significance
Nominal/ordinal	z-test for a binomial percentage
	chi-square goodness-of-fit test for a frequency distribution
	z-test of randomness for the number of runs
Interval/ratio	z-test for a mean (population variance known)
	t-test for a mean (population variance unknown)

Table 13.4 Tests of significance: two independent samples

Level of measurement	Test of significance
Nominal	chi-square test of independence for a crosstabulation (can also use a z-test for proportions on a binomial distribution)
Ordinal	z-test for the rank sum (also known as the Wilcoxon W test which is equivalent to the Mann Whitney U test)
Interval/ratio	t-test for the equality of two means

Table 13.5 Tests of significance: more than two independent samples

Level of measurement	Test of significance
Nominal	chi-square test for independence
Ordinal	Kruskal Wallis H test
Interval/ratio	ANOVA F-test for the equality of means

Table 13.6 Tests of significance: two dependent samples

Level of measurement	Test of significance
Nominal	McNemar z-test for change (equivalent to the sign test)
Ordinal	Wilcoxon signed-ranks z-test
Interval/ratio	t-test for the mean difference

When using these tables to select a test. it should be remembered that *any test that can be applied to a specific level of measurement can also be applied to higher levels of measurement.* Thus a test listed in the tables for nominal data can also be applied to ordinal and interval/ratio data. Similarly, ordinal tests can be applied to interval/ratio data. Looking at the situations under which the various tests are applicable will be the subject of the rest of the chapters on inference. The chapters are basically organized around these individual tests, so that the conditions under which each is applicable will be clearly delineated.

This chapter will cover the use of a single-sample z-test for a mean. The conditions that allow this test to be used are:

- the research question is interested in the central tendency of a variable, and the level of measurement is interval/ratio – the relevant descriptive statistic for summarizing the sample data, therefore, is the mean;

- the population is normally distributed along the variable; and/or
- the sample size is large ($n > 100$).

Either of these last two conditions, according to the central limit theorem, will guarantee that the sampling distribution of sample means is normal.

Step 3: Calculate the sample score

This is the process of transforming the relevant descriptive statistic into a standardized score such as a z-score by substituting the sample data into the relevant equation. As we described above, we can transform a sample mean into a z-score using the following equation:

$$z_{sample} = \frac{\overline{X} - \mu}{\sigma / \sqrt{n}}$$

From the table for the area under the standard normal curve (Table A1) we then determine the probability of obtaining a particular sample z-score if the null hypothesis is true. This is called the **significance** of the sample statistic, commonly called the 'p-value'.

Step 4: Establish the critical score(s) and critical region(s)

At what point does a sample value become so large, or its associated p-value become so small, that we decide to reject the null hypothesis? We decide this by defining a cut-off point which delineates 'high' scores from 'low' scores. This step can be broken down into three parts.

Choosing the level of significance

In the examples we used above to analyze the age of a sample of people, the decision whether to reject or not to reject the null hypothesis was easy. In the first instance, with a sample mean of 32 years, the probability that this sample came from a population with a mean of 35 was very small; in the second instance with a sample mean of 36 the probability was very large. But what if the sample result falls somewhere in between? At what point does the probability get small enough for us to say that the null hypothesis is not valid? Determining this cut-off point is called choosing the **level of significance**, or the **alpha (α) level**. We indicate a 0.05 level of significance as:

$$\alpha = 0.05$$

To understand the issues involved in selecting a level of significance we have to distinguish between a **type I error** (alpha error) and a **type II error** (beta error).

A **type I error** occurs when the null hypothesis of no difference is rejected, even though in fact there is no difference. In assessing whether the sample in the example above with a mean age of 32 came from a population with a mean age of 35, we rejected the null hypothesis of no difference. The chances of selecting from a population where the average is 35 years a sample with an average age of 32 or less is only 25 in 10,000. In other words, if we take 10,000 samples from a population with an average age of 35 years, only 25 will have an average age of 32 or less. However, we may have actually selected one of those fluke 25-in-10,000 samples. The sample may indeed have come from a population with an average age of 35 years, but the sample just happened to randomly pick up a few especially young people. There is always a chance of such an event – that is why we speak in terms of probabilities. It is a question of the chances we are prepared to take of making this error.

A **type II error** occurs when we fail to reject the null hypothesis when in fact it is false. For example, where the sample above had an average age of 36, we concluded that it did come from a population with an average age of 35 years. The difference between the sample statistic and the hypothesized parameter value is so small that it can be attributed to random variation. However, it may in reality be that the population from which the sample is drawn does not have an average age of 35, but our sample just happened to select some unrepresentative people.

The relationship between these two possible error types is summarized in Table 13.7.

Table 13.7 Error types

Decision based on hypothesis test	Truth about population	
	H_0 true	H_a true
Reject H_0	Type I error	Correct decision
Do not reject H_0	Correct decision	Type II error

It is clear that these two error types are the converse of each other so that *reducing the chance of one error occurring increases the chance of the other error occurring*. It is a question of which mistake we most want to avoid, and this depends on the research question. If we are testing a new drug that may have harmful side effects we want to be sure that it actually works. In other words, we don't want to make a type I error (conclude that the drug does make a difference when it doesn't) because the consequences could be devastating. The difference in the rate of improvement observed between a test group taking the drug and a control group that is not will have to be very large before we can say that such an improvement is not due to chance (say 1 in 1000). What we would be doing here is selecting a significance level of 0.001 before rejecting the hypothesis that the drug does not make a difference.

We can see the effect of choosing different levels of significance in Figure 13.3.

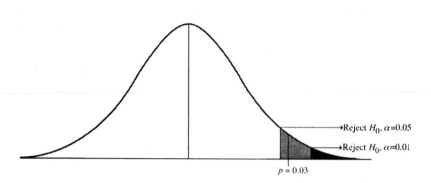

$p = 0.03$

Figure 13.3 Rejection regions for $\alpha = 0.05$ and $\alpha = 0.01$ (one-tail test)

A sample result has a probability of occurring of 0.03, if the null hypothesis of no difference is true. It is clear that the level of significance we choose will determine whether we reject or do not reject this assumption of no difference. If we choose $\alpha = 0.01$ then the difference between the sample and the population value can be attributed to random variation: do not reject the null. But if we choose $\alpha = 0.05$, then the same difference between the sample and the hypothesized parameter value will lead us to reject the null.

One-tail or two-tail test?

To calculate the critical score(s) we also decide whether to use a **one-tail** or **two-tail test**. Here we look at the alternative hypothesis as stated in Step 1 which states that the sample comes from a population with a value *different* to the hypothesized value, or from a population that has a value *larger or smaller* than the hypothesized value; that is, whether we are concerned with a difference or the direction of difference as well.

In our example, for instance, we may suspect that as an alternative to the null hypothesis of no difference the sample comes from a population that is on average *younger* than 35 years. Therefore a one-tail test is conducted because we are interested in whether the sample result falls far enough to the left of the population mean.

But say we had no a priori reason to believe this to be the case: this sample may come from a population either on average *younger or older*. In this case the critical region is split in two – one at each end of the sampling distribution. This is effectively how we proceeded in the example above.

If we have specified a direction of difference in the alternative hypothesis so that we need to use a one-tail test, we need to be careful that we refer to the appropriate tail of the sampling distribution. If the alternative hypothesis holds that the population value will be less than the specified value, the critical region will be in the left tail; if it holds that the population value will be greater than the specified value, the right tail is the relevant one (Table 13.8).

Table 13.8 Choosing a tail for a test

Alternative hypothesis	Tail of the sampling distribution
$H_a: \mu \neq X$	Both
$H_a: \mu < X$	Left
$H_a: \mu > X$	Right

Left-tail tests are normally used when we want to test to see if some *minimum* requirement has been met, whereas a right-tail test is normally used when we want to test whether some *maximum* limit or standard has not been exceeded. For example, if we wanted to see whether the average life of a piece of hospital equipment is at least 4.5 years, we would use a left-tail test. If we were interested in whether the time taken for a drug to have an effect on a patient was no greater than 1.5 minutes, then we would use a right-tail test.

Derive the critical score(s)

Once we have chosen a level of significance, and decided on a one-tail or two-tail test, we derive the critical score(s) (sometimes called the **test statistic**) that delineates the **critical region**.

The **critical region**, or **region of rejection**, is the range of scores that will cause the null hypothesis to be rejected.

To determine these critical scores we refer to the table for the area under the standard normal curve:

$$\alpha \rightarrow z_{critical}$$

With a two-tail test we refer to the column for the area under the curve beyond both points and read off both the positive and negative values for the z-score (Table 13.9); with a one-tail test we refer to the column for the area under the curve beyond one point and read off either the positive or the negative value for the z-score, depending on the appropriate tail. For example, the z-score that marks off the critical region, with a level of significance of $\alpha = 0.05$ on a two-tail test, is ± 1.96.

Thus a probability of 0.05 is divided into two regions of equal size, one at either tail of the distribution. Beyond a z-score of +1.96 is 0.025, or 2.5 percent, of the area under the curve, and beyond a z-score of −1.96 lies another 0.025 of the area under the curve (Figure 13.4).

Table 13.9 Areas under the standard normal curve

z	Area under curve between both points	Area under curve beyond both points	Area under curve beyond one point
±0.1	0.080	0.920	0.4600
±0.2	0.159	0.841	0.4205
±0.3	0.236	0.764	0.3820
±0.4	0.311	0.689	0.3445
±0.5	0.383	0.617	0.3085
±0.6	0.451	0.549	0.2745
±0.7	0.516	0.484	0.2420
±0.8	0.576	0.424	0.2120
±0.9	0.632	0.368	0.1840
±1	0.683	0.317	0.1585
±1.1	0.729	0.271	0.1355
±1.2	0.770	0.230	0.1150
±1.3	0.806	0.194	0.0970
±1.4	0.838	0.162	0.0810
±1.5	0.866	0.134	0.0670
±1.6	0.890	0.110	0.0550
±1.645	0.900	0.100	0.0500
±1.7	0.911	0.089	0.0445
±1.8	0.928	0.072	0.0360
±1.9	0.943	0.057	0.0290
±1.96	0.950	**0.050**	0.0250
±2	0.954	0.046	0.0230
⋮	⋮	⋮	⋮
±3	>0.996	<0.004	<0.0020

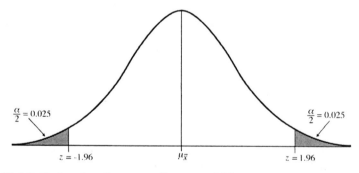

Figure 13.4 Critical regions for a two-tail test, $\alpha = 0.05$

The difference between a one-sided and two-sided test is illustrated in Figure 13.5. On a one-tail test, with an alpha level of 0.05, the critical region under the sampling distribution begins at either–1.645 or +1.645 but not both, depending on the direction of difference expressed in the alternative hypothesis. On a two-tail test this region has to be split in two because we are interested in a sample result *either* greater or smaller than the population value. This pushes the critical z-score outward to ±1.96.

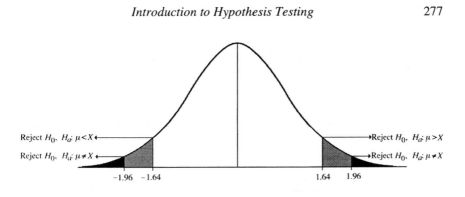

Figure 13.5 Critical regions for one-tail and two-tail tests, $\alpha = 0.05$

Certain alpha levels are conventionally chosen in most research contexts, and the associated critical z-scores for these conventional levels of significance become familiar through regular use. If you work often enough with inferential statistics the following information will eventually be memorized. This is especially so for an alpha level of 0.05, which is by far the most common significance level used in social research.

Table 13.10 Common critical scores

α	$z_{critical}$	
	Two-tail test	One-tail test
0.01	+ and – 2.58	+ or – 2.33
0.05	+ and – 1.96	+ or – 1.645
0.10	+ and – 1.645	+ or – 1.28

Step 5: Make a decision: comparing sample and critical scores

Now that we have calculated everything we need to calculate we can decide either to reject or not to reject the null hypothesis. Notice that the conclusion is always stated in terms of the null hypothesis: reject or fail to reject.

When making a decision we make either one of two comparisons:

compare z_{sample} with $z_{critical}$

or

compare the p-value with the alpha level

Since any given z-score is uniquely related to a particular probability, and vice versa, we will get the same answer regardless of the comparison we choose to make. The way a decision is reached is summarized in Table 13.11.

Table 13.11 Summary of hypothesis testing procedure

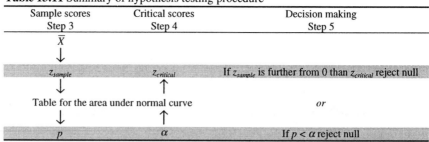

Sample scores	Critical scores	Decision making
Step 3	Step 4	Step 5
$\overline{X}$		
$\downarrow$		
z_{sample}	$z_{critical}$	If z_{sample} is further from 0 than $z_{critical}$ reject null
$\downarrow$	$\uparrow$	
Table for the area under normal curve		*or*
$\downarrow$	$\uparrow$	
p	α	If $p < \alpha$ reject null

It may be helpful at the decision-making stage actually to sketch a normal curve and plot the critical and sample values (as we have been doing above). This provides a quick visual indication as to whether the null should be rejected; if the sample score falls in the region of rejection.

A common confusion often arises right at this point of decision making. In observing the so-called 'p-value' of the sample score, students are often dismayed if it proves to be very close to zero. We are used to thinking that small numbers indicate that 'nothing is there' and therefore the difference we suspected or hoped to find has not eventuated. Here the opposite is true. Usually we do want to find a low p-value (lower than the alpha level), since this indicates that the null hypothesis of no difference should be rejected. A very high p-value, on the other hand, indicates that the null hypothesis of no difference should not be rejected.

When reporting the results of an hypothesis test, even if we are confident with the decision made about the null hypothesis, sufficient information should be provided so that the reader can make his or her own judgment. In particular, the exact probability associated with the sample z-score (and the z-score itself) should be reported, not just whether it is above or below the chosen alpha level. This allows readers to decide whether they feel the probability is sufficiently small for it to warrant rejecting the null. It leaves the decision making up to the reader, rather than just with the person conducting the test: the reader can compare the probability to the alpha level he or she thinks is warranted in the context rather than simply being told that a result 'is significant at the 0.05 level', or words to that effect. If the preceding statement is all that is reported, the sample probability could have been 0.049 or 0.00001 – there is no way of knowing without doing the calculations. This may be frustrating to a reader who feels that an alpha level of 0.01 is warranted in the circumstances rather than the stated alpha of 0.05. Stating the actual probability of the sample z-score, in other words, gives readers maximum information, so that they can arrive at their own conclusions about whether to reject or not to reject the null hypothesis, given their preparedness to make a type I or type II error.

We have seen that we reach one of either two decisions about the null hypothesis of no difference: reject or fail to reject. In either case, we need to ask ourselves whether we have 'proven' anything. The answer is 'no'! Remember that we are working with probabilities only, and we are simply deciding whether the null hypothesis is plausibly consistent with a sample result. Samples do not always exactly mirror the populations from which they are drawn, so making an inference from a sample to a population always involves a risk of error. Given this general point about the decisions we may reach, we will explore the specific meaning of each in turn.

What does it mean when we 'fail to reject the null hypothesis'?

Although we begin with the presumption that the null hypothesis is true, and then proceed to test this assumption, researchers are usually interested in rejecting the null. Normally we make comparisons because we believe a difference exists (we want a low 'p-value'); a decision to reject the null is usually the desired outcome. In other words, we are using the logic of proof by contradiction: we want to find support for the alternative hypothesis by showing that there is no support for its opposite, the null hypothesis.

Does this mean that if we fail to reject the null, the difference we are searching for does not exist? Not necessarily: failing to reject the null hypothesis of no difference simply means there is *not sufficient evidence* to think that the null hypothesis is wrong. This does not necessarily mean, however, that it is right. There might actually be a difference 'out there', but on the basis of the sample result such a difference has not been detected. This is a bit like the presumption of innocence in criminal law. A defendant is presumed not guilty unless the evidence is strong enough to justify a verdict of guilty. However, when someone has been found not guilty on the strength of the available evidence, it does not mean that the person is in fact innocent: all it means is that, given that either verdict is possible, we do not choose 'guilty' unless stronger evidence comes to light. Similarly, with a verdict of 'no difference', failing to reject the null hypothesis does not mean the alternative is wrong. It simply means that on the basis of the information available, the null can explain the sample result without stretching our notion of reasonable probability.

Therefore, failing to find a significant difference should not be seen as conclusive. If we have good theoretical grounds for suspecting that a difference really does exist, even though a test suggests that it does not, this can be the basis of future research. Maybe the variable has not been operationalized effectively, or the level of measurement does not provide sufficient information, or the sample was not appropriately chosen or was not large enough. In the context of social research, inference tests do not prove anything; they are usually evidence in an ongoing discussion or debate that rarely reaches a decisive conclusion.

What does it mean to 'reject the null hypothesis'?

What if our decision is the converse: we reject the null hypothesis? In formal language we say that we have found a **statistically significant** difference. So what? What have we learned about the world, and should we do anything about it? These questions are not ones that hypothesis testing as such can answer. A statistical difference is simply a difference between two numbers. A student who scores 60 in an exam is statistically different from a student who scores 61, or 66, or 90. Similarly, there may be a statistically significant difference between a sample of students that averages 60 in final exams and another sample with an average of 61, or 66, or 90. A statistically significant difference simply tells us that two numbers are not the same. Whether such a difference is of any *practical or theoretical* importance – whether it is 'significant' in any other sense of the word – is really something we as researchers or policy-makers have to decide for ourselves.

To give this a concrete application assume that I, as a statistics teacher, want to know whether the university should spend more money on computer workshops and hire extra instructors to help students with their statistics classes. The university argues that it will only do this if there is a 'significant' difference between grades in statistics courses and grades in other courses that these students undertake at university. I collect a sample of students and find that their average statistics mark is 55, and compare that with the university average for all other courses of 62, and find this to be statistically significant at an alpha level of 0.05. Have I won my argument with the university? Not necessarily. I might consider the difference in average marks to justify the extra expenditure because I think that statistics is very important to a well-rounded education. But the university has every right to say that given all the other possible ways it can spend its money, a difference of 7 marks is something it can live with. The university, in other words, may have no argument with me over the statistical difference; that is, it accepts that the difference really is there in the population and not just due to sampling variation. However, it may strongly disagree that this is of practical significance in the sense that it should prompt the university to spend money to try to close the gap.

This illustrates an all-too-often neglected point. It is not uncommon for researchers simply, and blandly, to state that a result is significant at the 0.05 or 0.01 level without further comment, as if this is all that needs to be said. In fact this should just be the entry point to the more creative and interesting (but usually more difficult) research problem: what does this tell us about the world and what can we do about it?

With all these general considerations in mind we will now turn to a number of examples that will familiarize us with the hypothesis testing procedure.

A two-tail z-test for a single mean

Suppose that a university is interested in the average academic ability of foreign students in a particular program. In this program, the university knows that the mean mark for all students is 62 with a standard deviation of 15. From a random sample of 150 foreign students the mean score is calculated as 60.5.

Step 1: State the hypotheses
Are foreign students on average different to the rest of the university population in terms of their average grade? Given this research question we form the following two hypotheses:

H_0: The population of foreign students has the same mean grade as the rest of the university population.

$$H_0: \mu = 62$$

H_a: There is a difference between the average grade of foreign students and the average grade of all other students.

$$H_a: \mu \neq 62$$

Step 2: Choose the test of significance
The important factor is that we are interested in the average, and the variable (academic performance) is measured at the interval/ratio level (final marks). Hence the descriptive statistic we calculate to summarize the data is the mean. These two factors allow us to conduct a z-test for a single mean.

Step 3: Calculate the sample scores
From the information derived from the sample we can calculate the test statistic:

$$z_{sample} = \frac{\overline{X} - \mu}{\sigma / \sqrt{n}} = \frac{60.5 - 62}{15 / \sqrt{150}}$$

$$= \frac{-1.5}{1.22}$$

$$= -1.2$$

Step 4: Establish the critical score(s) and critical region
Following convention we will choose the 0.05 level of significance:

$$\alpha = 0.05$$

The alternative hypothesis states that the average mark for foreign students is not equal to that for all students:

$$H_a: \mu \neq 62$$

Note that it does not specify whether the average mark of foreign students will be higher or lower than that of the rest. Since we do not have any reason to suspect that foreign students on average will perform any better or worse than local students – we are simply interested in whether they perform differently – a two-tail test is appropriate. From the table for the area under the standard normal curve (Table A1), we know that the critical scores for a two-tail test, with $a = 0.05$, will be:

$$z_{critical} = \pm 1.96$$

Step 5: Make a decision
We can immediately see that, by comparing the sample result with the critical score (Figure 13.6), it appears that the grades of foreign students are not sufficiently different from the hypothesized value for us to reject the null hypothesis of no difference.

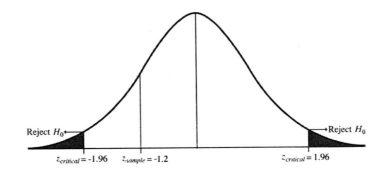

Figure 13.6 Critical and sample scores

We can see that the $z_{critical}$ of -1.96 is much further from 0 than the z_{sample} of -1.2. The 1.5 mark difference between the sample score for foreign students and the hypothesized value can simply be the result of random variation when drawing from a population with a mean grade of 62.

We can also make a decision by comparing the probabilities associated with these sample and critical values. The alpha we have chosen is 0.05. If we refer to the table for the normal distribution for a z-score of -1.2, we can see that the area under the curve beyond both points (the p-value) is 0.23. In other words, if the *population* of foreign students has an average grade of 62, 23 *samples* in every hundred drawn from this population will have an average grade of 1.5 marks or further from 62.

The procedure just outlined are summarized in Table 13.12.

Table 13.12 Summary of hypothesis testing procedure

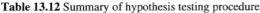

Sample scores Step 3	Critical scores Step 4	Decision making Step 5

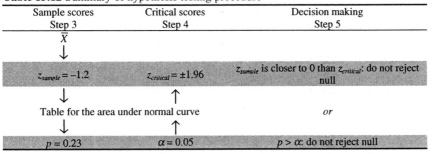

		z_{sample} is closer to 0 than $z_{critical}$: do not reject null
$z_{sample} = -1.2$	$z_{critical} = \pm 1.96$	
↓	↑	
Table for the area under normal curve		*or*
↓	↑	
$p = 0.23$	$\alpha = 0.05$	$p > \alpha$: do not reject null

A one-tail z-test for a single mean

A group of workers in a factory suspect that working conditions are unsafe and have caused them to suffer a high rate of respiratory illness. They call in a public health researcher who randomly selects 100 workers and asks each worker how many hours work they had lost the previous year as a result of respiratory illness. The average number of hours lost was 15 hours per worker. From information available from official sources, the researcher also knows that for all factory workers in the country, the average number of hours lost due to respiratory illness that year was 12 hours, with a standard deviation of 7.5 hours around this mean.

The workers argue that the sample result shows that they come from a population that has a higher rate of respiratory illness than other workers. Management, however, claims that the difference between the rate of respiratory illness in the sample and that for other workers is so small that it could easily be due to random variation from sampling. Obviously there is some difference between the sample of factory workers and the rest of the population but is this difference big enough to suggest that it is more than just random chance?

These claims can be formally tested.

Step 1: State the hypotheses
H_0: There is no difference between the rate of respiratory illness suffered by workers in this factory and the rate suffered by all factory workers.

$$H_0: \mu = 12 \text{ days}$$

H_a: There is a difference between the rate of respiratory illness suffered by workers in this factory and the rate suffered by all factory workers, and we expect that workers in this factory do have a *higher* rate of illness.

$$H_a: \mu > 12 \text{ days}$$

Notice that the alternative hypothesis does not just specify a difference, but also a direction of difference. The workers are only interested in rejecting the null if it shows that they have a *higher* incidence of illness to ground their claim for compensation. This will be important in determining whether to use a one-tail or two-tail test in Step 4.

Step 2: Choose the test of significance
We are interested in the average incidence of respiratory illness, which is measured at the interval/ratio level (number of hours lost). The appropriate descriptive statistic to summarize the data for this research question is therefore the mean. Since these conditions hold we conduct a z-test for a single mean.

Step 3: Calculate the sample score
The relevant information we need to calculate the sample score is:

$$n = 100$$

$$\sigma = 7.5 \text{ days}$$

$$\overline{X} = 15 \text{ days}$$

We put the sample data and hypothesized population value into the equation for z:

$$z_{sample} = \frac{\overline{X} - \mu}{\sigma / \sqrt{n}} = \frac{15 - 12}{7.5 / \sqrt{100}}$$

$$= 4$$

From the table for the area under the normal curve (Table A1) we find that the significance level associated with this sample z-score is:

$$p < 0.0001$$

Step 4: Establish the critical score(s) and critical region
Since management requires a lot of convincing, the workers want to show that the high rate of respiratory illness in the factory is extremely unlikely to be the result of sample selection. Therefore they set the level of significance at $\alpha = 0.01$. Since the alternative hypothesis does not just specify a difference, but also a direction of difference, we will use a one-tail (right-tail) test. From the table for the area under the normal curve this means that:

$$z_{critical} = 2.33$$

The direction of difference specified in the alternative hypothesis is that the average will be greater than 12, so the relevant tail is to the right of the distribution.

Step 5: Make a decision
If we compare the sample and critical values we see that our sample result falls in the critical region of rejection (Figure 13.7). That is, because our sample result is further from the mean than our critical score, we reject the null hypothesis that this sample came from a population with an average number of days lost due to illness of only 12: the workers do have a legitimate claim in arguing that the population of which they are members suffers a significantly higher rate of illness.

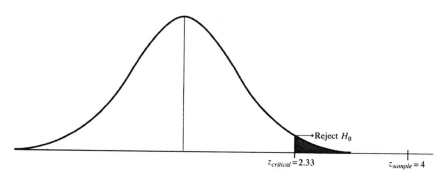

Figure 13.7 Critical and sample scores

Summary

We have just worked through the steps involved in the most basic of hypothesis testing procedures: the z-test of a single mean. However, in practice this test is very rarely employed because it requires a great deal of information about the population. We begin with it, though, because it provides the clearest exposition of the process of hypothesis testing. Having learnt this basic procedure we are now able to deal with more complicated situations that are more likely to arise in 'real life'. The following chapters detail the tests to be used in these situations.

Exercises

13.1   Under what conditions will the sampling distribution of sample means be normal in shape?

13.2   What is meant by type I and type II errors? How are they related?

13.3   How does the choice of significance level affect the critical region?

13.4   Specify some research questions that will involve one-tail tests. Which tail on the sampling distribution will hold the critical region in each situation?

13.5   Complete the following table:

Probability	Test	z-score
0.230		±1.2
0.100	Two-tail	
0.018		±2.1
	Two-tail	±2.3
	One-tail	±3.4

13.6   Sketch the critical region for the following critical scores:
(a) $z > 1.645$
(b) $z < -1.645$
(c) $z > 1.96$ or $z < -1.96$
What is the probability of a type I error associated with each of these critical regions?

13.7   For each of the following sets of results, calculate z_{sample}:

	μ	σ	$\bar{X}$	n
(a)	2.4	0.7	2.3	180
(b)	18	1.1	16.7	100

13.8   A sample with a mean of 12 years is tested to see whether it comes from a population with a mean of 15 years.
(a)   The significance level on a two-tail test proves to be 0.03. Explain in simple words what this indicates.
(b)   The significance level on a one-tail test proves to be 0.015. Explain in simple words what this indicates.

13.9   A sample of nurses finds that they work on average 4.3 hours of overtime per week. This is tested to see whether the average amount of overtime worked by all nurses is 0 hours. The significance level proves to be $p = 0.00002$. Does this prove that the sample did not come from a population with a mean number hours of overtime per week of 0 hours?

13.10   A particular judge has acquired a reputation as a 'hanging judge' because he is perceived as imposing harsher penalties for the same sentence. A random sample of 40 cases is taken from trials before this judge that resulted in a guilty verdict for a certain crime. The average jail sentence he imposed for this sample is 27 months. For all crimes of this type the average prison sentence is 24 months, with a standard deviation of 11 months (assume a normal distribution). Is this judge's reputation justified? (Pay close attention to the form of the alternative hypothesis.)

14

The One-sample *t*-test for a Mean

The previous chapter introduced the logic of hypothesis testing. The careful reader will have noticed that in conducting the one-sample *z*-test for a mean we used the population standard deviation to make an inference from the sample mean to the population mean. The careful *and critical* reader will have thought this a peculiar situation: the data used to calculate the standard deviation for the population should also allow us directly to calculate the mean; if we know the standard deviation for the population how can we *not know* the population mean? We should not need to make an inference from the sample to the population mean, but should be able directly to calculate it.

In other words, it is unlikely that we will ever find a situation where we do know the population standard deviation but do not know the population mean. Indeed, SPSS does not even provide an option for a *z*-test for a single mean. Before you suddenly decide that the previous chapter was a waste of time and tear it out of the book, let me justify why we spent so much time learning a test that we are unlikely ever to use in practice. We begin with the one-sample *z*-test for a mean because it is the simplest illustration of the hypothesis testing procedure. Having learnt the basic steps of hypothesis testing in this, albeit unrealistic, situation, we can then go on and apply it to more relevant, but slightly more complicated, situations. Thus the previous chapter allowed us to sharpen our hypothesis testing 'knife' so that we can use it to 'slice through' more real-life problems.

The tests that follow in the ensuing chapters are all variations of the basic hypothesis testing procedure. We will learn the specific conditions under which each test is relevant. These are the factors we look for in Step 2 of the hypothesis testing procedure to determine the test of significance to employ. The two key factors to consider (although there are others) are, first, the descriptive statistic that is used to summarize the sample data, and, second, the number of samples from which hypotheses are to be made. This chapter will detail the one-sample *t*-test for a mean, which is used instead of the one-sample *z*-test for a mean in the more common situation where neither the population mean nor the population standard deviation is known.

The Student's *t*-distribution

When we want to make an inference about a population mean but don't know the standard deviation of the population a slight change is required to the basic procedure outlined in the previous chapter. We no longer use the *z*-distribution to derive the sample and critical scores. This is because the sampling distribution of sample means will no longer be normal. Instead, the sampling distribution we use is the **Student's *t*-distribution**, and we conduct a ***t*-test**. (It is called the Student's *t*-distribution after W. Gossett who first defined its properties. As an employee of the Guinness brewing company, he was not permitted to publish under his own name. He therefore chose 'the Student' as his alias.) A *t*-distribution looks a lot like a *z*-distribution in that it is a smooth, unimodal, symmetrical curve. The difference is that a *t*-distribution is 'flatter' than the *z*-distribution. Exactly how much flatter depends on the sample size (Figure 14.1).

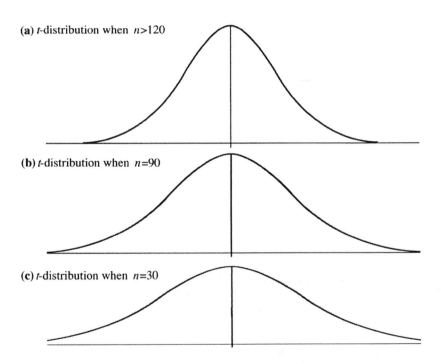

(a) *t*-distribution when *n*>120

(b) *t*-distribution when *n*=90

(c) *t*-distribution when *n*=30

Figure 14.1 *t*-distributions for sample sizes **(a)** *n* > 120, **(b)** *n* = 90, and **(c)** *n* = 30

The *t*-distribution, where sample size is 30, has much 'fatter tails'; these tails become thinner for a sample size of 90; and eventually are identical to the normal curve when sample size becomes very large (greater than 120).

The one-sample *t*-test for a mean

We will detail the one-sample *t*-test for a mean by working through an example using the five-step hypothesis testing procedure, indicating as we do the ways in which it varies from the *z*-test for a mean.

Assume that the Health Department is interested in whether the average age for the population in a certain region is over 40 years in order to decide how much money it should allocate to the local hospital. Unable to survey the whole area, the Department takes a random sample of 51 people from this population, which yields a sample average of 43 years and standard deviation of 10 years. Clearly the sample is on average older than 40 years. The Department is reluctant to conclude from this, however, that the *population* from which the sample is drawn is on average over 40 years of age. The Department argues that the sample could easily have come from a population with an average age of only 40 and the effect of random variation explains the slightly older sample result. We can test this claim using the one-sample *t*-test for a mean.

Step 1: State the null and alternative hypotheses
H_0: The population in this region is on average 40 years of age.

$$H_0: \ \mu = 40 \text{ years}$$

H_a: The population in this region is on average older than 40 years.

$$H_a: \ \mu > 40 \text{ years}$$

Notice the inequality in the statement of the alternative hypothesis. Given the Health Department's policy on funding we are not interested in whether the population in this region is on average younger than 40: its funding will only change if we find that the average age of the population is significantly *older* than 40 years.

Step 2: Choose the test of significance
We are interested in the *average* age for one sample, and since age is measured at the interval/ratio level the appropriate descriptive statistic is the mean. Unlike the examples in the previous chapter, we do not have any information regarding the population standard deviation, so we use the one-sample *t*-test for a mean.

Step 3: Calculate the sample score
When the population standard deviation is unknown we use, instead of the equation for *z*, the following equation for *t* to calculate the sample score. This equation substitutes the sample standard deviation for the population standard deviation.

$$t = \frac{\overline{X} - \mu}{s / \sqrt{n}}$$

We can substitute the data we have in our example to calculate the sample score:

$$t_{sample} = \frac{\overline{X} - \mu}{s / \sqrt{n}}$$

$$= \frac{43 - 40}{10 / \sqrt{51}}$$

$$= 2.1$$

Step 4: Establish the critical score(s) and critical region(s)
As with the procedure in the previous chapter, in order to determine the critical scores and regions we need to:

- decide between a one-tail and two-tail test, and
- select a level of significance (alpha level).

From the alternative hypothesis, which specifies a direction of difference, we will use a one-tail (right-tail) test. We will also follow social research convention and set the alpha level at $\alpha = 0.05$.

Given the alpha level and the number of tails, we then refer to the table for critical values for *t*-distributions in Table A2, and reproduced here as Table 14.1, to determine the critical score and critical region.

Since there is a different *t*-distribution for each sample size the table provides a set of critical values and *t*-scores for various **degrees of freedom** (*df*). The concept of degrees of freedom can be illustrated with a simple example. If there are five students and their final exam grades must have an average of 10, a restriction has been placed on the range of possible scores these students can get. For example, the first four marks could come out to be 12, 7, 15, and 11. Once I have recorded these first four marks, the fifth mark *must be* 5 for the total to produce the average of 10, which is the restriction I have imposed on the data. We have lost one degree of freedom (*df*) because we have imposed a certain result on the data. Instead of *n* degrees of freedom, where *n* is the sample size, we have $n - 1$. In this example, we have four degrees of freedom.

A similar correction applies when working with *t*-tests. The *t*-test is based on the *assumption that the population standard deviation* (which is unknown) *is equal to the sample standard deviation* (which is known). The imposition of this assumption on the data means we lose one degree of freedom.

$$df = n - 1$$

Table 14.1 Critical values for *t*-distributions

	Level of significance for one-tail test				
	0.10	0.05	0.02	0.01	0.005
	Level of significance for two-tail test				
df	0.20	0.10	0.05	0.02	0.01
1	3.078	6.314	12.706	31.821	63.657
2	1.886	2.920	4.303	6.965	9.925
3	1.638	2.353	3.182	4.541	5.841
4	1.533	2.132	2.776	3.747	4.604
5	1.476	2.015	2.571	3.365	4.032
6	1.440	1.943	2.447	3.143	3.707
7	1.415	1.895	2.365	2.998	3.499
8	1.397	1.860	2.306	2.896	3.355
9	1.383	1.833	2.262	2.821	3.250
10	1.372	1.812	2.228	2.764	3.169
11	1.363	1.796	2.201	2.718	3.106
12	1.356	1.782	2.179	2.681	3.055
13	1.350	1.771	2.160	2.650	3.012
14	1.345	1.761	2.145	2.624	2.977
15	1.341	1.753	2.131	2.602	2.947
16	1.340	1.746	2.120	2.583	2.921
17	1.333	1.740	2.110	2.567	2.898
18	1.330	1.734	2.101	2.552	2.878
19	1.328	1.729	2.093	2.539	2.861
20	1.325	1.725	2.086	2.528	2.845
21	1.323	1.721	2.080	2.518	2.831
22	1.321	1.717	2.074	2.508	2.819
23	1.319	1.714	2.069	2.500	2.807
24	1.318	1.711	2.064	2.492	2.797
25	1.316	1.708	2.060	2.485	2.787
26	1.315	1.706	2.056	2.479	2.779
27	1.314	1.703	2.052	2.473	2.771
28	1.313	1.701	2.048	2.467	2.763
29	1.311	1.699	2.045	2.462	2.756
30	1.310	1.697	2.042	2.457	2.750
35	1.306	1.690	2.030	2.438	2.724
40	1.303	1.684	2.021	2.423	2.704
45	1.301	1.679	2.014	2.412	2.690
50	1.299	1.676	2.009	2.403	2.678
55	1.297	1.673	2.004	2.396	2.668
60	1.296	1.671	2.000	2.390	2.660
70	1.294	1.667	1.994	2.381	2.648
80	1.292	1.664	1.990	2.374	2.639
90	1.291	1.662	1.987	2.368	2.632
120	1.289	1.658	1.980	2.358	2.617
∞	1.282	1.645	1.960	2.326	2.576

The number of degrees of freedom affects the value of the critical *t*-score. For any given alpha value, a select number of which are listed across the top of the table, the *t*-score that will mark off that area under the curve will be 'further out' with small samples (fewer degrees of freedom) than it will be for larger samples (more degrees of freedom). This means that the larger the sample size (and therefore degrees of freedom) the more likely that any difference between the sample mean and the test value will prove to be significant. For example, with a sample of 150 ($df = 149$), on a one-tail test with $\alpha = 0.05$, the value of $t_{critical}$ will be + or − 1.645. For a sample of only 51 ($df = 50$), as in our example, the critical region on a one-tail test with $\alpha = 0.05$ will be marked by t-scores of + or − 1.676 (Figure 14.2).

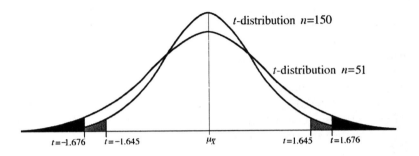

Figure 14.2 Critical regions for sample sizes $n = 150$ and $n = 51$

Since the t-distribution is 'flatter' with smaller samples, the critical scores lie further out compared with the t-distribution for the larger sample.

In our example, the critical score is +1.676, since the alternative hypothesis is concerned with whether the sample result indicates that the population has an average age greater than 40 years.

Step 5: Make a decision
We can compare the critical and sample scores by plotting them on the same t-distribution and observing whether the sample score falls in the region of rejection (Figure 14.3).

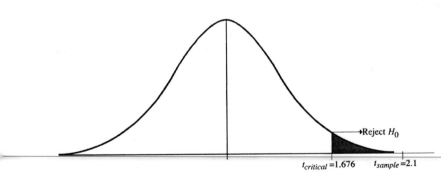

Figure 14.3 Critical and sample scores

Clearly the Health Department cannot argue that the population of this region has a mean age of only 40 years. It has a significantly higher average than 40 years. Although *it is possible* to draw a sample with a mean age of 43 from a population with a mean age of only 40, this will only occur less than five-in-every-hundred times. Given this low probability that random variation caused the sample to have a high average age, the Health Department should boost its funding to this region, even though it basis its decision on a sample rather than a survey of the whole population in the region.

Looking back at this example we can see that there are some slight changes to the hypothesis testing procedure we learnt in the previous chapter. These changes take account of the fact that we do not know the standard deviation for the population about which we want to make an inference. In particular:

- we use a slightly different formula in Step 3 to derive the sample score; and
- we refer to a slightly different sampling distribution in Step 4 to derive the critical score and critical region, one that requires us to consider the degrees of freedom we are working with.

Apart from these modifications the procedure is basically the same. In order to familiarize ourselves further with the one-sample *t*-test for a mean, we will now work through a number of examples.

Example: one-tail (left-tail) test

A large retail chain has recently been accused of discriminating against women in employment. One way of assessing whether it discriminates against women in job promotions is to look at the average number of women in management positions in each of the chain's stores. We know from national employment figures that for all similar establishments there are on average 2.5 women in management positions. We survey 31 of the retail chain's stores and find that they, on average, employ 1.9 women in management positions, with a standard deviation of 1. Can we say that this sample comes from a population with a mean number of women in management of 2.5?

Step 1: State the null and alternative hypotheses
H_0: The average number of women employed as managers by the retail chain is 2.5 per establishment.

$$H_0:\ \mu = 2.5$$

H_a: The average number of women employed as managers by the retail chain is less than that in other stores (the chain does discriminate against women).

$$H_a:\ \mu < 2.5$$

Step 2: Choose the test of significance
We are interested in the average for interval/ratio data, where the population standard deviation is unknown. Therefore, we will use a one-sample *t*-test for a mean, with degrees of freedom of 30:

$$df = n - 1 = 30$$

Step 3: Calculate the sample score
In shorthand we summarize the sample information as follows:

$$\overline{X} = 1.9$$

$$n = 31$$

$$s = 1$$

Using the formula for converting the sample value into a *t*-score, we get:

$$t_{sample} = \frac{\overline{X} - \mu}{s/\sqrt{n}} = \frac{1.9 - 2.5}{1/\sqrt{31}}$$

$$= -3.3$$

Step 4: Establish the critical score(s) and critical region
We will use $\alpha = 0.05$. Since we are interested in whether the retail chain discriminates against women in promotion, we will also use a one-tail test. From Table 14.2, which presents critical values for *t*–distributions, with 30 degrees of freedom, the critical value at this level of significance is –1.697.

Step 5: Make a decision
It is clear that t_{sample} is closer to the mean than our critical value, as illustrated in Figure 14.4.

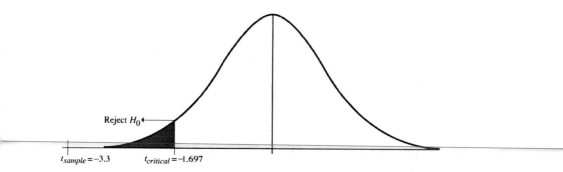

Figure 14.4 Critical and sample scores

Table 14.2 Critical values for *t*-distributions

	Level of significance for one-tail test				
	0.10	0.05	0.02	0.01	0.005
	Level of significance for two-tail test				
df	0.20	0.10	0.05	0.02	0.01
1	3.078	6.314	12.706	31.821	63.657
2	1.886	2.920	4.303	6.965	9.925
3	1.638	2.353	3.182	4.541	5.841
4	1.533	2.132	2.776	3.747	4.604
5	1.476	2.015	2.571	3.365	4.032
6	1.440	1.943	2.447	3.143	3.707
7	1.415	1.895	2.365	2.998	3.499
8	1.397	1.860	2.306	2.896	3.355
9	1.383	1.833	2.262	2.821	3.250
10	1.372	1.812	2.228	2.764	3.169
11	1.363	1.796	2.201	2.718	3.106
12	1.356	1.782	2.179	2.681	3.055
13	1.350	1.771	2.160	2.650	3.012
14	1.345	1.761	2.145	2.624	2.977
15	1.341	1.753	2.131	2.602	2.947
16	1.340	1.746	2.120	2.583	2.921
17	1.333	1.740	2.110	2.567	2.898
18	1.330	1.734	2.101	2.552	2.878
19	1.328	1.729	2.093	2.539	2.861
20	1.325	1.725	2.086	2.528	2.845
21	1.323	1.721	2.080	2.518	2.831
22	1.321	1.717	2.074	2.508	2.819
23	1.319	1.714	2.069	2.500	2.807
24	1.318	1.711	2.064	2.492	2.797
25	1.316	1.708	2.060	2.485	2.787
26	1.315	1.706	2.056	2.479	2.779
27	1.314	1.703	2.052	2.473	2.771
28	1.313	1.701	2.048	2.467	2.763
29	1.311	1.699	2.045	2.462	2.756
30	1.310	1.697	2.042	2.457	2.750
35	1.306	1.690	2.030	2.438	2.724
40	1.303	1.684	2.021	2.423	2.704
45	1.301	1.679	2.014	2.412	2.690
50	1.299	1.676	2.009	2.403	2.678
55	1.297	1.673	2.004	2.396	2.668
60	1.296	1.671	2.000	2.390	2.660
70	1.294	1.667	1.994	2.381	2.648
80	1.292	1.664	1.990	2.374	2.639
90	1.291	1.662	1.987	2.368	2.632
120	1.289	1.658	1.980	2.358	2.617
∞	1.282	1.645	1.960	2.326	2.576

$$t_{critical} = -1.697 \ (\alpha = 0.05, \ df = 30, \text{ one-tail})$$

We therefore do not reject the null. Despite the fact that the sample average was higher than the hypothesized value, we cannot reject the possibility that this is just due to random variation when sampling, and that all the stores in the region on average do not differ from the national average.

Example: two-tail test

According to AC Nielsen, a market research company, children in the Britain between the ages of 5 and 12 years watch on average 196 minutes of TV per day. For the sake of exposition we will assume that this is the value for the population of all British children in this age bracket. A survey is conducted by randomly selecting 20 Australian children within this age group to see if Australian children are significantly different from their British counterparts in terms of the average amount of TV watched per night.

The null hypothesis is that Australian children watch on average the same amount of TV each night as their British counterparts:

$$H_0: \ \mu = 196 \text{ minutes}$$

The alternative hypothesis is that Australian children on average watch a different amount of TV than their British counterparts:

$$H_a: \ \mu \neq 196 \text{ minutes}$$

Note that in this research question we are simply interested in whether there is a difference between Australian children and the hypothesized value of 196 minutes. We are not specifically concerned whether Australian children watch significantly more or significantly less, just whether they are different.

The descriptive statistics that summarize the results of this survey are:

$$\overline{X} \ = \ 166 \text{ minutes}$$
$$s \ = \ 29 \text{ minutes}$$
$$n \ = \ 20$$

Substituting this information into the equation for t, we get a sample t-score of:

$$t_{sample} \ = \ \frac{\overline{X} - \mu}{s/\sqrt{n}} \ = \ \frac{166 - 196}{29/\sqrt{20}}$$

$$= \ -4.6$$

From the table for the critical values for t-distributions, at 19 degrees of freedom and an alpha level of 0.05, the critical value for t is ± 2.093. Since we are conducting a two-tail test, on the basis of the alternative hypothesis, we have critical values on either side of the distribution (Figure 14.5).

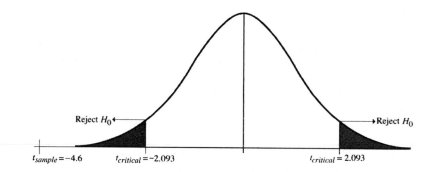

Figure 14.5 Critical and sample scores

We can clearly see that there is a significant difference: Australian children cannot be said to watch on average 196 minutes of TV per day.

The one-sample *t*-test using SPSS

We will now work through this example using SPSS. The data for the 20 Australian children are entered into SPSS. The procedure for generating a one-sample *t*-test on these data is as shown in Table 14.3 and Figure 14.6.

Table 14.3 The **One-Sample T Test** command using SPSS (file: **Ch14.sav**)

SPSS command/action	Comments
1 From the menu select **Analyze/Compare Means/One-Sample T Test**	This brings up the **One-Sample T Test** dialog box
2 Select **TV watched per night** from the source variables list	
3 Click on ▶	This pastes **TV watched per night** into the target list headed **Test Variable(s):**
4 In the text-box next to **Test value:** type **196**	
5 Click on **OK**	

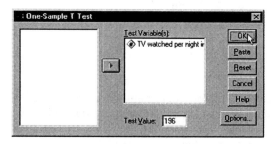

Figure 14.6 The **One-Sample T Test** dialog box

Figure 14.7 presents the output from this set of commands.

T-Test

One-Sample Statistics

	N	Mean	Std. Deviation	Std. Error Mean
TV watched per nght in minutes	20	165.85	29.29	6.55

One-Sample Test

	Test Value = 196					
					95% Confidence Interval of the Difference	
	t	df	Sig. (2-tailed)	Mean Difference	Lower	Upper
TV watched per nght in minutes	-4.603	19	.000	-30.15	-43.86	-16.44

Figure 14.7 SPSS **One-Sample T Test** output

The first **One-Sample Statistics** table provides all the descriptive statistics: the number of cases (20), the mean for the sample (165.85), and the standard deviation for the sample (29.29). The last figure for the first table, Std. Error of Mean, is the standard deviation of the sampling distribution for *t* for this number of degrees of freedom. This is the value in the denominator of the equation for *t*.

The second **One-Sample Test** table in the output contains the results of the inference test. The *t*-value is **-4.603**, as we have already calculated, which at 19 degrees of freedom (*df*) has a two-tail significance of less than 0.0005 (SPSS has rounded this off to 3 decimal places). The difference between the test value of 196 and the sample mean is the Mean Difference of -30.15. This is the numerator of the equation for *t*.

Given the very low probability of obtaining a sample with a mean of 165.85 or less from a population that watches on average 196 minutes of TV a day, we reject the hypothesis that the population mean is 196 minutes: Australian children do not watch the same amount of TV on average than children in Britain.

Another way of reaching the same conclusion is to look at the confidence interval constructed around the sample mean. This information is provided in the last column of the **One-Sample Test** table. At a 95 percent confidence level the interval for the difference between the sample and the test value ranges from a lower limit of **-43.86** to an upper limit of **-16.44**. In other words the difference between the average amount of TV watched by the two sets of children lies somewhere between this range, at a 95 percent confidence level. Since this range does not include the value of zero, which would indicate no difference, we can reject the hypothesis of no difference.

Summary

We have worked through, in this chapter, the one-sample t-test for a mean. It is in most respects equivalent to the one-sample z-test for a mean, which we introduced in the previous chapter, but is used in the more usual situation where we do not know the population standard deviation. In fact, the two tests are identical where the sample size is greater than 120. If we look at the last line of Table 14.1 for the t-distribution which has the infinity symbol, ∞ the scores should be familiar. For example, on a two-tail test at an alpha of 0.05 the t-score is 1.96. This is exactly the same value for z at this level of significance. In other words, when sample size is greater than 120, the t-distribution and the z-distribution are identical, so that the areas under the respective curves for any given scores are also identical.

An important, but often neglected, assumption behind the use of t-tests needs to be pointed out before moving on. With small samples, the sampling distribution of sample means will have a t-distribution only where the underlying population is normally distributed. This assumption is robust in that the sampling distribution will still approximate a t-distribution even where the population is moderately non-normal. Even so, we should be cautious about conducting a t-test without thinking about the validity of this assumption first. Chapter 16 provides a way of assessing this assumption based on the sample data, and if there is reason to believe that this assumption does not hold, a whole range of non-parametric tests are available. These will be investigated in the following chapters.

Exercises

14.1   What assumption about the distribution of the population underlies the t-test?

14.2   From the table for critical scores for t-distributions, fill in the following table:

t-score	Probability	Test	df
2.015		One-tail	5
	0.02	Two-tail	10
1.708	0.05	One-tail	
	0.05	Two-tail	65
	0.10	One-tail	228

14.3   Conduct a t-test, with $\alpha = 0.05$, on each of the following sets of data:

	Sample mean	s	H_0	H_α	n
(a)	62.4	14.1	$\mu = 68$	$\mu \neq 68$	61
(b)	62.4	14.1	$\mu = 68$	$\mu < 68$	61
(c)	2.3	1.8	$\mu = 3.1$	$\mu \neq 3.1$	25
(d)	2.3	1.8	$\mu = 3.1$	$\mu \neq 3.1$	190
(e)	102	45	$\mu = 98$	$\mu \neq 98$	210
(f)	102	45	$\mu = 90$	$\mu \neq 90$	210

14.4 Exercise 12.7 asked you to estimate the 95 percent and 99 percent confidence intervals for the following example. To gage the effect of enterprise bargaining agreements, union officials sampled a total of 120 workers from randomly selected enterprises across an industry. The average wage rise in the previous year for these 120 workers was $1018, with a standard deviation of $614. The union is worried that its workers have not reached its bargaining aim of securing a wage rise of $1150.

    (a) Conduct a two-tail *t*-test with alpha of 0.05 and alpha of 0.01 to assess whether this objective has been met.

    (b) Does this conform to your estimates based on the confidence interval?

14.5 The following data are ages, in years, at death for a sample of people who were all born in the same year:

34, 60, 72, 55, 68, 12, 48, 69, 78, 42, 60, 81, 72, 58, 70, 54, 85, 68, 74, 59, 67, 76, 55, 87, 70

    (a) Calculate the mean age at death and standard deviation for this sample.

    (b) What is the probability of randomly obtaining this sample from a population with an average life expectancy of 70 years?

    (c) Enter these data into SPSS and check your answers. Is the estimate of the 95 percent confidence interval consistent with your results?

14.6 A health worker wanted to gage the effect of hip fractures on people's ability to walk. On average, people walk at a rate of 1 meter per second. Walking speed for 43 individuals who had suffered a hip fracture 6 months previously averaged 0.44 m/s, with a standard deviation of 0.28 m/s. What should the health worker conclude?

14.7 AC Nielsen has provided the following figures for the average number of minutes of TV watched by children in some selected countries:

Country	Mean viewing time, minutes
Australia	159
Canada	140
Britain	196
Singapore	212

In the text we compared the hypothetical results of a survey of 20 Australian children, which had an average viewing time of 166 minutes and standard deviation of 29 minutes, with the 'population' value for the Britain. Compare this sample with the population values for Canada and Singapore, as well as the population value for Australia, and test whether there is a significant difference.

14.8 In Chapter 4 we used the following data for the weekly income of 20 people in a sample:

$0, $0, $250, $300, $360, $375, $400, $400, $400, $420, $425, $450, $462, $470, $475, $502, $520, $560, $700, $1020

The mean for these data we calculated to be $424.45, with a standard deviation of $216.

(a) Conduct a *t*-test, with $\alpha = 0.05$, to assess the probability that this sample is drawn from a population with a mean weekly income of $480.

(b) Enter these data into SPSS, and conduct the same *t*-test.

14.9 Open the **Employee data** file.

(a) Generate the mean and standard deviation for the current salary of workers in the sample.

(b) Assume that the average salary for all other workers is $25,000. Conduct by hand (showing all working) a one-sample *t*-test to assess whether there is a significant difference between the employees in this firm and all other employees. State your conclusion in simple terms.

(c) Conduct this test on SPSS and check that your hand calculations conform to the SPSS output.

(d) Assume that the average salary for all other workers is $33,000. Conduct by hand (showing all working) a one-sample *t*-test to assess whether there is a significant difference between the employees in this firm and all other employees.

(e) Conduct this test on SPSS and check that your hand calculations conform to the SPSS output.

(f) Assume that your research question is whether the employees in this firm are paid significantly *more* than other employees. Will your answer to part (d) be any different? Explain.

15

One-sample Tests for a Binomial Distribution

The previous chapters looked at z-tests and t-tests for a single **mean**. These procedures apply to research questions that direct our investigation to the central tendency of a distribution, and the variable we are interested in is measured at the interval/ratio level. We call such tests **parametric tests** because they test hypotheses about population parameters (in this instance the mean). However, there are many instances where we are interested in aspects of a variable's distribution other than its mean, such as its frequency distribution. We can usually calculate many descriptive statistics to summarize research data. But the descriptive statistics that are relevant to calculate are only those that will help answer our research question(s).

Take for example the problem we dealt with in the previous chapter, where the Health Department had a policy of allocating funds to a region depending on whether the average age of the population is over 40 years. Clearly, this policy rule directs our analysis to the *average* value for the variable of interest – age. Assume that the Health Department suddenly changes its policy rule and decides now to provide extra funding to a region's health services only if 20 percent or more of the population in that region is over 40 years of age. Suddenly the mean age of the population becomes irrelevant. We can still calculate the mean, but this will not assist us in making the policy decision about funding. The appropriate way to describe the data to deal with this new policy rule is to divide the sample into those people who are 40 years of age or less and those over 40, and calculate the percentage of people in each category. In effect we have organized the data into the simplest type of frequency distribution, called a **binomial distribution**.

A **binomial** (or **dichotomous**) **distribution** has only two categories or values.

Some variables are intrinsically dichotomous. A classic example is a coin toss which has only two possible outcomes: either heads or tails. Similarly, questions in opinion polls that allow only 'Yes/No' responses are dichotomous. Sex is another common example of a variable that intrinsically has a binomial distribution: someone is either male or female.

However, even where a variable does not initially have only two categories, it can be transformed into one that does. In fact, practically any variable measured at any level can be turned into a binomial by collapsing categories.

Nominal data

A nominal variable that does not intrinsically have only two categories can be collapsed into a binomial by simply specifying the number of cases that fall into an existing category (or combination of categories) or not. For example, a nominal distribution of cases according to religious denomination might begin with five classifications for religion: Catholic, Protestant, Jewish, Orthodox, and Muslim. These can be collapsed into a binomial distribution in one of two ways:

- by referring to the percentage of cases that fall into one of the existing categories or not, such as Catholic and Non-Catholic,

or

- by creating two entirely new categories by combining the existing ones, such as Christian and Non-Christian.

Each of these methods of collapsing categories is represented in Tables 15.1–15.4.

Table 15.1 Religious affiliation: original distribution

Religion	Frequency
Catholic	20
Protestant	15
Orthodox	12
Muslim	12
Jewish	7

Table 15.2 Religious affiliation: binomial distribution

Religion	Frequency
Catholic	20 (30%)
Non-Catholic	46 (70%)

Table 15.3 Religious affiliation: original distribution

Religion	Frequency
Catholic	20
Protestant	15
Orthodox	14
Muslim	10
Jewish	7

Table 15.4 Religious affiliation: binomial distribution

Religion	Frequency
Christian	49 (74%)
Non-Christian	17 (26%)

Ordinal and interval/ratio data

Ordinal or interval/ratio scales can be collapsed into a binomial distribution by simply specifying the number of cases that fall above or below a particular value on the scale. For example, a list of exam scores can be collapsed into a binomial by selecting 50 percent as the dividing line and organizing the scores into 'pass' and 'fail'.

The sampling distribution of sample percentages

After having arranged the data into a binomial distribution and calculated the relevant percentage of cases in each of the two categories, we can then proceed to conduct an inference test on these percentages. To do this we have to know the properties of **the sampling distribution of sample percentages**.

  In the previous chapters we had a sample mean and we were interested in making an inference from this sample mean to the mean for the population. To make this inference we constructed the sampling distribution of the sample means. This sampling distribution allows us to assess the probability of obtaining our actual sample mean from a population with a specific hypothesized value (the null hypothesis). When working with a binomial distribution, however, the descriptive statistic calculated from the sample is no longer the mean. Instead it is the percentage of cases that fall within one of the two possible categories of the variable. Having calculated the sample percentage we then need to make an inference about the percentage for the population as a whole. Thus we need to explore the properties of the sampling distribution of sample percentages: the distribution of sample percentages that will arise from repeated random samples of equal size.

  For example, we might know that 50 percent of all students at a (hypothetical) university are male and 50 percent are female. Despite this, if we take a random sample of 100 university students we will not necessarily get 50 males and 50 females. Random variation will cause some samples to include slightly more females, while other samples will include slightly more males. But most of these repeated samples will have a percentage of each sex either equal or close to 50 percent. In other words, while there is some variation in the distribution of repeated sample percentages, these sample percentages will cluster around the 'true' population value of 50 percent.

  If we take an infinite number of random samples of equal size from a population, and calculate the percentage of cases in each that have a certain value for a binomial distribution, the sampling distribution of these sample percentages will have the following properties:

- *The sampling distribution is approximately normal with a median percentage equal to the population value* It is only *approximately* normal because a binomial is a discrete variable, whereas the normal curve is continuous. However, the larger the sample size the more closely the distribution approximates the normal.

- The standard error of the sampling distribution will be defined by the following equation

$$\sigma_p = \sqrt{\frac{P_u(1 - P_u)}{n}}$$

where:
P_u is the population percentage.

These two pieces of information are very useful, as we discovered in previous chapters. Knowing the distribution of *all possible* sample percentages that could come from a particular population allows us to calculate the probability of getting any given sample result from a population with an hypothesized value. For example, if a *sample* has 60 percent females, we can calculate the probability that this was the result of sampling error when drawing from a *population* that only has 50 percent females. This is exactly the type of question the one-sample *z*-test for a percentage is designed to answer.

The *z*-test for a binomial percentage

Although we are describing the data by organizing it into a binomial distribution rather than by calculating a mean, the procedures for making an inference from a sample to the population are similar. In practical terms the steps involved in an hypothesis test for a percentage are exactly the same as when conducting an hypothesis test for a mean. We conduct an inference test, much like those in Chapters 13 and 14, but this time based upon the *percentage of the sample falling in one of the two categories of the binomial*, rather than based on the mean of the sample.

Since the sampling distribution is normal we conduct a *z*-test on the difference between the sample percentage and the hypothesized value (much in the same way as we conducted a *z*-test on the difference between the sample mean and the hypothesized population mean). The specific formulas used to calculate z_{sample} are:

$$z_{sample} = \frac{(P_s - 0.5) - P_u}{\sqrt{\dfrac{P_u(100 - P_u)}{n}}} \quad \text{where} \quad P_s > P_u$$

or

$$z_{sample} = \frac{(P_s + 0.5) - P_u}{\sqrt{\dfrac{P_u(100 - P_u)}{n}}} \quad \text{where} \quad P_s < P_u$$

where:
P_s is the sample percentage
P_u is the population percentage.

The addition or subtraction of 0.5 percent to or from the sample percentage in each of these equations is made because, strictly speaking, a binomial distribution is not exactly normal and the addition or subtraction of 0.5 (called a continuity correction) gives us a better approximation. With samples larger than

30 this approximation will be fairly accurate, but with less than 30 the approximation is not accurate and an exact binomial probability test should be used. Many statistics books print tables for the exact binomial distribution for various sample sizes, and these should be referred to in the small sample case rather than the standard normal table. SPSS automatically calculates an exact binomial probability in the small sample case.

Example

A researcher is concerned that the local area is harder hit by recession than the rest of the country. The researcher knows that the national unemployment rate is 11 percent. The researcher randomly asks 120 local people who are in the labor market if they are unemployed. The sample produces a result of 18 people unemployed. These raw data, for the purpose of answering the research question, are initially described by constructing the binomial distribution in Table 15.5.

Table 15.5 Distribution of respondents by employment status

Employment status	Frequency	Percentage
Employed	102	85%
Unemployed	18	15%
Total	120	100%

Does this indicate that this local area is harder hit by recession?

Step 1: State the null and alternative hypotheses
H_0: The local area has the same percentage of people unemployed as the rest of the nation.

$$H_0: P_u = 11\%$$

H_a: The local area has a higher percentage of people unemployed than the rest of the nation.

$$H_a: P_u > 11\%$$

Step 2: Choose the test of significance
The research question is interested in the percentage of people in a category of a binomial distribution (i.e. people unemployed). Therefore we use a single-sample z-test for a percentage.

Step 3: Calculate the sample score
The relevant sample data from the binomial distribution above are:

$$n = 120$$

$$P_s = \frac{18}{120} \times 100 = 15\%$$

We substitute these data into the equation to obtain the sample scores:

$$z_{sample} = \frac{(P_s - 0.5) - P_u}{\sqrt{\dfrac{P_u(100 - P_u)}{n}}} = \frac{(15 - 0.5) - 11}{\sqrt{\dfrac{11(100 - 11)}{120}}}$$

$$= 1.2$$

Step 4: Establish the critical score(s) and region(s)
The researcher chooses a 0.05 level of significance ($\alpha = 0.05$) and, suspecting that the local region is harder hit by recession, will use a one-tail test. Since the direction of difference specified in the alternative hypothesis is that the unemployment rate in this population is *higher* than the national figure, the relevant tail is to the right of the sampling distribution. From the table for the area under the standard normal curve, the critical value of z will be +1.645.

Step 5: Make a decision
The sample value of $z = 1.23$ is not greater than the critical value of 1.645 (Figure 15.1).

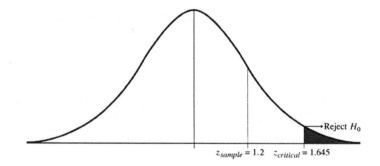

Figure 15.1 Sample and critical scores

Although the *sample* has a higher unemployment rate than the national figure, the difference is not big enough to suggest that the *population* in this area systematically suffers from a higher unemployment rate. We cannot reject, at this level of significance, the null hypothesis.

The z-test for a binomial percentage using SPSS

In order to work through this test on SPSS, the data for the previous example have been entered into a data file. SPSS calls the test for a percentage a binomial test, and the commands needed to carry out this test are as shown in Table 15.6 and Figure 15.2. Figure 15.3 presents the output from this analysis.

Table 15.6 The Binomial Test on SPSS (file: **Ch15-1.sav**)

SPSS command/action	Comments
1 From the menu select **Analyze/ Nonparametric Tests/Binomial**	This brings up the **Binomial Test** dialog box
2 From the source variable list click on **Employment status**	
3 Click on ▶	This pastes **Employment status** into the **Test Variable List:**
4 In the square next to **Test Proportion** type .11 over .50	The default setting is .50, which means that SPSS will compare the sample proportion against 0.5 unless we specify an alternative, as in this case where we specify 0.11 as the test proportion
5 Click on **OK**	

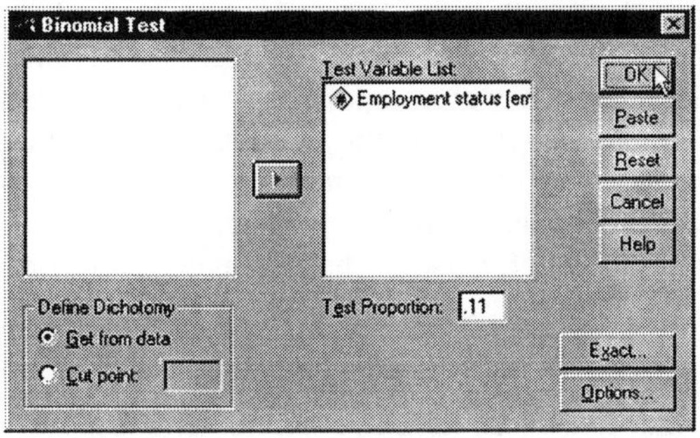

Figure 15.2 The **Binomial Test** dialog box

NPar Tests

Binomial Test

		Category	N	Observed Prop.	Test Prop.	Asymp. Sig. (1-tailed)
Employment status	Group 1	unemployed	18	.15	.11	.105[a]
	Group 2	employed	102	.85		
	Total		120	1.00		

a. Based on Z Approximation.

Figure 15.3 SPSS **Binomial Test** output

Notice that SPSS conducts the test in terms of proportions rather than percentages. This is not such a dramatic difference since we know that any proportion can be easily converted into an equivalent percentage simply by moving the decimal point two places to the right.

This result confirms the calculations above. In the **Binomial Test** table we have a column with the frequency of cases in each of the categories of the binomial distribution, and then a column indicating the relative frequencies as proportions. The last column headed **Asymp. Sig. (1-tailed)** is the important one for the purposes of the inference test. Although we are not given the value of z_{sample}, we are given the one-tail probability associated with it. Here the one-tail probability of .105 indicates that if the null were true (the population from which the sample is drawn has an unemployment rate of 11 percent) at least 1-in-10 samples will have an unemployment rate of 15 percent or more. This is not too unlikely: the assumption that the null is true cannot be rejected.

SPSS always produces a one-tail test when a test percentage is specified rather than the default value of 0.5. If the alternative hypothesis requires a two-tail test, then we simply double the one-tail probability. If one tail of the sampling distribution, at this z-score, contains 0.105 of the area under the curve, two tails will contain 0.21 of the area under the normal curve.

Example

A political scientist is interested in whether there has been a change in people's attitudes toward the two major political parties that normally contest elections in a particular political system. The researcher groups political parties into two distinct categories: major and non-major parties. At the previous election the percentage of people who voted for one of the two major parties was 85 percent. A survey of 300 eligible voters conducted 2 years since that election indicates that 216 (72 percent) plan to vote for one of the two major parties at the next election (Table 15.7).

Table 15.7 Support for major political parties

Who do you support?	Last election	Next election
Major parties	85%	72%
Other parties	15%	28%

Can we say that the level of support for the two major parties has changed since the last election? Since we are dealing with a situation where $P_s < P_u$ we use the following formula to calculate the test statistic:

$$z_{sample} = \frac{(P_s + 0.5) - P_u}{\sqrt{\frac{P_u(100 - P_u)}{n}}} = \frac{(72 + 0.5) - 85}{\sqrt{\frac{85(100 - 85)}{300}}}$$

$$= -6.1$$

At an alpha level of 0.05, on a two-tail test, the value of $z_{critical} = \pm 1.96$. Thus the sample result falls in the rejection region. We can reject the null hypothesis that the percentage of people planning to vote for one of the two major parties is the same as that in the previous election.

Estimating a population percentage

Chapter 12 detailed the procedure for estimating a confidence interval from a sample mean, within which the population mean falls. A similar procedure can be followed to construct a confidence interval from a sample percentage, within which the (unknown) population percentage falls.

Estimating population percentages is common in public opinion surveys. We often read in newspapers that a certain percentage of eligible voters favor one person over another as preferred Prime Minister or President. This percentage figure is not obtained by surveying all eligible voters, but rather through a sample of eligible voters. We therefore need to estimate the population value from this sample result. The formula involved in constructing the confidence interval for a percentage is:

$$ci = P_s \pm z \sqrt{\frac{P_s(100 - P_s)}{n}}$$

We can use this to construct the confidence interval for the estimated percentage of people who will vote for one of the two major parties at the next election, based on the data we used in the previous example. The sample data are:

$$n = 120$$
$$P_s = 15\%$$
$$\text{at } \alpha = 0.05, z = 1.96$$

From these data we can calculate the confidence interval:

$$ci = P_s \pm z \sqrt{\frac{P_s(100 - P_s)}{n}} = 15 \pm 1.96 \sqrt{\frac{15(100 - 15)}{120}}$$

$$= 15 \pm 6.4$$

Thus the lower limit of the confidence interval is 8.6 percent (15 − 6.4) and the upper limit is 21.4 percent (15 + 6.4).

Example

In a sample of 500 students enrolled in fee-paying postgraduate courses, 55 are from low socioeconomic backgrounds. What is the estimated percentage of all fee-paying postgraduate students that come from low socioeconomic backgrounds?

$$n = 500$$

$$P_S = \frac{55}{500} \times 100 = 11\%$$

at $\alpha = 0.05$, $z = 1.96$

$$ci = P_s \pm z\sqrt{\frac{P_s(100 - P_s)}{n}} = 11 \pm 1.96\sqrt{\frac{11(100 - 11)}{500}}$$

$$= 11 \pm 2.7$$

In other words, the percentage of students from low socioeconomic backgrounds in the population lies, with a 95 percent confidence level, between 8.3 percent and 13.7 percent.

Inference using the confidence interval for a percentage

The reason for conducting the above survey is to see if the introduction of fees for postgraduate courses has had an adverse effect on disadvantaged groups. A census of all postgraduate students *before* the introduction of university fees found that 16.8 percent of postgrads were from low socioeconomic backgrounds. Can we say that the introduction of fees has affected the recruitment of poorer students? We want to compare the population of postgraduate students before the introduction of fees with the population of students afterwards. We have information about the first pre-fees population, but we only have an *estimate* of the after-fees postgrad population, based on a sample. However, we can see that the estimate of the population percentage post-fees does not include the value of 16.8 percent. The percentage of disadvantaged students pre-fees does not fall into the 95 percent confidence interval within which, we estimate, lies the percentage of post-fees students from low socioeconomic backgrounds. In other words, on the basis of the sample result we argue that the percentage of disadvantaged students in the pre-fees period is significantly higher than that for the post-fees period. Fees do seem to have affected disadvantaged groups.

Thus we are able to conduct an inference test to see whether to reject an hypothesis about a population percentage through the construction of a confidence interval. This is an alternative to the hypothesis testing procedure we are familiar with. To drive the point home further, we will in fact conduct a one-sample z-test for a percentage to show that the conclusion is the same as that when using a confidence interval to make a decision about an hypothesis:

$$z_{sample} = \frac{(P_s - 0.5) - P_u}{\sqrt{\dfrac{P_u(100 - P_u)}{n}}} = \frac{(11 - 0.5) - 16.8}{\sqrt{\dfrac{16.8(100 - 16.8)}{500}}}$$

$$= -3.8$$

On a two-tail test the critical value of z, at a 0.05 significance level (the equivalent of the 95 percent confidence level), will be ±1.96.

Clearly, we can reject the hypothesis that this sample came from a population with a percentage of disadvantaged students of 16.8 percent.

The runs test for randomness

The proportion of the sample that falls into one category or the other of a binomial distribution is not the only descriptive statistic we might be interested in. We might have no interest in the question of what proportion of the total sample falls in one category or the other. Instead we might be interested in the *series or sequence of scores*: how each score follows on from the previous one. Usually we look at the sequence of cases with a particular question in mind: is a series of events **random**?

An event is **random** if its outcome in one instance is not affected by the outcome in other instances.

For example, if I toss a coin nine times, and each time the coin came down 'heads', then if it is an unbiased coin we should not expect that the next toss will be more likely to come down 'heads' (or 'tails').

To decide whether the value of a variable in one case is random with respect to the value it takes in other cases, we conduct a z-test on the number of sample runs – the 'runs test'.

The idea behind a runs test of randomness is simple. If the outcome of a coin toss is random, and an unbiased coin is tossed and comes up heads, the probability of the next toss being either heads or tails should be 50/50. There should be a fairly even spread of heads and tails after each toss. If any of the following three results occurs from tossing a coin 20 times we might get a little suspicious:

Set 1: T T T T T T T T T T T T T T T T T T T T

Set 2: H H H H H H H H H H H H H H H H H H H H

Set 3: H T H T H T H T H T H T H T H T H T H T

In each set, it seems that each case is not random. In the first two sets of tosses each flip leads to the same result in the next – tails seem to determine tails, and heads seem to determine heads. In the third set of tosses, tails determine heads and vice versa. Either way, the outcome of a coin toss does not appear to be random. But another interpretation could be that each of these outcomes occurred simply on the basis of chance. Coin tosses might be random, but we just happened by fluke to get these outcomes.

To decide between these explanations, we describe the results of each set of tosses by calculating the number of runs: how many sequences of like results there are. In the first two sets we have 1 run each:

Set 1
T T T T T T T T T T T T T T T T T T T T
1 run

Set 2
H H H H H H H H H H H H H H H H H H H H
1 run

In the third set of tosses we have 20 runs:

Set 3

H	T	H	T	H	T	H	T	H	T	H	T	H	T	H	T	H	T	H	T
1	2	3	4	5	6	7	8	9	10	11	12	13	14	15	16	17	18	19	20

20 runs

It is conceivable that I could toss an unbiased coin and get such results – they could happen just by chance. This is the null hypothesis of randomness. However, such results are very unlikely. The probability of getting either 1 run or 20 runs from 20 coin tosses, *if* the toss of a coin is truly random, is extremely low. On average, we expect to get between 1 and 20 runs. In fact, the value we expect to get if the results are random, and which we use in the null hypothesis, is given by the formula:

$$H_0 : \quad \mu_R \quad = \quad \frac{2n_1n_2}{n} + 1$$

where:
n_1 is the number of cases with a given value
n_2 is the number of cases with the other value
n is the total number of cases.

However, even though coin tosses are random, individual samples will not always have this many runs. The spread of possible sample results around the expected value is given by:

$$\sigma_R = \sqrt{\frac{n^2 - 2n}{4(n-1)}}$$

Given this information we can perform a z-test to determine whether the sample value of R is likely to be the result of chance or something systematic (where the sample is less than 20, the sampling distribution of sample runs will not be approximately normal, and therefore an exact probability test needs to be conducted; in our test we will only be working with samples larger than 20 where the normal approximation is applicable):

$$z_{sample} = \frac{(R + 0.5) - \mu_R}{\sigma_R} \quad \text{where } R < \mu_R$$

or

$$z_{sample} = \frac{(R - 0.5) - \mu_R}{\sigma_R} \quad \text{where } R > \mu_R$$

where:
R is the number of runs in the sample
μ_R is the number of runs expected from repeated sampling
σ_R is the standard error of the sampling distribution.

We simply follow the hypothesis testing procedure we have learnt and compare the sample z-score and probability with a pre-chosen critical value and decide either to reject or not to reject the null hypothesis. It is important when conducting this test that the data are ordered in the sequence in which they were generated. For example, when looking at time series, as we do below, the data are ordered according to year.

Example

One of the most common uses of the runs test is with time series data. Time series refer to a sequence of cases occurring over successive time periods. For example, we might be interested in people's propensity to save: how much do people set aside from their income instead of consuming? More specifically, is the proportion of saving out of household income in any given year related to the amount saved in the previous year? Do years of relatively high saving tend to follow each other and do years of low saving tend to follow each other?

Table 15.8 provides the raw data for a 33 year period. In order to conduct a runs test on such a time series of data we need first to categorize each year as exhibiting either a 'high' or a 'low' rate of saving, thereby collapsing the distribution into a binomial one. A number of options are available, but in this

Table 15.8 Saving rate Australia, 1949–1950 to 1981–1982

Year	Saving rate, %
1949–50	10.2
1950–51	16.2
1951–52	4.3
1952–53	10.2
1953–54	6.7
1954–55	6.8
1955–56	7.7
1956–57	7.9
1957–58	3.0
1958–59	6.6
1959–60	5.9
1960–61	6.2
1961–62	6.9
1962–63	6.8
1963–64	8.4
1964–65	8.3
1965–66	7.0
1966–67	9.1
1967–68	5.3
1968–69	8.5
1969–70	7.7
1970–71	9.0
1971–72	9.9
1972–73	12.4
1973–74	14.0
1974–75	14.4
1975–76	12.7
1976–77	11.9
1977–78	11.7
1978–79	11.8
1979–80	10.5
1980–81	10.9
1981–82	11.0

Source: Reserve Bank of Australia (1985) *Australian Economic Statistics*, Occasional Paper No. 8A, 146–147.

instance we will call any year with saving rate above the median a 'high saving' year, and any year with a rate below the 33 year median a 'low saving' year. The median for these 33 saving rates is 8.5 percent. To see whether years of low or high saving occur in 'patches' or are distributed randomly across years, we will put a plus or minus sign next to the rate for each year (Table 15.9), depending on whether it is above or below the median score of 8.5 (the median score is assigned a plus). Thus we are able to describe our sample result by saying that there are 9 runs. How likely is this to occur if the saving rate in any given year is random with respect to the rate in the previous year? To specify the null hypothesis we need to calculate:

$$\mu_R = \frac{2n_1 n_2}{n} + 1 = \frac{2(16)(17)}{33} + 1$$

$$= 17.5$$

Table 15.9 Determining the number of runs in a time series

Year	Saving rate %	Above or below median
1949–50	10.2	+ Run 1
1950–51	16.2	+
1951–52	4.3	– Run 2
1952–53	10.2	+ Run 3
1953–54	6.7	–
1954–55	6.8	–
1955–56	7.7	–
1956–57	7.9	–
1957–58	3.0	–
1958–59	6.6	– Run 4
1959–60	5.9	–
1960–61	6.2	–
1961–62	6.9	–
1962–63	6.8	–
1963–64	8.4	–
1964–65	8.3	–
1965–66	7.0	–
1966–67	9.1	+ Run 5
1967–68	5.3	– Run 6
1968–69	8.5	+ Run 7
1969–70	7.7	– Run 8
1970–71	9.0	+
1971–72	9.9	+
1972–73	12.4	+
1973–74	14.0	+
1974–75	14.4	+
1975–76	12.7	+ Run 9
1976–77	11.9	+
1977–78	11.7	+
1978–79	11.8	+
1979–80	10.5	+
1980–81	10.9	+
1981–82	11.0	+

Thus the null and alternative hypotheses will be:

$$H_0: \mu_R = 17.5$$

$$H_a: \mu_R \neq 17.5$$

The probability of getting the actual sample result of 9 runs, on the assumption that the null hypothesis is true, can be calculated:

$$z_{sample} = \frac{(R+0.5)-\mu_R}{\sqrt{\dfrac{n^2-2n}{4(n-1)}}} = \frac{9.5-17.5}{\sqrt{\dfrac{33^2-2(33)}{4(33-1)}}}$$

$$= -2.83$$

From the table for the area under the standard normal curve, this z-score has a probability of occurring (on a two-tail test) by chance less than 5 times in 1000. Therefore we reject the null hypothesis of randomness, and argue that the saving rate does seem to be affected by the rate in the previous year. In other words, there appears to be a cyclical process at work.

The runs test using SPSS

The data from this example have been entered into SPSS and to conduct a runs test we follow the procedure in Table 15.10 and Figure 15.4.

Table 15.10 The **Runs Test** on SPSS (file: **Ch15-2.sav**)

SPSS command/action	Comments
1 Select **Analyze/ Nonparametric Tests/Runs**	This brings up the **Runs Test** dialog box
2 Click on **Household saving rate** in the source variable list	
3 Click on ▶	This pastes **Household saving rate** into the **Test Variable List:**
4 In the area called **Cut Point** click on the square next to **Median**	This places × in the check-box to show that the median of the series will be used to decide whether a particular year is to be assigned as high or low
5 Click on **OK**	

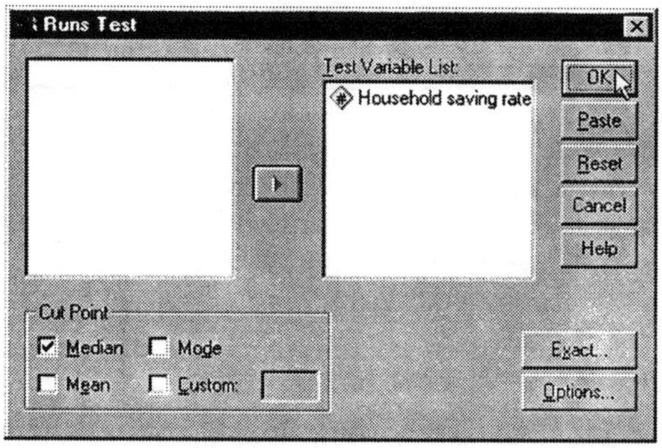

Figure 15.4 The **Runs Test** dialog box

Figure 15.5 presents the output from the runs test. This indicates that the Test Value is 8.5. This is the median saving rate which we use as the 'cut-point' for deciding whether any given year has a high or low saving rate. In effect this is the point on the saving rate scale which forms the dividing line of a binomial distribution. The next lines in the table indicate that there were 16 years in which the saving rate was below the median, and 17 years that were equal to or above the median. Provided the data are entered in chronological order, so that 1949–1950 is on the first row of data and 1981–82 is on the last, SPSS calculates that there are 9 runs. The z-score of -2.827 has a two-tail probability of 0.005, if the null hypothesis of randomness is true. (If we want to convert the two-tail probability into a one-tail probability, we halve its value.) This is so improbable that we reject the null hypothesis.

NPar Tests

Runs Test

	Household saving rate
Test Value[a]	8.50
Cases < Test Value	16
Cases >= Test Value	17
Total Cases	33
Number of Runs	9
Z	-2.827
Asymp. Sig. (2-tailed)	.005

a. Median

Figure 15.5 SPSS **Runs Test** output

Exercises

15.1 In order to estimate the percentage of a population giving a certain response to a survey we need to take a larger sample for larger populations. Is this statement true or false? Why?

15.2 For the following sets of statistics, conduct a z-test of percentages using both a one-tail and two-tail test, with alpha of 0.05:

(a)	(b)
$P_u = 52$	$P_u = 42$
$P_s = 61$	$P_s = 39$
$n = 110$	$n = 110$

15.3 A random sample of 900 jail prisoners is surveyed to gage the success of an in-prison resocialization program. Of the total, 350 stated that the program has been effective in reducing the likelihood of repeat offense. The program's target was a 40 percent success rate in reducing the likelihood of repeat offense.
(a) Using a z-test of percentages, can we say that the program was successful?
(b) Construct a 95 percent confidence interval to estimate the population value. How does this confirm the result of the z-test?

15.4   A survey polls 120 eligible voters the day before an election and 63 state that they will vote for the opposition candidate. This candidate declares that the election is a waste of time since she will clearly win. Is this argument justified? Explain.

15.5   A physiotherapist is interested in whether ankle taping has reduced the incidence of ankle sprains in basketball players. The incidence of ankle sprains in basketball players has been reported to be 8 percent. The physiotherapist randomly selects 360 basketball players who tape their ankles and finds that 11 have sprained their ankles. Does this suggest that taping reduces the incidence of ankle sprain?

15.6   A study of 500 people finds that 56 percent support the decriminalization of marijuana use. What is the 95 percent confidence interval for the percentage of all people in favor of decriminalization? Can we say that a majority of people are in favor of decriminalization?

15.7   A random survey of 60 firms in an industry finds that 15 are not meeting pollution emission control standards. What are the:
(a)   90 percent and
(b)   95 percent confidence intervals for the estimate of all firms in the industry not meeting the standards?

15.8   A hockey team captain has recorded the outcome of 20 coin tosses for the last 20 games. These tosses had the following sequence of results:

heads	tails	heads	heads	tails	tails	tails	heads
heads	heads	tails	heads	heads	tails	tails	heads
tails	tails	tails	tails				

(a)   Why is a runs test applicable to such data?
(b)   Conduct a runs test to see if the outcome of these tosses is random.
(c)   Enter these data into SPSS and confirm your results.

15.9   A hospital has kept a tally of the years in which a majority of boys were born and those in which a majority of girls were born. The sequence of results is as follows:

boys	boys	boys	girls	boys	boys	girls	boys
girls	boys	boys	boys	boys	boys	girls	boys
boys	girls	boys	boys	boys	boys	girls	

(a)   How many runs describe this sequence?
(b)   How many runs will we expect to get if the sex of each child born is purely random with respect to the previous year's outcome?

(c) At a 0.05 level of significance, can we say that the outcome is a non-random event?

(d) Enter these data on SPSS and conduct a runs test to confirm your own calculations.

15.10 Use the **Employee data** file to determine whether the proportion of employees in the company receiving a current salary of $25,000 or less is not greater than 35 percent (hint: in the **Binomial Test** dialog box use the **C̲ut point:** option to organize the distribution into a binomial one).

16

One-sample Tests for a Frequency Distribution

The previous chapters discussed situations where we tested an hypothesis about a population mean or a percentage of a binomial distribution. We hypothesize that the population mean or percentage is a specific value and then determine the likelihood of drawing from such a population a sample with a mean or percentage we actually obtain in the course of research. We do this by calculating a z-score or a t-score and looking up the corresponding probability in the appropriate table. If the difference between the sample statistic and the hypothesized population value is large, the corresponding probability that the sample is drawn from such a population will be low. In short, the question boils down to whether an observed difference between a sample statistic and a hypothesized population value is 'big enough'.

The chi-square goodness-of-fit test

This chapter will extend the analysis of the previous chapter. The previous chapter was interested in a very particular kind of frequency distribution: a binomial which is a scale with only two categories. We saw that often we construct a binomial by collapsing categories down into two. But what if responses do not, for example, fall into simple yes/no dichotomies and instead fall into a range of values such as 'strongly agree', 'agree', 'disagree', 'strongly disagree' and we are not prepared to collapse these categories down to two?

Where the research question we are addressing does not direct us to collapse the data down into two categories, but rather directs our attention to the frequency distribution of cases across a wide range of categories or values of a variable, we use the **chi-square goodness-of-fit test** (χ^2 – pronounced 'ki-square').

> The **chi-square goodness-of-fit test** is a non-parametric test for the frequency distribution of cases across a range of values for a single variable.

The nature of the question addressed by the goodness-of-fit test, as opposed to other tests we have encountered, is illustrated in Figure 16.1.

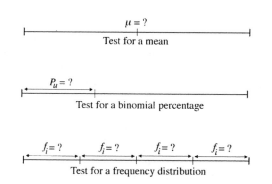

Figure 16.1 Comparison of inference tests

The chi-square goodness-of-fit test analyzes a frequency distribution, and since frequency distributions can be constructed for nominal and ordinal data as well as interval/ratio (as we saw in Chapter 3), it can be used for all levels of measurement. We will introduce the goodness-of-fit test as applied to nominal and ordinal data, where data are arranged into discrete categories. We will then show how this test can also be useful in analyzing the frequency distribution of interval/ratio data.

The test is called the 'chi-square' test because the sampling distribution we use to assess the probability of the null being true is a chi-square distribution. (A more detailed explanation of the chi-square distribution is presented in Chapter 20 for the two or more samples case, which is the most common use of the chi-square distribution. It may be helpful to return to the present chapter after reading Chapter 20. The one-sample case is presented here to maintain the overall logic of this book, which is to present all the one-sample tests first, before moving to tests for two or more samples.)

The chi-square distribution has the general shape shown in Figure 16.2.

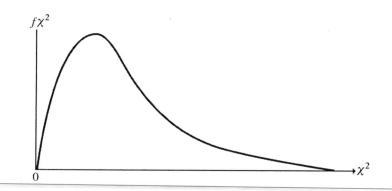

Figure 16.2 Distribution of chi-square (χ^2)

The chi-square distribution is constructed on the same basis as the other sampling distributions we have already encountered: it is the probability distribution of a sample statistic we will get from an infinite number of samples of the same size drawn from a population with certain specified features.

To illustrate the goodness-of-fit test we will try to answer the following question: is the crime rate affected by the seasons? Clearly, we are not interested in the average crime rate, but rather the *distribution of crime rates across the range of seasons*. We begin by making an hypothesis about the population distribution: we assume that there is no relationship between crime rates and seasons. On this hypothesis we will *expect* the number of crimes committed in any year to be evenly distributed across the four seasons.

$$f_e = \frac{\text{total number of crimes}}{4}$$

where:
f_e is the expected frequency in each category.

However, in any given year the crime rate might be affected by random events that cause the distribution to be a little bit different from this expected result. In other words, not every sample will conform with this expectation of an exactly equal number of crimes in each season. We can express the difference between the expected value and the observed value by calculating a sample chi-square statistic:

$$\chi^2_{sample} = \sum \frac{(f_o - f_e)^2}{f_e}$$

where:
f_e is the expected frequency in each category
f_o is the observed frequency in each category.

We can see that if the sample result conforms exactly to the expected result, the value of the sample chi-square (χ^2_{sample}) will be zero: if observed frequencies are the same as expected frequencies then subtracting one from the other will be zero.

What about situations in which the observed distribution is not exactly the same as the expected distribution? Looking at the formula for chi-square we can see that any difference will produce a positive value for sample chi-square. This is because any difference is squared, thereby eliminating negative values. We can also see that the larger the difference between the observed and expected frequencies, called the **residuals**, the higher the (positive) value of the sample chi-square. The question then becomes at what point does the value of the sample chi-square become so large that it suggests the sample was not selected from a population with a uniform spread of crime rates across seasons?

We choose this critical value for chi-square in the same way as with other tests. We choose an alpha level, such as 0.05, and look up the corresponding critical value from Table A4. To find the critical value of chi-square for a given alpha level we need to take into account the number of degrees of freedom. For any given distribution the number of degrees of freedom is given by:

$$df = k - 1$$

where:
k is the number of categories.

Thus if a variable has four categories, as in this case, the degrees of freedom will be:

$$df = 4 - 1 = 3$$

From the table for the critical values of chi-square, at an alpha level of 0.05 and with 3 degrees of freedom, we see that the critical region begins with a chi-square value of 7.815 (Table 16.1).

Table 16.1 Critical values for chi-square distributions

	Level of significance (α)									
df	0.99	0.90	0.70	0.50	0.30	0.20	0.10	0.05	0.01	0.001
1	0.00016	0.0158	0.148	0.455	1.074	1.642	2.706	3.841	6.635	10.827
2	0.0201	0.211	0.713	1.386	2.408	3.219	4.605	5.991	9.210	13.815
3	0.115	0.584	1.424	2.366	3.665	4.642	6.251	**7.815**	11.341	16.268
4	0.297	1.064	2.195	3.357	4.878	5.989	7.779	9.488	13.277	18.465
5	0.554	1.610	3.000	4.351	6.064	7.289	9.236	11.070	15.086	20.517
6	0.872	2.204	3.828	5.348	7.231	8.558	10.645	12.592	16.812	22.457
7	1.239	2.833	4.671	6.346	8.383	9.803	12.017	14.067	18.475	24.322
8	1.646	3.490	5.527	7.344	9.524	11.030	13.362	15.507	20.090	26.125
9	2.088	4.168	6.393	8.343	10.656	12.242	14.684	16.919	21.666	27.877
10	2.558	4.865	7.267	9.342	11.781	13.442	15.987	18.307	23.209	29.588

$$\chi^2_{critical} = 7.815\ (\alpha = 0.05,\ df = 3)$$

We can now calculate the sample value for chi-square to see if it falls within this critical region (region of rejection). For example, if we actually observe the (hypothetical) distribution of crime shown in Table 16.2 can we conclude that crime is indeed affected by the seasons?

Table 16.2 Distribution of crime by season

	Summer	Spring	Winter	Autumn	Total
Observed	300	270	200	250	1020
Expected	255	255	255	255	1020
Residual	45	15	–55	–5	

The expected values are simply the total divided by the number of seasons:

$$f_e = \frac{1020}{4}$$

$$= 255$$

The row labeled 'Residual' is the difference between the observed and expected values. To get a better picture of the logic behind this test, we have graphed the data in Figure 16.3.

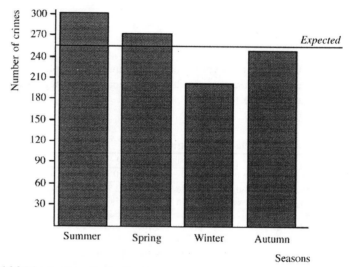

Figure 16.3 Distribution of crime by season

The straight line represents the height that the bars will be if the observed values are equal to the expected values. However, we can see that this is not the case: Summer and Spring have higher than expected values, whereas Winter and Autumn fall short. The gap between the line and each bar is the residual. We can now substitute the sample results into the formula for chi-square:

$$\chi^2_{sample} = \Sigma \frac{(f_o - f_e)^2}{f_e}$$

$$= \frac{(300-255)^2}{255} + \frac{(270-255)^2}{255} + \frac{(200-255)^2}{255} + \frac{(250-255)^2}{255}$$

$$= 20.78$$

In Figure 16.4 we graph both the sample and critical scores for chi-square to help us make a decision.

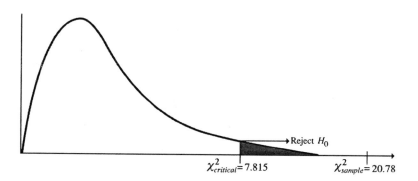

Figure 16.4 Distribution of chi-square ($df = 3$)

The value of the sample chi-square clearly falls into the critical region and therefore will cause us to reject the null hypothesis of an even distribution of crime across seasons.

Chi-square goodness-of-fit test using SPSS

The data from this test have been entered into SPSS. This data file comprises a column of 1020 numbers representing the season in which each crime was committed, which is given the variable name season. To conduct a one-sample chi-square test on these data we work through the procedure shown in Table 16.3 and Figure 16.5. Figure 16.6 presents the output from this set of instructions.

We can compare these results with the hand calculations above. The table in the output titled **Crime by season** contains the descriptive statistics that summarize the sample. In this case, the distribution of cases across the four seasons is provided. A column of expected frequencies is also generated, based on the assumption that an equal number of cases is expected in each season. The values in the **Expected N** column are subtracted from the **Observed N** column to give the **Residual** values. This is simply a replication of the frequency table we used above, but turned 'on its side' so that the seasons are down the left of the table rather than across the top.

Below this frequency table is the chi-square **Test Statistics** table. The sample chi-square is **20.784** (as we calculated above), which, with 3 degrees of freedom (df), has a probability of occurring if crime is evenly spread across seasons once in every 10,000 samples. Such a low probability leads us to reject the null hypothesis: crime rates do seem to be related to the seasons.

Table 16.3 Chi-square goodness-of-fit test using SPSS (file: **Ch16.sav**)

SPSS command/action	Comments
1 From the menu select **Analyze/Nonparametric Tests/Chi –Square**	This brings up the **Chi Square** dialog box
2 Click on **Crime by season** in the source list	This highlights **Crime by season**
3 Click on ▶	This pastes **Crime by season** into the **Test Variable List:**
4 Click on **OK**	

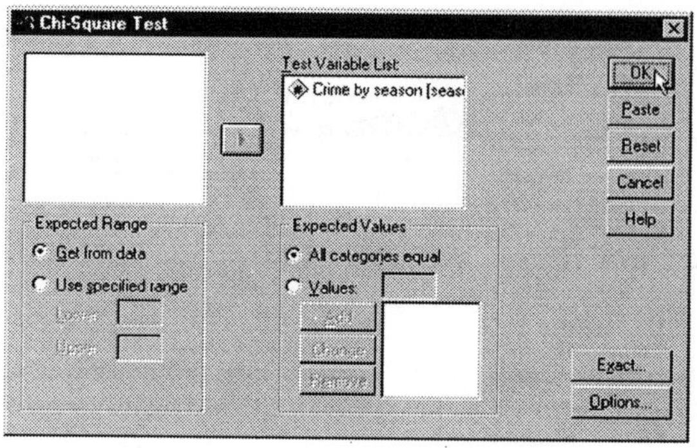

Figure 16.5 The **Chi-Square Test** dialog box

Chi-Square Test

Frequencies

Crime by season

	Observed N	Expected N	Residual
Summer	300	255.0	45.0
Spring	270	255.0	15.0
Autumn	200	255.0	-55.0
Winter	250	255.0	-5.0
Total	1020		

Test Statistics

	Crime by season
Chi-Square[a]	20.784
df	3
Asymp. Sig.	.000

a. 0 cells (0%) have expected frequencies less than 5. The minimum expected cell frequency is 255.0.

Figure 16.6 SPSS **Chi-Square Test** output

Notice in the **Chi-Square Test** dialog box, in the area called **Expected Values** that the radio button next to **All Categories equal** is selected. This is the default setting: SPSS will automatically calculate the number of expected cases in each category by dividing the total by the number of categories, which is what we desired in this example. The categories of the variables, however, do not need to have exactly equal numbers of expected cases. The chi-square test can be used for situations where, for some a priori reason, we hypothesize some unequal distribution of cases in the population. To enter user-specified expected values we select **Values:**, enter a value greater than 0 for each category of the test variable, and click on **Add**. Each time an expected value is added, it appears at the bottom of the value list. The order of the values is important: it corresponds to the ascending order of the category values of the test variable. The first value in the list corresponds to the category with the lowest value of the test variable, and the last expected frequency added corresponds to the highest value.

For example, assume that a region adjacent to the one we are investigating has the distribution of crime across seasons presented in the first column of Table 16.4.

Table 16.4 Distribution of crime by season

Season	Expected %	Expected number
Summer	35%	352
Spring	30%	306
Autumn	25%	255
Winter	10%	102
Total	100%	1020

We know, in other words, what the distribution of *all* crimes across the seasons is for this nearby region. Can we say that our region has the same distribution of crime? Given this research question we calculate the expected values on the basis of these percentages, producing the expected number of crimes in each season given in the second column. To conduct the chi-square test on SPSS using these expected values we first need to note the values given to each season in the coding scheme, which is 1 for Summer, 2 for Spring, 3 for Autumn, and 4 for Winter. We begin with the category with the lowest value which is Summer. We click on **Values:** and type 352 and then click on the **Add** button. We then type 306 and click on the **Add** button, and so on for each of the seasons.

Example

In 1996, 40 percent of sales by a car dealer were four-cylinder cars, 30 percent were six-cylinder, and 30 percent were eight-cylinder. A random sample of sales in recent months produced the distribution shown in Table 16.5.

Table 16.5 Observed sales distribution

Engine type	Observed number of sales
Four-cylinder	42
Six-cylinder	26
Eight-cylinder	12
Total	80

Can we say that this reflects a trend toward smaller cars? First we calculate the expected number of sales, based on the 1996 percentages (Table 16.6).

Table 16.6 Expected sales distribution

Engine type	Expected number of sales
Four-cylinder	$\dfrac{40}{100} \times 80 = 32$
Six-cylinder	$\dfrac{30}{100} \times 80 = 24$
Eight-cylinder	$\dfrac{30}{100} \times 80 = 24$
Total	80

Notice here that we are not expecting an *even* spread of cases across the categories, as we did in the example above regarding crime rates across seasons. This does not alter the test: our decision as to the frequencies to be expected in each category is determined primarily by our research question and the theory which informs it. Given these expected values we then conduct the chi-square test.

Substituting observed and expected frequencies into the formula for chi-square we get:

$$\chi^2_{sample} = \sum \frac{(f_o - f_e)^2}{f_e} = \frac{(42 - 32)^2}{32} + \frac{(26 - 24)^2}{24} + \frac{(12 - 24)^2}{24}$$

$$= 9.29$$

The critical value for chi-square, with 2 degrees of freedom and a 0.05 level of significance, is 5.991 (Figure 16.7).

We therefore reject the null – the frequency distribution of car sales by engine size is significantly different (in a statistical sense) to the distribution of engine size in 1994. Looking at the relative frequencies we can see that there is a trend toward smaller cars.

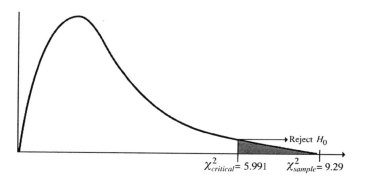

Figure 16.7 Distribution of chi-square ($df = 2$)

The chi-square goodness-of-fit test for normality

We have worked through examples of the chi-square goodness-of-fit test on nominal and ordinal data which fall into discrete categories. Any test that can be applied to nominal and ordinal data, though, can also be applied to the higher levels of measurement of interval/ratio. In the case of interval/ratio data we look at the frequency distribution of cases across the range of values or class intervals, in exactly the same way as when we looked at the distribution across discrete categories.

This logic makes the goodness-of-fit test particularly useful in assessing whether interval/ratio data come from a normal population. In this way, this non-parametric test can be a useful preliminary and complement to parametric tests, which require the assumption that a sample comes from a normal population.

Suppose that we have a sample and we want to assess whether it was drawn from a normal population. Remember from Chapter 6 that a normal distribution is defined by the frequency distribution shown in Table 16.7 and illustrated in Figure 16.8. We can use the percentage values in Table 16.7 to calculate the expected values we use in the formula for chi-square. Notice again that unlike the previous example of crime rates, we are not assuming that cases are evenly distributed across the categories; instead the expected frequencies are based on the characteristics of the normal curve.

Table 16.7 Distribution of the normal curve

Range of values	Percentage of cases
Further than 2 standard deviations below the mean	2%
Between 1 and 2 standard deviations below the mean	14%
Within 1 standard deviation below the mean	34%
Within 1 standard deviation above the mean	34%
Between 1 and 2 standard deviations above the mean	14%
Further than 2 standard deviations above the mean	2%

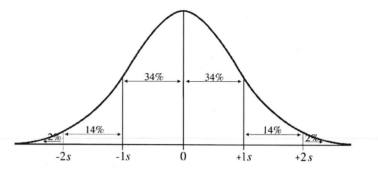

Figure 16.8 Areas under the normal curve

For example, assume that we have a sample of 110 people whose mean age is 45 years, with a standard deviation of 10 years. If this sample is normally distributed we will expect to find the numbers of people within the ranges shown in Table 16.8. The table includes the calculations for the first three ranges to show the method involved.

Table 16.8 Expected distribution of the sample

Range of values	Percentage of cases	Number of cases
25 years or less (further than 2 standard deviations below the mean)	2%	$\frac{2}{100} \times 110 = 2.2$
26–35 years (between 1 and 2 standard deviations below the mean)	14%	$\frac{14}{100} \times 110 = 15.4$
36–45 years (within 1 standard deviation below the mean)	34%	$\frac{34}{100} \times 110 = 37.4$
46–55 years (within 1 standard deviation above the mean)	34%	37.4
56–65 years (between 1 and 2 standard deviations above the mean)	14%	15.4
66 years or over (further than 2 standard deviations above the mean)	2%	2.2

However, we might actually get a sample distribution as shown in Table 16.9.

Table 16.9 Observed distribution of the sample

Range of values	Number of cases
25 years or less	5
26–35 years	17
36–45 years	33
46–55 years	33
56–65 years	17
66 years or over	5

There is obviously some difference between the observed and expected values: should this cause us to reject the hypothesis that the population is normally distributed? To answer this we need to calculate chi-square:

$$\chi^2_{sample} = \sum \frac{(f_o - f_e)^2}{f_e}$$

$$= \frac{(5 - 2.2)^2}{2.2} + \frac{(17 - 15.4)^2}{15.4} + \frac{(33 - 37.4)^2}{37.4} +$$

$$\frac{(33 - 37.4)^2}{37.4} + \frac{(17 - 15.4)^2}{15.4} + \frac{(5 - 2.2)^2}{2.2}$$

$$= 8.5$$

We need to compare this sample score with a critical value for chi-square, which depends on the degrees of freedom. Here we have six categories, so that degrees of freedom will be 6 – 1 = 5. At an alpha level of 0.05 the critical value for chi-square is 11.07 (Table 16.6).

Table 16.10 Critical values for chi-square distributions

df	0.99	0.90	0.70	0.50	0.30	0.20	0.10	0.05	0.01	0.001
1	0.00016	0.0158	0.148	0.455	1.074	1.642	2.706	3.841	6.635	10.827
2	0.0201	0.211	0.713	1.386	2.408	3.219	4.605	5.991	9.210	13.815
3	0.115	0.584	1.424	2.366	3.665	4.642	6.251	7.815	11.341	16.268
4	0.297	1.064	2.195	3.357	4.878	5.989	7.779	9.488	13.277	18.465
5	0.554	1.610	3.000	4.351	6.064	7.289	9.236	11.070	15.086	20.517
6	0.872	2.204	3.828	5.348	7.231	8.558	10.645	12.592	16.812	22.457
7	1.239	2.833	4.671	6.346	8.383	9.803	12.017	14.067	18.475	24.322

The sample value for chi-square is smaller than the critical value so we do not reject the hypothesis that the sample comes from a normally distributed population.

Summary

We have introduced a new test in this chapter: the chi-square test. Although the chi-square test involves slightly different calculations, it is very similar to the binomial test we looked at in the previous chapter. Whereas the z-test for a binomial percentage only applies to frequency distributions organized into a binomial distribution, the chi-square test is more general in that it applies to frequency distributions with any number of categories (thus the z-test for a binomial percentage can be considered a special case of the chi-square test). This gives the test a wide applicability, especially since (as we will see in Chapter 20), it can be extended in a direct way to the two-sample and more than two sample situations.

Exercises

16.1   What will be the number of degrees of freedom, and the value of $\chi^2_{critical}$ for both $\alpha = 0.10$ and $\alpha = 0.05$, for a goodness-of-fit test on a variable with:

(a)   three categories
(b)   five categories
(c)   eight categories

16.2   Conduct a goodness-of-fit test on the following data to test the hypothesis that the sample comes from a population with a uniform distribution of cases across categories:

(a)

Value	Number of cases
1	45
2	40
3	55
4	54
5	38

(b)

Value	Number of cases
1	120
2	111
3	119
4	125
5	120
6	127
7	118

16.3   According to a 1991 *Census of Population and Housing*, Australians between the ages of 25 and 34 years had the following distribution according to marital status:

Marital status	Number of persons
Never married	896,206
Married	1,591,010
Separated not divorced	104,296
Divorced	117,673
Widowed	14,216
Total	2,723,401

A survey of 350 residents aged between 25 and 34 is taken in a local area, which had the following distribution according to marital status:

Marital status	% of Sample ($n = 350$)
Never married	40
Married	50
Separated not divorced	6
Divorced	2
Widowed	2
Total	100

Using the census information to calculate the expected values, can we say that this area is significantly different from the rest of the population? In which direction are the differences?

16.4 Ninety people are surveyed and the amount of time they each spend reading each day is measured. The researcher wants to test the assumption that this sample comes from a normal population. The mean for the sample is 45 minutes, with a standard deviation of 15 minutes. The observed distribution of the sample across the following ranges of values is:

Range of values	Number of cases
less than 16 minutes	3
16–30 minutes	15
31–45 minutes	34
46–60 minutes	31
61–75 minutes	5
over 75 minutes	2

Using an alpha level of 0.05 test the assumption of normality for the population. Enter these data into SPSS and conduct the goodness-of-fit test.

16.5 Five schools are compared in terms of the proportion of students that proceed to university. A sample of 50 students who graduated from each school is taken and the number of those who entered university from each school are:

School	Number entering university
School 1	22
School 2	25
School 3	26
School 4	28
School 5	33

(a) Calculate the expected values and then conduct a chi-square goodness of fit test.

(b) What do you conclude about the prospects of entering university from each of the schools?

(c) Enter these data into SPSS and compare the results with your hand calculations.

16.6 Use the **Employee data** file to assess whether the sample data for the company indicates that its employment structure is 'top heavy'. This can be tested by assessing whether there are proportionately more employees in the Manager category than for similar companies. Assume that official data indicate that for similar firms the proportion of cases in each of the employment categories is Clerical 82 percent, Custodial 8 percent, and Managerial 10 percent.

(a) Calculate the expected number of employees in the sample for each employment category, on the assumption that this firm is no different to all others.

(b) Use these expected frequencies to test this assumption on SPSS.

PART 4

Inferential Statistics: Two or More
Independent Samples

17

The Two-sample *t*-test for the Equality of Means

All the tests covered thus far deal with the one-sample case. That is, they all involve making an inference about only one population: we don't have information about the population, so we infer it from the sample result.

This chapter will introduce hypothesis testing in the two-sample case. In the two-sample case we ideally want to compare two populations in terms of some descriptive statistic such as a mean, binomial percentage, or frequency distribution. However, we do not know the value of these statistics for either population so we take a sample from each population and make inferences from each of these samples.

For example, in Chapter 14 we worked through an example where we were interested in the average amount of TV watched by Australian and British children between the ages of 5 and 12 years. We wanted to compare the population means, but unfortunately we only had the mean for the population of British children. For Australian children, because we did not know the population value, we took a sample of 20 and made an inference based on the data from this sample (Figure 17.1).

What if we do not have information for the population of British kids either? The best we can do is take a random sample of British children as well, and make another inference from this second sample. In such a situation we conduct a **two-sample test of significance**. In this instance we conduct a survey of children from each country. Although in practice we may think in terms of one sample, which is made up of both Australian and British children, conceptually we say that we are working with two samples: one from each of the populations we want to compare. That is, although in the actual mechanics of data collection we have one big collection of children who have been surveyed as part of the same research process, when analyzing the data we treat the two groups of children as separate samples (Figure 17.2).

In fact, we could extend this to a situation in which we want to compare more than two populations. For example, we might be interested in comparing children from more than two countries in terms of their average amount of TV viewing and only have samples from each of these populations. Working with more than two samples requires a different test of significance which we will

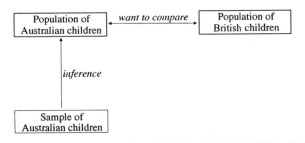

Figure 17.1 Hypothesis testing: the one-sample case

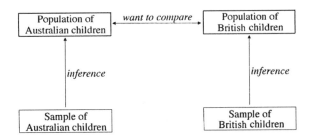

Figure 17.2 Hypothesis testing: the two-sample case

analyze in the following chapter. Generally, the choice of inference test is affected by the number of samples from which an inference is being made. In particular, it is common practice to distinguish between one-sample tests, two-sample tests, and tests for more than two samples. When making inferences from more than two samples we speak of tests for *k*-samples, where *k* is a number greater than two. Often the change involved in moving from the one-sample to the two-sample situation, or to the *k*-sample situation, will not be great, but as an organizing principle it is useful to keep in mind whether the number of samples from which an inference is being made is one, two, or more than two.

Let us look again at the example of comparing Australian and British children in terms of their average amount of TV viewing. In effect, we are collecting data on two variables: country of residence and amount of TV viewing. A child, in other words, can vary from another child in one of two ways. The child can be different in terms of the country he or she lives in, and/or different in terms of the amount of TV he or she watches.

We use one of these variables to sort cases into distinct samples, based on the populations we want to compare. SPSS calls this a **grouping variable**.

The **grouping variable** defines the number of samples from which inferences will be made.

The samples are then compared on the basis of another variable, which SPSS calls a **test variable**. Thus, in our example, children are first grouped according to the variable 'Country of residence', since this defines the populations we are interested in, and the two samples thus formed (Australian and British children) are compared in terms of a test variable, 'Amount of TV watched each night'.

In other words, each case (i,e, each child) is assigned two values. The first 'tags' each case as belonging to a group defined by country of residence. The second value is the amount of TV each child watches, which is the variable on which the groups will be compared.

Dependent and independent variables

We can think of this two-sample problem according to the notions of independent and dependent variables, which we introduced in Chapter 7. Usually the *grouping variable is the independent variable* and the *test variable is the dependent variable*.

A **dependent variable** is explained or affected by an independent variable.

In our example of children, we suspect that country of residence somehow affects or causes the amount of TV a child will watch (due possibly to factors such as the weather or the quality of programming in different countries). It is clear that in this situation we have a case of one-way causality that must run from place of residence to TV watching; it is unimaginable that children's TV viewing habits determine where they live! In other instances, however, the choice of appropriate model may be more contentious, as we discussed in Chapter 7 (it may help readers to return to that discussion before proceeding).

All these considerations involved in organizing data in the two-sample case are summarized in Table 17.1 and Figure 17.3.

Table 17.1

Type of variable	SPSS name	Function in inference test
Independent	Grouping variable	Sorts cases into a number of samples to be compared
Dependent	Test variable	Calculated to describe and compare the samples

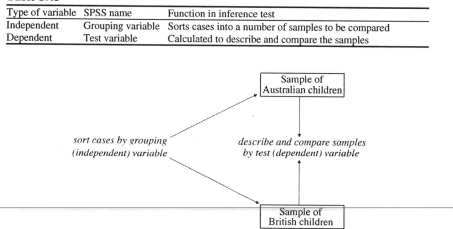

Figure 17.3 Two-sample significance test

The sampling distribution of the difference between two means

As with all other hypothesis tests, we begin by *assuming* that the null hypothesis of no difference is correct. On this assumption we build up a sampling distribution of the difference between two sample means. We then use this sampling distribution to determine the probability of getting an observed difference between two sample means from populations with no difference. Finally, we compare this probability to a critical (alpha) level to decide whether the null hypothesis should be rejected.

For example, let's begin by assuming that the average amount of TV watched by children is the same in both Australia and Britain. This null hypothesis of no difference is formally written as:

$$H_0: \mu_1 = \mu_2$$

or

$$H_0: \mu_1 - \mu_2 = 0$$

If this assumption is true, what will we get if we take repeated samples from each country and calculate the difference in means for each pair of samples? Intuitively, we expect that the most common result will be that the difference is small, if not zero. Since we are assuming no difference between the two populations, we expect the sample means to be equal as well (the three-dot triangle is mathematical shorthand for 'therefore').

$$\overline{X}_1 = \overline{X}_2 \quad \therefore \quad \overline{X}_1 - \overline{X}_2 = 0$$

This is illustrated in Figure 17.4.

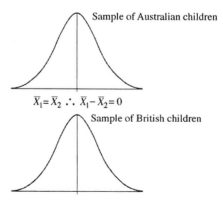

Sample of Australian children

$\overline{X}_1 = \overline{X}_2 \ \therefore \ \overline{X}_1 - \overline{X}_2 = 0$

Sample of British children

Figure 17.4 Two samples with means equal

But this will not always be the result. Occasionally we might draw a sample from Australia that has a lower than average amount of TV viewing coupled with a sample from Britain that has a higher than average amount of TV viewing (Figure 17.5).

$$\overline{X}_1 < \overline{X}_2 \quad \therefore \quad \overline{X}_1 - \overline{X}_2 < 0$$

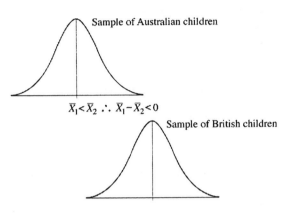

Figure 17.5 Two samples with means unequal

Similarly we might get, through the operation of random chance, the opposite situation:

$$\overline{X}_1 > \overline{X}_2 \quad \therefore \quad \overline{X}_1 - \overline{X}_2 > 0$$

If we take a large number of these repeated random samples and calculate the difference between each pair of sample means, we will end up with a sampling distribution of the difference between two sample means that has the following properties:

- It will be a *t*-distribution:

$$t = \frac{\overline{X}_1 - \overline{X}_2}{\sigma_{\overline{X}-\overline{X}}}$$

- The mean of the difference between sample means will be zero:

$$\mu_{\overline{X}-\overline{X}} = 0$$

- The spread of scores around this mean of zero will be defined by the formula:

$$\sigma_{\overline{X}-\overline{X}} = \sqrt{\frac{(n_1-1)s_1^2 + (n_2-1)s_2^2}{n_1+n_2-2}} \sqrt{\frac{n_1+n_2}{n_1 n_2}}$$

This is called the **pooled variance estimate**. This estimate assumes that the populations have equal variances. Sometimes this assumption cannot be sustained, in which case a **separate variance estimate** is used. As we shall see, SPSS will calculate t using each estimate, plus information that allows us to choose one or the other. But when doing hand calculations this pooled variance estimate is generally used since it is much easier to work with, and will usually lead to the same decision being reached as the separate variance estimate.

The two-sample t-test for the equality of means

We can use these properties of the sampling distribution to conduct a t-test for the equality of means. Assume our survey consists of 20 Australian children and 20 British children, and the research wants to assess whether TV viewing time is affected by country of residence. (Although it is the situation in this example, the two-sample t-test does not require the same number of cases in each sample.)

We will work through this example using the five-step hypothesis testing procedure.

Step 1: State the null and alternative hypotheses
H_0: There is no difference in the average amount of TV watched by children in Australia and Britain.

$$H_0: \mu_1 = \mu_2 \quad \text{or} \quad H_0: \mu_1 - \mu_2 = 0$$

H_a: There is a difference in the average amount of TV watched by children in Australia and Britain.

$$H_a: \mu_1 \neq \mu_2 \quad \text{or} \quad H_a: \mu_1 - \mu_2 \neq 0$$

Step 2: Choose the test of significance
The following two factors are relevant in choosing the test of significance:

1. We are making an inference from two samples: a sample of Australian children and a sample of British children. Therefore we need to use a two-sample test.
2. The two samples are being compared in terms of the average amount of time spent watching TV. This variable is measured at the interval/ratio level. Therefore the relevant descriptive statistic is the mean for each sample.

These factors lead us to choose the two-sample *t*-test for the equality of means as the relevant test of significance.

Step 3: Calculate the sample score(s)
We have the following results that describe the data for each sample (where Australian children are sample 1, and British children are sample 2):

$$\overline{X}_1 = 166 \text{ minutes}$$
$$s_1 = 29$$
$$n_1 = 20$$
$$\overline{X}_2 = 187 \text{ minutes}$$
$$s_2 = 30$$
$$n_2 = 20$$

The equation for calculating the sample *t*-score is:

$$t_{sample} = \frac{\overline{X}_1 - \overline{X}_2}{\sigma_{\overline{X} - \overline{X}}}$$

where:

$$\sigma_{\overline{X} - \overline{X}} = \sqrt{\frac{(n_1 - 1)s_1^2 + (n_2 - 1)s_2^2}{n_1 + n_2 - 2}} \sqrt{\frac{n_1 + n_2}{n_1 n_2}}$$

If we substitute the sample data into these equations we get:

$$\sigma_{\overline{X} - \overline{X}} = \sqrt{\frac{(20 - 1)29^2 + (20 - 1)\,30^2}{20 + 20 - 2}} \sqrt{\frac{20 + 20}{20 \times 20}} = 9.3$$

$$t_{sample} = \frac{166 - 187}{9.3} = -2.3$$

Step 4: Establish the critical score(s) and critical region
Since we have to assume that the sample variances are equal to the (unknown) population variances, we have imposed two restrictions on the data. This means that the number of degrees of freedom is:

$$df = n - 2 = 40 - 2 = 38$$

From the table for the *t*-distribution, with 38 degrees of freedom, at an alpha level of 0.05, and using a two-tail test (based on the alternative hypothesis), the critical values for *t* are as shown in Table 17.2.

Table 17.2 Critical values for *t*-distributions

df	0.10	0.05	0.02	0.01	0.005
	Level of significance for one-tail test				
	Level of significance for two-tail test				
df	0.20	0.10	0.05	0.02	0.01
1	3.078	6.314	12.706	31.821	63.657
2	1.886	2.920	4.303	6.965	9.925
3	1.638	2.353	3.182	4.541	5.841
4	1.533	2.132	2.776	3.747	4.604
5	1.476	2.015	2.571	3.365	4.032
6	1.440	1.943	2.447	3.143	3.707
7	1.415	1.895	2.365	2.998	3.499
8	1.397	1.860	2.306	2.896	3.355
9	1.383	1.833	2.262	2.821	3.250
10	1.372	1.812	2.228	2.764	3.169
11	1.363	1.796	2.201	2.718	3.106
12	1.356	1.782	2.179	2.681	3.055
13	1.350	1.771	2.160	2.650	3.012
14	1.345	1.761	2.145	2.624	2.977
15	1.341	1.753	2.131	2.602	2.947
16	1.340	1.746	2.120	2.583	2.921
17	1.333	1.740	2.110	2.567	2.898
18	1.330	1.734	2.101	2.552	2.878
19	1.328	1.729	2.093	2.539	2.861
20	1.325	1.725	2.086	2.528	2.845
21	1.323	1.721	2.080	2.518	2.831
22	1.321	1.717	2.074	2.508	2.819
23	1.319	1.714	2.069	2.500	2.807
24	1.318	1.711	2.064	2.492	2.797
25	1.316	1.708	2.060	2.485	2.787
26	1.315	1.706	2.056	2.479	2.779
27	1.314	1.703	2.052	2.473	2.771
28	1.313	1.701	2.048	2.467	2.763
29	1.311	1.699	2.045	2.462	2.756
30	1.310	1.697	2.042	2.457	2.750
35	1.306	1.690	2.030	2.438	2.724
40	1.303	1.684	2.021	2.423	2.704
45	1.301	1.679	2.014	2.412	2.690
50	1.299	1.676	2.009	2.403	2.678
55	1.297	1.673	2.004	2.396	2.668
60	1.296	1.671	2.000	2.390	2.660
70	1.294	1.667	1.994	2.381	2.648
80	1.292	1.664	1.990	2.374	2.639
90	1.291	1.662	1.987	2.368	2.632
120	1.289	1.658	1.980	2.358	2.617
∞	1.282	1.645	1.960	2.326	2.576

The table does not have a row of probabilities for 38 degrees of freedom. In such a situation, we refer to the row for the nearest reported number of degrees of freedom *below* the desired number, which in this instance is 35.

$$t_{critical} = \pm\,2.030\;(\alpha = 0.05,\, df = 35)$$

Step 5: Make a decision

Since the sample score falls within the critical region we reject the null hypothesis (Figure 17.6).

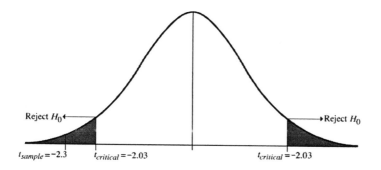

Reject H_0 ←   → Reject H_0

$t_{sample} = -2.3$ $t_{critical} = -2.03$ $t_{critical} = -2.03$

Figure 17.6 Critical and sample *t*-scores

We cannot say that Australian children watch on average the same amount of TV each night as British children.

The two-sample *t*-test using SPSS

We can now work through this example using SPSS. SPSS calls this test the independent samples *t*-test. The word 'independent' is very important because it raises both conceptual issues for hypothesis testing and practical issues for SPSS coding. We will define independent samples in Chapter 21, when we can compare them with dependent samples, since their basic character is most evident when compared with dependent samples.

In SPSS the data for the children have been coded for the two variables. Each of these variables occupies a separate column, so that we have a column of numbers for the amount of TV watched and a column of numbers indicating the country in which each child lives. All independent-samples tests have data entered in the same way: *one column for the test variable and one column for the grouping variable.*

The data for this example also contain information for hypothetical samples of children from Canada and Singapore that will be used in the next chapter where we consider the *k*-independent samples situation. The value labels for each country are:

1 = Singapore
2 = Australia
3 = Britain
4 = Canada

Thus in this example we want to compare values **2** (Australia) and **3** (Britain) for **Country of residence** (Table 17.3 and Figure 17.7).

Table 17.3 Independent-samples *t*-test using SPSS (file: **Ch17.sav**)

SPSS command/action	Comments
1 From the menu select **Analyze/Compare Means/Independent-Samples T Test**	This brings up the **Independent-Samples T Test** dialog box
2 Click on **Minutes of TV watched** in the source list	This highlights **Minutes of TV watched**
3 Click on the ▶ that points to the **Test Variable(s):** list	This pastes **Minutes of TV watched** into the **Test Variable(s):** list
4 Click on **Country of residence** in the source list	This highlights **Country of residence**
5 Click on the ▶ that points to the **Grouping Variable:** list	This pastes **Country of residence** into the **Grouping Variable:** list. Notice that in this list the variable appears as **country(? ?)**
6 Click on **Define Groups**	This brings up the **Define Groups** box
7 In the area next to **Group 1:** type **2**, and in the area next to **Group 2:** type **3**	This identifies the two groups to be compared, which are **Australia** and **Britain**.
8 Click on **Continue**	
9 Click on **OK**	

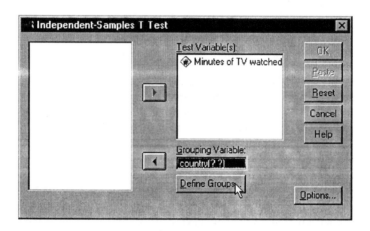

Figure 17.7(a) The **Independent-Samples T Test** dialog box

Figure 17.7(b) The **Define Groups** dialog box

Figure 17.8 presents the output generated by this command.

T-Test

Group Statistics

	Country of residence	N	Mean	Std. Deviation	Std. Error Mean
Minutes of TV Watched per night	australia	20	165.85	29.29	6.55
	britain	20	186.75	29.56	6.61

Independent Samples Test

		Levene's Test for Equality of Variances		t-test for Equality of Means						
									95% Confidence Interval of the Difference	
		F	Sig	t	df	Sig. (2-tailed)	Mean Difference	Std. Error Difference	Lower	Upper
Minutes of TV watched per night	Equal variances assumed	.025	.876	-2.246	38	.031	-20.90	9.31	-39.74	-2.06
	Equal variances not assumed			-2.246	37.997	.031	-20.90	9.31	-39.74	-2.06

Figure 17.8 SPSS T-Test output

The first table headed **Group Statistics** provides the descriptive statistics: the number of cases, the mean, and the standard deviation for each group.

The following table headed **Independent Samples Test** provides the inferential statistics. This table provides information for two different *t*-tests: one where the variances of the population are assumed to be equal and one where the population variances are not assumed to be equal. In calculating the *t*-score in the example above, we assumed that the variances of the two populations being compared were equal. In practical terms this means using the pooled variance estimate in the calculations. However, this may not always be a valid assumption. The validity of this assumption is tested in the columns headed **Levene's Test for Equality of Variances**. The value for **F** is the ratio of the two sample variances, and if this ratio is not equal to 1, it may reflect an underlying difference in the population variances. If the significance for this *F*-value (in the Sig. column) is less than 0.05 we conclude that the difference in variances observed in the samples reflects a difference in the variances of the populations from which the samples came. In such a situation we refer to the *t*-score in the first row of the table. In short, we therefore use the following rule:

- read across the first row labeled Equal variances assumed,

and

- if we find that the value under Sig. is less than 0.05 we continue along that line to assess whether the means are significantly different;

or

- if we find that the value under Sig. is greater than 0.05 we refer to the *t*-test in the next row labeled Equal variances not assumed.

Usually the two estimates will agree with each other in terms of whether to reject or not reject the null (as is the case here), but in strict terms, we should use the relevant estimate, either that for Equal or Unequal variances. Here the first row is the relevant one. Moving across the columns we see that the sample *t*-value is -2.246, which, with 38 degrees of freedom, has a two-tail significance of .031. These values all correspond to the values we generated by hand (with some slight differences due to rounding in the hand calculations). Since the sample probability of .031 is less than the alpha level of 0.05, we reject the null hypothesis of no difference.

We also have a column headed **Mean Difference**. This is the difference between the two sample means, -20.9, which in the equation used to calculate *t*-scores is represented by $\overline{X}_1 - \overline{X}_2$.

You will also notice that SPSS has generated a 95 percent confidence interval for the difference in sample means, which is printed as (−39.74, −2.06). This allows us to conduct the same inference test, but using the estimation procedures developed in Chapter 12. This confidence interval indicates that at a 95 percent level of confidence, the difference between the population means lies somewhere between −39.74 minutes and −2.06 minutes. Since this interval does not include the value of 0, we reject the hypothesis that the population means are equal.

One-tail and two-tail tests

In the above example we had no reason to suspect that either population watched more TV than the other, as reflected in the alternative hypothesis, which was simply a statement of difference:

$$H_a: \mu_1 \neq \mu_2$$

Given this formulation of the alternative hypothesis, a two-tail test is used. However, we might argue that because of the warmer weather Australian children might be less inclined to watch as much TV as children in Britain. Here we suspect not only a difference, but also a direction of difference. In this situation the alternative hypothesis will be:

$$H_a: \mu_1 < \mu_2$$

where μ_1 is the mean for the population of Australian children and μ_2 is the mean for the population of British children.

This form of the alternative hypothesis directs us to use a one-tail test. The SPSS output provides the two-tail significance as the default setting. To convert this into a one-tail significance we simply divide the two-tail probability in half. The area under the curve beyond a *t*-score of ±2.25 is 0.031 of the total area under the *t*-distribution. If two tails take up this amount of area, then one tail will take up half this amount:

$$\text{one-tail significance} = \text{two-tail} \div 2 = 0.031 \div 2$$

$$= 0.0155$$

Example

A study is conducted to investigate whether foreign-owned companies on average have a lower rate of conformity to local health and safety codes when compared with locally owned companies. A survey of 50 foreign-owned and 50 domestic companies of similar size and in similar industries is conducted. Inspectors record the number of breaches of health and safety regulations they observe when inspecting these establishments.

Step 1: State the null and alternative hypotheses
H_0: There is no difference in the average number of breaches between locally owned and foreign-owned firms.

$$H_0: \mu_1 = \mu_2 \quad \text{or} \quad H_0: \mu_1 - \mu_2 = 0$$

H_a: Foreign-owned firms have a higher average number of breaches than locally owned firms:

$$H_a: \mu_1 > \mu_2 \quad \text{or} \quad H_a: \mu_1 - \mu_2 > 0$$

Step 2: Choose the test of significance
We are making an inference from two samples. The two samples are being compared in terms of the average number of breaches of the health and safety code, measured at the interval/ratio level. Therefore the relevant descriptive statistic is the mean of each sample. We therefore use the two-sample t-test for the equality of means as the relevant test of significance.

Step 3: Calculate the sample score(s)
On average the 50 foreign firms are found to make 4.2 breaches per firm:

$$n_1 = 50$$
$$s_1 = 1.3$$
$$\overline{X}_1 = 4.2$$

The domestic firms are found to make 3.5 breaches per firm:

$$n_2 = 5$$
$$s_2 = 1.2$$
$$\overline{X}_2 = 3.5$$

We need first to calculate the standard error (assuming equal variances), and from this the sample t-score:

$$\sigma_{\overline{X}-\overline{X}} = \sqrt{\frac{(n_1-1)s_1^2+(n_2-1)s_2^2}{n_1+n_2-2}}\sqrt{\frac{n_1+n_2}{n_1 n_2}}$$

$$= \sqrt{\frac{(50-1)1.3^2+(50-1)1.2^2}{50+50-2}}\sqrt{\frac{50+50}{50\times50}}$$

$$= 0.25$$

$$t_{sample} = \frac{\overline{X}_1-\overline{X}_2}{\sigma_{\overline{X}-\overline{X}}} = \frac{4.2-3.5}{0.25}$$

$$= 2.8$$

Step 4: Establish the critical score(s) and critical region

With a combined sample size of 100 we have 98 degrees of freedom. Based on the way the alternative hypothesis is stated we use a one-tail (right-tail) test.

From the table for critical values for t-distributions (Table 17.2), with 98 degrees of freedom, at an alpha level of 0.05, and using a one-tail test, the critical value is +1.662. (Since the table does not have a row of probabilities for 98 degrees of freedom, we refer to the row for the nearest reported number of degrees of freedom below the desired number, which is 90.)

Step 5: Make a decision

We can see that the sample t-score is further from zero than the critical score (Figure 17.9). In other words, it falls in the region of rejection.

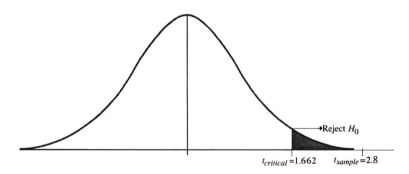

Figure 17.9 Critical and sample t-scores

We reject the null hypothesis of no difference. The results suggest that foreign firms are more inclined to breach local health and safety codes.

Exercises

17.1   What assumptions need to be made about the distribution of the populations before an independent-samples *t*-test is conducted?

17.2   For the following sets of results, test for a significant difference using a two-tail test and $\alpha = 0.05$ (assuming equal population variance):

		Mean	Standard deviation	Sample size
(a)	Sample 1	72	14.2	35
	Sample 2	76.1	11	50
(b)	Sample 1	2.4	0.9	100
	Sample 2	2.8	0.9	100
(c)	Sample 1	72	14.2	35
	Sample 2	76.1	11	50
(d)	Sample 1	450	80	120
	Sample 2	475	77	100

17.3   A researcher is interested in the effect that place of residency has on the age at which people begin to smoke cigarettes. The researcher divides a random sample of people into 91 rural and 107 urban residents and finds that rural dwellers started smoking at an average age of 15.75 years, with a standard deviation of 2.3 years, whereas the urban dwellers began to smoke at a mean age of 14.63 years, with a standard deviation of 4.1 years. Is there a significant difference (using the pooled variance estimate)?

17.4   A water utility wishes to assess the effectiveness of an advertising campaign to reduce water consumption. Before the campaign the utility randomly selects 100 households throughout a region and records water usage for a morning shower as averaging 87 liters, with a standard deviation of 15 liters. It then randomly selects another 100 households after the campaign. These households average 74 liters per shower, with a standard deviation of 14 liters. Is there a significant difference? What conclusions can the utility make about the advertising campaign? Should the test be a one-tail or two-tail test? What factors need to be considered when selecting the appropriate test?

17.5   A new form of organic pest control is developed for crop growing. Fifty plots of grain are sprayed with traditional pesticide, whereas 50 are sprayed with the new pest control. The output, in tonnes, of each set of plots, is recorded as follows:

	Old pesticide	Organic pesticide
Mean	1.4	2.20
Standard deviation	0.3	0.35

Since the organic pesticide is much more expensive, farmers want to be convinced that any improvement in yield is not due to chance. They therefore set an alpha level of 0.01. Conduct a *t*-test to assess the effectiveness of the new method. Should the test be a one-tail or two-tail test?

17.6 A study is conducted to investigate the political awareness of children in public (state-funded) and private schools. Twenty-four students from a private school and 20 students from a nearby public school are randomly selected, and asked a series of questions relating to the political system. The mean score for private school students is 46 and for public school students the mean score is 64. Both samples have a standard deviation of 18.5. Conduct an independent-samples *t*-test for the equality of means to confirm your decisions as to whether the two school systems are significantly different.

17.7 Use the **Employee data** file to determine whether there is a significant difference between the mean current salaries for employees based on minority classification.

18

The *F*-test for the Equality of More Than Two Means: Analysis of Variance

Hypothesis testing with more than two samples: the general idea

In Chapter 17 we considered the *t*-test for two independent samples, and tested the assumption that the samples came from populations with the same mean:

$$H_0: \mu_1 = \mu_2$$

We worked through an example where we had a sample of 20 children from Australia and 20 from Britain. Each child was asked how much TV, in minutes, they watched per night. We compared the samples in order to test the null hypothesis that there was no difference in the average amount of TV watched between children from the two countries (Figure 18.1).

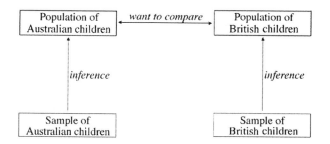

Figure 18.1 Hypothesis testing: the two-sample case

We call this a two-sample problem because we are using two samples to make inferences about each population. However, sometimes the problem we are addressing is slightly wider. Instead of just comparing two countries, we might be interested in comparing the average amount of TV watched by children in several countries. For example, we may have samples of 20 children from

Australia, Britain, Canada, and Singapore, and want to see if the means for all these four populations are equal:

$$H_0: \mu_1 = \mu_2 = \mu_3 = \mu_4$$

This is called the problem of k independent samples, where k is any number greater than two. Here k is four, and this example can be illustrated as in Figure 18.2.

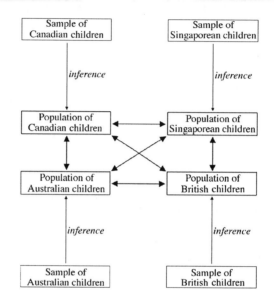

Figure 18.2 Hypothesis testing for more than two samples

One way to do this is simply to test all the possible two-sample combinations. With four samples the maximum number of combinations is six, illustrated in Figure 18.2 by the number of arrows running from each population to the others:

Australia by Singapore
Australia by Canada
Australia by Britain
Singapore by Canada
Singapore by Britain
Canada by Britain

Thus we can undertake six separate *t*-tests and assess whether there are any significant differences. When we are working with more than two samples, however, we can test for the equality of means all at once using the analysis of variance *F*-test (ANOVA). The reason why a single ANOVA is preferable to multiple *t*-tests is that the risk of making a type I error for the series of *t*-tests will be greater than the stated alpha level for each *t*-test. Thus if the alpha level for each individual *t*-test is 0.05, the chance of making a type I error for all the *t*-tests that can be conducted for a given number of samples will be greater than 0.05. The ANOVA test, on the other hand, has a stated alpha level equal to the risk of making a type I error.

The ANOVA procedure tests the null hypothesis that the samples come from populations whose means are equal. If the null hypothesis is true, samples drawn from such populations will have means roughly equal in value. In the example of children and TV time, the samples will all have roughly similar averages. Of course, we do not expect the sample means to be equal, even if the population means are the same, since random variation will affect the sampling process. The question we are addressing is whether the differences between the samples are consistent with the assumption of equality between the populations.

Consider the hypothetical sample results for our four groups of children shown in Table 18.1.

Table 18.1 Average amount of TV viewed per night, in minutes

TV watched per night	Country			
	Canada	Australia	Britain	Singapore
Mean	127	166	187	203
Standard deviation	27	29	30	26

We can see that there is a good deal of variation *between* the means of the four samples. In fact if we compare the highest with the lowest values, which are the means for Canada and Singapore, we can see a very large difference in average amounts of TV watched. Notice also the row for the standard deviation for each sample. We can see that *within* the sample for each country the results are clustered together, as indicated by the small standard deviations relative to the means. In other words, there are distinct differences from country to country, but similarity within each country. On the face of these descriptive statistics we might begin to question the hypothesis that the populations from which these samples came have the same mean.

This logic is exactly the same as that used by ANOVA. It compares the amount of variation between the samples with the amount of variation within each sample – hence the name 'analysis of variance'. Thus, although we are interested in the difference between the means, ANOVA actually works with the variance, which is the square of the standard deviation.

Before working through an ANOVA for our hypothetical survey of children from four countries, we will illustrate the logic behind the test. Consider the two hypothetical sets of distributions in Figure 18.3.

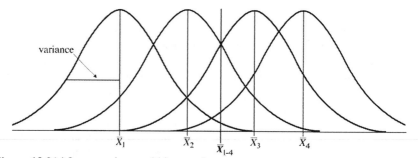

Figure 18.3(a) Large variance within samples

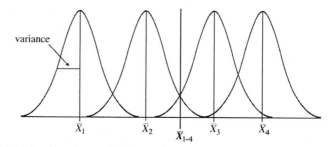

Figure 18.3(b) Small variance within samples

Four samples are randomly selected and the mean for each is calculated, together with the overall mean when the cases for all four samples are pooled together ($\overline{X}_{1-4}$). In both (a) and (b) we can see that the means are not equal: there is some variance between the sample means. We can also see that while the sample means are the same in the two sets of distributions, there is also an important and obvious difference. In (a) the spread of cases *within* each sample around the sample mean is quite wide, whereas in (b) the variance within each sample is relatively small. Each sample in (b) seems distinct from the others, whereas in (a) there is considerable overlap in the distributions, so that the samples seem to blend into each other. We would be more inclined to consider the second set of samples (b) to come from populations that are different from each other, whereas the first set (a) can be more easily explained as coming from identical populations, with random variation causing the *samples* to differ slightly from each other.

We can capture this difference by calculating two numbers and expressing one as a ratio of the other. The first number is the amount of variance *between* the sample means and the grand total mean. Consider the two sets of sample means shown in Figure 18.4. We can see in Figure 18.4 that in (a) the variance of the sample means around the overall mean (when the samples are pooled together) is small relative to the second situation. Thus the samples in (a) are less likely to form distinct clusters of cases that reflect underlying differences between the populations.

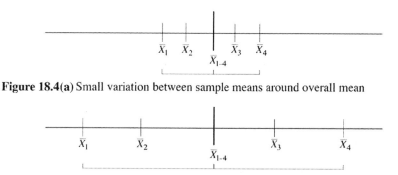

Figure 18.4(a) Small variation between sample means around overall mean

Figure 18.4(b) Large variation between sample means around overall mean

We cannot jump, however, to this conclusion about the populations just on the basis of the variance between sample means. As we saw in Figure 18.3, the variances within each sample in (a) might be very small, so that each sample forms a distinct 'spike' around each sample mean. The variances within each sample in (b), on the other hand, might be very wide so that the samples still blur into each other, despite the differences between the means. To capture these aspects of the distributions, we need to calculate a second number, which measures this variance within each sample around each sample mean. The extent to which samples will form these distinct spikes around their respective means will be expressed by the ratio of the **variance between samples** to the **variance within samples**.

The one-way analysis of variance *F*-test

We can now use these general concepts to determine whether there is a significant difference between children in different countries in terms of the average amount of TV they watch. To calculate the relevant test statistic we need to formalize some of these basic concepts. The first is the total amount of variation for the scores of all 80 cases sampled. This is measured by a concept called the **total sum of squares (TSS)**. This is calculated using the formula:

$$TSS = \Sigma\left(X_i - \bar{X}\right)^2$$

The value for the TSS can be divided into two components. The first is the amount of variation within each sample, called the **sum of squares within (SSW)**. The second is the amount of variation between each sample, called the **sum of squares between (SSB)**:

$$TSS = SSB + SSW$$

Each of these components of the TSS can be calculated in the following way:

$$SSW = \Sigma\left(X_i - \overline{X}_s\right)^2$$

$$SSB = \Sigma n_s\left(\overline{X}_s - \overline{X}\right)^2$$

where:
$\overline{X}_s$ is the mean for a given sample
n_s is the number of cases in a given sample.

These formulas should remind the reader of the formula for the standard deviation, since they embody the same principle that variance relates to the amount of difference between individual scores and the mean. As with the formula for the standard deviation, these definitional formulas can be difficult to work with. In particular, to calculate the TSS, it is easier to work with the formula:

$$TSS = \Sigma X_i^2 - n\overline{X}^2$$

Once we have TSS, we only need to calculate either SSW or SSB, and then use the formula *TSS = SSB + SSW* to calculate the other. In other words, if we calculate TSS and SSB, we substitute these into the following equation to arrive at SSW:

$$SSW = TSS - SSB$$

To see how this is done we will work through our example with the four samples of 20 children. These calculations are best done by constructing a listed data table (Table 18.2). The score for each case is listed, with the samples placed in separate columns. From this information we can calculate the mean for each sample, and the mean for all the samples combined:

$$\overline{X}_{canada} = \frac{2546}{20} = 127.3 \text{ minutes}$$

$$\overline{X}_{australia} = \frac{3317}{20} = 165.85 \text{ minutes}$$

$$\overline{X}_{britain} = \frac{3735}{20} = 186.75 \text{ minutes}$$

$$\overline{X}_{singapore} = \frac{4063}{20} = 203.15 \text{ minutes}$$

Table 18.2 Calculations for ANOVA

Canada		Australia		Britain		Singapore	
X_i	X_i^2	X_i	X_i^2	X_i	X_i^2	X_i	X_i^2
89	7921	102	10,404	124	15,376	156	24,336
92	8464	120	14,400	135	18,225	165	27,225
95	9025	132	17,424	156	24,336	174	30,276
105	11,025	134	17,956	165	27,225	179	32,041
106	11,236	145	21,025	167	27,889	180	32,400
108	11,664	149	22,201	172	29,584	184	33,856
110	12,100	156	24,336	178	31,684	189	35,721
113	12,769	162	26,244	182	33,124	189	35,721
116	13,456	165	27,225	184	33,856	196	38,416
125	15,625	165	27,225	185	34,225	203	41,209
128	16,384	165	27,225	186	34,596	204	41,616
135	18,225	174	30,276	187	34,969	207	42,849
138	19,044	179	32,041	189	35,721	210	44,100
139	19,321	180	32,400	198	39,204	218	47,524
140	19,600	187	34,969	209	43,681	221	48,841
146	21,316	189	35,721	212	44,944	228	51,984
146	21,316	196	38,416	218	47,524	231	53,361
154	23,716	201	40,401	223	49,729	238	56,644
167	27,889	206	42,436	225	50,625	241	58,081
194	37,636	210	44,100	240	57,600	250	62,500
$\Sigma X_i = 2546$		$\Sigma X_i = 3317$		$\Sigma X_i = 3735$		$\Sigma X_i = 4063$	
$\Sigma X_i^2 = 337,732$		$\Sigma X_i^2 = 566,425$		$\Sigma X_i^2 = 714,117$		$\Sigma X_i^2 = 838,701$	

$$\overline{X} = \frac{(2546 + 3317 + 3735 + 4063)}{80} = 170.8 \text{ minutes}$$

Using this information we can calculate the TSS and SSB:

$$TSS = \Sigma X_i^2 - n\overline{X}^2$$

$$= (337,732 + 566,425 + 714,117 + 838,701) - 80(170.8)^2$$

$$= 124,189$$

$$SSB = \Sigma n_s \left(\overline{X}_s - \overline{X} \right)^2$$

$$= 20(127.3 - 170.8)^2 + 20(165.85 - 170.8)^2 + 20(186.75 - 170.8)^2 +$$
$$20(203.15 - 170.8)^2$$

$$= 64,353$$

$$SSW = TSS - SSB = 124,189 - 64,353$$

$$= 59,836$$

The actual test statistic we use to determine whether the between-samples variance is significantly different from the within-samples estimate is called the *F*-ratio. We have actually encountered this test statistic before when analyzing SPSS output for a two-sample *t*-test. Just as in that case, the *F*-ratio tests for a difference between variances. The *F*-ratio is a ratio of the two variances, the SSB and SSW, each corrected for the appropriate degrees of freedom:

$$F_{sample} = \frac{\frac{SSB}{k - 1}}{\frac{SSW}{n - k}}$$

where:
k is the number of samples.

Substituting the relevant numbers into this equation we get:

$$F_{sample} = \frac{\frac{SSB}{k - 1}}{\frac{SSW}{n - k}} = \frac{\frac{64,353}{4 - 1}}{\frac{59,836}{80 - 4}}$$

$$= 27.25$$

As with the other test statistics we have come across, namely *z*-scores, *t*-scores, and chi-square, we need to compare this sample value with a critical value in order to decide whether to reject or not reject the null hypothesis. To find the critical value we refer to the table for the distribution of *F* (Table A3). To determine a critical value for *F* from Table A3 we have to take into account the following three factors:

The degrees of freedom for the estimate of the variance between samples This is the number of samples minus one, and appears in the numerator of the *F*-ratio:

$$dfb = k - 1$$

The degrees of freedom for the estimate of the variance within the samples This is the total number of cases minus the number of samples, and appears in the denominator of the *F*-ratio:

$$dfw = n - k$$

The alpha level The number of degrees of freedom for both the within and between estimates change from research problem to research problem. The alpha level on the other hand is usually set at 0.05. Table A3 (and that in most textbooks) therefore provides the *F*-scores for various degrees of freedom at the given probability level of 0.05. We would need a different table if the alpha level were not equal to 0.05.

In this example, we will use an alpha level of 0.05. We have four samples and a total of 80 cases, so that the relevant numbers of degrees of freedom are:

$$dfb = k - 1 = 4 - 1$$

$$= 3$$

$$dfw = n - k = 80 - 4$$

$$= 76$$

A 'cut-down' version of the table is reproduced in Table 18.3 to show how we determine critical scores of *F*.

Table 18.3 Critical values for *F*-distributions ($\alpha = 0.05$)

| $n - k$ | \multicolumn{10}{c}{Degrees of freedom for estimates of variance between samples $k - 1$} |
	1	2	3	4	5	6	7	8	9	∞
1	161.4	199.5	215.7	224.6	230.2	234.0	236.8	238.9	240.5	254.3
2	18.51	19.00	19.16	19.25	19.30	19.33	19.35	19.37	19.38	19.50
3	10.13	9.55	9.28	9.12	9.01	8.94	8.89	8.84	8.81	8.53
4	7.71	6.94	6.59	6.39	6.26	6.16	6.09	6.04	6.00	5.63
5	6.61	5.79	5.41	5.19	5.05	4.95	4.88	4.82	4.77	4.36
⋮	⋮	⋮	⋮	⋮	⋮	⋮	⋮	⋮	⋮	⋮
40	4.08	3.23	2.84	2.61	2.45	2.34	2.25	2.18	2.12	1.51
50	4.03	3.18	2.79	2.56	2.38	2.29	2.20	2.13	2.07	1.44
60	4.00	3.15	2.76	2.52	2.37	2.25	2.17	2.10	2.04	1.39
80	3.96	3.11	2.72	2.48	2.33	2.21	2.12	1.99	1.91	1.32
100	3.94	3.09	2.70	2.46	2.30	2.19	2.10	2.03	1.97	1.28
120	3.92	3.07	2.68	2.45	2.29	2.17	2.09	2.02	1.96	1.25
∞	3.84	2.99	2.60	2.37	2.21	2.09	2.01	1.94	1.88	1.00

Notice that Table 18.3 does not have a line for the degrees of freedom within equal to 76. In fact, whole ranges of values are skipped after the first 30. This is because the critical scores do not decrease very much for incremental increases in the degrees of freedom after 30. Where we have degrees of freedom that do not appear in the table, we refer to the closest value that appears in the table *below* the desired number. Here the closest value below 76 that appears in the table is 60. Thus the critical value for *F* in this instance is 2.52. We reject the null hypothesis of no difference if the sample value for F is greater than the critical value:

$$\text{reject null if } F_{sample} > F_{critical}$$

Here $F_{sample} = 27.25$, and $F_{critical} = 2.52$. We therefore reject the null hypothesis. At least one of the populations of children is different from the others.

Notice the particular wording of the conclusion: *at least* one population differs from the rest. The F-test itself does not tell us which of the populations, and how many, differ. Obviously, if there are differences, then at the very least these must include the groups with the highest and the lowest sample averages, in this instance Canada and Singapore. But whether any other possible combinations are significantly different cannot be answered by the F-test.

To determine which samples are significantly different, after having performed an F-test and rejected the null, we turn to a set of techniques called *post hoc* comparisons. Unfortunately, there is little agreement within the literature as to which comparison to use. When in doubt, the most conservative test should be used; namely, the one that is the least likely to find a significant difference and this usually is the **Scheffe** *post hoc* comparison, which we will use in the course of explaining the SPSS ANOVA procedure.

ANOVA using SPSS

The data from the previous example have been entered into SPSS. We have two columns, one for the variable indicating how much TV each child watches, and another indicating their country of residence. To conduct an ANOVA we work through the procedures in Table 18.4 and Figure 18.5. Figure 18.6 presents the results of this set of commands.

Table 18.4 One-Way ANOVA on SPSS (file: **Ch18.sav**)

SPSS command/action	Comments
1 From the menu select **Analyze/Compare Means/ One-Way ANOVA**	This brings up the **One-Way ANOVA** dialog box
2 Click on **Minutes of TV watched** in the source variable list	This highlights **Minutes of TV watched**
3 Click on ▶ pointing to the box below **Dependent List:**	This pastes **Minutes of TV watched** in the dependent variable target list, which is the variable used to compare the samples
4 Click on **Country of residence** in the source list	This highlights **Country of residence**
5 Click on ▶ pointing to the box below **Factor:**	This pastes **Country of residence** in the **Factor** variable target list, which will form the samples to be compared
6 Click on OK	

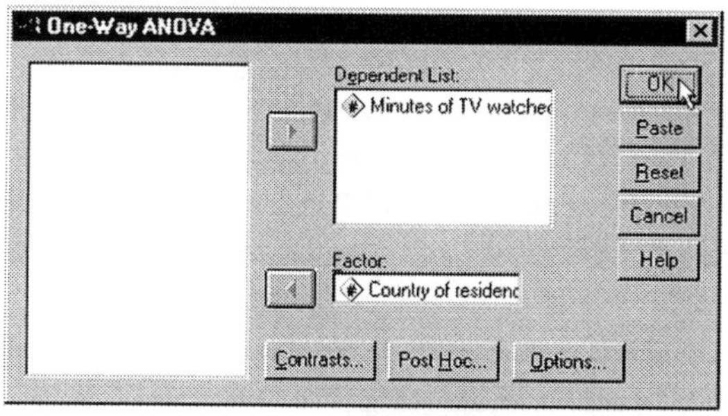

Figure 18.5 The ANOVA dialog box

Oneway

ANOVA

Minutes of TV watched per night

	Sum of Squares	df	Mean Square	F	Sig.
Between Groups	64353.438	3	21451.146	27.246	.000
Within Groups	59835.050	76	787.303		
Total	124188.488	79			

Figure 18.6 SPSS ANOVA output

Looking at the SPSS output we can see the results we calculated by hand. The sum of squares between, the sum of squares within, and the total sum of squares are in the first column of the **ANOVA** table, together with the relevant degrees of freedom in the third column. From these, the *F*-ratio is **27.246**, which is the same as that calculated above (allowing for rounding). The probability is printed as .000. This does not mean that the probability of obtaining an *F*-ratio of 27.25 is zero. SPSS rounds off the probability to 3 decimal places, so that this result is read as 'less than 5 in 10,000'.

We must stop at this point and be clear about what this *F*-test ANOVA has determined. The null hypothesis is that the samples come from populations with the same mean:

$$H_0: \mu_1 = \mu_2 = \mu_3 = \dots = \mu_k$$

As noted in the earlier discussion, by rejecting the null hypothesis after conducting an *F*-test, we have decided that *at least one of these populations has a mean that is not equal to the others*. However, the *F*-test itself does not tell us which of these populations is different.

Thus when conducting an *F*-test we normally ask for some follow-up information to be provided, so that if we do discover a statistically significant difference, we can determine which of the populations differ(s) from the others. These are called *post hoc* comparisons, which are available as an option in the **One-Way ANOVA** dialog box by clicking on the **Post Hoc** button. This will bring up the **One-Way ANOVA Post Hoc Multiple Comparisons** dialog box (Figure 18.7), which provides us with a range of options for comparing the samples so that we can determine exactly which ones come from populations different from the others.

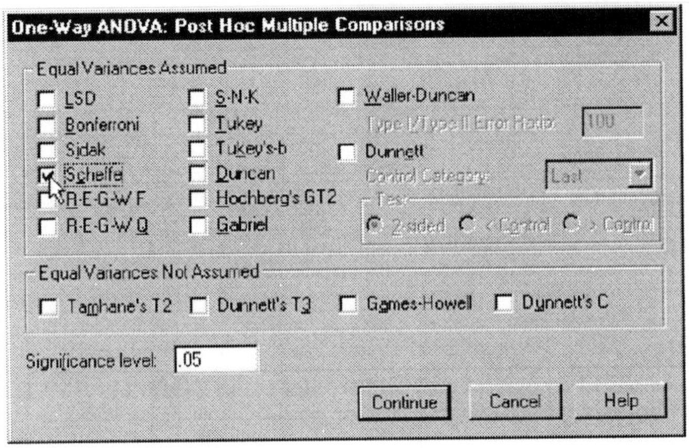

Figure 18.7 The **Post Hoc Multiple Comparisons** dialog box

We will not explore the subtle differences between the choices; in most situations they will all lead to the same conclusions. The most commonly used is the Scheffe test, so by clicking on the box next to it, the output in Figure 18.8 will be generated along with the ANOVA output we generated in Figure 18.6.

This table provides a comparison of means for each country of residence against each other country of residence. The first rows compare Singapore with each of Australia, Britain, and Canada. The second set of rows compare the mean amount of TV watched by the Australian sample with each of the other three countries, and so on. Notice that this results in the same comparison being repeated. For example, in the first set of rows we see that the difference between the means when comparing Singapore with Australia is 37.3 minutes, and in the second set of rows when comparing Australia with Singapore the mean difference is –37.3 minutes, since this is effectively the same comparison looked at the other way.

The important aspect to this table is the * next to some of the mean differences. This indicates a significant difference (at the SPSS default significance level of 0.05) between the means of the two samples being compared. This is verified in the last column which provides the exact significance for the difference between any two means. Where this is less than 0.05 there is also an * next to the value in the Mean Difference column.

Multiple Comparisons

Dependent Variable: Minutes of TV Watched per Night
Scheffe

(I) Country of Residence	(J) Country of Residence	Mean Difference (I-J)	Std. Error	Sig.	95% Confidence Interval Lower Bound	Upper Bound
singapore	australia	37.30*	8.873	.001	11.93	62.67
	britain	16.40	8.873	.339	-8.97	41.77
	canada	75.85*	8.873	.000	50.48	101.22
australia	singapore	-37.30*	8.873	.001	-62.67	-11.93
	britain	-20.90	8.873	.145	-46.27	4.47
	canada	38.55*	8.873	.001	13.18	63.92
britain	singapore	-16.40	8.873	.339	-41.77	8.97
	australia	20.90	8.873	.145	-4.47	46.27
	canada	59.45*	8.873	.000	34.08	84.82
canada	singapore	-75.85*	8.873	.000	-101.22	-50.48
	australia	-38.55*	8.873	.001	-63.92	-13.18
	britain	-59.45*	8.873	.000	-84.82	-34.08

*. The mean difference is significant at the .05 level.

Homogeneous Subsets

Minutes of TV Watched per Night

Scheffe[a]

Country of Residence	N	Subset for alpha = .05 1	2	3
canada	20	127.30		
australia	20		165.85	
britain	20		186.75	186.75
singapore	20			203.15
Sig.		1.000	.145	.339

Means for groups in homogeneous subsets are displayed.
a. Uses Harmonic Mean Sample Size = 20.000.

Figure 18.8 SPSS **Post Hoc Multiple Comparisons** output

Collecting these * together we can see that a significant difference exists between the means for each of the following pairwise comparisons:

Singapore by Australia
Singapore by Canada
Australia by Canada
Britain by Canada

In other words, for each of these pairwise combinations, we can reject the hypothesis that the mean amounts of TV watched per night by children are the same.

Example

Three children are compared in terms of their reading abilities. Each child is asked to complete 12 reading tasks, and the number of mistakes made during each reading task is recorded (Table 18.5).

Table 18.5 Number of mistakes per child

Task number	Alexandra	Katherine	Evelyn
1	8	15	12
2	6	9	6
3	14	20	8
4	9	15	9
5	14	6	10
6	8	9	14
7	12	17	16
8	19	12	5
9	6	6	18
10	11	13	21
11	8	13	15
12	15	5	11

Can we say that these children differ in their readings abilities?

Step 1: State the null and alternative hypotheses
H_0: The average number of mistakes made by each child are equal.

$$H_0: \mu_1 = \mu_2 = \mu_3$$

H_a: The average number of mistakes made by each child are not all equal.

$$H_a: \mu_1 \neq \mu_2 \neq \mu_3$$

Step 2: Choose the test of significance
The research question is interested in the average number of mistakes, which are measured at the interval/ratio level. Therefore we will be comparing means to see if they are equal. We also have three samples, so we are comparing means across more than two samples. The appropriate test is therefore the ANOVA F-test for the equality of means.

Step 3: Calculate the sample score
In conducting an ANOVA it is helpful to set up a listed data table with the relevant calculations (Table 18.6). From this information we calculate the mean for each sample, and the mean for all the samples combined.

$$\overline{X}_{alexandra} = \frac{130}{12} = 10.8$$

$$\overline{X}_{katherine} = \frac{140}{12} = 11.7$$

$$\overline{X}_{evelyn} = \frac{145}{12} = 12.1$$

Table 18.6 Calculations for ANOVA

Alexandra		Katherine		Evelyn	
X_i	X_i^2	X_i	X_i^2	X_i	X_i^2
8	64	15	225	12	144
6	36	9	81	6	36
14	196	20	400	8	64
9	81	15	225	9	81
14	196	6	36	10	100
8	64	9	81	14	196
12	144	17	289	16	256
19	361	12	144	5	25
6	36	6	36	18	324
11	121	13	169	21	441
8	64	13	169	15	225
15	225	5	25	11	121
$\Sigma X_i = 130$	$\Sigma X_i^2 = 1588$	$\Sigma X_i = 140$	$\Sigma X_i^2 = 1880$	$\Sigma X_i = 145$	$\Sigma X_i^2 = 2013$

$$\overline{X} = \frac{(130 + 140 + 145)}{36} = 11.5$$

These are the descriptive statistics for the sample data. Clearly there is a difference between the samples in terms of the average number of mistakes made. Could this be due to random variation when sampling from populations with no difference?

To determine this we first calculate the TSS and SSB:

$$TSS = \Sigma X_i^2 - n\overline{X}^2 = (1588 + 1880 + 2013) - 36(11.5)^2$$
$$= 720$$

$$SSB = \Sigma n_s (\overline{X}_s - \overline{X})^2$$
$$= 12(10.8 - 11.5)^2 + 12(11.7 - 11.5)^2 + 12(12.1 - 11.5)^2$$
$$= 10.7$$

$$SSW = TSS - SSB = 720 - 10.7$$
$$= 709.3$$

From this we can finally calculate the sample F-statistic that we use in the test of significance:

$$F_{sample} = \frac{\dfrac{SSB}{k-1}}{\dfrac{SSW}{n-k}} = \frac{\dfrac{10.7}{3-1}}{\dfrac{709.3}{36-3}}$$

$$= 0.25$$

Step 4: Establish the critical score(s) and critical region(s)
From the table for critical values for the F-distribution (Table A3), where $k = 2$ and $n = 36$, the critical value for F is:

$$F_{critical} = 3.32 \ (\alpha = 0.05)$$

Step 5: Make a decision
If we plot both the sample score and critical score on the graph for the F-distribution (Figure 18.9) we can see that the null hypothesis cannot be rejected.

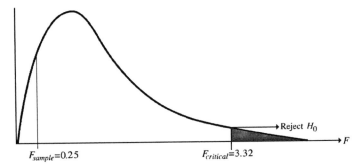

Figure 18.9 Critical and sample scores

Despite the differences in the sample means we cannot say that these reflect differences between any of the underlying populations. The differences, in other words, we attribute to random variation.

Exercises

18.1   A comparison is made between five welfare agencies in terms of the average number of cases handled by staff during a month. The research is aimed at finding whether the workload is significantly different between agencies.
(a)   Explain why an ANOVA should be used to explore this issue.
(b)   State the null hypothesis for this research in words and using mathematical notation.
(c)   From the following hypothetical results calculate the F-ratio and make a decision about the null ($\alpha = 0.05$).

Variation	Sum of squares	Degrees of freedom
Between Agencies	50	4
Within Agencies	7210	110
Total	7260	114

18.2 A university instructor uses different teaching methods on three separate classes. The instructor wants to assess the relative effectiveness of these methods by testing for a significant difference between the classes. The data on final grades are:

Method A	Method B	Method C
21	28	19
19	28	17
21	23	20
24	27	23
25	31	20
20	38	17
27	34	20
19	32	21
23	29	22
25	28	21
26	30	23

(a) Calculate the mean and standard deviation for each sample. Can you anticipate from these descriptive statistics the result of an ANOVA conducted on these data?

(b) Conduct the ANOVA to assess your expectations.

18.3 The prices ($) of an item are collected from the stores of three separate retail chains:

Chain A	Chain B	Chain C
3.30	3.20	2.99
3.30	3.35	3.00
3.45	3.15	3.30
3.35	3.10	3.45
3.20	2.99	3.40
3.25	3.30	3.25
3.30	3.15	3.25

(a) Using a significance level of 0.05, can we say that these chains do not price this good differently?

(b) Enter these data in SPSS and confirm your results. Note that you will need two columns: one column to indicate the sample each case falls into, and one column indicating each case's measurement for the dependent variable.

(c) If you find a significant difference use the Scheffe *post hoc* comparison to determine which group(s) are different.

18.4 The following data were obtained from a hypothetical study of the effects of blood alcohol levels on driving performance. Subjects were randomly assigned into four groups, with each group being assigned a different blood alcohol level. Each group was then measured by time in seconds spent on target when steering a car in a simulated environment.

Level 1	Level 2	Level 3	Level 4
216	178	180	166
187	144	132	145
166	176	172	148
242	132	137	136
229	188	154	126
276	168	154	176
233	204	176	133
166	187	178	184
208	165	169	155
224	193	188	177
213	201	175	189
254	197	186	165
227	183	179	172
203	176	168	172
206	196	188	179
221	182	176	166
219	202	185	180
220	190	195	176
196	202	177	165
230	188	186	193

(a) Using an ANOVA *F*-test, determine whether driving ability is significantly reduced with higher blood alcohol levels.

(b) Enter these data in SPSS and confirm your results. Note that you will need two columns: one column to indicate the sample each case falls into, and one column indicating each case's measurement for the dependent variable.

(c) If you find a significant difference use the Scheffe *post hoc* comparison to determine which group(s) are different.

18.5 The following data are from a hypothetical sample of 20 children from the USA, representing the number of minutes of TV watched per night:

195	184	165	162	168	196	217	190	212	232
204	205	217	210	230	197	180	192	190	198

(a) How will the addition of this sample to the ANOVA of Australian, British, Canadian, and Singaporean children affect the number of degrees of freedom?

(b) Enter these data into the file with the data for the Australian, British, Canadian, and Singaporean children and recalculate the ANOVA and *post hoc* analysis on SPSS.

(c) What do you conclude about the amount of TV watched between children from different countries?

18.6 Enter into SPSS the data from the example in the text above regarding the reading ability of three children and conduct a comparison of the means to see if there is a significant difference.

18.7   Using the **Employee data** file determine whether there is a significant difference across employment categories in terms of current salary.

19

Rank-order Tests for Two or More Samples

The previous two chapters discussed situations where two or more samples are compared in terms of their means for a particular variable. These tests are very handy because the mean is such an important descriptive statistic in social research. However, there are many instances where a comparison of means is not the appropriate analysis to undertake, especially for the following three reasons.

The research question is not interested in the central tendency of the distribution We are not always interested in the average for a variable; our research question may direct our attention to some other aspect of the distribution such as the frequency of cases across the range of values.

The level at which the variable is measured may not be interval/ratio Even where we are interested in the central tendency of the distribution, the data we have collected may not be measured at the interval/ratio level for us to calculate the mean as the relevant descriptive statistic. In the social and health sciences we do not always work with interval/ratio data but ordinal-level data instead. Sometimes this ordinal data looks interval/ratio, especially with attitude scales that have a large number of points. For example, we might construct an 'index of satisfaction', whereby we ask individuals to rate themselves on a scale of 1 to 10, with 1 indicating 'Not at all satisfied' and 10 indicating 'Extremely satisfied':

```
1-------2-------3-------4-------5-------6-------7-------8-------9-------10
```
Not at all   *Extremely*
satisfied   *satisfied*

Such an index is ordinal because the numbers assigned to each group are purely arbitrary. We can just as easily, and just as validly, label the grades on the index 2, 5, 8, 12, 100, 133, 298, 506, 704, 999, rather than 1, 2, 3, 4, 5, 6, 7, 8, 9, 10. All we need to do in constructing an index is preserve the ranking of cases, since we are not measuring satisfaction by some unit of measurement, as we do when measuring age in years. All we can say is that one case is more or less satisfied than the other; we do not have a unit of measurement that allows us to say *by how much* one case is more or less satisfied than the other. For example, we cannot say that someone with a score of 6 is three times more satisfied than someone with a score of 2. In fact, instead of using numbers to label the categories, we could have used terms like 'Moderately satisfied and 'Very satisfied' without losing any information at all. The problem is that when we use a long ordinal scale with numbers for labels, like 1,2,3,...,10, there is the *appearance* of interval/ratio data. This might tempt us to calculate a mean in order to compare two samples that have been measured on this scale. This is, strictly speaking, not a correct procedure.

Unfortunately, calculating a mean on essentially ordinal data is not an infrequent occurrence. Market research companies do this as a standard procedure when describing survey data. Indeed, this writer's own academic institution, the University of New South Wales, has introduced course evaluation measures, much like the above satisfaction scale, and uses the means of such scales to compare student evaluations of courses and instructors. What a score of 5.6 is meant to signify, however, and whether this is different in any meaningful way to a score of say 5.3, is not very obvious. Clearly, even such an august institution as this is not immune from statistical silliness!

We cannot assume that the population is normally distributed Even if it is legitimate to calculate the mean as the descriptive statistic for a set of data, to conduct an inference test on this mean requires the additional assumption (especially when working with small samples) that the population is normally distributed. This assumption is sometimes suspect. For example, we know that income in the population is not normally distributed: it is usually skewed to the right. Therefore, it is inappropriate to conduct a *t*-test for mean income. Fortunately, there is a range of significance tests, called **distribution-free** (or **non-parametric**), tests that *do not require any assumption about the shape of the underlying population distribution*. A distribution-free test that operates in a similar way to the *t*-test for the equality of two means, but on data that only need to be rank-ordered, is the **two-sample z-test for the rank sum**, also known for short as the **Wilcoxon W test**.

To see the logic of this test, we need to remind ourselves of the relationship between descriptive and inferential statistics. We begin with the raw data from a sample, and then calculate a descriptive statistic that somehow captures the 'essence' of these data that will help us answer a specific research problem. We then use inferential statistics to see if we can generalize from this sample result to the population. For any of the reasons we have just discussed the mean may not be an appropriate descriptive statistic. We might need to generate a different descriptive statistic from a sample, and then apply our inferential statistics to it.

The rank sum and mean rank as descriptive statistics

With data measured at least at the ordinal level, we can order cases from lowest to highest according to the 'score' each case receives on the scale. Once arranged in this order, each case can be assigned a **rank** that indicates where in the order it appears: first, second, third, and so on. Think of the way that tennis players are given a ranking, with the best player ranked number one, the second best ranked two, and so on. These numbers do not measure tennis playing ability as such, they merely indicate a position in an ordered series based on tennis playing ability. Just as we can rank-order people according to their tennis playing ability, we can rank-order cases according to any variable measured at least at the ordinal level.

To see how we use the **rank sum** and the **mean rank** as descriptive statistics for such data, we will elaborate the example we have used in the preceding chapters regarding the TV viewing habits of Australian and British children. Let us assume that in trying to assess whether there is a difference between Australian and British children in terms of their TV watching behavior, the researcher is dissatisfied with using just viewing time measured in minutes as the operationalization of TV viewing behavior. The researcher believes that a child may sit in front of the TV for long periods of time, but this does not indicate the *intensity* with which the child watches TV, the level of interest in what is actually screened.

To incorporate this factor into the measurement of TV watching behavior the researcher observes 20 children from Australia and 20 children from Britain, taking note of their level of attention and their responses to what they see on the screen. Based on these observations, each child is given a score between 0 and 100 indicating their level of intensity of TV viewing. A score of 0 indicates a child who is completely disinterested with what is on TV, while a score of 100 indicates a child who shows an extremely high interest in the TV. The raw data from this research are listed in Table 19.1.

Table 19.1 Scores on viewing intensity index: raw data from a (hypothetical) survey of children's TV viewing behavior

Australia	Britain
3	1
9	4
12	5
19	10
20	14
25	21
33	24
37	30
38	35
45	37
56	40
58	43
64	50
69	59
73	62
75	65
78	70
80	74
83	76
89	95

Clearly, this listing of the raw data, even when rank-ordered as in this table, is difficult to interpret. One British child shows the least interest in what he or she watches, but another British child is also the most highly engaged. What about the *overall* distribution across the range of scores? Before proceeding, 'eyeball' these data and try make a judgment about any difference between these two samples in terms of their intensity of TV viewing.

You have probably concluded that the scores for British children tend to be clustered at the low end of the scale (relatively uninterested in TV), while the Australian children tend to be clustered at the other end (relatively interested in TV). We might be inclined to take just the mean for each set of scores and compare them. However, we need to resist this temptation because this is only an ordinal scale and therefore the mean will not 'mean' anything. We might more usefully calculate the median for each sample: I will leave it to you to calculate that the median for the Australian children is 50.5 and for British children it is 38.5. This gives us a better sense of the distribution, but since the median only makes use of the central score(s) of a distribution, rather than all the data points, it can at times be misleading as a summary measure.

The best way of describing these 40 pieces of data in a more digestible way is to assign each case a rank and to sum the ranks for each sample. If one sample tends to cluster at the low end of the scale then the sum of the ranks for this sample will be smaller than that for the other sample.

Let us first assign ranks to each case in our survey. To do this imagine that all 40 children are lined up with the British child who scored 1 at the head of the line, followed by the Australian child who scored 3, and so on down to the British child who scored 95 at the end of the line. Each child is then given a number indicating their place, or **rank**, in the line as in Table 19.2.

A problem arises in assigning ranks when two or more cases score the same value for the variable. These are called **tied ranks**. For example, an Australian child and British child each scored 37 on the index.

To assign ranks to tied cases divide the **sum** of the ranks to be filled by the **number** of ranks to be filled.

These two children occupied positions 17 and 18 in line, so their average rank is 17.5:

$$\text{average rank} = \frac{17+18}{2} = 17.5$$

Having allocated ranks to all the cases we simply then sum them for each sample. This produces **rank sums** of 441.5 and 378.5 for Australian and British children respectively. We can now easily compare these two numbers rather than compare the two sets of 20 numbers that made up the raw data, and make an assessment of our research findings. The higher rank sum for Australian children indicates that they tended to cluster toward the high end of the scale, indicating that they watch TV with more intensity than British children.

Table 19.2 Scores and ranks on viewing intensity index

Australia Score	Britain Score	Rank
	1	1
3		2
	4	3
	5	4
9		5
	10	6
12		7
	14	8
19		9
20		10
	21	11
	24	12
25		13
	30	14
33		15
	35	17.5
37	37	17.5
38		19
	40	20
	43	21
45		22
	50	23
56		24
58		25
	59	26
	62	27
64		28
	65	29
69		30
	70	31
73		32
75		33
	74	34
	76	35
78		36
80		37
83		38
89		39
	95	40
$\Sigma R = 441.5$	$\Sigma R = 378.5$	

In this example we conveniently have two samples with the same number of cases. If we had samples of unequal size, the rank sums would not be so easily compared because they will be affected by the number of cases in each sample rather than just the relative positions of the cases in the rank-ordering. To compensate for this problem with rank sums, an even more meaningful way of describing rank-ordered raw data is to calculate the **mean rank** ($\bar{R}$) for each sample, which is the rank sum divided by the number of cases in a sample. For our data the mean ranks will be:

$$\bar{R}_{australia} = \frac{441.5}{20} = 22$$

$$\bar{R}_{britain} = \frac{378.5}{20} = 19$$

On average Australian children are 22nd in line, whereas on average British children are 19th in line. We can immediately see by comparing these two numbers, rather than by comparing the original 40 numbers from which these mean ranks are derived, that British children watch TV with less interest than Australian children. We can also see that this difference does not appear to be very great.

To sharpen this notion of the rank sum and mean rank as descriptive statistics for long ordinal scales, let us consider the extreme situation depicted in Table 19.3.

Table 19.3 Scores on viewing intensity index: raw data from a (hypothetical) survey of children's TV viewing behavior

Australia	Britain
48	1
52	3
52	5
56	5
58	8
62	10
65	12
69	15
69	15
72	19
73	20
78	23
79	28
85	29
86	31
86	31
89	38
91	39
92	44
95	46

We can immediately see that if we lined these children up according to their index scores the British children will occupy the first 20 ranks, while the Australian children will occupy ranks 21, 22, 23, ..., 40. The mean ranks for each sample will be (the rank sums are in the numerator of each equation):

$$\bar{R}_{britain} = \frac{1+2+3+...+20}{20} = \frac{210}{20}$$
$$= 10.5$$

$$\overline{R}_{australia} = \frac{21 + 22 + 23 + \ldots + 40}{20} = \frac{610}{20}$$

$$= 30.5$$

These two mean ranks clearly and concisely describe the basic difference in the distributions, which is the clustering of cases from one sample at one end of the scale and the clustering of cases from the other sample at the other end of the scale.

The two-sample z-test for the rank sum

We have observed two samples in Table 19.1 that differ in terms of the variable with which we are comparing them: intensity of viewing TV. In particular, we have found that the sample of Australian children tends to watch TV with more interest than the sample of British children. Can we draw an inference from this to the entire populations of Australian and British children?

Let us assume that in fact there is no difference between the two populations of children in terms of this variable. If there is no difference between these two populations (remember, this is just a hypothesis) we expect that the two *samples* will not differ. It is possible to select randomly two samples that produce the extreme rank sums from Table 19.3, even though there is no difference between the populations. Such a result, however, is highly improbable. If the two populations do not differ, the more likely result is that the sample of Australian and the sample of British children will be evenly spread through the joint distribution. In this case the rank orders for the two samples will be identical so that each Australian child will tie with a British child on the intensity scale. Where the two samples are evenly spread through the rank-ordering, the rank sums for either sample will be equal to:

$$\mu_W = \frac{1}{2} n_1 (n_1 + n_2 + 1)$$

where:
n_1 is the sample with the fewest cases
n_2 is the sample with the most cases

In this example, each sample has 20 cases, so if the samples conformed exactly with our hypothesis of no difference between the populations, we will generate rank sums of:

$$\mu_W = \frac{1}{2} n_1 (n_1 + n_2 + 1) = \frac{1}{2} 20(20 + 20 + 1)$$

$$= 410$$

The actual rank sums that we observe in our samples do not conform to this, reflecting the fact that one sample tended to cluster higher up the scale than the other. The rank sum for the sample of Australian children is 441.5 and for the sample of British children the rank sum is 378.5. We know, however, that random samples do not always exactly reflect the populations from which they are drawn. Random variation will often cause samples to differ from each other, even though the populations from which they are drawn are not different. What is the probability, in other words, of drawing samples that are as different in their index scores as that which we observe from populations that are not different?

To determine this probability for sample sizes of 20 or more we conduct a z-test on the difference between the smallest of the two rank sums (which is given the symbol W) and the value for μ_W.. (Strictly speaking, the sampling distribution of W is only approximately normal, but this a reasonable approximation for sample sizes larger than 20. A table for the exact distribution for W should be used to look up probabilities in the small sample case. In the small sample case SPSS will automatically conduct an exact test rather than use the normal approximation.)

The smallest of the two rank sums we have observed is that for British children:

$$W = 378.5$$

The formula involved is:

$$z_{sample} = \frac{W - \mu_W}{\sigma_W}$$

where:

$$\sigma_W = \sqrt{\frac{1}{12} n_1 n_2 (n_1 + n_2 + 1)}$$

We substitute our sample results into these equations to determine the sample z-score:

$$\sigma_W = \sqrt{\frac{1}{12} n_1 n_2 (n_1 + n_2 + 1)} = \sqrt{\frac{1}{12} 20(20)(20 + 20 + 1)}$$

$$= 37$$

$$z_{sample} = \frac{W - \mu_W}{\sigma_W} = \frac{378.5 - 410}{37}$$

$$= -0.85$$

On a two-tail test, with an alpha level of 0.05, the critical level for z is ±1.96. We can see in Figure 19.1 that the sample result does not fall in the region of rejection.

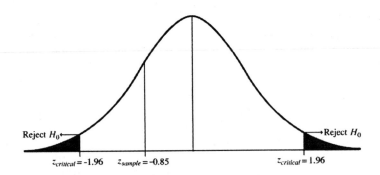

Reject H_0 Reject H_0

$z_{critical} = -1.96$ $z_{sample} = -0.85$ $z_{critical} = 1.96$

Figure 19.1 Critical and sample scores

In plain words, although our *samples* differ, the difference is not so great that it suggests the samples come from *populations* that differ. We cannot reject the hypothesis that the populations of Australian and British children do not differ in terms of TV viewing intensity and the sample difference is due just to random variation.

Example

We want to see if people from rural areas are more or less conservative than people from urban areas. We asked a random sample of 22 people from rural areas and 22 people from urban areas a detailed set of questions, and from their responses constructed an 'index of conservatism' which ranges from 1 to 40. A score of 40 indicates someone who is extremely conservative, while a score of 0 indicates someone who is not at all politically conservative. All 44 scores are listed in Table 19.4.

Now imagine lining up these 44 people from lowest to highest (rank-ordering the cases). An urban resident scored the lowest with 0, and so appears first in line, while a rural dweller had the highest score of 39, and appears at the end of the line. Ranks are assigned to each person (indicated in the brackets) according to their position in the line-up.

Just to remind ourselves of how to assign tied ranks, look at the one rural and two urban dwellers who each scored 18 on the index of conservatism. Together, these three people occupy three spaces, which are 19th, 20th, and 21st in line:

$$\frac{19 + 20 + 21}{3} = 20$$

Table 19.4 Scores on conservatism index: Samples of rural and urban residents

Urban	Rural
0 *(1)*	2 *(3)*
1 *(2)*	3 *(4)*
4 *(5)*	6 *(7)*
5 *(6)*	7 *(8)*
10 *(11)*	8 *(9)*
11 *(12)*	9 *(10)*
13 *(14)*	12 *(13)*
14 *(15)*	17 *(18)*
15 *(16)*	18 *(20)*
16 *(17)*	19 *(22)*
18 *(20)*	21 *(24)*
18 *(20)*	22 *(25)*
20 *(23)*	24 *(27)*
23 *(26)*	25 *(28)*
26 *(29)*	28 *(31)*
27 *(30)*	29 *(32)*
31 *(34)*	30 *(33)*
32 *(35)*	33 *(36.5)*
35 *(39.5)*	33 *(36.5)*
35 *(39.5)*	34 *(38)*
37 *(42)*	36 *(41)*
38 *(43)*	39 *(44)*

Therefore they are each assigned a rank of 20. Notice that in assigning this rank of 20 to each of these three cases we do not use ranks 19 or 21 for the cases immediately preceding or following them in line.

If we sum and average the ranks for each group, we get descriptive statistics which indicate the relative spread of the two groups in the joint distribution:

$$\Sigma R_1 = 480, \quad \bar{R}_1 = 21.82$$

$$\Sigma R_2 = 510, \quad \bar{R}_2 = 23.18$$

These rank sums and mean ranks give a sense as to whether one sample is more or less conservative than the other. Here we see that the mean rank for the urban sample is 21.82, whereas for the rural sample it is 23.18. This indicates that urban residents tended to have lower scores on the conservatism scale than rural residents.

What does this tell us about the populations from which these samples are drawn? To make this inference we work through our five-step hypothesis testing procedure.

Step 1: State the null and alternative hypotheses
In this example with sample sizes of 22, the value of μ_W is:

$$\mu_W = \frac{1}{2}n_1(n_1 + n_2 + 1) = \frac{1}{2}22(22 + 22 + 1)$$

$$= 495$$

Remember, this is the rank sum we will get on average from samples drawn from populations that are no different in terms of the conservatism scale. Therefore the null and alternative hypotheses for this example are:

$$H_0: \mu_w = 495$$

$$H_a: \mu_w \neq 495$$

Step 2: Choose the test of significance
In this example we are comparing *two random samples* to see if they differ in terms of their rank sums. The appropriate test, therefore, is the Wilcoxon z-test for the rank sum.

Step 3: Calculate the sample statistic
Here the smallest of the two rank sums is that for urban dwellers, so that:

$$W = 480$$

This is obviously different to the value assumed in the null hypothesis, indicating that the samples differ. Can we conclude from this that the *populations* are different as well? The Wilcoxon test analyzes whether 480 is 'different enough' from the expected value of 495 to suggest that there is also a difference between the populations.

The standard error of the sampling distribution of rank sums (σ_w) for this example is:

$$\sigma_w = \sqrt{\frac{1}{12} 22 \times 22(22 + 22 + 1)}$$

$$= 42.6$$

The z-test for W produces the following result:

$$z_{sample} = \frac{W - \mu_w}{\sigma_w} = \frac{480 - 495}{42.6}$$

$$= -0.352$$

Step 4: Calculate the critical scores and critical regions
On a two-tail test (we do not expect in the alternative hypothesis that one group will tend to be *more* conservative than the other), with an alpha level of 0.05 the critical score is:

$$z_{critical} = \pm 1.96$$

Step 5: Make a decision

We can see that the sample score does not fall in the region of rejection (Figure 19.2).

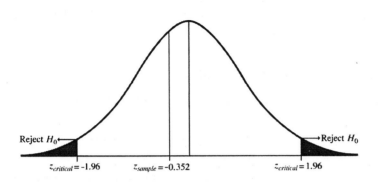

Figure 19.2 Critical and sample scores

Despite the difference between the samples we cannot say that this is due to a difference between the two populations. We therefore do not reject the null hypothesis of no difference.

Another way of arriving at this conclusion is by comparing the probability associated with the sample score against the alpha level of 0.05. Looking at the sample z-score of −0.352, we can see from the table for the area under the standard normal curve, on a two-tail test, that the probability of drawing samples with this much difference in their conservatism rating (or more) from populations with no difference is around 0.72. Since we do not have a table with z-scores listed at more than 1 decimal place, we take the two z-scores either side of 0.352 in Table 19.5 and estimate the probability as somewhere roughly between 0.689 and 0.764.

Table 19.5 Area under the standard normal curve

z	Area under curve between both points	Area under curve beyond both points	Area under curve beyond one point
±0.1	0.080	0.920	0.4600
±0.2	0.159	0.841	0.4205
±0.3	0.236	0.764	0.3820
±0.4	0.311	0.689	0.3445
±0.5	0.383	0.617	0.3085
±0.6	0.451	0.549	0.2745
±0.7	0.516	0.484	0.2420
±0.8	0.576	0.424	0.2120
±0.9	0.632	0.368	0.1840
±1	0.683	0.317	0.1585
⋮	⋮	⋮	⋮
±3	>0.996	<0.004	<0.0020

Even if there is no difference between the two populations in terms of their conservatism ratings, around 70 in every 100 *samples* drawn from such populations will have a difference as large or larger than that which we have actually observed. In other words, the difference between the two samples in their rank sums is not large enough for it to be attributed to a difference between the two populations.

Wilcoxon's rank-sum z-test using SPSS

To conduct a rank-sum test on these data we follow Table 19.6 (Figure 19.3).

Table 19.6 Wilcoxon's rank-sum test using SPSS (file: **Ch19.sav**)

SPSS command/action	Comments
1 From the menu select **Analyze/ Nonparametric Tests/2 Independent Samples**	This brings up the **Two-Independent-Samples Tests** dialog box. Notice that in the area for **Test Type** the tick-box next to **Mann-Whitney U** has ✓ indicating that this is the default test. This is the same test as the Wilcoxon. In other words, the Wilcoxon test is the default test which will automatically be generated under this command
2 Click on **Score on conservatism index** in the source variables list	This highlights **Score on conservatism index**
3 Click on ▶ that points to the **Test Variable List:**	This pastes **Score on conservatism index** into the **Test Variable List:**
4 Click on **Area of residence** in the source variables list	This highlights **Area of residence**
5 Click on ▶ that points to the area headed **Grouping Variable:**	This pastes **Area of residence** into the **Grouping Variable:** list. Notice that in this list the variable appears as **area(? ?)**
6 Click on **Define Groups**	This brings up the **Define Groups** box
7 In the area next to **Group 1:** type **1**, and in the area next to **Group 2:** type **2**	This identifies the two groups to be compared, which are urban and rural residents
8 Click on **OK**	

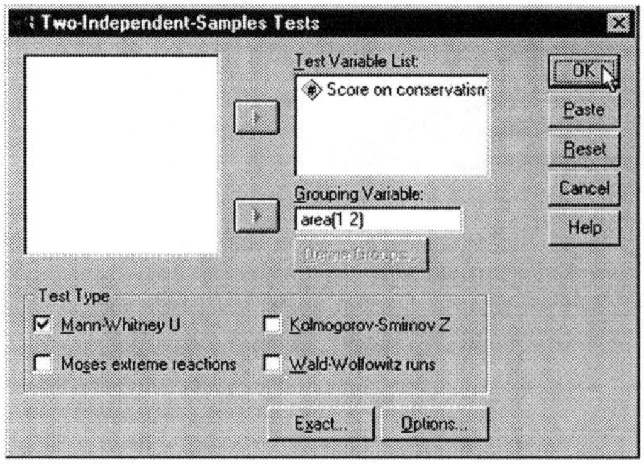

Figure 19.3(a) The **Two-Independent-Samples Tests** dialog box

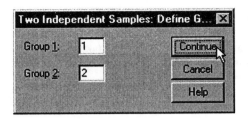

Figure 19.3(b) The **Define Groups** dialog box

The results from this set of instructions are presented in Figure 19.4.

NPar Tests

Mann-Whitney Test

Ranks

	Area of residence	N	Mean Rank	Sum of Ranks
Score on conservatism index	urban	22	21.82	480.00
	rural	22	23.18	510.00
	Total	44		

Test Statistics[a]

	Score on conservatism index
Mann-Whitney U	227.000
Wilcoxon W	480.000
Z	-.352
Asymp. Sig. (2-tailed)	.725

a. Grouping Variable: Area of residence

Figure 19.4 SPSS rank-sum test output

The first thing you will notice is that the output is titled **Mann-Whitney Test**. As we show in the Appendix to this chapter (for those interested) the Mann–Whitney and Wilcoxon tests are equivalent ways of reaching the same conclusion.

The **Ranks** table provides the relevant descriptive statistics for the two samples we are comparing: the number of cases in each and in total, the mean ranks, and the sum of ranks. These figures all correspond to the values we calculated by hand above.

Below this descriptive information is the table providing the **Test Statistics**. The footnote indicates the samples have been formed on the basis of their area of residence variable. The value for Wilcoxon W is **480.000** (the smallest of the two rank sums from the **Ranks** table). The value for Z is **-.352**, which is the same as our sample z-score calculated above. This has a two-tail probability, if the null hypothesis of no difference is true, of .725. Clearly, the difference between the samples of rural and urban residents should not be taken to indicate a difference between the population of rural and the population of urban residents. We do not reject the null hypothesis of no difference.

Other non-parametric tests for two or more samples

This chapter has worked through one of the most common non-parametric tests: the Wilcoxon test for two independent samples. The other common non-parametric test is the chi-square test, which we introduced in Chapter 16, but which will be detailed for the two or more samples case in Chapter 20. A researcher, in fact, can tackle most problems with a sound knowledge of the Wilcoxon and the chi-square tests. However, there are many other non-parametric tests available, to which some reference should be made. Indeed, the attentive reader will have noticed that SPSS offered a number of choices in the **Test Type** area when conducting a test of two independent samples. This range of choices is further extended when we consider situations where more than two samples are being compared.

Kruskal–Wallis H test on more than two samples

The Wilcoxon test compares two samples in terms of a variable measured at least at the ordinal level. In the example, we had a sample of rural and a sample of urban residents. But what if we have more than two samples that we want to compare? What if we want to compare urban, rural, and semi-rural residents, rather than just urban and rural residents?

One way of doing this is simply to conduct multiple Wilcoxon tests, using all the possible combinations of samples:

Urban by Rural
Urban by Semi-Rural
Rural by Semi-Rural

Thus with three samples to compare we will need to undertake three separate two-sample Wilcoxon tests. In practical terms, on SPSS, this will involve specifying under **Define Groups,** one test at a time, each possible combination of values for the grouping variable, and then rerunning the test. This is obviously a cumbersome procedure.

When we have more than two samples, a more direct path is to conduct a Kruskal–Wallis H Test. The Kruskal–Wallis Test compares all possible combinations of the samples in one go. It has very similar logic to the Wilcoxon test, in that it compares rank sums for each sample being compared. The test statistic, though, is no longer a z-score. The Kruskal–Wallis test uses a chi-square test to assess the null hypothesis that the populations have the same distribution in some ordinal scale.

The difference between the Wilcoxon W and Kruskal–Wallis H tests is analogous to the difference between a two-samples t-test and an ANOVA. These latter tests compare the relevant number of samples in terms of the difference between means, whereas the W and H tests compare samples in terms of rank sums.

Wald–Wolfowitz runs test

This test uses the same logic as the one-sample runs test we introduced in Chapter 15. It can be used in similar situations to the Wilcoxon test, where the cases in the two samples are pooled and ordered in terms of their scores on an ordinal scale. The number of runs of cases from each same sample is counted, and this number of runs is the sample statistic tested. In the extreme case, using the example above, all 22 rural residents will be at one end of the distribution and all 22 urban residents at the other end, thus forming only two runs. Such a sample result will strongly suggest that the two populations are different in terms of this ordinal scale. On the other hand, if the two samples were scattered throughout the combined distribution, the number of runs will be much higher. The Wald–Wolfowitz runs test conducts a z-test on the difference between the number of runs from the samples and the expected number of runs, if the null hypothesis of no difference is true. One limitation of this test though is that it is seriously affected by tied ranks.

Appendix: the Mann–Whitney U test

In generating the results of the Wilcoxon test on SPSS, we actually clicked on the box under **Test Type** next to **Mann-Whitney**. The SPSS output produced, along with the Wilcoxon W, another statistic called a Mann–Whitney U. This is also common in many textbooks, and is based on a slightly different calculation. Since it is a little more complicated than simply looking at the sum of the ranks, and will always result in the same probability value as the Wilcoxon rank-sum test, we have detailed the latter in the text. However, for those who are interested, the logic of the Mann–Whitney U is presented here. In the example, the 44 respondents in the sample were lined up from highest to lowest rank on the conservatism scale. We ask the rural resident who scored 39 to step out of the line and count how many urban residents he or she is ranked above. This of course will be all 22 urban residents. We then ask the second highest ranked rural dweller to step out of the line and count how many urbanites he or she is ahead of in the line. If we get each rural resident to do this and add up all the figures, the number obtained is the sample U-statistic. This sample statistic can be calculated for any sample using the following formula:

$$U = n_1 n_2 + \frac{n_1(n_1 + 1)}{2} - \Sigma R_1$$

where:

n_1 is the smaller of the two samples

n_2 is the larger of the two samples

ΣR_1 is the sum of ranks for the smaller sample.

If the two samples came from populations that were not different in terms of this variable, then we would on average randomly select samples that produced a U-statistic given by:

$$\mu_U = \frac{n_1 n_2}{2}$$

In this example, the expected value of U will be:

$$U = \frac{22(22)}{2} = 242$$

From the SPSS output we see that the sample U is 227. We can conduct a z-test to see if the difference between the sample and expected values of U is large enough to warrant the rejection of the null hypothesis.

$$z_{sample} = \frac{U - \mu_u}{\sigma_u}$$

where:

$$\sigma_U = \sqrt{\frac{n_1 n_2(n_1 + n_2 + 1)}{12}}$$

The z-score obtained will be exactly the same as that derived from conducting a Wilcoxon test on the same data, and therefore, regardless of the test used, the conclusion regarding the null hypothesis will be the same.

Exercises

19.1   Determine the correct rank for the score of 10 in each of the following series:

(a)   2, 9, 17, 10, 11, 6

(b)   2, 9, 17, 10, 11, 6, 8

(c)   2, 9, 17, 10, 10, 11, 6

(d)   2, 9, 17, 10, 10, 11, 6, 8, 11

(e)   3, 20, 15, 10, 22, 4, 10, 9, 16, 10

19.2 Identify and assign the correct rank to the score immediately following
10 in each of the following rank-ordered series:
(a) 2, 6, 9, 10, 11, 17
(b) 2, 6, 8, 9, 10, 11, 17
(c) 2, 6, 9, 10, 10, 11, 17
(d) 2, 6, 8, 9, 10, 10, 11, 11, 17
(e) 3, 4, 9, 10, 10, 10, 15, 16, 20, 22

19.3 When comparing two samples, under what conditions will you use a
Wilcoxon z-test for the rank sum rather than a t-test for the equality of
means?

19.4 (a) Order the following data, assigning ranks to each case:

Group 1	Group 2
1	12
15	25
12	29
16	8
23	15
9	20
11	7

(b) What are the rank sums and mean ranks for each group?
(c) Which rank sum is the sample statistic for conducting the
Wilcoxon test?
(d) Calculate the value for μ_w.
(e) Conduct a Wilcoxon test to assess whether there is a significant
difference in rankings.

19.5 A trial is used to evaluate the effectiveness of a specific exercise
program to improve standing up performance of individuals who have
suffered a stroke. Twenty subjects are randomly assigned to either a
treatment or control group, and their individual scores on a Motor
Assessment Scale (MAS), which measures standing up performance
for stroke patients on a scale of 0 to 6, are recorded:

Treatment group		Control group	
Subject	MAS	Subject	MAS
1	0	11	3
2	4	12	1
3	5	13	0
4	6	14	2
5	4	15	3
6	4	16	6
7	6	17	1
8	3	18	2
9	6	19	2
10	2	20	2

Using the Wilcoxon rank-sum test assess the effectiveness of the exercise program. Enter these data on SPSS and conduct the test.

19.6   Enter into SPSS the data for the example in the text for the comparison of Australian and British children.

(a)   Conduct a Wilcoxon rank-sum test on these data and compare the results with the calculations in the text.

(b)   The following data are the viewing intensities for a sample of 23 American children:

5, 8, 16, 21, 26, 35, 39, 45, 45, 54, 59, 61, 78, 79, 83, 85, 85, 90, 97, 99

Add these data to the SPSS file and conduct another Wilcoxon rank-sum test to see if there is a significant difference between British and American children.

(c)   Conduct the same Wilcoxon test by hand and compare your results with the SPSS output.

19.7   Use the **Employee data** file to determine whether there is a significant difference in the starting salaries of employees based on their minority status. Why might we use the Wilcoxon test rather than the two-sample *t*-test to make this comparison?

20

The Chi-square Test for Independence

This chapter will look at the technique for conducting an hypothesis test for categorical data arranged in a crosstabulation. This is the **chi-square test for independence**, which is similar to the one-sample test we have already encountered in Chapter 17. To understand the place of the chi-square test as one choice in the 'menu' of inference tests available to us it is helpful to review the general criteria for choosing an inference test.

The chi-square test and other tests of significance

The earlier chapters emphasized that the choice of inference test is determined by two main considerations:

- The descriptive statistic used to describe the raw data for a sample.
- The number of samples being described and from which an inference is being made.

The descriptive statistic used to describe the raw data

This factor is itself a function of two specific issues. The first is the research question we want to answer. The research question almost invariably directs our interest to a specific characteristic of the distribution for a given variable. A public health research worker might be concerned with the question of whether a population is on average 'young' or 'old', a research problem that directs one to look at the central tendency of the variable. A political scientist may also be concerned with the age distribution of this population, but the specific interest may be the relative number of people that are above voting age. For this research problem the political scientist will organize the data into a binomial distribution and calculate the proportion of the sample above and below the voting age. Both researchers are interested in the same population, and both have exactly the same raw data in front of them, but their respective research questions decide whether they are interested in the central tendency of the distribution, or the proportion of cases above or below a certain point on the scale.

The second issue which determines the descriptive statistic used to summarize data is the level of measurement for the variable. The level of measurement often limits the way we can describe the particular characteristic of the distribution we are interested in. For example, assume we are interested in the central tendency for the age distribution of a sample. Whether we collect data at the interval/ratio level or at the ordinal level determines which of the measures of central tendency (mode, median, or mean) we actually use as the descriptive statistic to summarize the raw data. If we measure age in years (interval/ratio) then the descriptive statistic we use to summarize the data is the mean. If we classify people into age categories ranging from 'very young' to 'very old' (ordinal) then the appropriate descriptive statistic is the median.

These two factors, the research question and the level of measurement, combine to determine the actual descriptive statistic upon which inference tests are conducted.

The number of samples to be compared

We saw in Chapter 14 that when we collect data from only one sample we have a certain range of inference tests to choose from. The range of choices is different when we have two samples and therefore need to make an inference about each of the two populations from which the samples are drawn. Similarly, with more than two samples we are then confronted with another range of tests to choose from. For example, when comparing means, a *t*-test for sample means is used with one or two samples, whereas ANOVA is used for more than two samples. Similarly, the Wilcoxon rank-sum test is designed for the two-sample case when comparing rank orders, whereas with three or more samples the Kruskal–Wallis *H* test is employed to compare rank orders.

With this discussion in mind, we can now look at the conditions under which the chi-square test is appropriate.

The descriptive statistic upon which the chi-square test for independence is conducted is the frequency distribution contained in a bivariate table We investigated the construction and use of bivariate tables that crosstabulate data on two variables in Chapter 8. We saw that crosstabs are a convenient way of summarizing and displaying categorical data when we are interested in the overall frequency distribution of cases across the whole range of categories, rather than just the central tendency. Nominal and ordinal data come 'pre-packaged' in categories, and hence crosstabs are a very common way of describing such data. It should also be remembered, however, that interval/ratio data can be collapsed down into discrete categories, as we do when we organize people's dollar incomes into clusters such as 'low', 'middle', and 'high income' groups. Hence, a crosstab can also potentially be a means of describing interval/ratio data, as well as nominal and ordinal data.

The chi-square test is basically the same, regardless of whether we have one, two, or more than two samples We have already encountered the chi-square test as a one-sample test for a frequency distribution. Unlike other tests, the chi-square test can be extended to the two-sample and more than two samples cases without much modification: we follow the same basic procedure, and use the same formula, regardless of the number of samples being compared (although in the one-sample case it is called a goodness-of-fit-test, whereas with two or more samples it is called a test for independence).

Statistical independence

We construct crosstabulations to get a visual sense of whether the two variables under investigation are **independent** of each other.

Two variables are statistically **independent** if the classification of cases in terms of one variable is not related to the classification of those cases in terms of the other variable.

Take the example we used in Chapter 8 to construct a crosstab between 'income' and 'place of residence' (Table 20.1).

Table 20.1 Place of residence by income level

Place of residence	Income		
	Low	High	Total
Rural	205	118	323
	55%	34%	45%
Urban	167	230	397
	45%	66%	55%
Total	372	348	720
	100%	100%	100%

We make a visual, or 'eyeball', inspection of the relative frequencies in each cell of the table and assess whether *in the sample* the two variables are independent or whether in fact some kind of a relationship exists. We observe from this that there is some relationship (or pattern of dependence) between these two variables. It seems that low income tends to be associated with living in rural areas, while high income is associated with living in urban areas.

In addition to the crosstab we calculated an appropriate measure of association to quantify this observed relationship between these two variables. With at least one variable measured at the nominal level, the appropriate measure is lambda and we calculated the value of lambda for this table to be 0.12, indicating that a weak relationship exists in the sample.

However, our conclusion is based on sample data, and we must therefore be wary that it may be due to random variation when sampling from populations in which there is no relationship between income and place of residence. The chi-square test for independence assesses this possibility.

The chi-square test for independence

The starting point for conducting a chi-square test for independence, as with all inference tests, is the statement of the null and alternative hypotheses. In the example we are using, the hypotheses take the form of:

H_0: Income and place of residence are independent of each other
H_a: Income and place of residence are not independent of each other

The statement of independence forms the null hypothesis for the test, and if the null is rejected, we conclude that the two variables are not independent in the population. Conversely if we do not reject the null hypothesis we argue that the variables are truly independent, even though a dependence is observed in the samples.

Looking at our actual example, we have determined that the variables are not independent in the sample – there does appear to be some relationship – but can we draw this inference about the populations from which the samples came?

To see how the chi-square test helps us assess whether these two variables are truly independent of each other, even where there is a dependence in the samples, we begin by looking at the raw and relative frequencies for the row totals in Table 20.1 (Table 20.2).

Table 20.2 Place of residence: all respondents

Place of residence	Total	Percentage
Rural	323	45%
Urban	397	55%
Total	720	100%

These row totals and percentages are the basic reference points from which the chi-square test is conducted. The argument is that if 45 percent of *all* respondents live in a rural setting, then we should expect 45 percent of *each group* (low income and high income) also to live in a rural setting, if the two variables are independent.

Under the null hypothesis of independence the relative frequencies for each group are expected to be the same as that for the groups combined.

In other words, we expect to find in each cell of the table, if the two variables are independent, the relative frequencies in Table 20.3.

Table 20.3 Expected relative cell frequencies

Place of residence	Income		
	Low	High	Total
Rural	45%	45%	45%
Urban	55%	55%	55%
Total	100%	100%	100%

However, even if the null hypothesis of independence is true, we should not always expect random samples of low and high income earners to reflect this. For example, we might occasionally draw samples of low and high income groups and get one of the three separate results shown in Table 20.4.

Table 20.4(a) Sample 1

Place of residence	Income		
	Low	High	Total
Rural	47%	44%	45%
Urban	53%	56%	55%
Total	100%	100%	100%

Table 20.4(b) Sample 2

Place of residence	Income		
	Low	High	Total
Rural	52%	40%	45%
Urban	48%	60%	55%
Total	100%	100%	100%

Table 20.4(c) Sample 3

Place of residence	Income		
	Low	High	Total
Rural	65%	30%	45%
Urban	35%	70%	55%
Total	100%	100%	100%

Sample 1 represents a situation in which the observed percentages very closely reflect the expected percentages, assuming that the two variables are independent. Occasionally we might find the situation shown in sample 2, where there is a greater variation between the groups, but it is not too great. Sample 3 shows an extreme situation in which we happened to pick up cases from either end of the scale, causing the relative frequencies in the first two columns to diverge a great deal from those in the Total column. Although this is a possibility when random sampling from populations where there is no relationship, it is also highly unlikely.

In fact, we can take an infinite number of random samples from populations where the two variables are independent and observe the spread of results. Obviously most would be like samples 1 and 2, and very few like sample 3.

The **chi-square statistic** is a means by which we can capture this difference between observed and expected frequencies.

The **chi-square statistic** is calculated from the difference between the observed and expected frequencies in each cell of a bivariate table.

The **chi-square distribution** is the probability distribution of the chi-square statistic for an infinite number of random samples of the same size drawn from populations where the two variables are independent of each other.

The exact formula for calculating chi-square is:

$$\chi^2 = \sum \frac{\left(f_o - f_e\right)^2}{f_e}$$

where:
f_o is observed cell frequencies
f_e is expected cell frequencies.

Occasionally we draw samples that are 'true' to the population so that there is no difference between the actual and expected frequencies. In other words, we get cell frequencies like those in Table 20.3. In this case the value of chi-square will be zero:

$$f_o = f_e \;\; \rightarrow \;\; \left(f_o - f_e\right)^2 = 0 \;\; \rightarrow \;\; \chi^2 = 0$$

This will not be the case for every sample. We will occasionally take samples that, through random chance, do not fully reflect the populations from which they are drawn. The result is that chi-square will take on a positive value:

$$f_o \neq f_e \;\; \rightarrow \;\; \left(f_o - f_e\right)^2 > 0 \;\; \rightarrow \;\; \chi^2 > 0$$

The greater the difference between the observed frequencies and the expected frequencies, the larger the value of chi-square. In the formula for chi-square, notice that differences between observed and expected frequencies are squared. This ensures that the range of all possible chi-square values must start at zero and increase in a positive direction. Regardless of whether the expected frequency is larger than the observed frequency or vice versa, squaring any difference will produce a positive number. (Since chi-square is calculated on the basis of the difference between expected and actual scores *squared*, and not on the *direction* of difference, there is no sense in which we have to choose between a one-tail or two-tail inference test. All differences between observed and expected scores, regardless of whether they are due to the observed scores being above or below the expected scores, will take on a positive value.)

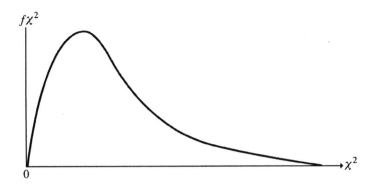

Figure 20.1 The chi-square distribution

The chi-square distribution has a long tail (Figure 20.1), reflecting the fact that it is possible to select random samples that yield a very high value for chi-square, even though the variables are independent, but this is highly improbable. It will be a fluke just to happen to select a sample from one group in which all cases come from one end of the distribution and another sample from the other group that comes from the other end of the distribution, if the null hypothesis of independence is true. Therefore the area under the curve for very large chi-square values is small, reflecting the low probability of this happening by chance.

> From the sampling distribution of chi-square we can determine the probability that the difference between observed and expected scores is due to random variation when sampling from populations in which the two variables are independent.

For example, we might find that sample 3 above will be drawn one time in a thousand ($p = 0.001$) if the two variables are independent of each other. This will be considered so unlikely as to warrant us to argue that our assumption about independence should be dropped – there really is a dependence between income and place of residence.

We will now use the example of income and place of residence to provide a concrete illustration of this procedure. The (hypothetical) survey, you will recall, consists of 323 people from rural areas and 397 people from urban areas, with the distribution of responses as shown in Table 20.5.

The first number in each cell is the actual count of low and high income earners who live in each of the two types of areas. The percentage figure is the number of people in that cell as a proportion of the column total. That is, 55 percent of all low income earners surveyed live in rural areas, which is 205 people. On the other hand, only 34 percent of all high income earners surveyed live in rural areas.

Table 20.5 Place of residence by income level: observed frequencies

Place of residence	Income		
	Low	High	Total
Rural	205	118	45%
	55%	34%	
Urban	167	230	55%
	45%	66%	
Total	372	348	720
	100%	100%	100%

Another way to visualize this result is with a stacked bar graph, which I have generated on SPSS (Figure 20.2).

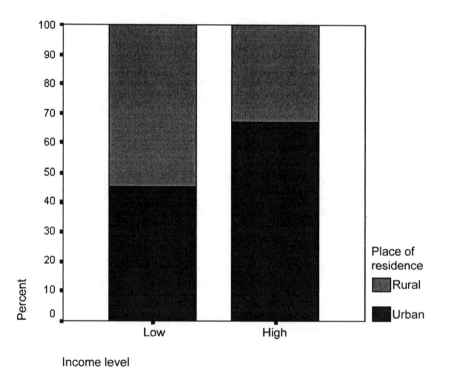

Figure 20.2 A stacked bar chart of place of residence by income level

This is exactly the same information as contained in Table 20.5 but graphically described. We can easily see that there is obviously a difference between low and high income earners in terms of where they live, but could this be due to random variation?

To answer this we need to calculate the expected frequencies: the numbers we expect to find in each cell if the two variables are independent. We use the percentage figures in the Total column and apply them to the individual income groups, as illustrated in Table 20.6.

Table 20.6 Place of residence by income level: expected frequencies

Place of residence	Income		
	Low	High	Total
Rural	$\frac{45}{100} \times 372 = 167.4$	$\frac{45}{100} \times 348 = 156.6$	45%
Urban	$\frac{55}{100} \times 372 = 204.6$	$\frac{55}{100} \times 348 = 191.4$	55%
Total	372	348	100%

The number of respondents we expect to find in each cell, if the variables are independent, is calculated for each cell. For example, if 45 percent of *all* respondents live in rural areas, then we expect to find 45 percent of just low income earners in rural areas. There are 372 low income earners in total, and 45 percent of 372 gives 167.4 low income earners *expected* to live in rural areas. Effectively we are calculating the numbers we would need so that exactly the same percentage of low and high income earners live in each area type.

Thus we have two numbers for each cell in the table, one for the expected frequencies based on the null hypothesis, and the other is the actual observed frequencies we obtain from our research. We show both of these sets of numbers in Table 20.7, with the expected frequencies in brackets.

Table 20.7 Place of residence by income level: observed and expected frequencies

Place of residence	Income		
	Low	High	Total
Rural	205 (167.4)	118 (156.6)	323
Urban	167 (204.6)	230 (191.4)	397
Total	372	348	720

We can see that in each cell there is a difference between the observed and expected frequencies, and we can use the formula for chi-square to express this difference in a single number. Table 20.8 illustrates how we go through the mechanics of calculating the chi-square statistic from these differences.

Table 20.8 Calculations for chi-square

Place of residence	Income		
	Low	High	Total
Rural	$\chi^2 = \dfrac{(205 - 167.4)^2}{167.4} = 8.5$	$\chi^2 = \dfrac{(118 - 156.6)^2}{156.6} = 9.5$	323
Urban	$\chi^2 = \dfrac{(167 - 204.6)^2}{204.6} = 6.9$	$\chi^2 = \dfrac{(230 - 191.4)^2}{191.4} = 7.8$	397
Total	372	348	720

Having calculated these values for each cell we can add them together to get an overall χ^2 for the crosstab as a whole. In other words, the chi-square statistic gathers up these individual values so that we get a single number for the whole table that expresses the fact that the actual sample result does not conform perfectly to the null hypothesis of independence:

$$\chi^2_{sample} = \sum \frac{(f_o - f_e)^2}{f_e}$$

$$= \frac{(205 - 167.4)^2}{167.4} + \frac{(118 - 156.6)^2}{156.6} + \frac{(167 - 204.6)^2}{204.6} +$$

$$\frac{(230 - 191.4)^2}{191.4}$$

$$= 8.5 + 9.5 + 6.9 + 7.8$$

$$= 32.7$$

The distribution of chi-square

So we have obtained a value for chi-square of 32.7. What does this tell us? In and of itself it does not tell us a great deal, apart from the fact that it is not equal to zero and therefore indicates that there is some dependence between these variables in the sample data. Whether this should cause us to reject the null hypothesis of independence depends on the probability of obtaining this sample chi-square value of 32.7 from populations where the two variables are independent. To determine this probability we refer to the table for the critical values of chi-square printed as Table A4.

In using this table to work out the probability of obtaining a sample chi-square of 32.7 just by random chance, we need to take into account the degrees of freedom. For any table the number of degrees of freedom will be:

$$df = (r-1)(c-1)$$

where:
r is the number of rows
c is the number of columns.

In a 2-by-2 table such as this, therefore, there is 1 degree of freedom.

We can now refer to the table for the critical values of chi-square and determine the relevant probability. To illustrate how this is done a portion of the table is reproduced in Table 20.9.

Table 20.9 Critical values of chi-square

df	\multicolumn{10}{c}{Level of significance}
	0.99	0.90	0.70	0.50	0.30	0.20	0.10	0.05	0.01	0.001
1	0.00016	0.0158	0.148	0.455	1.074	1.642	2.706	3.841	6.635	10.827
2	0.0201	0.211	0.713	1.386	2.408	3.219	4.605	5.991	9.210	13.815
3	0.115	0.584	1.424	2.366	3.665	4.642	6.251	7.815	11.341	16.268
4	0.297	1.064	2.195	3.357	4.878	5.989	7.779	9.488	13.277	18.465
5	0.554	1.610	3.000	4.351	6.064	7.289	9.236	11.070	15.086	20.517
⋮	⋮	⋮	⋮	⋮	⋮	⋮	⋮	⋮	⋮	⋮
30	14.953	20.599	25.508	29.336	33.530	36.250	40.256	43.773	50.892	59.703

$$\chi^2_{critical} = 3.841 \ (\alpha = 0.05, \ df = 1)$$

This table is very similar to that for the distribution of *t*, with the critical values for chi-square in the body of the table, the number of degrees of freedom down the side, and a select set of significance levels across the top. As Siegel and Castellan state, 'if an observed value of chi-square is equal to or greater than the value given in [the table] ... for a given level of significance, at a particular *df*, then H_0 may be rejected' (S. Siegel and N.J. Castellan (1988) *Nonparametric Statistics for the Behavioral Sciences*, New York: McGraw-Hill).

In our example, if we choose an alpha level of 0.05, with 1 degree of freedom, the critical value will be 3.841. The sample chi-square is 32.7 and, as evident in Figure 20.3, this falls in the critical region of rejection, so we reject the null hypothesis of independence: place of residence and income are not independent.

It is of the utmost importance to note, however, that the test itself does not tell us what the nature of the relationship is. All we can conclude is that there is some association between these variables. We have chosen to characterize this as a one-way dependent relationship from income to place of residence. Someone else could just as easily claim that the causality runs in the other direction, or we have mutual dependence between the two variables. The chi-square test does not decide this issue for us. It merely tells us that the variables are not independent; that is, they are related. How we choose to characterize the relationship is a matter for theoretical debate that statistical analysis can inform, but never decide.

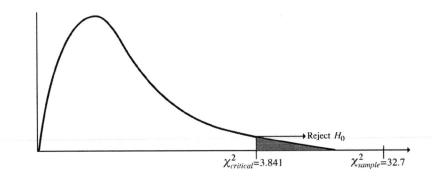

Figure 20.3 Critical and sample scores

The chi-square test using SPSS

In Chapter 7 we introduced the commands for generating a crosstab on these data in SPSS. The chi-square test appears as an option within the procedure for generating a crosstab, much like the way in which we added lambda to the crosstab in Chapter 8. Table 20.10 and Figure 20.4 repeat the steps for generating a crosstab in SPSS, but with the addition of the relevant chi-square statistic.

Table 20.10 Generating crosstabs with chi-square on SPSS (file: **Ch20.sav**)

SPSS command/action	Comments
1 From the menu select **Analyze/ Summarize/Crosstabs**	This brings up the **Crosstabs** dialog box
2 Click on the variable in the source list that will form the rows of the table, in this case **Place of residence**	This highlights **Place of residence**
3 Click on ▸ that points to the target list headed **Row(s):**	This pastes **Place of residence** into the **Row(s):** target list
4 Click on the variable in the source list that will form the columns of the table, in this case **Income level**	This highlights **Income level**
5 Click on ▸ that points to the target list headed **Column(s):**	This pastes **Income level** into the **Column(s):** target list
6 Click on the **Statistics** button	This brings up the **Crosstabs: Statistics** box. In the top-left corner you will see **Chi-square** with a tick-box next to it
7 Select **Chi-square** by clicking on the box next to it	This places ✓ in the tick-box to show that it has been selected
8 Click on **Continue**	
9 Click on **OK**	

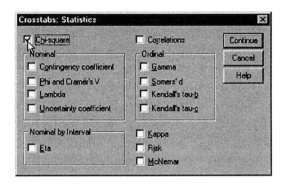

Figure 20.4 The **Crossstabs: Statistics** dialog box

This set of commands will produce the necessary information for conducting a chi-square test. However, I have found it useful to instruct SPSS also to include the relative column frequencies in the crosstab. This is done by clicking on the **Cell** button in the **Crosstabs** dialog box, which provides a range of options for information to be printed in each cell of the table (Figure 20.5).

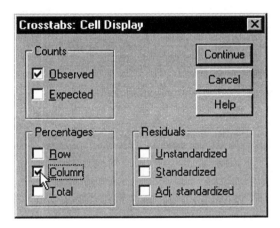

Figure 20.5 The **Crossstabs: Cell Display** dialog box

By clicking on the check-box next to **Column** we instruct SPSS also to include the column percentages in the output. While the choice of information to be calculated and printed in each cell is really up to the person conducting the research, and what they think is needed to make a reasonable eyeball assessment, the column percentages allow us to look at the data and make a preliminary judgment as to whether we think the two variables are independent or not.

The output generated from these commands will be as shown in Figure 20.6.

Crosstabs

Case Processing Summary

	Cases					
	Valid		Missing		Total	
	N	Percent	N	Percent	N	Percent
Place of residence * Income level	720	100.0%	0	.0%	720	100.0%

Place of residence * Income level Crosstabulation

			Income level		Total
			Low	High	
Place of residence	Urban	Count	167	230	397
		% within Income level	44.9%	66.1%	55.1%
	Rural	Count	205	118	323
		% within Income level	55.1%	33.9%	44.9%
Total		Count	372	348	720
		% within Income level	100.0%	100.0%	100.0%

Chi-Square Tests

	Value	df	Asymp. Sig. (2-sided)	Exact Sig. (2-sided)	Exact Sig. (1-sided)
Pearson Chi-Square	32.667[b]	1	.000		
Continuity Correction[a]	31.816	1	.000		
Likelihood Ratio	32.965	1	.000		
Fisher's Exact Test				.000	.000
Linear-by-Linear Association	32.622	1	.000		
N of Valid Cases	720				

a. Computed only for a 2x2 table

b. 0 cells (.0%) have expected count less than 5. The minimum expected count is 156.12.

Figure 20.6 SPSS chi-square output

We get a table headed **Place of residence * Income level Crosstabulation** which is an SPSS version of Table 20.5. We then get a table headed **Chi-Square Tests**. The relevant part of this table is the first row labeled Pearson Chi-Square. Under Value we see 32.667, which is the sample χ^2 value we calculated above. With 1 degree of freedom, we see that the significance level is reported to be .000, although this really means 'less than 5-in-10,000' chances of obtaining samples with this distribution from populations where the variables are independent. This very low *p*-value leads us to reject the null hypothesis of independence.

Example

A random sample of 50 migrants from non-English-speaking backgrounds (NESB) and a random sample of 50 migrants from English-speaking backgrounds (ESB) are asked whether or not they feel they have ever been discriminated against in seeking employment or promotion. We suspect that perception of discrimination is somehow dependent on language background, so that we will form crosstabs with language background as the independent variable and perception of discrimination as the dependent variable. However, this suspicion may not be correct. These two variables may in fact be independent of each other, so that knowing if a migrant is ESB or NESB tells us nothing about whether that migrant feels a stronger or weaker sense of discrimination.

The results for all 100 respondents are shown in Table 20.11.

Table 20.11 Perception of discrimination

Discrimination	Total
No	40
Yes	60
Total	100

If the two variables are independent we should expect to find the percentage distribution of 'Yes' and 'No' responses for each migrant group to be the same as that for the two groups combined.

Table 20.12 Expected distribution of responses

Discrimination	Status		Total
	NESB	ESB	
Yes	$\frac{50 \times 60}{100} = 30$	$\frac{50 \times 60}{100} = 30$	60
No	$\frac{50 \times 40}{100} = 20$	$\frac{50 \times 40}{100} = 20$	40
Total	50	50	100

Table 20.12 illustrates the simplest way to calculate expected frequencies.

To calculate the expected frequency for each cell multiply the column total by the row total and divide the product by the total number of cases.

However, instead of these expected values, the sample produced the observed frequencies shown in Table 20.13.

Table 20.13 Actual distribution of responses

Discrimination	Migrant status		
	NESB	ESB	Total
No	5	35	40
Yes	45	15	60
Total	50	50	100

We could stop here and let the descriptive statistics contained in these tables speak for themselves. NESB migrants do have a relatively higher perception of being discriminated against than ESB migrants. However, we must remember that because we are only working with samples rather than populations, the result can simply be due to random variation. We might just happen to select a high proportion of NESB migrants who feel discriminated against and/or a slightly lower proportion of ESB migrants who feel discriminated against, even though in the populations there is no difference. This is where the chi-square test helps. Table 20.14 uses the expected and observed values for each cell to calculate their respective contributions to the total chi-square value.

Table 20.14 Calculations for chi-square

Discrimination	Migrant status		
	NESB	ESB	Total
No	$\chi^2 = \dfrac{(5-20)^2}{20} = 11.25$	$\chi^2 = \dfrac{(35-20)^2}{20} = 11.25$	40
Yes	$\chi^2 = \dfrac{(45-30)^2}{30} = 7.5$	$\chi^2 = \dfrac{(15-30)^2}{30} = 7.5$	60
Total	50	50	100

$$\chi^2_{sample} = \sum \frac{(f_o - f_e)^2}{f_e}$$

$$= \frac{(5-20)^2}{20} + \frac{(35-20)^2}{20} + \frac{(45-30)^2}{30} + \frac{(15-30)^2}{30}$$

$$= 11.25 + 11.25 + 7.5 + 7.5$$

$$= 37.5$$

In a 2-by-2 table such as this, there is 1 degree of freedom. Looking at the table for the distribution of chi-square, with 1 degree of freedom, the critical value for chi-square at an alpha level of 0.05 is 3.841 (Table 20.15).

Table 20.15 Critical values of chi-square

df	0.99	0.90	0.70	0.50	0.30	0.20	0.10	0.05	0.01	0.001
					Level of significance					
1	0.00016	0.0158	0.148	0.455	1.074	1.642	2.706	3.841	6.635	10.827
2	0.0201	0.211	0.713	1.386	2.408	3.219	4.605	5.991	9.210	13.815
3	0.115	0.584	1.424	2.366	3.665	4.642	6.251	7.815	11.341	16.268
4	0.297	1.064	2.195	3.357	4.878	5.989	7.779	9.488	13.277	18.465
5	0.554	1.610	3.000	4.351	6.064	7.289	9.236	11.070	15.086	20.517
⋮	⋮	⋮	⋮	⋮	⋮	⋮	⋮	⋮	⋮	⋮
30	14.953	20.599	25.508	29.336	33.530	36.250	40.256	43.773	50.892	59.703

$$\chi^2_{critical} = 3.841 \ (\alpha = 0.05, \ df = 1)$$

The probability of getting a sample χ^2 of 37.5, if the two variables are truly independent, is less than 0.05. As indicated in Figure 20.7, the sample score falls in the region of rejection, so we reject the hypothesis of independence.

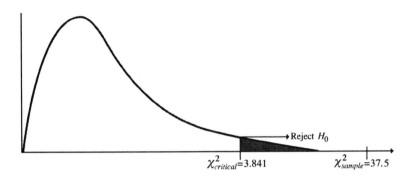

Reject H_0

$\chi^2_{critical} = 3.841$ $\chi^2_{sample} = 37.5$

Figure 20.7 Critical and sample scores

In fact we can see in Table 20.15 that the sample chi-square is even larger than that for an alpha level of 0.001. We can therefore say that the probability of getting frequencies such as those we observe, if the two variables are independent, is less than 0.001 (less than one in a thousand).

Therefore we reject the null hypothesis of independence, and argue that the perception of discrimination does systematically differ between migrant groups, such that NESB migrants have a systematically higher perception of discrimination than ESB migrants.

Problems with small samples

You may have noticed the footnote attached to the Pearson chi-square value in the SPSS output we generated above:

b. 0 cells (.0%) have expected count less than 5. The minimum expected count is 156.12

This is a check to see whether any cells in the crosstab have an expected frequency of 5 or less. SPSS basically runs through the table and determines how many, and what percentage of, cells have an expected frequency of less than 5. It then indicates what the lowest expected frequency in the table is – in this case 156.12. You can confirm this for yourself by referring to our calculations of expected frequencies in Table 20.12.

The reason why SPSS goes through such a procedure to indicate how many, if any, cells have an expected frequency of less than 5, is because a problem can arise with the use of a chi-square test when working with small samples. If the use of small samples leads to either of the following situations, the chi-square statistic becomes difficult to interpret:

- Any cell in the bivariate table has an expected frequency of less than 1.
- The expected frequency of cases in a large percentage of cells is 5 or less. Usually 20 percent of cells is considered too high, but any cells with expected values of 5 or less can create a problem.

If the footnote to the chi-square value in the SPSS output indicates that one of these conditions has been violated, the chi-square test cannot be meaningfully interpreted. In such situations there are some alternatives, depending on the dimensions of the table.

With 2-by-2 tables some writers suggest using Yate's correction for continuity:

$$\chi_c^2 = \sum \frac{\left(|f_o - f_e| - 0.5\right)^2}{f_e}$$

Other writers suggest that for 2-by-2 tables, Fisher's exact probability test should be used. SPSS calculates both of these alternatives in the relevant situations (See H.T. Reynolds (1977) *The Analysis of Cross-classification*, London: Free Press, 9–10, for a discussion of these procedures.)

With tables larger than 2 by 2 the only possible solution is to collapse categories together for either or both variables so as to increase expected frequencies. Before doing this, though, we need to justify the procedure because information is lost when categories are collapsed together. Originally there was enough information to say that one case differed from another case in terms of a variable, but if these cases are now in the same category after the original categories are combined, we are saying that such cases are the same. For example, we might need to collapse the four-point scale shown in Figure 20.8 into a two-point scale (in SPSS using the **Recode** command) in order to avoid small expected frequencies.

Thus cases that were previously classified into separate groups, such as Low and Very low, now are classified in the same group, namely Low. The scale was originally constructed for supposedly good theoretical reasons, and we should be wary of abandoning that scale simply to allow us to use a statistical procedure.

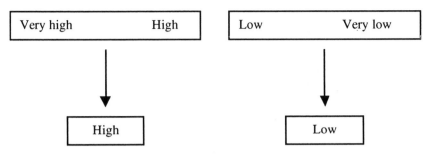

Figure 20.8 Collapsing four categories into two

Problems with large samples

The other main problem with the use of chi-square as a test of independence is that it is especially sensitive to large samples. The chance of finding a significant difference between samples always increases with sample size, regardless of whether we use z-tests, or t-tests, or F-tests, or chi-square. This in itself is not a problem; in fact, we should place greater faith in the results of larger samples rather than small samples, since large samples are more reliable. However, especially with chi-square, we may risk overstating the importance of a statistically significant difference.

To illustrate this problem, imagine that you are looking at two people standing far away. With the naked eye they appear to have the same height. But through a pair of binoculars it is evident that one person is slightly taller than the other. The more powerful the looking device we use to make our observation, the more likely slight differences will be detected. However, this example should also highlight the important distinction between statistical difference and meaningful difference. There may be a statistical difference in height of 1 inch between two people, but for all practical purposes they are as tall as each other. Using too powerful a looking device may complicate a picture by exaggerating slight statistical differences that aren't really worth worrying about in practice. When performing inference tests, increasing sample size has the effect of intensifying the 'looking device' we are employing and thereby accentuating slight differences that may not be important.

Increasing the sample size increases the chance of detecting a statistical difference that smaller samples may attribute to random variation.

Of all the tests we cover, chi-square is especially sensitive to sample size and might result in a statistically significant difference even though a difference is trivial. To see this, assume that we have respondents grouped according to their respective level of education. Level of education is measured by asking if the respondent has had a university education or not. We are interested in whether this affects enjoyment of work, measured according to whether respondents find their job 'Exciting', 'Routine', or 'Dull'. The distribution, when expressed as percentages of the total for each group is shown in Table 20.16.

Table 20.16 Enjoyment of work by education level: relative frequencies

Enjoyment of work	University education		
	No	Yes	Total
Dull	47.0%	45.7%	46.8%
Routine	48.2%	47.9%	48.2%
Exciting	4.8%	6.4%	5.0%
Total	100%	100%	100%

If these percentages are derived from a total of 1461, consisting of 1242 people without university education and 219 people with university education, the figures for observed and expected values will be as listed in Table 20.17.

Table 20.17 Enjoyment of work by education level

Enjoyment of work	University education		
	No	Yes	Total
Dull	584	100	684
	(581.5)	(102.5)	
Routine	599	105	704
	(598.5)	(105.5)	
Exciting	59	14	73
	(62)	(11)	
Total	1242	219	1461

Just by looking at the table it is clear that there is little difference between the observed frequencies and the expected frequencies (shown in brackets). As a matter of common sense we will say that the difference between the distribution of those without a university education and those with a university education in terms of job satisfaction is so slight that it could easily be put down to chance: the null hypothesis of independence is not rejected. In fact, the chi-square for this table is:

$$\chi^2_{sample} = 1.08148$$

The probability of getting this by chance alone, with 2 degrees of freedom, is:

$$p_{sample} = 0.58$$

However, if we obtain exactly the same pattern of responses, but from a sample size 10 times as large ($n = 14,610$) the conclusion is different. The bivariate table will be as shown in Table 20.18.

Table 20.18 Enjoyment of work by education level: observed and expected frequencies

Enjoyment of work	University education		
	No	Yes	Total
Dull	5840	1000	6840
	(5815)	(1025)	
Routine	5990	1050	7040
	(5985)	(1055)	
Exciting	590	140	730
	(620)	(110)	
Total	12,420	2190	14,610

All that has happened is that the value in each cell has been multiplied by 10. The chi-square for this table will also be exactly 10 times the value for that calculated from the previous table:

$$\chi^2_{sample} = 10.8148$$

This is now significant at the 0.01 level: the difference between observed and expected frequencies is large enough to allow us to reject the null hypothesis of independence. The pattern of responses is the same *relatively*, yet the conclusion is reversed. This shows that *any relative difference in frequency distributions can be significant if it comes from sufficiently large samples*.

One possible solution is to do the opposite to that when confronted with a small sample: use even finer scales to measure the dependent and/or independent variables. For example, here we could use more than three possible responses for the question: 'How much do you enjoy your work?' Unfortunately, by the time this problem arises – the data analysis stage of research – it is usually too late to change the scale and resurvey the respondents. At best it is a solution to an anticipated problem, but it does indicate the value of allowing for a wide range of possible responses when working with nominal/ordinal data on large samples.

If this problem is not anticipated and a significant result is obtained that might be due to sample size, then we should look at the percentage distribution of responses alone and make a judgment based on these percentages, without adding the complication of chi-square (i.e. work with the 'naked eye' rather than the statistical binoculars).

To aid this decision, we can refer to the appropriate measure of association and see if these measures indicate a negligible association between the two variables. If we calculate gamma for either of these tables it will equal 0.04, since measures of association are not affected by sample size when relative frequencies stay the same. This indicates that the relationship is so weak as to be negligible; we should not even bother to proceed to determine whether such a trivial relationship derives from a relationship in the population.

Example

We will work through one more example using the five-step hypothesis testing procedure to see it in the familiar context. We have the data presented in Table 20.19 showing the joint distribution of 800 children in terms of their sex and whether or not they watch the news on TV?

Table 20.19 Children's TV newswatching by sex

Watch news on TV?	Sex		
	Girl	Boy	Total
Yes	377	363	740 (92%)
No	25	35	60 (8%)
Total	402	398	800

Step 1: State the null and alternative hypotheses
H_0: Sex and TV newswatching are independent of each other.
H_a: Sex and TV newswatching are not independent of each other.

Step 2: Choose the test of significance
We are analyzing sample data arranged in a bivariate table to see if there is a relationship between two variables, which makes the chi-square test for independence the appropriate inference test.

Step 3: Calculate the sample score
To do this we first need to calculate the expected frequencies based on the Total column percentages in Table 20.20.

Table 20.20 Children's TV newswatching by sex: expected frequencies

Watch news on TV?	Sex		
	Girl	Boy	Total
Yes	371.8	368.2	740
No	30.2	29.8	60
Total	402	398	800

$$\chi^2_{sample} = \sum \frac{(f_o - f_e)^2}{f_e}$$

$$= \frac{(377 - 371.8)^2}{369.8} + \frac{(363 - 368.2)^2}{366.2} + \frac{(25 - 30.2)^2}{30.2} + \frac{(35 - 29.8)^2}{29.8}$$

$$= 1.95$$

Step 4: Establish the critical score and critical region
We have a 2-by-2 table, so that there is only 1 degree of freedom. At an alpha level of 0.05 the critical value for chi-square is:

$$\chi^2_{critical} = 3.841 \ (\alpha = 0.05, \ df = 1)$$

Step 5: Make a decision
We can see in Figure 20.9 that the sample score does not fall in the critical region of rejection.

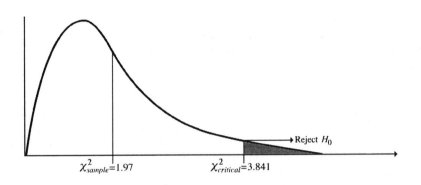

$\chi^2_{sample}=1.97$ $\chi^2_{critical}=3.841$

Figure 20.9 Critical and sample scores

We therefore do not reject the null hypothesis that these variables are independent.

Appendix: hypothesis testing for two percentages

This chapter discussed a widely used test of significance – the chi-square test of independence. The reason for its popularity is that it is applicable in situations in which we have categorical (nominal and ordinal) data and we are interested in the frequency distribution across the categories of the variable. This situation is very common in research. The chi-square test looks at the distribution of responses in a bivariate table and assesses whether a pattern of dependence exists. In the case of a 2-by-2 bivariate table (i.e. when both variables are binomial) a z-test of percentages can also be carried out on the same data; in fact, the two tests are equivalent ways of analyzing the same data and yield the same result. Indeed, the z-test of percentages can be considered a special case of the chi-square test, and since it is commonly used in research, it is worth knowing the mechanics of its calculation.

This appendix will work through an example of a z-test of sample percentages and then use a chi-square test to show that the results will be the same.

The z-test for two percentages

A (hypothetical) survey is conducted to investigate the level of support for social welfare reform, and whether this varies by age. Respondents are grouped according to whether they are aged 'under 45' or '45 or over'. Each respondent is also asked whether the government should do more to alleviate poverty. This is put to respondents as a simple 'yes/no' question.

The null hypothesis is that the percentage of under 45s responding 'yes' (P_1) is the same as the percentage of those 45 or over responding 'yes' (P_2):

$$H_0: P_1 = P_2$$

If this is true, samples taken from such populations will usually reflect the equality. In other words, the difference between any two sample percentages, if there is no difference between the populations, should be zero or close to it.

But this will not always be the case. Samples do not always exactly reflect the populations from which they are drawn. Random variation may cause us to pick up a few 'extra' young people who are in favor of welfare reform, and a few 'extra' older people who are opposed, causing the sample percentages to differ considerably. This means that if there is a difference between the two sample percentages, we cannot automatically conclude it reflects an underlying difference in the populations. However, larger differences between the sample percentages are less likely to be due to random chance. The z-test for percentages gives us the precise probability of such unlikely events occurring.

The survey consisted of 600 people under the age of 45 and 400 people aged 45 years or older. The percentage of each group responding 'yes', the government should do more to alleviate poverty, is:

$$\text{under } 45: P_1 = \frac{490}{600} \times 100 = 82\%$$
$$n_1 = 600$$

$$45 \text{ or older}: P_2 = \frac{232}{400} \times 100 = 58\%$$
$$n_2 = 400$$

Does this reflect an underlying difference between the age groups on this issue? To determine this we begin with the following formula:

$$P_u = \frac{n_1 P_1 + n_2 P_2}{n_1 + n_2}$$

This is basically a weighted average of the two sample percentages, a sort of mid-point between the two results. If we substitute the relevant numbers into the equation we get:

$$P_u = \frac{n_1 P_1 + n_2 P_2}{n_1 + n_2} = \frac{600(82) + 400(58)}{600 + 400}$$

$$= 72.2\%$$

This calculation allows us to determine the standard error of the sampling distribution of all possible sample differences. One standard error is defined by:

$$\sigma_{p-p} = \sqrt{P_u(100 - P_u)}\sqrt{\frac{n_1 + n_2}{n_1 n_2}} = \sqrt{72.2(100 - 72.2)}\sqrt{\frac{600 + 400}{600(400)}}$$

$$= 29\%$$

The actual difference between our two samples in terms of z-scores is:

$$z_{sample} = \frac{P_1 - P_2}{\sigma_{p-p}} = \frac{82 - 58}{29}$$

$$= 8.3$$

This z-score is significant at the 0.01 level: we reject the null hypothesis of no difference and argue that support for government assistance to the poor does vary with age.

Chi-square test for independence

The alternative way of analyzing these data is to organize them into a 2-by-2 bivariate table (Table 20.21).

Table 20.21 Attitude to government policy by age group

Agree	Age group		
	Under 45	45 or over	Total
No	110	168	278
	(166.8)	(111.2)	27.8%
Yes	490	232	722
	(433.2)	(288.8)	72.2%
Total	600	400	1000

The figures in brackets are the expected values based on the percentage of total respondents who said 'yes' or 'no'. Notice that 72.2 percent of all respondents agreed with the need for welfare reform. From this figure we calculate the number of 'under 45' respondents and '45 or over' respondents who are expected to agree. The 72 percent is the same figure that popped up in the two-sample z-test for percentages as the reference point for calculating the standard deviation of the sampling distribution. In fact, when we calculate chi-square:

$$\chi^2 = \sum \frac{(f_o - f_e)^2}{f_e}$$

$$= \frac{(110 - 166.8)^2}{166.8} + \frac{(168 - 111.2)^2}{111.2} + \frac{(490 - 433.2)^2}{433.2} +$$

$$\frac{(232 - 288.8)^2}{288.8}$$

$$= 67$$

From the table for the distribution of chi-square the probability of getting this value (or greater) from identical populations is 0.005 – the same as that for the z-test.

The conclusion to draw from this is that while two-sample binomial z-tests are very common, and therefore worth knowing, they are in fact a special case of chi-square. Since the formula for the z-test is more cumbersome, and the logic not as intuitively clear, it is probably best to use chi-square in most situations. Also SPSS cannot conduct two-sample z-tests of proportions, but it can calculate a chi-square on a 2-by-2 table.

Exercises

20.1   How many degrees of freedom are there for tables with each of the following dimensions:
(a) 2 by 4
(b) 4 by 2
(c) 6 by 4
(d) 3 by 5?

20.2   What will be the critical value for χ^2, with $\alpha = 0.05$ and $\alpha = 0.10$, for tables with the following dimensions:
(a) 2 by 4
(b) 4 by 2
(c) 6 by 4
(d) 3 by 5?

20.3 If a chi-square test, with $n = 500$, produces $\chi^2 = 24$, what will χ^2 be with the same relative distribution of responses, but with:
(a) $n = 50$
(b) $n = 1000$?

20.4 For the following table, calculate the expected frequencies for each cell and identify the ones that violate the rules for using chi-square.

	a	b	c	d	Total
a	1	0	6	48	55
b	2	0	7	40	49
Total	3	0	13	88	104

20.5 For the data in Exercise 8.2, which you used to construct a bivariate table, conduct a chi-square test to test your hypotheses about independence. Conduct this test on SPSS and compare the results with your hand calculations.

20.6 In earlier chapters we compared hypothetical samples of children from Australia, Canada, Singapore, and Britain, in terms of the amount of TV they watch. Assume that this variable was not measured at the interval/ ratio level, but rather on an ordinal scale. The results of this survey are:

Amount of TV	Country				
	Canada	Australia	Britain	Singapore	Total
Low	23	25	28	28	104
Medium	32	34	39	33	138
High	28	30	40	35	133
Total	83	89	107	96	375

Can we say that the amount of TV watched is independent of country of residence?

20.7 A sample of 162 men between the ages of 40 and 65 years is taken and the state of health of each man recorded. Each man is also asked whether he smokes cigarettes on a regular basis. The results are crosstabulated using SPSS, the results of which are shown over the page.
(a)   What are the variables and what are their respective levels of measurement?
(b)   Should we characterize any possible relationship in terms of one variable being dependent and the other independent? Justify your answer.
(c)   Calculate by hand the column percentages and the expected values if the null hypothesis of independence is true, and confirm that they are the same as those in the SPSS table.

Health level * Smoking habit Crosstabulation

			Smoking habit		
			Doesn't smoke	Does smoke	Total
Health level	Poor	Count	13	34	47
		Expected Count	28.1	18.9	47.0
		% within Smoking habit	13.4%	52.3%	29.0%
	Fair	Count	22	19	41
		Expected Count	24.5	16.5	41.0
		% within Smoking habit	22.7%	29.2%	25.3%
	Good	Count	35	9	44
		Expected Count	26.3	17.7	44.0
		% within Smoking habit	36.1%	13.8%	27.2%
	Very good	Count	27	3	30
		Expected Count	18.0	12.0	30.0
		% within Smoking habit	27.8%	4.6%	18.5%
Total		Count	97	65	162
		Expected Count	97.0	65.0	162.0
		% within Smoking habit	100.0%	100.0%	100.0%

(d) Looking at the column percentages, do you think that differences in health level between smokers and non-smokers could be the result of sampling variation rather than a difference in the populations?

(e) Conduct a chi-square test of independence on these data. Does it confirm your answer to (d)?

20.8 The following information was obtained from a survey of 50 'blue-collar' and 50 'white-collar' workers. The survey asked respondents if they could sing the National Anthem from start to finish. The results are 'Blue collar': Yes=29, No=21; 'White collar': Yes=22, No=28.

(a) Arrange these data into a bivariate table, and conduct a chi-square test of independence.

(b) (optional) Conduct a two-sample test for proportions on the same data and compare your results.

20.9 Use the **Employee data** file to assess whether minority classification and employment category are independent.

21

The *t*-test for a Correlation Coefficient

In Chapter 10 we calculated the regression line, and the correlation statistics that go along with it, for a set of cases measured in terms of two interval/ratio scales. We introduced these descriptive statistics in the context of investigating the relationship between unemployment and civil unrest across cities. The result we arrived at was:

$$\text{civil unrest} = 4.4 + 0.53(\text{unemployment rate})$$

$$r = 0.81$$

These statistics tell us that in *our sample* there is a strong, positive association between civil unrest and unemployment rates. But this is a result that obtains in the sample, and therefore might not reflect what is happening *in all cities*. As with any other descriptive statistics that we may calculate for a sample, we need to determine whether the correlation coefficient that describes the sample data reflects the population from which it is drawn. There may be no correlation between these variables in the population of all cities (r_μ) and it is only sampling error that has caused us to select five cities that are not like the rest. We therefore need to conduct an inference test on the value of the correlation coefficient we have obtained.

The *t*-test for Pearson's correlation coefficient

The null hypothesis for this test is that there is no correlation in the population, whereas the alternative hypothesis is that there is some correlation:

$$H_0: r_\mu = 0$$

$$H_a: r_\mu \neq 0$$

Obviously the sample correlation coefficient of 0.81 does not conform to the null hypothesis. But can we reject the hypothesis of no correlation in the population on the basis of this sample result? What is the probability of obtaining a sample of five cities with a correlation between civil disturbances and unemployment of 0.81 from a population where the correlation is zero? To obtain this probability we conduct a *t*-test, using the following formulas:

$$t_{sample} = \frac{r - r_\mu}{s_r}$$

$$s_r = \sqrt{\frac{1 - r^2}{n - 2}}$$

If we substitute the values for *r* and r^2 into this equation, we get:

$$s_r = \sqrt{\frac{1 - r^2}{n - 2}} = \sqrt{\frac{1 - (0.81)^2}{5 - 2}}$$

$$= 0.34$$

$$t_{sample} = \frac{r - r_\mu}{s_r} = \frac{0.81 - 0}{0.34}$$

$$= 2.38$$

In determining the critical *t*-score we refer to Table 21.1 which presents critical values of *t* for *n* – 2 degrees of freedom.

Table 21.1 Critical values for *t*-distributions

	Level of significance for one-tail test				
	0.10	0.05	0.02	0.01	0.005
	Level of significance for two-tail test				
df	0.20	0.10	0.05	0.02	0.01
1	3.078	6.314	12.706	31.821	63.657
2	1.886	2.920	4.303	6.965	9.925
3	1.638	2.353	3.182	4.541	5.841
4	1.533	2.132	2.776	3.747	4.604
5	1.476	2.015	2.571	3.365	4.032
⋮	⋮	⋮	⋮	⋮	⋮
∞	1.282	1.645	1.960	2.326	2.576

At an alpha level of 0.05 and a two-tailed test, the critical score is:

$$t_{critical} = \pm 3.182 \ (\alpha = 0.05, df = 3)$$

If we put all this information on a graph (Figure 21.1) we can see that we fail to reject the null hypothesis of no correlation.

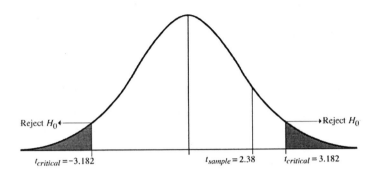

Reject H_0 Reject H_0

$t_{critical} = -3.182$ $t_{sample} = 2.38$ $t_{critical} = 3.182$

Figure 21.1 Critical and sample scores

It is important to stop and consider what has happened. In the sample we measured a strong positive correlation between unemployment and civil unrest. The inference test tells us that despite this the sample result might be due to chance when sampling from a population where these variables are not correlated. To see why we cannot conclude that the sample result reflects a relationship in the population, it is helpful to look again at the scatter plot of data (Figure 21.2).

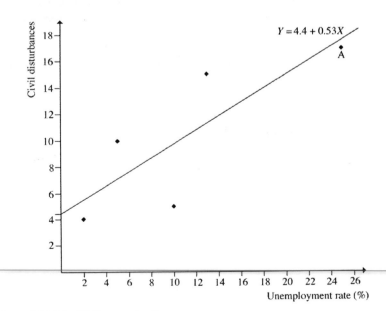

Figure 21.2 The OLS regression line

We can see that the regression line has been heavily influenced by the one score for City A with an unemployment rate of 25 percent and 17 civil disturbances. Because we are working with such a small sample ($n = 5$) one extreme case can throw out the results for the whole sample. If this one score was different, the regression line would also be very different. Since this is possible, even strong correlations may not turn out to be significant when working with very small samples.

Testing the significance of Pearson's correlation coefficient using SPSS

The test of significance for Pearson's product moment correlation coefficient is generated as part of the output when conducting a regression analysis. The procedures we followed in Chapter 10 for generating regression statistics therefore are the same as those for generating the necessary information for conducting an inference test on these statistics. There is also an alternative means by which we can generate the correlation coefficient between two variables and the associated *t*-score and significance level. This is through the **Bivariate Correlations** command (Table 21.2, Figure 21.3). We use this command if we wish to generate just the correlation coefficient without all the additional information that comes with a complete regression analysis.

Table 21.2 Bivariate Correlation with a *t*-test using SPSS (file: **Ch21-1.sav**)

SPSS command/action	Comments
1 From the menu select **A̲nalyze/C̲orrelate/ Bivariate**	This brings up the **Bivariate Correlations** window
2 Click on **Number of civil disturbances**	This highlights **Number of civil disturbances**
3 Click on the ▶ that points to the **V̲ariables:** target list	This pastes **Number of civil disturbances** into the **V̲ariables:** target list
4 Click on **Unemployment rate**	This highlights **Unemployment rate**
5 Click on the ▶ that points to **V̲ariables:** target list	This pastes **Unemployment rate** into the **V̲ariables:** target list
6 Click on **OK**	

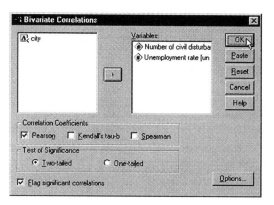

Figure 21.3 The **Bivariate Correlation** dialog box

Notice that the radio button under **Test of Significance** and next to **two-tailed** is selected indicating that a two-tail *t*-test is the default setting. This command will generate the output in Figure 21.4.

Correlations

Correlations

		Unemployment rate	Number of civil disturbances
Unemployment rate	Pearson Correlation	1.000	.807
	Sig. (2-tailed)	.	.099
	N	5	5
Number of civil disturbances	Pearson Correlation	.807	1.000
	Sig. (2-tailed)	.099	.
	N	5	5

Figure 21.4 SPSS bivariate correlation output

With two variables being correlated the table produces four correlation coefficients. One is between Unemployment rate and itself and the other is between Number of civil disturbances and itself, each of which produces a coefficient of 1.000. This is necessarily so since any variable is perfectly correlated with itself. In the first row the table also provides the correlation between Unemployment rate and Number of civil disturbances which is .807, and the significance of this coefficient which is .099. This indicates that the coefficient, despite its strength, is not significant at the 0.05 level, and therefore could be the result of sampling variation. The next row of the table provides the correlation coefficient between Number of civil disturbances and Unemployment rate which is exactly the same as that in the first row of the table since it is the same correlation looked at the other way.

The *t*-test for Spearman's rank-order correlation coefficient

We have, in earlier chapters, actually learnt the techniques for calculating two different correlation coefficients: Pearson's *r* and Spearman's rho (r_s). The former is used to investigate the association between two variables measured at the interval/ratio level, whereas the latter is used when at least one of the two variables is measured on an ordinal scale. However, if we look closely at the procedures for calculating the two types of correlation coefficients we see that they are almost identical. The difference is that Pearson's *r* uses the raw data in the computations, whereas Spearman's rho is calculated on the *ranks* of the data.

Given the basic mathematical equivalence between the two measures of correlation, the test of significance for each is the same. That is, the formula for calculating the sample *t*-score is the same regardless of whether we are testing for the significance of Pearson's correlation coefficient or Spearman's correlation coefficient:

$$t_{sample} = \frac{r_s - \rho}{s_r}$$

$$s_r = \sqrt{\frac{1 - r_s^2}{n - 2}}$$

where:

ρ is the hypothesized value for Spearman's correlation coefficient for the population.

To see how we actually conduct a test for Spearman's rho we will use the five-step hypothesis testing procedure on the example we introduced in Chapter 9.

Step 1: State the null and alternative hypotheses

H_0: There is no correlation between age and mobility scores.

$$H_0: \rho = 0$$

H_a: There is a correlation between age and mobility scores.

$$H_a: \rho \neq 0$$

Step 2: Choose the test of significance

Since we are investigating the correlation between two variables measured at the ordinal level, the data have been described by calculating Spearman's rho. The appropriate inference test is therefore the *t*-test for a correlation coefficient.

Step 3: Calculate the sample score

We calculated the correlation between age and mobility scores for 16 physiotherapy patients to be:

$$r_s = -0.8$$

To see whether this correlation might result from random variation when sampling from a population where these variables are not correlated, we first need to calculate the standard error for the sampling distribution of rho:

$$s_r = \sqrt{\frac{1 - r_s^2}{n - 2}} = \sqrt{\frac{1 - (-0.8)^2}{16 - 2}}$$

$$= 0.16$$

The sample *t*-score will therefore be:

$$t_{sample} = \frac{r_s - \rho}{s_r} = \frac{-0.8 - 0}{0.16}$$

$$= -5$$

Step 4: Calculate the critical score(s) and region(s)
With an alpha level of 0.05, on a two-tail test, we refer to Table 21.3 for the critical values for *t*-distributions, to determine the critical value for *t* with 14 degrees of freedom.

Table 21.3 Critical values for *t*-distributions

df	Level of significance for one-tail test				
	0.10	0.05	0.02	0.01	0.005
	Level of significance for two-tail test				
	0.20	0.10	0.05	0.02	0.01
1	3.078	6.314	12.706	31.821	63.657
2	1.886	2.920	4.303	6.965	9.925
3	1.638	2.353	3.182	4.541	5.841
⋮	⋮	⋮	⋮	⋮	⋮
11	1.363	1.796	2.201	2.718	3.106
12	1.356	1.782	2.179	2.681	3.055
13	1.350	1.771	2.160	2.650	3.012
14	1.345	1.761	**2.145**	2.624	2.977
15	1.341	1.753	2.131	2.602	2.947
⋮	⋮	⋮	⋮	⋮	⋮
∞	1.282	1.645	1.960	2.326	2.576

$$t_{critical} = \pm 2.145 \ (\alpha = 0.05, df = 14)$$

Step 5: Make a decision
If we graph the sample and critical scores (Figure 21.5) we can see that we reject the null hypothesis.

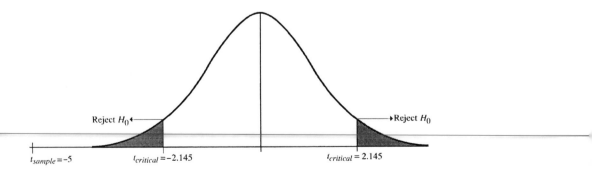

Figure 21.5 Critical and sample scores

On the basis of the strong relationship we find in the sample we cannot say that there is no correlation in the population.

Testing the significance of Spearman's correlation coefficient using SPSS

As with testing for the significance of Pearson's r, the relevant inferential statistics are automatically generated when we ask SPSS to calculate Spearman's rho. Thus the procedures we introduced in Chapter 9 (Table 21.4, Figure 21.6) provide the relevant information.

Table 21.4 Generating Spearman's rho on SPSS (file: **Ch21-2.sav**)

SPSS command/action	Comments
1 From the menu select **Analyze/Correlate/ Bivariate**	This brings up the **Bivariate Correlation:** dialog box
2 Click on **age** in the source variable list	This highlights **age**
3 Click on ▶	This pastes **age** into the **Variables:** target list
4 Click on **Score on mobility test** in the source variable list	This highlights **Score on mobility test**
5 Click on ▶	This pastes **Score on mobility test** into the **Variables:** target list
6 Click on the tick-box next to **Pearson**	This removes ✓ from the tick-box so that Pearson's coefficient is no longer selected. Pearson's coefficient is the default correlation
7 Click on the tick-box next to **Spearman**	This places ✓ in the tick-box to show that it is selected
8 Click on **OK**	

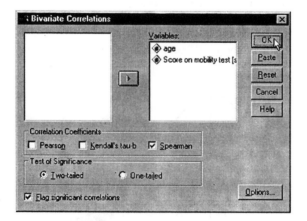

Figure 21.6 The **Bivariate Correlations** dialog box

Figure 21.7 present the output from this command.

Nonparametric Correlations

Correlations

			AGE	Score on mobility test
Spearman's rho	AGE	Correlation Coefficient	1.000	-.814*⃰
		Sig. (2-tailed)	.	.000
		N	16	16
	Score on mobility test	Correlation Coefficient	-.814*⃰	1.000
		Sig. (2-tailed)	.000	.
		N	16	16

** . Correlation is significant at the .01 level (2-tailed).

Figure 21.7 SPSS **Bivariate Correlations** output

SPSS calculates a correlation coefficient between each variable selected and all the other variables selected in the target list, including itself. Thus with only two variables selected in this example, we end up with four correlations: age with mobility score, mobility score with age, age with age, mobility score with mobility score. The correlations for each variable and itself are irrelevant since any variable is always perfectly correlated with itself – hence the value of 1.000 in the SPSS table. The correlation for age and score on mobility test is –.814. This is the same as the correlation for score on mobility test and age, since it is exactly the same relationship. Notice the ** next to this correlation coefficient. As the footnote to the table states, ** signals a value for rho that is significant at the 0.01 level on a two-tail test. In fact we can see that the exact significance is reported to be .000, which indicates that a probability of less than 5 in every 10,000 samples drawn from a population where these variables are not related will have a correlation coefficient this strong or stronger.

Exercises

21.1 In Chapter 9 we calculated the rank-order correlation coefficient for a set of 15 students to see if there is a relationship between performance in exams and performance in presentations. The correlation coefficient was found to be –0.26. Assuming that these data came from all the students in the class, do we need to conduct an inference test?

21.2 In Exercise 9.10 you were asked to calculate the value for rho for a sample of wines, relating price to quality. Conduct a *t*-test to assess whether the result reflects a non-zero correlation for the population of all wines. Check your SPSS output to confirm your results.

21.3   A survey of employed workers found that the correlation coefficient between the number of years of post-secondary education and current annual income measured in dollars is 0.54. The sample size for this survey was 140. The significance of this correlation coefficient was tested using a *t*-test, which gave a *t*-value of 7.54. What conclusion should be drawn about the nature of the relationship between these two variables?

21.4   The firm from which the **Employee data** file is generated is interested in whether starting salaries are correlated with current salaries. Generate the necessary information to determine whether any observed correlation in the sample is due to sampling variation or whether it reflects an underlying relationship for all employees in the firm.

PART 5

Inferential Statistics: Two Dependent Samples

22

The *t*-test for the Mean Difference

Dependent and independent samples

In Chapters 17–20 we looked at inference tests for two or more **independent samples**.

> **Independent samples** are those where the criteria for selecting the cases that make up one sample do not affect the criteria for selecting cases that make up the other sample(s).

For example, to compare Australian and British children in terms of average amounts of TV watched, we selected any random sample of Australian children and any random sample of British children. However, there are research questions that require us to choose samples that are not independent. We sometimes want to link our samples so that if a certain case is included in one sample this necessitates a specific case being included in the other. Samples that are linked in this way are called **dependent** samples.

> **Dependent samples** are those where the criteria for selecting the cases that make up one sample affect the criteria for selecting cases that make up the other sample(s).

There are generally two situations in which such dependence is required:

When the same subject is observed under two different conditions This is often used in a before-and-after experiment (sometimes called a pre-test–post-test design). For example, a new drug may be tested to see its impact on blood pressure. The blood pressure of a group of subjects is taken and then these *same* participants take the drug and their blood pressure is again measured. Obviously, to isolate the effect of the drug, a person who is included in the 'before treatment' sample is also included in the 'after treatment' sample. The measurement for each person in the 'before' sample is then matched with their respective measurement after receiving the new drug to see if it has improved their condition.

When subjects in different samples are linked for some special reason   An example may be where we want to compare the amount of TV watched by a parent with the amount of TV watched by his or her particular child. If we choose a certain set of parents, we cannot choose any set of children to compare them with: the sample needs to be comprised of the children of the people making up the parent sample.   This is sometimes called a **matched-pairs** technique.

It is clear that in either situation the make-up of one sample determines the make-up of the other sample.   The advantage of a dependent-sample method is that it controls in a loose fashion for other variables that might affect the dependent variable. For example, consider further the issue of whether parents and children differ in the amount of TV they watch. If we take a random sample of parents and a random sample of *any* children and compare the means for each sample, we might find that there is a statistically significant difference. But this might not be due to family status. There might be another variable, such as socioeconomic status, that affects TV watching, and because our sample of parents has more cases from one socioeconomic group than does the sample of children, a difference has emerged.

  It might be safe to assume, however, that any given parent-and-child pair falls into the same socioeconomic group. By taking parent-and-child pairs, therefore, and looking at *the difference for each pair*, the effect of other variables such as socioeconomic status is mitigated. In effect we are saying that all other variables that might determine TV watching are the same for each member of a given pair, and therefore only family relationship differs between them, allowing us to isolate its impact on the dependent variable.

The dependent samples *t*-test for the mean difference

To illustrate the use of a dependent (or paired) samples *t*-test we will work through the following example. A survey of 10 families is conducted and a parent from each household and a child from each household are asked to keep a diary of the amount of TV in minutes they watch during a set time period. For each parent-child pair the amount of TV watched is recorded (Table 22.1).

  Since the variable of interest, amount of TV watching, is measured at the interval/ratio level, the mean for each sample has been calculated. If we are comparing independent samples of adults and children, we then conduct a *t*-test on the difference between these two sample means. This procedure for the *independent samples t*-test can be summarized as follows:

  1. Calculate the mean for *each* sample.
  2. Then calculate the difference between the two sample means.

However, here we have selected these two samples so that we can match each member of one with a member of the other. To conduct a dependent-samples *t*-test, we reverse the order of the two steps:

Table 22.1 Amount of TV watched by household pair

Household	Minutes of TV watched by child	Minutes of TV watched by parent
1	45	23
2	56	25
3	73	43
4	53	26
5	27	21
6	34	29
7	76	32
8	21	23
9	54	25
10	43	21
Mean	$\overline{X} = \dfrac{\Sigma X}{n} = 48.2$	$\overline{X} = \dfrac{\Sigma X}{n} = 26.8$

1. Calculate the difference for each pair of cases (D).
2. Then calculate the mean of the differences $\left(\overline{X}_D\right)$.

To put it even more succinctly, an independent-samples t-test looks at the *difference between the means*, while a dependent-samples t-test looks at the *mean of the differences*.

Table 22.2 goes through the first step involved in performing a dependent-samples t-test by calculating the difference in the amount of TV watched for each pair.

Table 22.2 Difference in the amount of TV watched by household pairs

Household	Difference in minutes of TV watched (D)
1	45–23 = 22
2	56–25 = 31
3	73–43 = 30
4	53–26 = 27
5	27–21 = 6
6	34–29 = 5
7	76–32 = 44
8	21–23 = -2
9	54–25 = 29
10	43–21 = 22
Mean difference	$\overline{X}_D = \dfrac{\Sigma D}{n} = 21.4$

You may notice that the mean difference is equal to the difference between means; this will always be the case. So why go through this alternative procedure for calculating the difference between two means? Although the mean difference will always equal the difference between the means, the variances will not be the same; the *variance* around the mean difference is much smaller than the variance around the difference between means. Because of this we may fail to reject a difference if it is treated as a difference between means, when we would have rejected it if it were treated as a mean difference.

We can see in Table 22.2 that there is on average a difference for each of the pairs that make up the samples. Let us assume that in the population as a whole there is no difference in the amount of TV watched between parents and their respective children. The null hypothesis is written in the following way:

$$H_0: \mu_D = 0$$

When sampling from such a population, occasionally we might find a parent who watches more TV than his or her child, and occasionally we might find that a child watches a little more than his or her parent, but *if the null hypothesis of no difference is true*, on average the positive differences will cancel out the negative differences. In other words, it is not unreasonable to expect that random variation might occasionally result in a few extra households in which the parent watches less TV than the corresponding child, or vice versa, so that the mean difference between the samples is not zero. The bigger the difference between the sample result and the expected result of zero mean difference, though, the less likely that this will be due to random variation and the more likely that it reflects an underlying difference between parents and their children.

In this example the average of the differences is 21.4 minutes. Should this difference between the samples cause us to reject the hypothesis that there is no difference between the populations?

The formulas involved in conducting a *t*-test for the mean difference are:

$$t = \frac{\overline{X}_D}{s_D / \sqrt{n}}$$

where:

$$s_D = \sqrt{\frac{\Sigma D^2 - \frac{(\Sigma D)^2}{n}}{n-1}}$$

Note that *n* refers to the number of pairs, and not the total number of cases. In this example *n*=10, even though we have a total of 20 cases made up of 10 parents and 10 children. The sample score will be:

$$s_D = \sqrt{\frac{\Sigma D^2 - \frac{(\Sigma D)^2}{n}}{n-1}} = \sqrt{\frac{6400 - \frac{45,796}{10}}{10-1}}$$

$$= 14.2$$

$$t_{sample} = \frac{\overline{X}_D}{s_D/\sqrt{n}} = \frac{21.4}{14.2/\sqrt{10}}$$

$$= 4.8$$

Here we have 9 degrees of freedom (the 10 pairs minus one). At an 0.05 level of significance, the critical score is as shown in Table 22.3.

Table 22.3 Critical values for *t*-distributions

df	Level of significance for one-tail test				
	0.10	0.05	0.02	0.01	0.005
	Level of significance for two-tail test				
df	0.20	0.10	0.05	0.02	0.01
1	3.078	6.314	12.706	31.821	63.657
2	1.886	2.920	4.303	6.965	9.925
3	1.638	2.353	3.182	4.541	5.841
4	1.533	2.132	2.776	3.747	4.604
5	1.476	2.015	2.571	3.365	4.032
6	1.440	1.943	2.447	3.143	3.707
7	1.415	1.895	2.365	2.998	3.499
8	1.397	1.860	2.306	2.896	3.355
9	1.383	1.833	2.262	2.821	3.250
10	1.372	1.812	2.228	2.764	3.169
⋮	⋮	⋮	⋮	⋮	⋮
∞	1.282	1.645	1.960	2.326	2.576

$$t_{critical} = \pm 2.262 \ (\alpha = 0.05, \ df = 9)$$

If we graph these sample and critical scores for *t* (Figure 22.1) we can see that the null should be rejected.

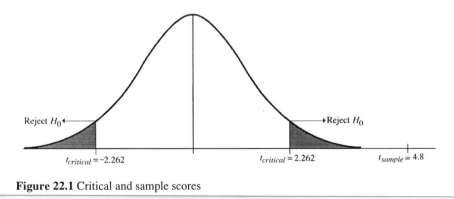

Reject H_0 $t_{critical} = -2.262$ $t_{critical} = 2.262$ $t_{sample} = 4.8$ Reject H_0

Figure 22.1 Critical and sample scores

There is a significant difference in the amount of TV watched between parents and their children.

The dependent-samples *t*-test using SPSS

In order for SPSS to do this same calculation, we first need to note the special way in which data are entered in order to conduct a dependent-samples *t*-test. When coding data for paired samples, *each pair has to be treated as one case so that the information for each parent-and-child pair has to appear along the same row of data* (Figure 22.2). The unit of analysis is the pair, not the individual people. Thus, in our example, there will only be 10 rows of data.

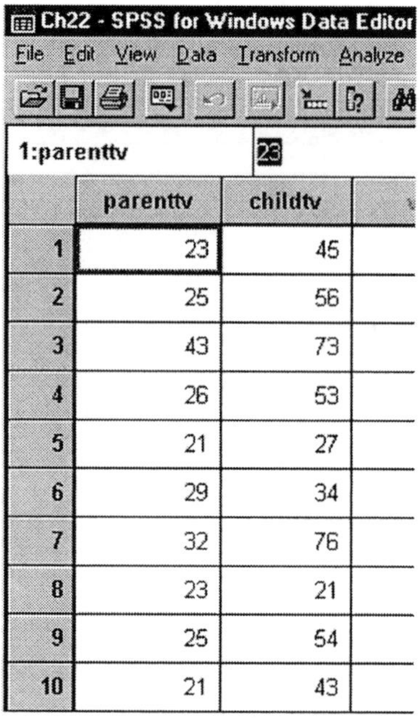

	parenttv	childtv	
1	23	45	
2	25	56	
3	43	73	
4	26	53	
5	21	27	
6	29	34	
7	32	76	
8	23	21	
9	25	54	
10	21	43	

Figure 22.2 SPSS data entered for dependent-samples test

By placing each pair on the same row of data, we can match responses according to household. This produces a column for the amount of TV the parent watches, which is given the variable name **parenttv**, and a second column for the amount of TV the child watches, which has been given the variable name **childtv**. Thus each row has an entry for the amount of TV the child watches and the amount of TV the parent watches. (If, on the other hand, we were treating the two samples as independent, we enter all 20 scores in the *same column*, so that there are 20 rows of data. We would then have a second column for the variable indicating the status of each case within a family – either parent or child.)

Once data have been entered in the appropriate way for a dependent-samples *t*-test, which SPSS calls a paired-samples *t*-test, the following set of instructions is used (Table 22.4, Figure 22.3).

Table 22.4 Paired-samples *t*-test using SPSS

SPSS command/action	Comments
1 Select from the menu **Analyze/Compare Means/ Paired-Samples T Test**	This brings up the **Paired-Samples T Test** dialog box. In the top left of the box will be an area with a list of the variables entered in the data page
2 Click on **Minutes of TV watched – parent**, and then click on **Minutes of TV watched – child** in the source variable list	This highlights the two variables that will be matched
3 Click on ▸	This pastes the highlighted variables into the **Paired Variables:** target list
4 Click on **OK**	

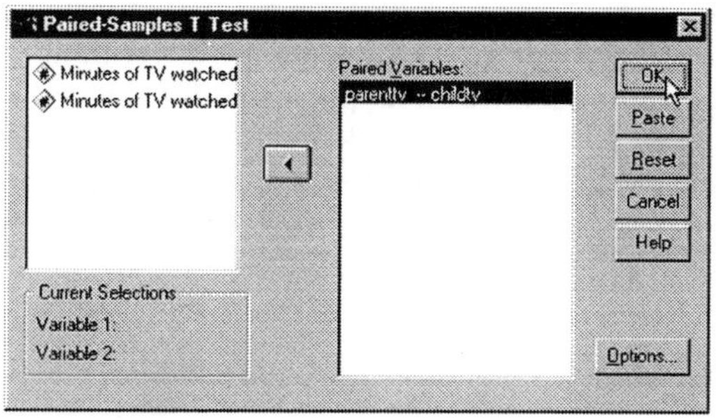

Figure 22.3 The **Paired-Samples T Test** dialog box

These procedures will generate the results presented in Figure 22.4.

T-Test

Paired Samples Statistics

		Mean	N	Std. Deviation	Std. Error Mean
Pair 1	Minutes of TV watched - parent	26.80	10	6.65	2.10
	Minutes of TV watched - child	48.20	10	18.05	5.71

Paired Samples Correlations

		N	Correlation	Sig.
Pair 1	Minutes of TV watched - parent & Minutes of TV watched - child	10	.699	.024

Paired Samples Test

		Paired Differences							
					95% Confidence Interval of the Difference				
		Mean	Std. Deviation	Std. Error Mean	Lower	Upper	t	df	Sig. (2-tailed)
Pair 1	Minutes of TV watched - parent - Minutes of TV watched - child	-21.40	14.22	4.50	-31.57	-11.23	-4.758	9	.001

Figure 22.4 SPSS paired-samples *t*-test output

The output begins with a table called **Paired Samples Statistics**. This provides the descriptive statistics for the paired samples: the mean of 48.20 minutes for the 10 children and 26.80 minutes for the 10 parents. The next table with the correlation information is not relevant to our discussion here. The important table is the last one labeled **Paired Samples Test**. This contains the information on the dependent-samples *t*-test, and confirms the calculations above. The mean difference is calculated as -21.4 minutes. The *t*-test for this value is -4.758. From the last column we see that, with 9 degrees of freedom, a mean difference this large or greater will occur, if the null hypothesis of no difference is true, less than one time in every thousand samples (.001). This is well below any normal alpha level, such as 0.05 or 0.01, so we reject the null hypothesis of no difference.

The output also provides the 95 percent confidence interval for the estimate of the difference. The upper limit of the estimate is -11.23 while the lower limit is -31.57. We can use this information to conduct the hypothesis test. Since the interval does not include the value of 0, we can conclude that the difference in the population as to the amount of TV watched by parents and their children is not zero.

Example

A teacher is interested in the effect of a new study technique on the ability of students to complete basic arithmetic. The teacher selects five students and asks them to complete a basic arithmetic test. The teacher then introduces the new study technique and after a month selects the same five students and asks them to complete a similar test. The results are presented in Table 22.5

Table 22.5 Results of arithmetic test

Student	Time to complete test – pre	Time to complete test – post
Stacey	7.3	6.8
Chloe	8.5	7.9
Billie	6.4	6.0
Alana	9.0	8.4
Timothy	6.9	6.5
Mean	$\bar{X} = 7.62$	$\bar{X} = 7.12$

Initially the teacher treats these as independent samples. The average time for the pre-test is 7.62 minutes while for the post-test it is 7.12 minutes. Using the *independent-samples* *t*-test for the difference between sample means, the teacher obtains a sample *t*-score of 0.75, which is not significant at the 0.05 level. Feeling disheartened that, although the sample results looked promising, the inference test did not reject the possibility that the improvement came about by chance, the teacher decides to abandon the new study method.

Fortunately a colleague knows a little more about statistics and realizes that, since the same students make up each sample, a dependent-samples test is required for this research design. They work through the data with the following results.

Step 1: State the null and alternative hypotheses

$$H_0: \mu_D = 0$$

$$H_a: \mu_D \neq 0$$

Step 2: Choose the test of significance
Here we are comparing two dependent samples in terms of mean differences. Therefore we use the two dependent-samples t-test for the mean difference.

Step 3: Calculate the sample scores
To help in calculating the mean difference between the samples and the associated t-score we construct Table 22.6.

Table 22.6 Calculations for dependent-samples t-test

Student	Time to complete test – pre	Time to complete test – post	Difference	D^2
Stacey	7.3	6.8	0.5	0.25
Chloe	8.5	7.9	0.6	0.36
Billie	6.4	6.0	0.4	0.16
Alana	9.0	8.4	0.6	0.36
Timothy	6.9	6.5	0.4	0.16
Sum			$\Sigma D = 2.5$	$\Sigma D^2 = 1.29$
Mean			$\overline{X}_D = 0.5$	

Substituting this information into the equation for the standard error and then for t_{sample} we get:

$$s_D = \sqrt{\frac{\Sigma D^2 - \frac{(\Sigma D)^2}{n}}{n-1}} = \sqrt{\frac{1.29 - \frac{(2.5)^2}{5}}{5-1}}$$

$$= 0.1$$

$$t_{sample} = \frac{\overline{X}_D}{s_D / \sqrt{n}} = \frac{0.5}{0.1 / \sqrt{5}}$$

$$= 11.8$$

Step 4: Establish the critical score(s) and critical region(s)
At an alpha level of 0.05 with 4 degrees of freedom the critical value for t is 2.776.

Step 5: Make a decision
The t-score, when calculated on the basis of dependent samples rather than independent samples, is now clearly significant at even the 0.01 level. The teacher can reject the hypothesis that the improvement came about only by random chance.

Exercises

22.1   (a)   What is the mean difference for the following 10 pairs of observations?

Pair	Observation 1	Observation 2
1	12	15
2	10	13
3	8	13
4	14	14
5	12	18
6	15	13
7	14	18
8	9	9
9	18	11
10	13	14

   (b)   What is the standard error?
   (c)   Conduct a dependent-samples t-test on the following data, with a 0.05 level of significance.

22.2   Test the following hypotheses using the data provided:

	H_0	H_a	Mean difference	s_D	n	α
(a)	$\mu_D = 0$	$\mu_D \neq 0$	2.3	1.4	20	0.10
(b)	$\mu_D = 0$	$\mu_D < 0$	−3.2	20	41	0.05

22.3   One hundred and forty patients are given a new treatment for lowering blood pressure. The mean difference between systolic blood pressure for these patients before and after the treatment is −9, with a standard deviation of 8. The treatment will only be adopted if it is significant at a 0.01 level. Should it be adopted?

22.4   A company wants to investigate whether changes in work organization can significantly improve productivity levels. It randomly selects 10 workplaces and measures productivity levels in terms of units per hour produced. It then introduces a program in these workplaces giving workers greater discretion over conditions and job structure, and measures productivity levels 6 months later. The results are:

Workplace	Productivity before change	Productivity after change
1	120	165
2	121	154
3	145	120
4	112	155
5	145	164
6	130	132
7	134	154
8	126	162
9	137	130
10	128	142

Has the program significantly improved productivity levels (note the form of the alternative hypothesis)?

22.5 The following data list the asking and selling prices (in dollars) for a random sample of 10 three-bedroom homes sold during a certain period:

Home	Asking price ($)	Selling price ($)
1	140,000	144,300
2	172,500	169,800
3	159,900	155,000
4	148,000	150,000
5	129,900	129,900
6	325,000	315,000
7	149,700	146,000
8	147,900	149,200
9	259,000	259,000
10	223,900	219,000

Why is a dependent-samples test appropriate in this situation? Using a dependent-samples *t*-test, do people receive the price they want when selling their home? Enter these data in SPSS and conduct this test. Compare the results with your hand calculations.

22.6 A nutritionist is interested in the effect that a particular combination of exercise and diet has on weight loss. The nutritionist selected a group of people and measured their weight in kilograms before and after a program of diet and exercise. A paired-samples *t*-test was conducted on SPSS with the results shown over the page.
  From this output determine the:
  (a) variable names assigned to the before-and-after measurements;
  (b) number of pairs in the test;
  (c) mean weight for the pre-test sample;
  (d) mean weight for the post-test sample;
  (e) mean difference between the two samples;
  (f) value of t_{sample} and the number of degrees of freedom;

Paired Samples Statistics

		Mean	N	Std. Deviation	Std. Error Mean
Pair 1	Weight in Kg Pre-Test	70.10	21	11.19	2.44
	Weight in Kg Post Test	66.43	21	9.64	2.10

Paired Samples Correlations

		N	Correlation	Sig.
Pair 1	Weight in Kg Pre-Test & Weight in Kg Post Test	21	.974	.000

Paired Samples Test

		Paired Differences					t	df	Sig. (2-tailed)
					95% Confidence Interval of the Difference				
		Mean	Std. Deviation	Std. Error Mean	Lower	Upper			
Pair 1	Weight in Kg Pre-Test - Weight in Kg Post Test	3.67	2.82	.61	2.38	4.95	5.966	20	.000

(g) probability of obtaining this mean difference if the null hypothesis of no difference is true;

(h) upper limit of the confidence interval for the estimate of the difference;

(i) lower limit of the confidence interval for the estimate of the difference.

(j) What should the nutritionist conclude about the effect of the program?

22.7   From the previous question if this nutritionist considered an average weight loss of 5 kg or more to be the measure of success of this program, can we say that the program was successful? What does this say about the difference between practical and statistical significance?

22.8   Using the data for the example in the text regarding the study technique to improve mathematical skills, enter the data into SPSS, first to conduct an independent-samples test and second to conduct a dependent-samples test. What explains the difference?

22.9   Using the **Employee data** file determine whether there has been a significant increase in salaries since employees began working at the company. If the research question was, alternatively, whether any increase was significantly greater than $15,000, what would you conclude?

23

Non-parametric Tests for Two Dependent Samples

The previous chapter discussed the t-test for the mean difference. This test is equivalent to the t-test for the equality of two means, but applied to dependent rather than independent samples. In fact, for each test for independent samples there is usually an analogous test for dependent samples.

This chapter will consider tests that can be applied to dependent samples compared in terms of nominal or ordinal data:

The McNemar test/the sign test These tests are used to compare two dependent samples in terms of their distribution across a binomial variable. These two tests are equivalent, in the sense that they will always produce the same p-value for any given difference between the samples. In the text we will detail the McNemar test, since the SPSS output for this test provides slightly more information than with a sign test. After working through the McNemar test we will conduct a sign test on the same data to show the difference in the presentation of the results.

The Wilcoxon signed-ranks test This test is used to compare two dependent samples in terms of their frequency distribution across a range of categories for a variable measured at least at the ordinal level.

The McNemar chi-square test for change

A binomial variable, such as a coin toss, only has two possible outcomes. The McNemar test compares the outcome for each case in one sample with the outcome for its respective pair in the other sample. For example, a political scientist might be interested in whether televized debates between political candidates have an effect on voting intentions. The researcher randomly selects 137 people and asks them whether they plan to vote Progressive or Conservative at the forthcoming election, ignoring all other candidates. The researcher then asks the same question of *the same* 138 people after they have watched a televized debate between the Progressive and Conservative candidates.

In comparing each individual in the 'before' stage with his or her own particular response after the debate, there are four possibilities (Figure 23.1).

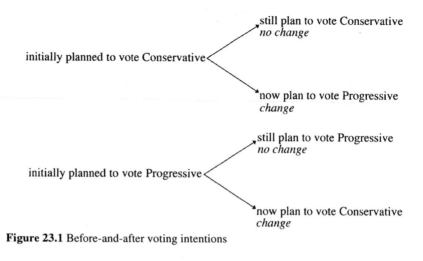

initially planned to vote Conservative
- still plan to vote Conservative
  no change
- now plan to vote Progressive
  change

initially planned to vote Progressive
- still plan to vote Progressive
  no change
- now plan to vote Conservative
  change

Figure 23.1 Before-and-after voting intentions

Table 23.1 illustrates these possibilities.

Table 23.1 Joint distribution of survey results

Before	After	
	Conservative	Progressive
Conservative	No change (a)	Change (b)
Progressive	Change (c)	No change (d)

The McNemar test only considers those pairs for which a change has occurred, and analyzes whether any changes tend to occur in one direction (e.g. Conservative to Progressive) *or* the other (Progressive to Conservative). The total number of pairs registering a change will be cells (b) and (c) in Table 23.1. If the changes induced by watching the TV debate do not favor a shift in one direction or the other, then we should *expect* to find 50 percent of the total number of changes in cell (b), and 50 percent in cell (c).

Of course, random variation will cause samples to differ from the expected result, even if the debate did not affect the overall opinion of the population. It is possible (although very unlikely) to select a random sample where 90 percent of all pairs registering a change in opinion are in cell (b), even if in the whole population the changes are similar in either direction. The greater the difference between the observed cell frequencies and the expected cell frequencies, however, the less likely that such an event can be attributed to sampling error.

This discussion of expected and observed cell frequencies should sound similar to the chi-square test. In fact the McNemar test (with large samples) is a chi-square test for the difference between expected and observed cell frequencies. This test statistic is calculated using the following formula:

$$\chi_M^2 = \frac{(n_1 - n_2 - 1)^2}{n_1 + n_2}$$

where:

n_1 is the observed number of cases in cell (b) or cell (c), whichever is *largest*
n_2 is the observed number of cases in cell (b) or cell (c), whichever is *smallest*.

The distribution of responses to this hypothetical study is as shown in Table 23.2.

Table 23.2 Voting intentions before and after TV debate

Before	After	
	Conservative	Progressive
Conservative	28	55
Progressive	27	28

We can immediately see that the total number of cases that did not change their opinion (the unshaded cells) is:

$$28 + 27 = 55$$

whereas the total number of cases that *did* record a change (the shaded cells) is:

$$55 + 27 = 82$$

Obviously the sample result differs from the expected result, but is the difference big enough to warrant rejecting the null hypothesis? Using the formula for the McNemar statistic we get:

$$\chi_M^2 = \frac{(n_1 - n_2 - 1)^2}{n_1 + n_2} = \frac{(55 - 27 - 1)^2}{55 + 27}$$

$$= 8.89$$

From Table A4 for the critical values of chi-square, with 1 degree of freedom, the critical value of chi-square at the 0.01 level is 6.635 (Figure 23.2). This leads us to reject the null hypothesis. The TV debate does have an affect on voting intentions. Looking back at the table of raw numbers, it is clear that the direction of change is from Conservative to Progressive.

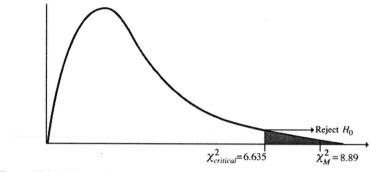

Figure 23.2 Critical and sample scores

The McNemar test using SPSS

Table 23.3 and Figure 23.3 go through the steps involved in conducting a McNemar test on these data. Figure 23.4 presents the output from this set of instructions.

The first table in the output contains the descriptive statistics for the sample data, and is basically the same as Table 23.3 below. The second table labeled **Test Statistics** contains the information for the McNemar chi-square test on the cells in the first table reflecting a change. The difference between the observed and expected frequencies produces a chi-square value for the sample of 8.890. With 1 degree of freedom, the exact probability of getting this sample chi-square just by random variation is .003. This is well below any normal alpha level such as 0.05. The researcher concludes that the TV debate is likely to favor a change in opinion, from Conservative to Progressive.

Table 23.3 McNemar test on SPSS (file: **Ch23-1.sav**)

SPSS command/action	Comments
1 From the menu select **Analyze/ Nonparametric Tests/2 Related Samples**	This brings up the **Two-Related-Samples Tests** dialog box. You will notice that in the area to the bottom right of the window headed **Test Type** the small square next to **W**ilcoxon is selected. This indicates that the Wilcoxon test for two dependent samples is the default test. Here we want to conduct a McNemar test so we need to 'unselect' Wilcoxon and select McNemar instead
2 Click on the square next to **W**ilcoxon	This removes ✓ from the tick-box
3 Click on the square next to **Mc**Nemar	This places ✓ in the tick-box, indicating that it is the selected test
4 Click on **Voting intention pre debate** and then click on **Voting intention post debate** in the source variables list	These two variable names will be highlighted
5 Click on ▶	This pastes the highlighted two variables into the **T**est Pairs: target list indicating that responses for these two variables will be matched
6 Click on **OK**	

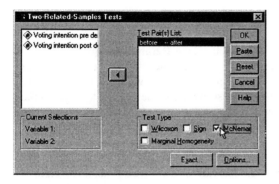

Figure 23.3 The **Two-Related-Samples Tests** dialog box

McNemar Test
Crosstabs

Voting intention pre debate & Voting intention post debate

	Voting intention post debate	
Voting intention pre debate	1	2
1	28	55
2	27	27

Test Statistics[b]

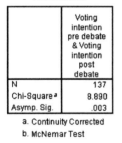

	Voting intention pre debate & Voting intention post debate
N	137
Chi-Square[a]	8.890
Asymp. Sig.	.003

a. Continuity Corrected
b. McNemar Test

Figure 23.4 SPSS McNemar test output

Before leaving the discussion of the McNemar test, we should note that since it is a special application of the chi-square test, it also suffers from the same limitations. In particular, from Chapter 20 we know that the chi-square test is only appropriate when expected cell frequencies are 5 or more. This rule applies to the McNemar test, and the same correction is taken. When cell sizes are small, SPSS will automatically conduct the test using the binomial approximation to the normal curve, and print the two-tail probability associated with this approximation.

The sign test

You will notice that under **Test Type** in the **Two-Related-Samples** dialog box there are three options for conducting an inference test on two dependent samples. One is the McNemar chi-square test which we have just discussed. Another is the Wilcoxon signed-ranks test, which is the default test, and which we will discuss in detail below. The third is the **sign test**. The sign test conducts a binomial z-test, much like that detailed in Chapter 15. The pairs in which there is a change in one direction (such as Conservative to Progressive) are given a positive sign, and the pairs in which there is a change in the other direction (such as Progressive to Conservative) are given a negative sign. A binomial z-test is then conducted by comparing the proportion of positive changes (or negative changes) with the test proportion of 0.5.

In the above SPSS procedure, if we had selected the sign test rather than the McNemar test under **Test Type** in the **Two-Related-Samples** dialog box, the output would be like that illustrated in Figure 23.5.

Sign Test

Frequencies

		N
Voting intention post debate - Voting intention pre debate	Negative Differences[a]	27
	Positive Differences[b]	55
	Ties[c]	55
	Total	137

a. Voting intention post debate < Voting intention pre debate

b. Voting intention post debate > Voting intention pre debate

c. Voting intention pre debate = Voting intention post debate

Test Statistics[a]

	Voting intention post debate - Voting intention pre debate
Z	-2.982
Asymp. Sig. (2-tailed)	.003

a. Sign Test

Figure 23.5 SPSS sign test output

In the first table we have the sample descriptive statistics, which is just another way of presenting the same information as Table 23.2. The **Test**

Statistics table presents the information on the binomial z-test for the signs. Note that the two-tailed probability of .003 for the sample z-score of -2.982 is the same as that for chi-square in the McNemar test. The probability obtained through the sign test is always exactly the same as that obtained from a McNemar test applied to the same data. Therefore the same decision is made regarding the null hypothesis, regardless of which test is used. The advantage of the McNemar test is that the crosstab that is generated as part of the SPSS output provides a more detailed breakdown of the pairs than the output that comes with the sign test. This makes it easier to interpret the data since it allows us to see in which direction the changes move.

Example

A study is conducted to investigate attitudes toward computer games. Fifty people are randomly chosen and asked if they believe video games to be of any educational value, with responses restricted to 'yes' or 'no'. After playing a range of video games each person is asked the same question. The distribution of responses is recorded in Table 23.4, with the cells indicating a change in attitude highlighted.

Table 23.4 Attitude to video games before and after playing

After	Before	
	No	Yes
No	15	18
Yes	10	7

Substituting this information into the formula for the McNemar test produces the following result.

$$\chi_M^2 = \frac{(n_1 - n_2 - 1)^2}{n_1 + n_2} = \frac{(18 - 10 - 1)^2}{18 + 10}$$

$$= 1.75$$

From the distribution for chi-square table, the critical value with 1 degree of freedom is 3.841. The sample score does not fall in the region of rejection. We therefore do not reject the null hypothesis: playing video games does not seem to change people's attitude in one particular way or the other.

The Wilcoxon signed-ranks z-test

In Chapter 19 we saw that hypothesis tests for ordinal data, when comparing independent samples, use the ranks of the cases rather than the raw scores. The same principle applies when working with ordinal data and we want to compare dependent samples. Since we can't calculate a mean on the raw scores, we first rank the *pairs* of cases and use these rank scores in the calculations. For dependent samples compared on an ordinal scale the appropriate test is the **Wilcoxon signed-ranks test**, and is very similar in logic to the Wilcoxon rank-sum test for independent samples.

For example, assume that the researcher (in the example above) who conducted the McNemar test to assess people's attitude to video games is dissatisfied with the results. The researcher suspects that playing video games really does affect a person's attitude to the educational value of such games, and that the simple binomial scale used in the original study was not sensitive enough to detect this change. The researcher therefore conducts another study involving 15 people who are asked to rate on a 10-point scale whether they believe video games have any educational value, with 1 indicating no educational value and 10 indicating very high educational value. Each of these 15 people is then asked to play a variety of video games and again rate whether they believe video games are of educational benefit. What effect does actually playing the game have on opinion?

The scores for each person, before and after playing, are recorded in Table 23.5, together with the difference, for each pair.

Table 23.5 Rating of video games before and after use

Person	Before	After	Difference in scores
1	3	5	+2
2	5	5	0
3	2	8	+6
4	3	4	+1
5	8	7	−1
6	6	3	−3
7	4	4	0
8	7	6	−1
9	2	7	+5
10	6	7	+1
11	1	9	+8
12	9	7	−2
13	8	1	−7
14	5	5	0
15	6	2	−4

The first step is to exclude the cases with no change in scores, which are those shaded in the table. As with the McNemar test, cases that show no change are not used in the analysis. Here cases 2, 7, and 14 record no change in their scores before and after.

It would be tempting simply to calculate an average change in scores and conduct a *t*-test on the difference. However, we are working with an ordinal scale and such averages are not appropriate. Instead we take a slightly more difficult route. We rank the cases, starting with those registering the smallest change in scores (these will be cases 4, 8, 5, and 10, which each registered a change of ±1) and continuing through to the case with the largest change (case 11 with a change of 8). Pairs, that is, are ordered according to the absolute difference between their 'Before' and 'After' scores (Table 23.6).

Table 23.6 Ordering of all non-tied pairs

Pair number	4	5	8	10	1	12	6	15	9	3	13	11
Difference	+1	−1	−1	+1	+2	−2	−3	−4	+5	+6	−7	+8
Rank	2.5	2.5	2.5	2.5	5.5	5.5	7	8	9	10	11	12

Notice that cases that have the same absolute change in scores have been assigned an average rank. For example, four cases each changed their score by one point on the scale. Since collectively these cases occupy ranks 1, 2, 3, and 4, the average rank for these four cases is:

$$\frac{1+2+3+4}{4} = 2.5$$

If playing video games has no effect on attitudes regarding their educational value, there should not be a tendency for pairs with either positive or negative changes to bunch up at one end of the ranking or the other. Another way of assessing this is to compare the rank sum for pairs registering a positive change in attitude to the rank sum for pairs registering a negative change in attitude. If the positive and negative changes are equally distributed through the ranks, the sum of these ranks will be equal, and can be calculated using the following formula:

$$\mu_T = \frac{n(n+1)}{4}$$

The value of μ_T is the rank sum we expect from samples drawn from a population where attitude to video games does not change systematically in one direction or the other, and is the value we use in stating the null hypothesis. For these data we obtain:

$$\mu_T = \frac{12(12+1)}{4} = 39$$

The null hypothesis in this instance will therefore be:

$$H_0: \mu_T = 39$$

However, even if this is the case, random samples drawn from such a population will not always produce a value of 39. We need to compare this hypothesized value with the sample statistic we obtain, and assess whether any difference can be attributed to random variation.

We derive this sample statistic by separating out those cases that have a positive change (increase) in their score after playing the video games from those cases that have a negative change (reduction) in score. We then sum the ranks for each group (Table 23.7).

Table 23.7 Ordering of pairs

Pair number	5	8		12	6	15		13		
Difference	−1	−1		−2	−3	−4		−7		
Negative rank	2.5	2.5		5.5	7	8		11		
Pair number	4		10	1			9	3		11
Difference	+1		+1	+2			+5	+6		+8
Positive rank	2.5		2.5	5.5			9	10		12

In this example we have rank sums of 36.5 and 41.5. What is the probability of obtaining such a sample result if the null hypothesis is true? The sample statistic, called Wilcoxon's T, is the smallest rank sum, which in this case is the rank sum for the positives. We conduct a z-test on the difference between the value of μ_T and the sample value, T, where:

$$z_{sample} = \frac{T - \mu_T}{\sigma_T}$$

$$\sigma_T = \sqrt{\frac{n(n+1)(2n+1)}{24}}$$

If we substitute the data from the example into these equations, we get:

$$\sigma_T = \sqrt{\frac{n(n+1)(2n+1)}{24}} = \sqrt{\frac{12(12+1)(2 \times 12+1)}{24}}$$

$$= 12.75$$

$$z_{sample} = \frac{T - \mu_T}{\sigma_T} = \frac{36.5 - 39}{12.75}$$

$$= -0.2$$

This value for z, from the table for the area under the standard normal curve, has a two-tail probability of 0.8445. We cannot reject the null hypothesis since the differences observed in the pairs could easily come about through sampling error when drawing from a population in which playing video games has no effect on attitude to their educational value.

The Wilcoxon signed-ranks test using SPSS

The actions required to conduct this test in SPSS are listed in Table 23.8 and Figure 23.6.

Table 23.8 Wilcoxon signed-ranks test on SPSS (file: **Ch23-2.sav**)

SPSS command/action	Comments
1 From the menu select **Analyze/ Nonparametric Tests/2 Related Samples**	This brings up a window headed **Two-Related-Samples Tests**. You will notice that in the area to the bottom left of the window headed **Test Type** the small square next to **Wilcoxon** is selected. This indicates that the Wilcoxon test for two dependent samples is the default test
2 Click on **after** and while holding down the command key click on **before**	These two variable names will be highlighted
3 Click on ▶	This pastes the highlighted variables into the area headed **Test Pairs List:**
4 Click on **OK**	

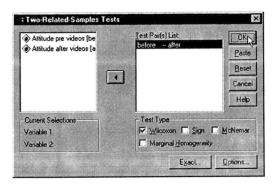

Figure 23.6 The **Two-Related-Samples Tests** dialog box

Figure 23.7 present the output that results from this set of instructions. The SPSS output gives us the same results as those we calculated by hand. As with many of the other tests we have covered, the first part of the output presents the descriptive statistics for the samples, followed by the information from the inference test. In the table labeled **Ranks** we first see that there are six pairs that registered an increase in score after playing videos (Attitude after videos > Attitude pre videos). There are also six pairs that registered a decrease (Attitude after videos < Attitude pre videos), and three pairs whose score did not change (Attitude after videos = Attitude pre videos).

Wilcoxon Signed Ranks Test

Ranks

		N	Mean Rank	Sum of Ranks
Attitude after videos - Attitude pre videos	Negative Ranks	6[a]	6.08	36.50
	Positive Ranks	6[b]	6.92	41.50
	Ties	3[c]		
	Total	15		

a. Attitude after videos < Attitude pre videos

b. Attitude after videos > Attitude pre videos

c. Attitude pre videos = Attitude after videos

Test Statistics[b]

	Attitude after videos - Attitude pre videos
Z	-.197[a]
Asymp. Sig. (2-tailed)	.844

a. Based on negative ranks.

b. Wilcoxon Signed Ranks Test

Figure 23.7 SPSS Wilcoxon test output

Second, SPSS calculates the mean ranks and rank sums for the positives and negatives. If we multiply these mean ranks by the number of cases in each group we get the sum of ranks:

$$\Sigma R_- = 6.92 \times 6 = 41.5$$

$$\Sigma R_+ = 6.08 \times 6 = 36.5$$

The **Test Statistics** table, which contains the information on the z-test for the rank sums, indicates that we should not reject the null hypothesis, given that the probability of .844 is greater than the alpha level of 0.05. In other words, even if playing video games makes no difference in attitude toward their educational value, we will still get sample results with this amount of difference or greater more than 8 times out of 10.

Exercises

23.1   Conduct a McNemar test on the following data ($\alpha = 0.05$):

(a)

After	Before	
	1	2
1	27	22
2	34	28

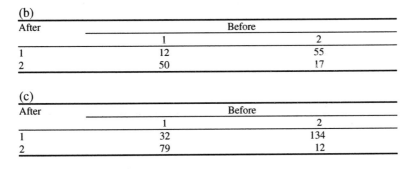

(b)

After	Before	
	1	2
1	12	55
2	50	17

(c)

After	Before	
	1	2
1	32	134
2	79	12

23.2 Brothers and sisters are matched and asked if they play regular sport. The results are:

Sister	Brother	
	Yes	No
Yes	18	11
No	16	15

(a) Conduct a McNemar test to assess whether there is a difference between brothers and sisters in terms of sport playing.
(b) Enter these data in SPSS, and conduct a McNemar test. Compare the SPSS output with your hand calculations.

23.3 The following are scores of 8 matched pairs in a before-and-after experiment:

Before	After
75	65
63	67
82	51
37	43
46	47
59	61
39	52
33	85

Use the Wilcoxon signed-ranks test to assess whether there is a difference (use $\alpha = 0.05$).

23.4 Ten people are asked to rate the effectiveness of two training programs, with 1 equal to 'Very poor' and 10 equal to 'Very good'. The responses are summarized in the table over the page.

(a) Can we say that one program is preferred over another, at a 0.01 level of significance?
(b) Enter these data into SPSS and confirm your results.

Program1	Program 2
3	5
2	6
3	7
2	7
1	4
4	2
5	5
1	8
6	9

PART 6

Multivariate Descriptive Statistics

24

Elaborating Crosstabs: Adding Control Variables

Chapters 7–10 analyzed the relationship between two variables. In those chapters it was assumed that any association observed in the data between two variables is due to a simple and direct relationship. A strong association in a bivariate table, however, does not necessarily mean that a simple direct relationship *in fact* exists; this is only how we have *interpreted* the data. There may be more complex relationships buried in the data, but we have not dug deep enough to find them.

The simplest way of extending – **elaborating** – the relationship discovered in a crosstab is to look at the possible impact that a third variable has on the original bivariate association. Depending on the outcome of this elaboration we may have to adjust our model of the relationship between the original two variables to take into account the influence of the third variable.

There are three possible conclusions we can reach when we introduce a third variable into the analysis:

1. a direct relationship still exists (the third variable has no effect); or
2. either a spurious or intervening relationship exists; or
3. a conditional relationship exists.

We will investigate these possible outcomes by looking at examples of each type of relationship in turn.

Direct relationship

We begin with an example where the original bivariate relationship does not change when we introduce a third variable. When the introduction of a third variable does not alter the original bivariate relationship, this will provide evidence that the simple direct model is the appropriate way of characterizing the relationship.

For example, we may have data relating income and TV watching, arranged in a crosstab (Table 24.1).

Table 24.1 TV watching by income level

TV watching	Income		Total
	Low	High	
Low	115 57%	95 32%	210
High	88 43%	204 68%	292
Total	203	299	502
Gamma=0.47			

We initially model the relationship between these two variables as a direct one (Figure 24.1).

Income ⎯⎯⎯⎯⎯⎯▶ TV watching

Figure 24.1 A direct relationship

Our theoretical model argues that income directly affects the amount of TV someone watches, and the statistics tell us that this is a moderate to strong, positive relationship. When we argue that there is a direct relationship between two variables we are effectively arguing that the relationship will be the same regardless of any other variable which may cause cases to vary from each other. In this example, we think income affects TV watching in the same way and to the same degree, regardless of any other variable that may cause cases to vary, such as sex, age, hair color, etc.

This direct bivariate model, however, may appear to be overly simplistic. Surely there are other variables which impact on the amount of TV someone watches. Another researcher, for example, may feel that level of education also affects the amount of TV watched by individuals.

To assess the possible impact this new variable (level of education) has on the observed relationship between income and amount of TV watched, we divide the sample into two sub-groups: those who have no post-secondary education and those who have completed some post-secondary education. In technical terms we have introduced education level as a **control variable**.

A **control variable** decomposes the data into sub-groups based on the categories of the control variable.

The effect of this control variable is to **generate a separate crosstab for each of the sub-groups defined by the control variable**. In this example, we first take *only those cases with no post-secondary education* and create a crosstab between their income and TV watching, ignoring those cases with some post-secondary education. We then take *only cases with some post-secondary* *education* and create a crosstab between their income and TV watching, ignoring people with no post-secondary education.

The resulting crosstabs are called **partial tables** and *we generate as many partial tables as there are categories for the control variable* (Table 24.2, Table 24.3). Here the control variable, 'Education level', only has two categories; we therefore generate two partial tables. (If we had three categories for the control variable, say 'no post-secondary', 'some post-secondary', 'a lot of post-secondary', we would generate three partial tables.)

Table 24.2 TV watching by income level: controlling for education level (no post-secondary education)

TV watching	Income		
	Low	High	Total
Low	78	22	100
	57%	31%	
High	58	48	106
	43%	69%	
Total	136	70	206
Gamma = 0.49			

Table 24.3 TV watching by income level: controlling for education level (post-secondary education)

TV watching	Income		
	Low	High	Total
Low	37	73	110
	55%	32%	
High	30	156	186
	45%	68%	
Total	67	229	296
Gamma = 0.45			

With this outcome we can see that the original relationship is reproduced almost exactly for each partial table. The value for gamma for each of the two partial tables is almost the same as that for the original table, before we controlled for education. In other words, regardless of the level of education, the relationship between income and TV watching still holds. The direct relationship we first observed is preserved even after controlling for the third variable. No matter how cases vary according to income level, the direct bivariate relationship remains basically the same, so we will not alter our initial model which characterized income and TV watching in a direct relationship.

Elaboration of crosstabs using SPSS

We can add control variables when generating a crosstab (Table 24.4, Figure 24.2) as part of the **Analyze/Descriptive Statistics/Crosstabs** command we introduced in Chapter 7.   Note that Steps 8 and 9 are only optional when elaborating crosstabs, but the additional information they provide will help us interpret the results.

Table 24.4 Crosstabs with control variables on SPSS (file: **Ch24.sav**)

SPSS command/action	Comments
1 From the menu select **Analyze/Descriptive Statistics/Crosstabs**	This brings up the **Crosstabs** dialog box
2 Click on the **TV watching**	This highlights **TV watching**
3 Click on ▶ that points to the target list headed **Row(s):**	This pastes **TV watching** into the **Row(s):** target list
4 Click on **Income**	This highlights **Income**
5 Click on ▶ that points to the target list headed **Column(s):**	This pastes **Income** into the **Column(s):** target list
6 Click on **Education level**	This highlights **Education level**
7 Click on ▶ that points to the target list below **Layer 1 of 1**	This pastes **Education level** into the target list that contains the control variable. A crosstab will be generated for each value of the variable in this list
8 Click on the **Statistics** button and select Gamma	This will produce the gamma value for each partial table
9 Click on the **Cells** button and select column percentages	This will generate the relative frequencies for each partial table
10 Click on **OK**	

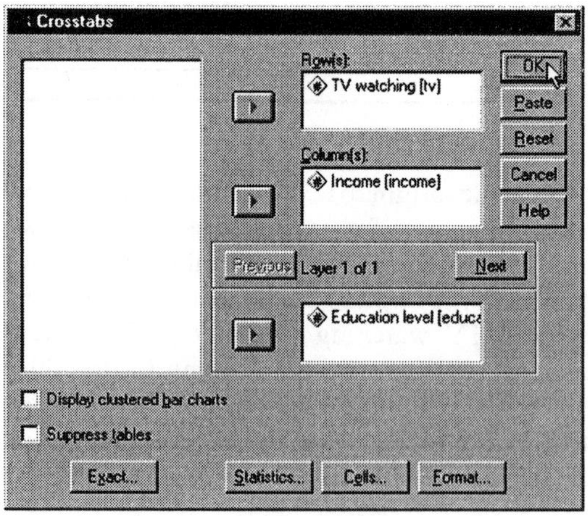

Figure 24.2 The **Crosstabs** dialog box

These commands will produce the crosstab in Figure 24.3.

Crosstabs

TV watching * Income * Education level Crosstabulation

Education level					Income		Total
					Low	High	
No post-secondary	TV watching	Low	Count		78	22	100
			% within Income		57.4%	31.4%	48.5%
		High	Count		58	48	106
			% within Income		42.6%	68.6%	51.5%
	Total		Count		136	70	206
			% within Income		100.0%	100.0%	100.0%
Post-secondary	TV watching	Low	Count		37	73	110
			% within Income		55.2%	31.9%	37.2%
		High	Count		30	156	186
			% within Income		44.8%	68.1%	62.8%
	Total		Count		67	229	296
			% within Income		100.0%	100.0%	100.0%

Symmetric Measures

Education level			Value	Asymp. Std. Error[a]	Approx. T[b]	Approx. Sig.
No post-secondary	Ordinal by Ordinal	Gamma	.492	.118	3.657	.000
	N of Valid Cases		206			
Post-secondary	Ordinal by Ordinal	Gamma	.450	.113	3.317	.001
	N of Valid Cases		296			

a. Not assuming the null hypothesis.

b. Using the asymptotic standard error assuming the null hypothesis.

Figure 24.3 SPSS **Crosstabs** command output with a control variable

This is actually two crosstabs combined into one. The first half of the table is the crosstab of income and TV watching for cases with no post-secondary education, and immediately below it is the crosstab for those cases with post-secondary education. The percentage of cases that watches a certain level of TV is the same for all income categories, *regardless of education level.*

This is reinforced by the values for gamma presented in the **Symmetric Measures** table. These are the same as those we calculated above. The relationship between income and TV watching retains its strength and direction for each of the partial tables.

Spurious or intervening relationship

Assume that when we introduce level of education into the analysis we instead obtain the following partial tables (Tables 24.5 and 24.6), rather than those in Tables 24.2 and 24.3. The relationship between income and TV watching that we observed in the original table has suddenly disappeared for each of the partial tables. It is clear to the naked eye that there is no association to speak of between income and TV watching, once we have controlled for education level. The original association we found has been 'washed out' by the introduction of the control variable. A more precise way of reaching this conclusion is to calculate the **partial gamma** from the gamma values for each partial table.

Table 24.5 TV watching by income level: controlling for education level (no post-secondary education)

TV watching	Income		
	Low	High	Total
Low	102	50	152
	75%	71%	
High	34	20	54
	25%	29%	
Total	136	70	206
Gamma = 0.09			

Table 24.6 TV watching by income level: controlling for education level (post-secondary education)

TV watching	Income		
	Low	High	Total
Low	13	45	58
	19%	20%	
High	54	184	238
	81%	80%	
Total	67	229	296
Gamma = –0.007			

Partial gamma

The gamma values we have calculated for each of the partial tables are very useful for uncovering a spurious or intervening relationship. We can see that these gamma values are negligible in strength, unlike the combined gamma for the original bivariate table. In the original table, where the cases are not separated by level of education, gamma is 0.47. But the gamma values for each of the partial tables are very close to zero.

In Chapter 9 we discussed the logic behind the calculation of gamma, which involved calculating the number of concordant pairs and the number of discordant pairs. Concordant pairs, you remember, are pairs of cases which are ranked the same on each of the two variables, and thereby embody a positive relationship between the variables. Discordant pairs on the other hand are pairs of cases which are ranked differently on the two variables and thereby embody a negative relationship between the variables.

If we add the concordant pairs across both partial tables and the discordant pairs across both partial tables we can calculate the **partial gamma**, which measures the direct relationship between the two variables we started with, *controlling for the third variable*. It is calculated by summing the concordant and discordant pairs across the partial tables. We still use all the cases in determining the partial gamma, but we are now doing it *after* separating the cases into two separate partial tables.

The process of calculating the partial gamma for these data is presented in Table 24.7.

Table 24.7 Calculating partial gamma

	Concordant pairs	Discordant pairs	Gamma
Original bivariate table	$204 \times 115 = 23{,}460$	$88 \times 95 = 8360$	0.47
Partial table 1	$20 \times 102 = 2040$	$34 \times 50 = 1700$	0.09
Partial table 2	$13 \times 184 = 2392$	$54 \times 45 = 2430$	–0.07
Total across partial tables	$2040+2392 = 4432$	$1700+2430 = 4130$	0.04

The partial gamma value for these data is only 0.04, indicating that there is very little *direct* relationship between income and TV watching, once we add level of education as a control.

Spurious or intervening relationship?

When the partial gamma is much lower than the original gamma calculated on the combined crosstab we should conclude that there is either a **spurious** relationship or **intervening** relationship between the first two variables. Before explaining each of these types of relationship, we need to point out that deciding which one explains the results of the elaboration is a *theoretical and not a statistical issue*. Having found that the original relationship disappears after elaborating a crosstab, it is up to us to decide how the three variables fit together, based on our understanding of how the world operates.

We might, for example, believe that the model represented in Figure 24.4 best explains the results we just analyzed.

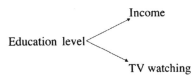

Figure 24.4 A spurious relationship

This represents a spurious relationship between income and TV watching in the sense that a relationship does not exist between the original two variables we looked at; it is only a statistical outcome based on their respective relationships with the control variable. Education level separately affects income and TV watching, but the latter two variables are not linked to each other.

The classic example of a spurious relationship is the observed association between the presence of storks in an area and the birth rate (although it is not clear whether this study was ever undertaken, or whether it is part of statistics mythology). It was observed that where there were many storks there was also a higher birth rate. The storks must be responsible for delivering babies! Of course this is a ridiculous argument and highlights the difference between a **statistical** relationship and a **causal** relationship. The observed relationship was explained by arguing that the same factors which caused the number of storks to vary across regions also caused the birth rate to vary. Specifically, rural areas attract storks, and they also attract people looking to start a family (at the time the study was supposedly undertaken).

In other words, the relationship between the number of storks and the birth rate in a region is spurious. It does not really exist but is an artefact of two other relationships: the relationship between the type of region (rural, non-rural) and the number of storks, and the type of region and the birth rate.

Another researcher may look at the results of our elaboration of the crosstab between income and TV watching and instead characterize the relationship as in Figure 24.5.

Income —————→ Education level —————→ TV watching

Figure 24.5 An intervening relationship

This researcher could make the argument that higher income earners can afford to undertake post-secondary education and then this affects how much TV they watch. Whether you think this argument is a good one or not is a matter for theoretical debate. Whether it is a more appropriate explanation of the results of the elaboration than the model of spurious relationship is open to discussion, but the statistical analysis itself cannot decide between the issue. The results of the statistical analysis merely indicate that *one* of these models best explains the results.

Conditional relationship

Assume that a researcher is interested in the extent to which patients respond to a program of exercise aimed at improving their cardiovascular system. The researcher organizes patients into low exercise and high exercise groups and observes whether there is any improvement in their cardiovascular systems (Table 24.8).

A visual inspection of Table 24.8, looking particularly at the (shaded) modal cells for each column, suggests that there is a strong, positive relationship between the variables. The exercise program does seem to work. To reinforce this impression the researcher calculates gamma, which produces a value of 0.68.

Table 24.8 Cardiovascular improvement by exercise level

Improvement	Exercise level		
	Low	High	Total
No	38 / 73%	11 / 34%	49
Yes	14 / 27%	21 / 66%	35
Total	52	32	84

The researcher could leave the results here, and conclude that a direct relationship has been observed between the independent variable (level of exercise) and the dependent variable (improvement level). However, the researcher believes that the actual relationship is more complex than this, and that there may be other factors left out of this analysis which may determine whether a patient's cardiovascular system improves. In particular, the researcher believes that whether a person has been a regular smoker will affect their chances of responding to the exercise program.

The researcher therefore reruns the crosstabulation, this time controlling for smoking level. The results of this analysis are presented in Table 24.9 and Table 24.10.

Table 24.9 Cardiovascular improvement by exercise level: smokers only

Improvement	Exercise level		
	Low	High	Total
No	28 / 74%	7 / 70%	35
Yes	10 / 26%	3 / 30%	13
Total	38	10	48
Gamma = 0.09			

Table 24.10 Cardiovascular improvement by exercise level: non-smokers only

Improvement	Exercise level		
	Low	High	Total
No	10 / 71%	4 / 18%	14
Yes	4 / 29%	18 / 82%	22
Total	14	22	36
Gamma = 0.84			

When comparing these partial tables against the complete table we started with it is clear that the relationship works differently depending on smoking history. Regular smokers gained no improvement in their health levels as a result of the exercise program. But for non-smokers the relationship is even stronger than was evident in the complete table, a result that was 'diluted' by the inclusion of the smokers for whom the relationship does not seem to hold.

This is reinforced by looking at the gamma values for each of these tables. For non-smokers, the value of gamma is 0.84, as opposed to 0.68 for the table as a whole. For smokers, though, there is practically no benefit from the exercise program. We can see that in gaging the effect of the control variable the measure of association is extremely useful, since it quantifies the changes that are brought about when the control variable is added.

As a result of this observation, the researcher changes the model which may tie the variables together. Instead of a simple one-way direct relationship, the researcher depicts the association in terms of a **conditional relationship**, as in Figure 24.6.

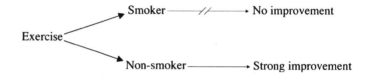

Figure 24.6 A conditional relationship

A conditional relationship is sometimes called **interaction**. Interaction exists where the relationship between two variables depends on the particular values of a third variable. Sometimes we might find that the relationship is reversed depending on the value of the control variable; for one sub-group the relationship might be positive, whereas for another sub-group the relationship might be negative.

Example

We want to investigate the relationship between intelligence and income. Intelligence is measured by a standard IQ test and respondents are divided into low and high IQ. Respondents are also divided into low or high income groups, depending on whether they earn below or above the median national income level.

The combined results for all 1000 people surveyed is presented in Table 24.11. This table illustrates a moderate association between intelligence, as measured by IQ, and income, and might lead to an interpretation that variation in intelligence causes the variation in income levels. People's earning capacity is to some extent predetermined by their respective IQs.

In order to avoid such a conclusion, we might argue that the IQ test as a measure of intelligence is biased. In particular we may feel that IQ scores are themselves a reflection of social class background, and this variable is a key determinant of income. To assess this we construct two partial tables, dividing the 1000 respondents into high social class and low social class sub-groups, producing the results in Tables 24.12 and 24.12.

Table 24.11 Income and intelligence

IQ	Income		Total
	Low	High	
Low	165	95	260
	36%	18%	
High	295	445	740
	64%	82%	
Total	460	540	1000
Gamma = 0.48			

Table 24.12 Income and intelligence: high social class only

IQ	Income		Total
	Low	High	
Low	20	60	80
	18%	14%	
High	90	380	470
	82%	86%	
Total	110	440	550
Gamma = 0.17			

Table 24.13 Income and intelligence: low social class only

IQ	Income		Total
	Low	High	
Low	145	35	180
	41%	35%	
High	205	65	270
	59%	65%	
Total	350	100	450
Gamma = 0.13			

We can see that the strength of the bivariate relationship is greatly diminished once we control for social class. There is little difference in the pattern of relative frequencies across the two partial tables. In fact, the partial gamma calculated on the basis of the partial tables is only 0.15. We have either a spurious relationship or an intervening relationship.

Summary

We have looked at the way in which the introduction of a third variable may alter a relationship we had previously observed between two variables. Indeed, the story can get even more complex when we allow for the impact of even more variables on the original bivariate relationship. Taking into account the possible effects of other variables involves **multivariate analysis**, and we have only just skimmed the surface in this chapter.

To help in drawing conclusions from the elaboration of crosstabs, Table 24.14 provides a useful guide to decision making (adapted from J. Healey (1993) *Statistics: A Tool for Social Research*, Belmont, CA: Wadsworth, 428).

Table 24.14 Possible results when controlling for a third variable

Partial tables when compared with crosstab show:	Model	Implications for further analysis	Likely next step in statistical analysis	Theoretical implications
Same relationship between X and Y	Direct relationship	Disregard control variable	Select another control variable to test further the directness of the relationship	Model that X causes Y in a direct way is supported
Weaker or no relationship between X and Y	Spurious relationship	Incorporate control variable	Focus on the relationship between these three variables	Model that X causes Y is not supported
	or			
	Intervening relationship	Incorporate control variable	Focus on the relationship between these three variables	Model that X causes Y is partially supported but must be revised to take control into account
Mixed relationships	Interaction/ conditional relationship	Incorporate control variable	Analyze sub-groups based on control variable separately	Model that X causes Y partially supported but must be revised to take control into account

Exercises

24.1   A study finds a strong positive relationship between a child's shoe size and the child's skills at mathematical problem solving. Explain.

24.2   What conclusion would you draw about the relationship between X and Y based on the following elaboration?

All cases

Y	X		
	1	2	Total
1	177	146	323
2	51	346	397
Total	228	492	720

Controlling for C(1)

Y	X		
	1	2	Total
1	153	52	205
2	44	123	167
Total	197	175	372

Controlling for C(2)

Y	X		
	1	2	Total
1	24	94	118
2	7	223	230
Total	31	317	348

24.3 An investigation of the relationship between age, concern for the environment, and political affiliation produces the following gamma values:

Gamma (age and concern for the environment): −0.57
Gamma (age and concern for the environment, liberals only): −0.22
Gamma (age and concern for the environment, conservatives only): −0.67
Partial gamma: −0.38

What conclusion should be drawn about the relationship, if any, between these three variables?

24.4 The following tables are based on a study of the likelihood of US courts to impose the death penalty, based on the racial characteristics of the victim and the defendant (M. Radelet (1981) Racial characteristics and the imposition of the death penalty. *American Sociological Review*, 46, 918-927).

All cases

Death penalty	Victim		
	White	Black	Total
No	184	106	290
Yes	30	6	36
Total	214	112	326

White defendant only

Death penalty	Victim		
	White	Black	Total
No	132	9	141
Yes	19	0	19
Total	151	9	160

Black defendant only

Death penalty	Victim		
	White	Black	Total
No	52	97	149
Yes	11	6	17
Total	63	103	163

What conclusions can you draw about the relationship between the race of the victim, the race of the defendant, and likelihood to impose the death penalty?

25

Multiple Regression

Review of bivariate regression

In Chapter 10, Exercise 10.10, we considered the following problem. A real-estate agent wants to explore the factors affecting the selling price of a house. The agent collects data on these two variables for 12 houses, with the results given in Table 25.1.

Table 25.1 House size and selling prices

Selling price ($,000)	House size (squares)
260	20
240	15
245	20
210	13
230	18
242	14
295	28
235	16
287	24
252	20
270	23
275	25

The purpose of the analysis is to explain the variation in selling price, which is the dependent variable. The agent believes that the main factor explaining the variation in selling prices is the variation in house sizes. We formally call this a **model** of the factors determining the sale price of a house, since it is a theoretical depiction of a relationship that may or may not hold up to empirical scrutiny. Let us compare for example two houses from the sample, such as the house that sold for $252,000 and the one that sold for $230,000. Indeed, we find that the more expensive house is also the larger house, so that these two houses seem to be consistent with the agent's model. Does this relationship hold true for all the 12 houses?

A simple regression analysis on these data from Exercise 10.10, using the method of ordinary least squares, produces the following results:

$$Y = 157 + 4.88X$$
$$r = 0.92$$
$$r^2 = 0.85$$

On the basis of these results we can conclude the following:

- There is a positive relationship between house size and selling price.
- for every one square increase in house size the selling price increases by $4880.
- The relationship is strong and highly reliable for making predictions.
- The variation in house size does not *perfectly* predict selling price. The coefficient of determination is high (0.85), but not equal to one. Therefore other factors also affect the sale price of houses in our sample.

This last point means that on a scatter plot of the data in Table 25.1 not all the data points lie right on the regression line, as evident in Figure 25.1, which presents an SPSS-generated scatter plot with the regression line for these data.

Graph

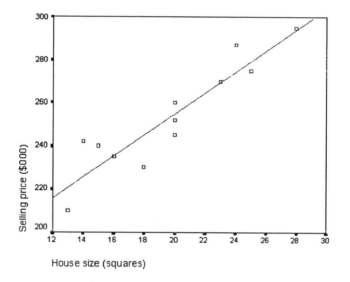

Figure 25.1 SPSS scatter plot with regression line

The actual sale price for any given house can in fact be expressed by the following equation:

$$\text{selling price} = a + b(\text{house size}) + e$$

This equation states that the sale price of houses varies primarily because of differences in their size, but also because of random factors, represented by the **error term** (*e*). The error term expresses the difference between what we predict the price of a house will be given its size and what it actually sells for.

We should stop for a moment and be clear about what we mean by the 'error term' and 'random variation'. We can all agree that many factors affect the specific price at which a house sells. It would not be hard to provide a long list of such factors. Our bivariate model of the sale price argues that among all these factors there is one variable – house size – that plays a major role in determining sale price and it does so in a systematic and consistent way. This is why we have singled out the variable 'house size' and given it an explicit position in the equation. But we also do not want to ignore all the other factors. The error term bundles up all these other factors, factors that affect the sale price of houses in a haphazard, unsystematic way. One house may have sold at a high price because the estate agent was particularly aggressive in his or her sales pitch; another house may have sold well because the buyers particularly liked the color scheme; still another may have sold for a low price because that particular vendor had to sell quickly in order to repay a bad debt. It is because these and other factors spring up randomly from one sale to the next that we do not treat them as separate independent variables, but allow the error term to capture their collective influences together. Sometimes these random factors cause the sale price to be higher than what we predict based on knowledge of the house's size, and sometimes they cause the sale price to be below the predicted value. Knowing a house's size will allow us to predict a value for sale price which will be close to the mark, but we concede that for any given house the effect of these random factors will mean that the actual sale price will not necessarily equal the predicted sale price.

Introduction to multiple regression

We may, however, regard the bivariate model as overly simplistic. We may feel that there are factors other than house size that are not random, but which operate in a systematic way to cause sale prices of houses to vary independently of their size. In other words, if we compare two houses *of the same size*, the difference in their respective sale prices is not only due to random factors such as those we just discussed. We have three houses in our sample, for example, that are each 20 squares in size. One sold for $260,000, the other $245,000, and the third for $252,000. Why the differences in sale price? We could put faith in our bivariate model and argue that random factors explain these differences, or we could argue that another model which allows for the operation of other variables systematically to affect sale price offers a better explanation.

We may, for instance, believe that the *age* of a house also (partly) explains its sale price. That is, the age of a house is not a variable that may occasionally impact on the sale price of a house, but instead is a common factor that *regularly* impacts on the prices that houses sell for. Our new model may hold that it is reasonable to expect that the older the house the cheaper will be its price. That is, we expect there to be a *negative relationship* between house prices and their age.

If we suspect this to be the case, we need to extend our regression analysis to include the operation of this other variable, much in the same way that in the previous chapter we extended our simple bivariate crosstab analysis to account for the possible effects of third variables. When working with interval/ratio data (as we have here) this is the task of **multivariate regression**.

Multivariate regression investigates the relationship between two or more independent variables on a single dependent variable.

With this new multivariate model in mind we collect data in Table 25.2 for the ages (in years) of the 12 houses we originally surveyed (this example is adapted from A. Slevanathan *et al.* (1994) *Australian Business Statistics*, Melbourne: Thomas Nelson).

Table 25.2 Selling price, house size, and age of 12 houses

Selling price ($,000)	House size (squares)	Age (in years)
260	20	5
240	15	12
245	20	9
210	13	15
230	18	9
242	14	7
295	28	1
235	16	12
287	24	2
252	20	5
270	23	5
275	25	5

Generally we can express the relationship between any dependent variable and any (k) number of independent variables in the following way:

$$Y = a + b_1X_1 + b_2X_2 + ... + b_kX_k + e$$

For the specific example we are investigating we therefore can represent the model of the relationship in the following terms:

$$\text{selling price} = a + b_1(\text{house size}) + b_2(\text{age}) + e$$

In other words, we believe that the sale price of a house is pulled in one direction or another by its age and its size. We expect an old house that is also relatively small to have its price pulled in a downward direction through the independent operation of both age and size. Conversely, we expect a new house that is also relatively large to have its price pulled upwards. In other instances, house size and age may be pulling in opposite directions.

In our equation we still allow for random factors to have an influence so that age and price do not *exactly* determine sale price in every instance. But if this multivariate model is a better explanation of house selling prices than the bivariate model, *the amount of variation left over to be explained by the error term will be much smaller than in the bivariate model we started with.* If, on the other hand, introducing age into the equation does not reduce the proportion of sale price variation attributed to the error term then knowing a house's age does not improve our ability to predict its sale price. We have wasted time and energy gathering information on a variable that is not helpful.

The task of multivariate regression is to try and apportion the variation in house prices to each of these competing 'pulls' on the dependent variable. Does one dominate the determination of selling price, such that we can say age or size is clearly more important, or do they have similar influences? And what is the role left over to random factors? Multivariate analysis, through the calculation of the **regression coefficients** and the **partial correlations** for each variable, gives us precise measures of the respective influence of these independent variables on the dependent variable.

It is possible to use numerical techniques to calculate the regression coefficients between each of these independent variables and the dependent variable. However, these techniques are very cumbersome, and with large data sets, overwhelmingly time consuming. No one today would consider conducting multiple regression by hand. To save ourselves the hassle we will leave it to SPSS to conduct the calculations, and we will simply interpret the results.

Multiple regression with SPSS

The procedure for calculating the equation statistics for multiple regression is the same as that for simple bivariate regression from Chapter 10, except for the fact that we paste more than one variable into the **Independent(s)** variable target list (Table 25.3, Figure 25.2).

Table 25.3 Multiple regression using SPSS (file: **Ch25.sav**)

SPSS command/action	Comments
1 From the menu select **Analyze/Regression/ Linear**	This brings up the **Linear Regression** dialog box
2 Click on **Selling price** in the source variable list	This highlights **Selling price**
3 Click on the ▸ that points to the **Dependent:** target variable list	This pastes **Selling price** as the dependent variable
4 Click on **House size** in the source variable list and while holding down the **Shift** key click on **Age in years**	This highlights both **House size** and **Age in years**
5 Click on the ▸ that points to the **Independent(s):** target variables list	This pastes both **House size** and **Age in years** as the independent variables
6 Click on **OK**	

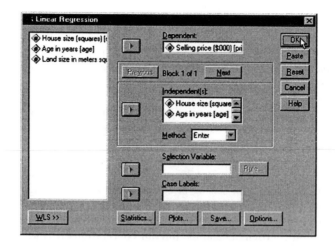

Figure 25.2 The **Linear Regression** dialog box

The output is presented in Figure 25.3. A great deal of information is generated so we will concentrate on just the most important parts. The table headed **Variables Entered/Removed** provides a simple verbal description of the models we are estimating. It is possible in SPSS to run several multiple regressions simultaneously, using different combinations of independent variables to see which combination best explains the variation in the dependent variable. Here we have only estimated one model, called Model 1, which uses the variables Age in years and House size in squares as the predictors of the dependent variable Selling price ($000).

The second table, headed **Model Summary**, provides the correlation coefficient, which indicates the strength of the relationship between the combination of independent variables in the model and the dependent variable. The value for R of .959 indicates a very strong relationship. R is the multivariate equivalent for the bivariate correlation coefficient, *r*. Of more interest is the value for R Square (the multiple regression coefficient of determination) which is .919. When we used the bivariate model to explain selling price (correlating it only with house size) the value for the coefficient of determination was 0.85. When we use both house size *and* the age of the house to predict selling price the coefficient of determination rises to .919. This indicates that our ability to explain (or predict) the selling price of a house has increased when we also have information about its age as well as its size. Part of the variation in sale price that we had previously attributed to random factors is actually due to the systematic effect of age.

The next table, headed **ANOVA,** contains inferential statistics that allow us to make an inference from the sample to the population of all houses. We are at the moment concentrating just on the descriptive statistics for the sample, so we will skip this part of the output for now, and return to it in the discussion below.

Regression

Variables Entered/Removed[b]

Model	Variables Entered	Variables Removed	Method
1	Age in years, House size (squares)	.	Enter

a. All requested variables entered.

b. Dependent Variable: Selling price ($000)

Model Summary

Model	R	R Square	Adjusted R Square	Std. Error of the Estimate
1	.959[a]	.919	.901	7.80

a. Predictors: (Constant), Age in years, House size (squares)

ANOVA[b]

Model		Sum of Squares	df	Mean Square	F	Sig.
1	Regression	6248.759	2	3124.379	51.298	.000[a]
	Residual	548.158	9	60.906		
	Total	6796.917	11			

a. Predictors: (Constant), Age in years, House size (squares)

b. Dependent Variable: Selling price ($000)

Coefficients[a]

Model		Unstandardized Coefficients B	Std. Error	Standardized Coefficients Beta	t	Sig.
1	(Constant)	224.290	26.222		8.553	.000
	House size (squares)	2.578	.973	.487	2.650	.026
	Age in years	-2.974	1.076	-.508	-2.764	.022

a. Dependent Variable: Selling price ($000)

Figure 25.3 SPSS **Linear Regression** output

The table headed **Coefficients** provides the elements of the regression equation we have estimated, which can be written:

sale price ($,000) $= 224.29 + 2.578$(house size in squares) $- 2.974$(age in years)

When reading a regression equation it is important to keep in mind the units of measurement in which the variables have been measured. Here we see that for every one square increase in house size, the selling price increases by $2578. Independently of this relationship we also find that for every one year increase in the age of a house, its selling price decreases (note the negative sign) by $2974.

To give this slightly more practical meaning let us assume that we are now presented with a house that is going up for sale. We measure it as being 15 squares in size and also 5 years old. What do we predict it will sell for? We place the information into the regression equation

$$\text{selling price (\$,000)} = 224.29 + 2.578(15) - 2.974(5)$$

$$= 224.29 + 38.67 - 14.87$$

$$= 248.09$$

Of course we do not expect $248,090 to be the exact price realized when the house is actually sold, because random factors will still play a role. But given the high value of the coefficient of determination, these random factors should not cause the actual sale price to deviate much from this predicted value.

It is difficult to use the regression coefficients to assess the *relative* importance of each independent variable in determining the value of the dependent variable, since each independent variable is measured with different units (one is measured in years, the other in squares). If we measured house size in another unit, such as square feet, the regression coefficient for this variable would be different because of the unit of measurement. In other words, we cannot say that, because the coefficient for house size is 2.578, whereas the coefficient for age is -2.974, age is a more powerful force acting on selling price. The table therefore provides a column of **Standardized Coefficients**. Without going into the details of how these standardized coefficients, also called **beta-weights**, are calculated, we simply note that they 'wash out' the effect of the units of measurement. We can see that age (-.508) has a slightly stronger 'pull' on sale price than does house size (.487).

Table 25.4 summarizes the role that the various measures generated by SPSS play.

Table 25.4 Interpretation of SPSS output

Regression coefficient	Allows us to make predictions for the dependent variable based on the values of the independent variables, in terms of the original units of measurement
Standardized coefficient	Allows us to distinguish the relative importance of each independent variable in determining the value of the dependent variable
R	Indicates the strength of the relationship between the combination of independent variables and the dependent variable
R-squared	Indicates the amount of variation in the dependent variable explained by the combination of independent variables in the model, thereby indicating whether the model is a good predictor of the dependent variable

Testing for the significance of the multivariate model

You may have noticed in the output some of the inferential statistics we came across in previous chapters. As they do in other situations, these statistics tell us whether we can generalize from a sample result, such as that in our example, to the population from which the sample is drawn. Will the relationship between selling price and house size and age still hold if we surveyed all houses sold in the area?

The critical information for this inference testing is contained in the table headed **ANOVA**. SPSS conducts an *F*-test on the whole model, which tests the hypothesis that the correlation coefficients for all the variables included in the model are zero. In this example, the *F*-statistic for the model has a significance level of 0.000. This tells us that at least one of the correlations between each of the independent variables and the dependent variable is not equal to zero in the population.

This conclusion is confirmed in the **Coefficients** table, where we can see that the *t*-statistics for each independent variable are significant at the 0.05 level. Thus we use the *F*-test to see whether at least some of the independent variables in our model are significant, and the *t*-statistics for each individual variable indicate which ones are significant.

Stepwise regression

Our real-estate agent may have observed all of these calculations and may yet believe that we have still left out other important factors that determine the selling price of houses in the area. Despite the high explanatory power of our model with only two independent variables, the agent may argue that our ability to predict the sale price of houses will be even further improved if we include the size of the land as *another* independent variable. The agent therefore goes back and gathers the data for the 12 houses we are analyzing, measuring the land area in meters squared (Table 25.5).

Table 25.5 Selling price, house size, age, and land size of 12 houses

Selling price ($,000)	House size (squares)	Age (in years)	Land size (meters squared)
260	20	5	420
240	15	12	640
245	20	9	600
210	13	15	590
230	18	9	700
242	14	7	720
295	28	1	624
235	16	12	590
287	24	2	710
252	20	5	630
270	23	5	700
275	25	5	710

We now have three models to explain the sale price of houses. We have the bivariate model we started with which relates sale price just with the size of the house. We have a multivariate model which relates sale price to house size and age of the house. We now also have another multivariate model which includes the size of the land as an explanatory variable:

selling price $= a + b_1$(house size) $+ e$

selling price $= a + b_1$(house size) $+ b_2$(age) $+ e$

selling price $= a + b_1$(house size) $+ b_2$(age) $+ b_3$(land size) $+ e$

We have already discussed that the way we judge whether a variable adds to the explanatory power of a model is by looking at the impact its inclusion has on the value for R-squared. If the value for R-squared increases significantly when a variable is added to the model, then the extra information provided by this variable increases the model's ability to explain the variation in sale price.

One way to decide between the various models is to undertake separate linear regressions based on the particular combination of independent variables we want to include. We can then compare the R-squared values to see the extent to which our ability to explain the variation in sale price is maximized by each combination of independent variables. For example, if we do conduct a multiple regression including land size R-squared will be 0.922, which is the same as that for the model with only age and house size. In other words, land size does not increase our ability to explain selling prices; the time and effort in measuring this variable is wasted.

The problem with this approach is that it is tedious to run separate regressions for each of the possible models we can construct. It is also difficult to judge how much of an increase in R-squared justifies the inclusion of a variable in our model. Fortunately, SPSS provides a way around this. This is the method of **stepwise regression**. The method of stepwise regression allows us to determine which combination of possible independent variables best explains the dependent variable. It does this by adding in and taking out variables from the calculations according to whether each makes a statistically significant change to the value of R-squared.

But before illustrating how this is done, we need to raise one word of caution. We can potentially provide SPSS with a whole list of variables that may or may not affect a particular dependent variable, and then run a stepwise regression on SPSS to find the 'best' combination. This kind of fishing expedition is not appropriate since it selects variables based on statistical results alone. We should at all times be guided by our theories of the world and/or past research as to the variables that we should consider for analysis. Having determined a 'short-list' of variables we believe may influence the dependent variable (on the basis of theory or past research), we can then use stepwise regression to home in on the specific variables that actually do have significant influence.

The stepwise regression method is an option available within the linear regression dialog box (Table 25.6, Figure 25.4).

Table 25.6 Stepwise multiple regression using SPSS (file: **Ch25.sav**)

SPSS command/action	Comments
1 From the menu select **Analyze/Regression/ Linear**	This brings up the **Linear Regression** dialog box
2 Click on **Selling price** in the source variable list	This highlights **Selling price**
3 Click on the ▶ that points to the **Dependent:** target variable list	This pastes **Selling price** as the dependent variable
4 Click on **House size** in the source variable list and while holding down the **Shift** key click on **Age in years** and then on **Land size**	This highlights **House size, Age in years**, and **Land size**
5 Click on the ▶ that points to the **Independent(s):** target variables list	This pastes **House size, Age in years**, and **Land size** as the independent variables
6 Click on ▼ next to **Enter**	A drop-down menu appears
7 In the drop-down menu click on **Stepwise**	This selects stepwise regression as the method for including and excluding variables from the regression
8 Click on **OK**	

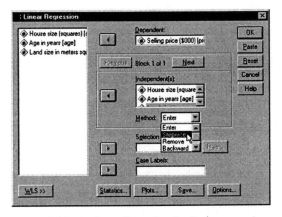

Figure 25.4 The **Stepwise** option for linear regression

The results of this procedure will be as shown in Figure 25.5. In the first table headed **Variables Entered/Removed** we see that SPSS has generated two models from the three variables we suggested: one with Age in years only (our original bivariate model) which SPSS calls Model 1, and another with age and House size (squares) which SPSS calls Model 2. The rest of the output is basically same as that we generated separately before for each of these models; here we have the two models presented in the same analysis.

The new part of the output is the last table, headed **Excluded Variables**. This tells us that on the basis of the F-test on changes in R-squared, land size is not a useful variable to include in any of the models. All of this means that complicating the model by adding this new variable does not 'buy' us any more accuracy in terms of estimating the dependent variable. Parsimony suggests that we should leave it out of the picture.

Regression

Variables Entered/Removed[a]

Model	Variables Entered	Variables Removed	Method
1	Age in years	.	Stepwise (Criteria: Probability-of-F-to-enter <= .050, Probability-of-F-to-remove >= .100).
2	House size (squares)	.	Stepwise (Criteria: Probability-of-F-to-enter <= .050, Probability-of-F-to-remove >= .100).

a. Dependent Variable: Selling price ($000)

Model Summary

Model	R	R Square	Adjusted R Square	Std. Error of the Estimate
1	.925[a]	.856	.842	9.88
2	.959[b]	.919	.901	7.80

a. Predictors: (Constant), Age in years

b. Predictors: (Constant), Age in years, House size (squares)

ANOVA[c]

Model		Sum of Squares	df	Mean Square	F	Sig.
1	Regression	5820.999	1	5820.999	59.646	.000[a]
	Residual	975.918	10	97.592		
	Total	6796.917	11			
2	Regression	6248.759	2	3124.379	51.298	.000[b]
	Residual	548.158	9	60.906		
	Total	6796.917	11			

a. Predictors (Constant), Age in years

b. Predictors (Constant), Age in years, House size (squares)

c. Dependent Variable: Selling price ($000)

Coefficients[a]

Model		Unstandardized Coefficients B	Unstandardized Coefficients Std. Error	Standardized Coefficients Beta	t	Sig.
1	(Constant)	292.702	5.832		50.193	.000
	Age in years	-5.419	.702	-.925	-7.723	.000
2	(Constant)	224.290	26.222		8.553	.000
	Age in years	-2.974	1.076	-.508	-2.764	.022
	House size (squares)	2.578	.973	.487	2.650	.026

a. Dependent Variable: Selling price ($000)

Excluded Variables[c]

Model		Beta In	t	Sig.	Partial Correlation	Collinearity Statistics Tolerance
1	House size (squares)	.487[a]	2.650	.026	.662	.265
	Land size in meters squared	.015[a]	.115	.911	.038	.973
2	Land size in meters squared	.015[b]	.147	.886	.052	.973

a. Predictors in the Model: (Constant), Age in years

b. Predictors in the Model: (Constant), Age in years, House size (squares)

c. Dependent Variable: Selling price ($000)

Figure 25.5 SPSS stepwise regression output

The assumptions behind multiple regression

While multiple regression is a powerful tool for assessing the impact of many independent variables on a dependent variable, there are a number of assumptions behind it that limit its applicability. All the assumptions we covered in the discussion of bivariate regression in Chapter 10 still apply in the case of multiple regression. To this list, though, we need to add another very important assumption. Multiple regression *assumes* that each of the independent variables is independent of each other (there is no **multicollinearity**). In our example this can be depicted as shown in Figure 25.6.

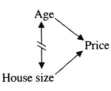

Figure 25.6

Age and house size each affect price *but do not affect each other*. This may seem fairly reasonable for these particular variables: if a house was suddenly enlarged, this would not also suddenly make it older or younger! Similarly, as a house grows older it does not usually grow larger or smaller.

This assumption underlying multiple regression makes it a little more restricted than the multivariate techniques we looked at in the previous chapter. There we used multivariate analysis to *determine* which model out of a range of models best explains the relationship between three or more variables. With regression analysis we *assume* a specific model, as depicted in Figure 25.3.

Exercises

25.1 The study described in Exercise 10.12 investigating the factors that cause employees to be absent due to illness at a certain factory is extended to include data on the employees' ages.

Hours of exercise	Days lost	Age in years
3	12	36
8	10	35
1	10	54
0	15	42
0	18	41
4	7	25
7	7	32
2	14	39
5	9	43
0	16	29
9	8	32
3	10	50

(a)   Which variable is the dependent variable?

(b)   What do you expect the sign in front of the independent variables to be?

(c)   Enter these data into SPSS and conduct a multiple regression. What is the regression equation?

(d)   Has the inclusion of age added anything to our ability to predict number of working hours lost due to illness?

25.2   In Exercise 10.13 you were asked to generate, from the **World95** data file that comes with SPSS, the regression equation relating female life expectancy and birth rate per 1000 people. Are there any other variables in the data file which you feel should be included in the equation? Test your model by running the appropriate regression on SPSS.

25.3   Using the **Employee data** file, select variables you think will be good predictors of current salary, and conduct a stepwise regression to see which ones are actually worth including in your model.

Appendix

Table A1 Area under the standard normal curve

z	Area under curve between both points	Area under curve beyond both points	Area under curve beyond one point
±0.1	0.080	0.920	0.4600
±0.2	0.159	0.841	0.4205
±0.3	0.236	0.764	0.3820
±0.4	0.311	0.689	0.3445
±0.5	0.383	0.617	0.3085
±0.6	0.451	0.549	0.2745
±0.7	0.516	0.484	0.2420
±0.8	0.576	0.424	0.2120
±0.9	0.632	0.368	0.1840
±1	0.683	0.317	0.1585
±1.1	0.729	0.271	0.1355
±1.2	0.770	0.230	0.1150
±1.3	0.806	0.194	0.0970
±1.4	0.838	0.162	0.0810
±1.5	0.866	0.134	0.0670
±1.6	0.890	0.110	0.0550
±1.645	0.900	0.100	0.0500
±1.7	0.911	0.089	0.0445
±1.8	0.928	0.072	0.0360
±1.9	0.943	0.057	0.0290
±1.96	0.950	0.050	0.0250
±2	0.954	0.046	0.0230
±2.1	0.964	0.036	0.0180
±2.2	0.972	0.028	0.0140
±2.3	0.979	0.021	0.0105
±2.33	0.980	0.020	0.0100
±2.4	0.984	0.016	0.0080
±2.5	0.988	0.012	0.0060
±2.58	0.990	0.010	0.0050
±2.6	0.991	0.009	0.0045
±2.7	0.993	0.007	0.0035
±2.8	0.995	0.005	0.0025
±2.9	0.996	0.004	0.0020
±3	0.997	0.003	0.0015
±3.1	0.998	0.002	0.0001
±3.2	0.9986	0.0014	0.0007
±3.3	0.9990	0.0010	0.0005
±3.4	0.9993	0.0007	0.0003
±3.5	0.9995	0.0005	0.00025
±3.6	0.9997	0.0003	0.00015
±3.7	0.9998	0.0002	0.00010
±3.8	0.99986	0.00014	0.00007
±3.9	0.99990	0.00010	0.00005
±4	>0.99990	<0.00010	<0.00005

Table A2 Critical values for t-distributions

	Level of significance for one-tail test				
	0.10	0.05	0.02	0.01	0.005
	Level of significance for two-tail test				
df	0.20	0.10	0.05	0.02	0.01
1	3.078	6.314	12.706	31.821	63.657
2	1.886	2.920	4.303	6.965	9.925
3	1.638	2.353	3.182	4.541	5.841
4	1.533	2.132	2.776	3.747	4.604
5	1.476	2.015	2.571	3.365	4.032
6	1.440	1.943	2.447	3.143	3.707
7	1.415	1.895	2.365	2.998	3.499
8	1.397	1.860	2.306	2.896	3.355
9	1.383	1.833	2.262	2.821	3.250
10	1.372	1.812	2.228	2.764	3.169
11	1.363	1.796	2.201	2.718	3.106
12	1.356	1.782	2.179	2.681	3.055
13	1.350	1.771	2.160	2.650	3.012
14	1.345	1.761	2.145	2.624	2.977
15	1.341	1.753	2.131	2.602	2.947
16	1.340	1.746	2.120	2.583	2.921
17	1.333	1.740	2.110	2.567	2.898
18	1.330	1.734	2.101	2.552	2.878
19	1.328	1.729	2.093	2.539	2.861
20	1.325	1.725	2.086	2.528	2.845
21	1.323	1.721	2.080	2.518	2.831
22	1.321	1.717	2.074	2.508	2.819
23	1.319	1.714	2.069	2.500	2.807
24	1.318	1.711	2.064	2.492	2.797
25	1.316	1.708	2.060	2.485	2.787
26	1.315	1.706	2.056	2.479	2.779
27	1.314	1.703	2.052	2.473	2.771
28	1.313	1.701	2.048	2.467	2.763
29	1.311	1.699	2.045	2.462	2.756
30	1.310	1.697	2.042	2.457	2.750
35	1.306	1.690	2.030	2.438	2.724
40	1.303	1.684	2.021	2.423	2.704
45	1.301	1.679	2.014	2.412	2.690
50	1.299	1.676	2.009	2.403	2.678
55	1.297	1.673	2.004	2.396	2.668
60	1.296	1.671	2.000	2.390	2.660
70	1.294	1.667	1.994	2.381	2.648
80	1.292	1.664	1.990	2.374	2.639
90	1.291	1.662	1.987	2.368	2.632
120	1.289	1.658	1.980	2.358	2.617
∞	1.282	1.645	1.960	2.326	2.576

Table A3 Critical values for F-distributions ($\alpha = 0.05$)

$n - k$	Degrees of freedom for estimates of variance between samples $k - 1$									
	1	2	3	4	5	6	7	8	9	∞
1	161.4	199.5	215.7	224.6	230.2	234.0	236.8	238.9	240.5	254.3
2	18.51	19.00	19.16	19.25	19.30	19.33	19.35	19.37	19.38	19.50
3	10.13	9.55	9.28	9.12	9.01	8.94	8.89	8.84	8.81	8.53
4	7.71	6.94	6.59	6.39	6.26	6.16	6.09	6.04	6.00	5.63
5	6.61	5.79	5.41	5.19	5.05	4.95	4.88	4.82	4.77	4.36
6	5.99	5.14	4.76	4.53	4.39	4.28	4.21	4.15	4.10	3.67
7	5.59	4.74	4.35	4.12	3.97	3.87	3.79	3.73	3.68	3.23
8	5.32	4.46	4.07	3.84	3.69	3.58	3.50	3.44	3.39	2.93
9	5.12	4.26	3.86	3.63	3.48	3.37	3.29	3.23	3.18	2.71
10	4.96	4.10	3.71	3.48	3.33	3.22	3.14	3.07	3.02	2.54
11	4.84	3.98	3.59	3.36	3.20	3.09	3.01	2.95	2.90	2.40
12	4.75	3.88	3.49	3.26	3.11	3.00	2.91	2.85	2.80	2.30
13	4.67	3.80	3.41	3.18	3.02	2.92	2.83	2.77	2.71	2.21
14	4.60	3.74	3.34	3.11	2.96	2.85	2.76	2.70	2.65	2.13
15	4.54	3.68	3.29	3.06	2.90	2.79	2.71	2.64	2.59	2.07
16	4.49	3.63	3.24	3.01	2.85	2.74	2.66	2.59	2.54	2.01
17	4.45	3.59	3.20	2.96	2.81	2.70	2.61	2.55	2.49	1.96
18	4.41	3.55	3.16	2.93	2.77	2.66	2.58	2.51	2.46	1.92
19	4.38	3.52	3.13	2.90	2.74	2.63	2.54	2.48	2.42	1.88
20	4.35	3.49	3.10	2.87	2.71	2.60	2.51	2.45	2.39	1.84
21	4.32	3.47	3.07	2.84	2.68	2.57	2.49	2.42	2.37	1.81
22	4.30	3.44	3.05	2.82	2.66	2.55	2.46	2.40	2.34	1.78
23	4.28	3.42	3.03	2.80	2.64	2.53	2.44	2.38	2.32	1.76
24	4.26	3.40	3.01	2.78	2.62	2.51	2.42	2.36	2.30	1.73
25	4.24	3.38	2.99	2.76	2.60	2.49	2.40	2.34	2.28	1.71
26	4.22	3.37	2.98	2.74	2.59	2.47	2.39	2.32	2.27	1.69
27	4.21	3.35	2.96	2.73	2.57	2.46	2.37	2.30	2.25	1.67
28	4.20	3.34	2.95	2.71	2.56	2.44	2.36	2.29	2.24	1.65
29	4.18	3.33	2.93	2.70	2.54	2.43	2.35	2.28	2.22	1.64
30	4.17	3.32	2.92	2.69	2.53	2.42	2.33	2.27	2.21	1.62
40	4.08	3.23	2.84	2.61	2.45	2.34	2.25	2.18	2.12	1.51
50	4.03	3.18	2.79	2.56	2.38	2.29	2.20	2.13	2.07	1.44
60	4.00	3.15	2.76	2.52	2.37	2.25	2.17	2.10	2.04	1.39
80	3.96	3.11	2.72	2.48	2.33	2.21	2.12	1.99	1.91	1.32
100	3.94	3.09	2.70	2.46	2.30	2.19	2.10	2.03	1.97	1.28
120	3.92	3.07	2.68	2.45	2.29	2.17	2.09	2.02	1.96	1.25
∞	3.84	2.99	2.60	2.37	2.21	2.09	2.01	1.94	1.88	1.00

Degrees of freedom for estimates of variance within samples

Table A4 Critical values for chi-square distributions

df	\multicolumn{10}{c}{Level of significance}
	0.99	0.90	0.70	0.50	0.30	0.20	0.10	0.05	0.01	0.001
1	0.00016	0.0158	0.148	0.455	1.074	1.642	2.706	3.841	6.635	10.827
2	0.0201	0.211	0.713	1.386	2.408	3.219	4.605	5.991	9.210	13.815
3	0.115	0.584	1.424	2.366	3.665	4.642	6.251	7.815	11.341	16.268
4	0.297	1.064	2.195	3.357	4.878	5.989	7.779	9.488	13.277	18.465
5	0.554	1.610	3.000	4.351	6.064	7.289	9.236	11.070	15.086	20.517
6	0.872	2.204	3.828	5.348	7.231	8.558	10.645	12.592	16.812	22.457
7	1.239	2.833	4.671	6.346	8.383	9.803	12.017	14.067	18.475	24.322
8	1.646	3.490	5.527	7.344	9.524	11.030	13.362	15.507	20.090	26.125
9	2.088	4.168	6.393	8.343	10.656	12.242	14.684	16.919	21.666	27.877
10	2.558	4.865	7.267	9.342	11.781	13.442	15.987	18.307	23.209	29.588
11	3.053	5.578	8.148	10.341	12.899	14.631	17.275	19.675	24.725	31.264
12	3.571	6.304	9.034	11.340	14.011	15.812	18.549	21.026	26.217	32.909
13	4.107	7.042	9.926	12.340	15.119	16.985	19.812	22.362	27.688	34.528
14	4.660	7.790	10.821	13.339	16.222	18.151	21.064	23.685	29.141	36.123
15	5.229	8.547	11.721	14.339	17.322	19.311	22.307	24.996	30.578	37.697
16	5.812	9.312	12.624	15.338	18.418	20.465	23.542	26.296	32.000	39.252
17	6.408	10.085	13.531	16.338	19.511	21.615	24.769	27.587	33.409	40.790
18	7.015	10.865	14.440	17.338	20.601	22.760	25.989	28.869	34.805	42.312
19	7.633	11.651	15.352	18.338	21.689	23.900	27.204	30.144	36.191	43.820
20	8.260	12.443	16.266	19.337	22.775	25.038	28.412	31.410	37.566	45.315
21	8.897	13.240	17.182	20.337	23.858	26.171	29.615	32.671	38.932	46.797
22	9.542	14.041	18.101	21.337	24.939	27.301	30.813	33.924	40.289	48.268
23	10.196	14.848	19.021	22.337	26.018	28.429	32.007	35.172	41.638	49.728
24	10.856	15.659	19.943	23.337	27.096	29.553	33.196	36.415	42.980	51.179
25	11.524	16.473	20.867	24.337	28.172	30.675	34.382	37.652	44.314	52.620
26	12.198	17.292	21.792	25.336	29.246	31.795	35.563	38.885	45.642	54.052
27	12.879	18.114	22.719	26.336	30.319	32.912	36.741	40.113	46.963	55.476
28	13.565	18.939	23.647	27.336	31.391	34.027	37.916	41.337	48.278	56.893
29	14.256	19.768	24.577	28.336	32.461	35.139	39.087	42.557	49.588	58.302
30	14.953	20.599	25.508	29.336	33.530	36.250	40.256	43.773	50.892	59.703

Key Equations

The mean of a population: listed data

$$\mu = \frac{\Sigma X_i}{N}$$

N is the size of the population
X_i is each score in a distribution

The mean of a sample: listed data

$$\overline{X} = \frac{\Sigma X_i}{n}$$

n is the size of the sample

The mean of a sample: frequency data

$$\overline{X} = \frac{\Sigma fX_i}{n}$$

f is the frequency of each value in a distribution

The mean of a sample: class intervals

$$\overline{X} = \frac{\Sigma fm}{n}$$

m is the mid-point of a class interval

The standard deviation of a population: listed data

$$\sigma = \sqrt{\frac{\Sigma(X_i - \mu)^2}{N}}$$

The standard deviation of a sample: listed data

$$s = \sqrt{\frac{\Sigma\left(X_i - \overline{X}\right)^2}{n-1}}$$

$$s = \sqrt{\frac{\Sigma X_i^2 - \dfrac{\left(\Sigma X_i\right)^2}{n}}{n-1}}$$

The standard deviation of a sample: frequency data

$$s = \sqrt{\frac{\Sigma f X_i^2 - \dfrac{\left(\Sigma f X_i\right)^2}{n}}{n-1}}$$

Coefficient of relative variation

$$CRV = \frac{s}{\overline{X}} \times 100$$

Index of qualitative variation

$$IQV = \frac{\text{observed differences}}{\text{maximum possible differences}}$$

$$\text{maximum possible differences} = \frac{n^2(k-1)}{2k}$$

k is the number of categories.

Z-score for describing a population

$$Z = \frac{X_i - \mu}{\sigma}$$

z-score for describing a sample

$$z = \frac{X_i - \overline{X}}{s}$$

Lambda

$$\lambda = \frac{E_1 - E_2}{E_1}$$

E_1 is the number of errors without information for the independent variable

E_2 is the number of errors with information for the independent variable

Cramer's *V*

$$V = \sqrt{\frac{\chi^2}{n(k-1)}}$$

χ^2 is the chi-square statistic for the crosstab

k is the number of rows or the number of columns, whichever is smaller

Gamma

$$G = \frac{N_c - N_d}{N_c + N_d}$$

N_s is the number of concordant pairs

N_d is the number of discordant pairs

Somers' *d*

$$d = \frac{N_s - N_d}{N_s + N_d + T_y}$$

T_y is the number of cases tied on the dependent variable but varying on the independent variable

Kendall's tau-*b*

$$\text{tau-}b = \frac{N_c - N_d}{\sqrt{(N_c + N_d + T_y)(N_c + N_d + T_x)}}$$

T_x is the number of cases tied on the independent variable but varying on the dependent variable

Kendall's tau-*c*

$$\text{tau-}c = \frac{2k(N_c - N_d)}{N^2(k-1)}$$

Spearman's rank-order correlation coefficient

$$r_s = 1 - \frac{6\Sigma D^2}{n(n^2 - 1)}$$

Equation for a straight line

$$Y = a \pm bX$$

Y is the dependent variable
X is the independent variable
a is the Y-intercept (the value of Y when X is zero)
b is the slope of the line
+ indicates positive association
− indicates negative association

Regression coefficient

$$b = \frac{\Sigma(X_i - \overline{X})(Y_i - \overline{Y})}{\Sigma(X_i - \overline{X})^2}$$

$$b = \frac{n\Sigma(X_i Y_i) - (\Sigma X_i)(\Sigma Y_i)}{n\Sigma X_i^2 - (\Sigma X_i)^2}$$

Pearson's product moment correlation coefficient

$$r = \frac{\Sigma(X_i - \overline{X})(Y_i - \overline{Y})}{\sqrt{\left[(X_i - \overline{X})^2\right]\left[(Y_i - \overline{Y})^2\right]}}$$

$$r = \frac{n\Sigma(X_i Y)_i - (\Sigma X_i)(\Sigma Y_i)}{\sqrt{\left[n\Sigma X_i^2 - (\Sigma X_i)^2\right]\left[n\Sigma Y_i^2 - (\Sigma Y_i)^2\right]}}$$

Confidence interval for a mean

$$\text{lower limit} = \overline{X} - z\left(\frac{s}{\sqrt{n}}\right)$$

$$\text{upper limit} = \overline{X} + z\left(\frac{s}{\sqrt{n}}\right)$$

z-test for a single mean

$$z = \frac{\overline{X} - \mu}{\sigma/\sqrt{n}}$$

t-test for a single mean

$$t = \frac{\overline{X} - \mu}{s/\sqrt{n}}$$

z-test for a binomial percentage

$$z = \frac{(P_s - 0.5) - P_u}{\sqrt{\dfrac{P_u(100 - P_u)}{n}}} \quad \text{where} \quad P_s > P_u$$

or

$$z = \frac{(P_s + 0.5) - P_u}{\sqrt{\dfrac{P_u(100 - P_u)}{n}}} \quad \text{where} \quad P_s < P_u$$

$$\sigma_p = \sqrt{\frac{P_u(1 - P_u)}{n}}$$

P_u is the population percentage

Runs test

$$z = \frac{(R+0.5) - \mu_R}{\sigma_R} \quad \text{where } R < \mu_R$$

or

$$z = \frac{(R-0.5) - \mu_R}{\sigma_R} \quad \text{where } R > \mu_R$$

$$\mu_R = \frac{2n_1 n_2}{n} + 1$$

$$\sigma_R = \sqrt{\frac{n^2 - 2n}{4(n-1)}}$$

R is the number of runs in the sample
n_1 is the number of cases with a given value
n_2 is the number of cases with the other value

Chi-square test for independence and goodness of fit

$$\chi^2 = \sum \frac{(f_o - f_e)^2}{f_e}$$

f_o is the observed frequency in each category
f_e is the expected frequency in each category

$$df = (r-1)(c-1)$$

r is the number of rows
c is the number of columns

The *t*-test for the equality of two means

$$t = \frac{\overline{X}_1 - \overline{X}_2}{\sigma_{\overline{X} - \overline{X}}}$$

$$\sigma_{\overline{X} - \overline{X}} = \sqrt{\frac{n_1 s_1^2 + n_2 s_2^2}{n_1 + n_2 - 2}} \sqrt{\frac{n_1 + n_2}{n_1 n_2}} \quad \text{(pooled variance estimate)}$$

ANOVA *F*-test for more than two sample means

$$F = \frac{\dfrac{SSB}{k-1}}{\dfrac{SSW}{n-k}}$$

$$TSS = SSB + SSW$$

$$TSS = \Sigma X_i^2 - n\overline{X}^2$$

$$SSW = \Sigma \left(X_i - \overline{X}_s \right)^2$$

$$SSB = \Sigma n_s \left(\overline{X}_s - \overline{X} \right)^2$$

$\overline{X}_s$ is the mean for a given sample
n_s is the number of cases in a given sample.

The two-sample *z*-test for the rank sum (Wilcoxon's rank-sum test)

$$z = \frac{W - \mu_W}{\sigma_W}$$

$$\mu_W = \frac{1}{2} n_1 \left(n_1 + n_2 + 1 \right)$$

$$\sigma_W = \sqrt{\frac{1}{12} n_1 n_2 \left(n_1 + n_2 + 1 \right)}$$

n_1 is the sample with the fewest cases
n_2 is the sample with the most cases

The dependent-samples *t*-test for the mean difference

$$t = \frac{\overline{X}_D}{s_D / \sqrt{n}}$$

$$\overline{X}_D = \frac{\Sigma D}{n}$$

$$s_D = \sqrt{\frac{\Sigma D^2 - \frac{(\Sigma D)^2}{n}}{n-1}}$$

The McNemar chi-square test for change

$$\chi^2_M = \frac{(n_1 - n_2 - 1)^2}{n_1 + n_2}$$

n_1 is the observed number of cases in cell (b) or cell (c), whichever is *largest*
n_2 is the observed number of cases in cell (b) or cell (c), whichever is *smallest*

The Wilcoxon signed-ranks z-test for dependent samples

$$z = \frac{T - \mu_T}{\sigma_T}$$

$$\sigma_T = \sqrt{\frac{n(n+1)(2n+1)}{24}}$$

$$\mu_T = \frac{n(n+1)}{4}$$

Glossary

Arithmetic mean The sum of all scores in a distribution divided by the total number of cases.

Asymmetric measures of association Measures of association whose value depends on which variable is specified as independent and which variable is specified as dependent.

Binomial distribution A distribution that has only two possible values or categories.

Bivariate descriptive statistics A class of statistics that can be used to analyze whether a relationship exists between two variables.

Bivariate table A table that displays the joint frequency distribution for two variables.

Case An entity that displays or possesses the traits of a variable.

Census An investigation that includes every member of the population.

Central limit theorem A theorem which states that if an infinite number of random samples of equal size are selected from a population, the sampling distribution of the sample means will approach a normal distribution as sample size approaches infinity.

Class interval A range of values on a distribution that are grouped together for presentation and analysis.

Coefficient of relative variation A descriptive statistic that expresses the standard deviation of a distribution as a percentage of the mean.

Conceptual definition The use of literal terms to specify the qualities of a variable (also called the **nominal definition**).

Concordant pair Two cases in a joint distribution that are ranked the same on both variables.

Confidence level The probability that an interval estimate will include the value of the population parameter being estimated.

Constant An attribute or quality that does not vary from one case to another.

Contingency table See **Bivariate table**.

Continuous variable A variable that can vary in quantity by infinitesimally small degrees.

Coordinate A point on a scatter plot that simultaneously indicates the values a given case takes for each variable.

Critical region The range of scores that will cause the null hypothesis to be rejected at a specified significance level.

Crosstabulation See **Bivariate table**.

Cumulative frequency table A table that shows, for each value in a distribution, the number of cases up to and including that value.

Cumulative relative frequency table A table that shows, for each value in a distribution, the percentage or proportion of the total number of cases up to and including that value.

Dependent samples Samples for which the criterion for inclusion in one sample is affected by the composition of the other samples.

Descriptive statistics The numerical, graphical, and tabular techniques for organizing, presenting, and analyzing data.

Dichotomous variable A variable that has only two possible values.

Discordant pair Two cases in a joint distribution whose rank on one variable is different to their rank on the other variable.

Discrete variable A variable that has a countable number of values.

Error term See **Residual**.

Frequency The number of times that a particular score appears in a set of data.

Frequency table A table that reports, for each value of a variable, the number of cases that have that value.

Hypothesis A statement about some characteristic of the distribution of a population.

Hypothesis testing The procedure for deciding whether some aspect of a population distribution has a specified characteristic.

Independence Two variables are independent if the pattern of variation in the scores for one variable is not related to the pattern of variation in the scores for the other variable.

Index of qualitative variation The number of differences between scores in a distribution expressed as a proportion of the total number of possible differences.

Inferential statistics The numerical techniques used for making conclusions about a population distribution, based on the data from a random sample drawn from that population.

Interquartile range The difference between the upper limits of the first quartile and the third quartile; the range for the middle 50 percent of cases in a rank-ordered series.

Interval scale A level of measurement that has units measuring intervals of equal distance between values on the scale.

Mean See **Arithmetic mean**

Measurement The process of determining and recording which of the possible traits of a variable an individual case exhibits or possesses.

Measures of association Descriptive statistics that indicate the extent to which a change in the value of one variable is related to a change in the value of the other variable.

Measures of central tendency Descriptive statistics that indicate the typical or average value for a distribution

Measures of dispersion Descriptive statistics that indicate the spread or variety of scores in a distribution.

Median A measure of central tendency which indicates the value in a rank-ordered series that divides the series in half.

Missing cases Cases in a data set for which measurements of a variable have not been taken.

Mode A measure of central tendency which indicates the value in a distribution with the highest frequency.

Multivariate regression A technique that investigates the relationship between two or more independent variables and a single dependent variable.

Nominal definition See **Conceptual definition**

Nominal scale A level of measurement that only indicates the category of a variable that a case falls into.

Non-parametric test A test of an hypothesis about some feature of a population distribution other than its parameters.

Operational definition The specification of the procedures and criteria for taking a measurement of a variable for individual cases.

Ordinal scale A level of measurement that, in addition to the function of classification, allows cases to be ordered by degree according to measurements of a variable.

Ordinary least squares regression A rule which states that the line of best fit for a linear regression is the one that minimizes the sum of the squared residuals.

Parameter A statistic that describes some feature of a population.

Parametric test A test of an hypothesis about the parameters of a population distribution.

Percentages Statistics that standardize the total number of cases to a base value of 100.

Perfect association A statistical relationship where all cases with a particular value for one variable have a certain value for the other variable.

Population The set of all cases of interest.

Proportions Statistics that standardize the total number of cases to a base value of one.

Random selection A sampling method where each member of the population has the same chance of being selected in the sample.

Range The difference between the lowest and highest scores in a distribution.

Rank A number that indicates the position of a case in an ordered series.

Ratio scale A level of measurement which assigns a value of 0 to cases which possess or exhibit no quantity of a variable.

Region of rejection See **Critical Region**.

Regression coefficient A descriptive statistic that indicates by how many units the dependent variable will change, given a one-unit change in the independent variable.

Relative frequencies Statistics that express the number of cases within each value of a variable as a percentage or proportion of the total number of cases.

Residual The difference between the observed and expected value of a variable.

Run A sequence of cases in an ordered series that have the same value for a variable.

Sample A set of cases that does not include every member of the population.

Sampling distribution The theoretical probability distribution of an infinite number of sample outcomes for a statistic, using random samples of equal size.

Scatter plot A graphical technique for describing the joint distribution for two continuous variables.

Standard deviation A measure of dispersion that is the square root of the variance.

Stated class limits The upper and lower bounds of an interval that determine its width.

Symmetric measures of association Measure of association whose strength will be the same regardless of which variable is specified as independent and which variable is specified as dependent.

Type I error The error of rejecting the null hypothesis of no difference when in fact it is correct.

Type II error The error of failing to reject the null hypothesis when in fact it is false.

Valid cases Cases in a data set for which measurements of a variable have been taken.

Variable A condition or quality that can vary from one case to another.

Variance A statistic that expresses the mean deviation of scores from the mean of a distribution.

z-scores Numbers that express the interval between a point and the mean of a normal distribution as a proportion of the standard deviation of that normal distribution.

Answers

1.1 (a) Not exhaustive: no option for people not eligible to vote.
Not mutually exclusive: someone can be either of the first two options and did not vote at the last election.

(b) Not exhaustive: needs an 'other category' at least for students enrolled in other courses.
Not mutually exclusive: social sciences is a broader category that includes sociology and economics.

(c) Not mutually exclusive: someone can have multiple reasons for joining the military.

1.2 (a) interval/ratio
(b) nominal
(c) nominal
(d) interval/ratio
(e) nominal
(f) nominal
(g) ordinal
(h) interval/ratio
(i) ordinal
(j) nominal
(k) interval/ratio
(l) nominal
(m) ordinal
(n) interval/ratio
(o) ordinal
(p) nominal

1.5 (a) discrete
(b) continuous
(c) continuous
(d) discrete
(e) continuous
(f) continuous

3.1 A proportion standardizes totals to a base of 1, whereas a percentage standardizes totals to a base of 100.

3.2 A percentage is calculated using the same formula as a proportion multiplied by 100, ensuring that the percentage will be a higher number (by a factor of 100) than the corresponding proportion.

3.3 (a) 0.01 (1%)
       (b) 0.13 (13%)
       (c) 1.24 (124%)
       (d) 0.0045 (0.45%)

3.4 (a) 12% (0.12)
       (b) 13.4% (0.134)
       (c) 167% (1.67)
       (d) 3.5% (0.035)

3.5

Time to complete fitness trial

Interval	Mid-point	Frequency	Cumulative frequency	Percent	Cumulative percent
1–9	5	0	0	0.0%	0.0%
10–19	15	5	5	12.5%	12.5%
20–29	25	7	12	17.5%	30.0%
30–39	35	14	26	35.0%	65.0%
40–49	45	6	32	15.0%	80.0%
50–59	55	4	36	10.0%	90.0%
60–69	65	0	36	0.0%	90.0%
70–79	75	1	37	2.5%	92.5%
80–89	85	3	40	7.5%	100.0%

Heart rate in minutes

Interval	Mid-point	Frequency	Cumulative frequency	Percent	Cumulative percent
60–69	65	4	4	10.0%	0.0%
70–79	75	10	14	25.0%	25.0%
80–89	85	14	28	35.0%	60.0%
90–99	95	11	39	27.5%	87.5%
100–109	105	1	40	2.5%	90.0%

3.6

Region	People attending public libraries	Relative frequency, %	People attending popular music concerts	Relative frequency, %
A	1409	31.7	1166	33.7
B	1142	25.7	870	25.2
C	713	16.1	604	17.5
D	423	9.5	280	8.1
E	497	11.2	332	9.6
F	130	2.9	99	2.9
G	90	2.0	32	0.9
H	38	0.9	74	2.1
Total	4442	100	3456	100

3.10 (a) 104
        (b) 21.9%
        (c) 77%
        (d) 27%

4.1 No; the numbers on an ordinal scale are values which have no quantitative significance. They are merely labels which preserve the ordering of cases. To calculate a mean we need to perform the mathematical operation of addition and this requires interval/ratio data.

4.2 The advantage of the range is that it is very easy to calculate and everyone understands it. Its disadvantage is that because it only uses two scores it does not use all the information available in a distribution. For the same reason it is very sensitive to extreme values.

4.3 μ is the mean for a population; s is the standard deviation for a sample; σ is the standard deviation for a population; $\overline{X}$ is the mean for a sample.

4.4 2

4.5 (a) mean=23.3; median=14; range=67; standard deviation=24.9
   (b) mean=267.4; median=289; range=332; standard deviation =120.6
   (c) mean=2.9; median=2.4; range=4; standard deviation =1.4

4.6 This student had a lower than average IQ in the first class, and a higher than average IQ for the class the student joined.

4.7 (a) 9, 11, 20, 22, 36, 36, 39, 43, 45, 50, 56, 57, 59, 60, 66, 68, 68, 73, 75, 80, 87
      Median=56
   (b) 50.5 (rounded to 1 decimal place)
   (c) The median is greater than the mean, therefore the distribution is skewed to the **left**.
   (d) Mean=57
      Median=56.5
      The median is a relatively stable measure of central tendency that is not sensitive to extreme outliers, whereas the mean, by including every value in its calculation, is affected by the addition of one extreme score.

4.8 (a) mean=$33,500; median=$32,500; mode=$22,000
   (b) range=$60,000; IQR=$30,000; standard deviation=$14,183

4.9 (a) mean (ungrouped)=29.6 minutes; mean (grouped)=28.25 minutes
      median (ungrouped)=31.5 minutes; median (grouped)=31–40 minutes
      The differences are due to the fact that class intervals do not provide as much information as a listing of the raw scores. Since we use class mid-points rather than the actual data in calculating the mean, the answer will vary. With median and mode we can only report the class, rather than the specific value.

4.10   Degree of enrollment
(a)   Nominal
(b)   mode=Arts

Time spent studying in library
(a)   Interval/ratio
(b)   mean =3.275 hours; median=2 hours; mode=4 hours

Satisfaction with employment
(a)   Ordinal
(b)   mode=satisfied; median=satisfied

4.11   (a)   mean=8.7 years; median=9–12 years; mode=9–12 years
(b)   distribution is skewed to the right

4.12   No; the value that occurs the most is Europe. The mode is not the frequency with which it occurs.

4.13   (a) $17,403
(b)   The *CRV* for beginning salaries is 46.4%. The *CRV* for current salaries is 49.6%. Therefore current salaries have slightly more variation.
(c)   10 years, 1 month

5.1   A pie chart emphasizes the contribution that the frequency for each category makes to the total, whereas a bar graph emphasizes the frequency of each category relative to each other.

5.2   A bar graph expresses the distribution of discrete variables whereas a histogram expresses the distribution of continuous variables.

5.4   This is continuous interval/ratio data, so that a frequency polygon is the best technique, given the number of values in the distribution. If these data were organized into class intervals a histogram could also be constructed.

5.5   (a)

Price	Frequency
7000–8499	2
8500–9999	3
10000–11499	6
11500–12999	3
13000–14499	1

5.6   The pie graph should illustrate the large proportion of migrants from Europe in the total.

5.7 (a) A pie graph will highlight that clerical workers make the most significant contribution, in terms of employment categories, to the total.

(b) You should have a bar chart with three spikes, one for each of the employment categories. The spikes should be divided into males and females. The graph will reveal that women are highly concentrated in clerical positions, whereas men dominate managerial and, especially, custodial positions.

(c) The curve is highly skewed to the right.

6.1 (a) 0.097
(b) 0.903
(c) 0.3082
(d) 0.9665
(e) 0.0915
(f) 0.110
(g) 0.050

6.2 (a) ±1
(b) +2.1
(c) −1.645
(d) ±1.5

6.3 (a) 0
(b) −0.8
(c) 2.5
(d) −1.7
(e) 1.3

6.4 The z-score for the poverty line is −0.83. The proportion for $z = -0.8$ is 0.212, and the proportion for $z = -0.9$ is 0.184. Therefore the proportion of all families headed by a single mother also living in poverty is between 0.212 and 0.184 or around 1 in 5.

6.5 $z = -1.6$, and the area under curve is 0.055. Therefore 5.5% of light bulbs last 462 hours or less.

6.6 (a) $z = -1.65$, area under curve is 0.05.
(b) $z = \pm1.96$; for $z = -1.96$ the selling price is $15,292; for $z = 1.96$ the selling price is $24,308. Therefore the range is $15,292–$24,308.

6.7 (a) $z = 1.4$, probability is 0.081
(b) $z = 1.645$, distance is 48.225 meters

6.8 (a) for 18 years $z = -1.3$, proportion between mean and 18 is 0.403

for 65 years $z = 2.1$, proportion between mean and 65 is 0.486
proportion between 18 and 65 years is 0.403+0.486=0.889

(b)   middle 50%: closest probability in Table is 0.516 with $z = \pm0.7$
for $z = -0.7$ the age is 26, for $z = 0.7$ the age is 45 (both figures rounded to nearest whole year)

6.9   (a)   At $1.7 million $z = 1$, which has a one-tail probability of 0.1585
(b)   At $1.2 million $z = -1.5$, which has a one-tail probability of 0.067

6.10   At 15 km/h $z = 0.5$, which has a probability of 0.3085. This means that the wind speed will be over 15 km/h 30 percent of the time, which meets the proposal requirements.

7.1   The conclusion drawn incorrectly about the causality of the relationship from the observed statistical association. It is more appropriate to regard the causality as running in the opposite direction: the higher injury rate 'causes' the higher number of ambulance officers attending the accident.

7.2   (a)

Dependent	Independent		
	1	2	Total
1	40%	55%	44%
2	60%	45%	56%
Total	100%	100%	100%

(b)

Dependent	Independent			
	1	2	3	Total
1	79%	57%	16%	53%
2	21%	43%	84%	47%
Total	100%	100%	100%	100%

7.3   (a)

Dependent	Independent		
	1	2	Total
1	33%	67%	100%
2	47%	53%	100%
Total	41%	59%	100%

(b)

Dependent	Independent			
	1	2	3	Total
1	53%	38%	9%	100%
2	16%	32%	47%	100%
Total	35%	35%	30%	100%

7.4 (a) It is most likely that since a father's voting preference is formed before his own child's that this is the independent variable and the child's voting preference is the dependent variable. Voting preferences are measured at the ordinal level.

(b)

Own voting preference	Father's voting preference			
	Progressive	Conservative	Other	Total
Progressive	22	4	4	30
Conservative	5	19	6	30
Total	27	23	10	60

(c) Adding column percentages will help determine by eye whether there is any dependence. The pattern of dependence suggests that children tend to vote in a similar way to their respective father.

7.5 After calculating the relative frequencies there appears to be no relationship between country of residence and amount of TV watched.

7.6 (a) Smoking habit is ordinal, and health level is ordinal.

(b) Both of these are behavioral variables so any plausible explanation which has either variable as the independent, or mutually dependent, is permissible.

(c)

Health level	Smoking level		
	Doesn't smoke	Does smoke	Total
Poor	13	34	47
	13.4%	52.3%	29.0%
Fair	22	19	41
	22.7%	29.2%	25.3%
Good	35	9	44
	36.1%	13.8%	27.2%
Very Good	27	3	30
	27.8%	4.6%	18.5%
Total	97	65	162
	59.9%	40.1%	100%

7.7 (a) 84
(b) 254
(c) 74
(d) 88.1%
(e) 0

8.1 An asymmetric measure will be affected by the choice of which variable is specified as the dependent and which variable is specified as independent. A symmetric measure will yield the same value for the strength of association irrespective of the model of the relationship. A symmetric measure is therefore the appropriate one.

8.2   It is important to specify the dependent and independent variables since lambda is an asymmetric measure of association, whose value is therefore affected by this choice. If the pattern of dependence is not thought to be that of one-way dependence, the symmetric version of Lambda should be used.

8.3   (a) Lambda=0.11 (very weak association)
(b) Lambda=0.42 (moderate association)
(c) Lambda=0 (this does not necessarily indicate no association. Looking at the table it is clear that there is some variation between columns, but the modal response for all values of the independent variable is one, causing lambda to equal zero).

8.4   Lambda=0.54. Looking at the table the moderate association is due to the higher proportion of gun owners in favor of capital punishment.

8.5

Can sing anthem?	Job classification		
	Blue collar	White collar	Total
Yes	29	22	51
No	21	28	49
Total	50	50	100

Lambda = 0.12

8.6   The study indicates that the strength of the association has increased in recent times. In a *relative* sense we might say that the association is strong, but this is only in relation to the past studies, rather than in some absolute sense.

8.7   (a) $V = 0.17$
(b) $V = 0.33$
(c) $V = 0.09$

8.8   (a) Lambda = 0.19 (with current income dependent)
(b) Lambda = 0.262 (with current income dependent)

9.1   Negative

9.2   Nominal variables do not have a direction of change

9.3   (a) 14(60)=840
(b) 24(8)=192
(c) 19(12+17+20)=931
(d) 16(12+17+10+14+22)=1200

9.4   (a) 14(12)=168

(b) 32(24+12)=1152
(c) 24(32)=768
(d) 11(25+42+19+24)=1210

9.5 (a) 8(14+32)=1472
(b) 32(14+8)=1472
(c) 24(60+12)=1728
(d) 11(6+16+20)=462

9.6 The number of cases tied on the dependent but not on the dependent variable is 5030. The value of Somers' d is 0.25.

9.7 Concordant pairs:
26(20+58+15+62) + 23(20+58) + 62(20+15) +62(20) = 5359
Discordant pairs:
12(58+22+62+23) + 15(58+22) + 62(22+23) + 62(22) = 7274
Gamma = –0.15; therefore a very weak, negative relationship between these variables.

9.8 (a) Inspection of the table by eye reveals a negative association, since health level seems to decrease as smoking level increases (it is helpful to calculate the column percentages to see this). This will appear as a negative sign in front of any measure of association calculated on these data.
(b) The value for gamma is –0.69, indicating a moderate to strong negative association.

9.9 Rho = 0.85. There is a strong positive association between these variables.

9.10 Rho = 0.51

9.11 Rho = –0.19

9.12 Somers' d with current income as dependent is 0.794 and Gamma is 0.914 indicating a strong, positive relationship. Tau-b is not useful because there is not the same number of columns and rows.

10.1 The purpose of drawing a scatter plot is to make judgment about whether the conditions for using a linear regression hold. In particular, we can assess visually whether there is a linear relationship, rather than a curvilinear relationship.

10.2 The Y-intercept indicates the expected value for the dependent variable when the independent variable is zero. It is equal to a in the regression equation.

10.3   The principle, often called the ordinary least squares regression line, is to draw a line that minimizes the sum of the squared residuals between each point in a scatter plot and the regression line.

10.4   (a) positive
             (b) negative
             (c) positive
             (d) no relationship
             (e) negative

10.6   The correlation coefficient is a standardized measure of correlation that ranges from –1 to 1, regardless of the units in which the variables are measured. The coefficient of the regression line indicates the amount of change in the dependent variable expected from a one-unit change in the independent variable. It is therefore sensitive to the units of measurements.

10.7   (d) $Y = 27.165 - 0.15(X)$; when $X = 12$, $Y = 24.885$

10.8   (a) When $X = 0$, $Y = 40$ years
             (b) $Y = 40 + 0.7(30) = 61$ years (note that we use 30 in the equation not 30,000, since the units of measurement are $,000).
             (c) We cannot use the regression coefficient of +0.7 to assess the strength of the correlation. To do this we need to calculate the correlation coefficient.

10.9   (a) $Y = 33.4 + 0.511(X)$
             (b) The value for r indicates a strong, positive relationship.
             (c) When hours (X) are zero, $Y=33.4$, indicating a fail.
             (d) $50 = 33.4 + 0.511(X)$, $X = 32.6$ hours. The high value of r^2 indicates that the student can be very confident in the prediction. It is wrong to use the regression line in this way because it is not a deterministic relationship: there is an element of error. The student may not actually work when in the library, thinking that just spending the time will be sufficient.

10.10   (a) $Y = 157 + 4.88(X)$, $r = 0.92$, $r^2 = 0.85$
             (b) The regression coefficient changes to 4880. Since r and r^2 are standardized coefficients their values are unaffected by the units of measurement.

10.12   (a) $r = -0.77$
             (b) days lost = 14.4 – 0.88(hours of exercise); for 8 hours of exercise, days lost equals 7.4

10.15   current salary = $1928 + 1.9(beginning salary)

The value for r^2 is 0.755 indicating that using beginning salary to predict current salary will produce reliable predictions.

11.1 A sample statistic is a numerical measure of a **sample** while a parameter is a measure of some feature of a **population**.

11.2 Descriptive statistics summarize the data from a sample, inferential statistics attempt to generalize from a random sample to the population.

11.3 Random variation is the variation in sample outcomes brought about by random selection from a population. It requires us to use probability theory when generalizing to a population.

11.4 (a) False; it is evident from the equation for the standard error that the size of the population is not a factor affecting the reliability of a sample.
  (b) True
  (c) False; the standard error is equal to the standard deviation of the population *divided* by the square root of the sample size and therefore must be smaller than the standard deviation of the population.
  (d) False; provided the sample size is large (i.e. greater than 12) the central limit theorem states that the sampling distribution of sample means will be normal, even where the population from which the samples are drawn is not normal.

11.5 In either case the mean of the sampling distribution is 40.

11.6 The standard error is the standard deviation of a sampling distribution. It is always smaller than the standard deviation of the population since the effect of any extreme individual scores included in a sample will be muted by more representative scores included in the sample.

11.7 The difference is that where $n = 30$ the distribution has fatter tails than the distribution for $n = 200$; that is, the standard error is smaller in the larger sample. They are similar because they both approximate the normal curve and are centered on the population mean.

11.8 It appears to be random because each letter in the hat has an equal chance of being selected; however, since there may not be the same number of students for every letter it does not mean every *student* in the class has an equal chance of being selected. For example, if there were a lot of people with a surname beginning with G in the class the sample would over-represent that particular group.

11.9   The sampling method is random if every book in the library has an equal chance of being borrowed and then returned on a Thursday and there is nothing about Thursday that will influence the condition of books returned on that day.

11.11   The theorem is important because it allows the use of a normal sampling distribution to carry out statistical analysis, even where samples are drawn from non-normal populations, and such populations are very common in social research.

11.12   There is far greater variation in the sample means from the $n = 20$ samples. The spread of scores still should be centered on the population mean.

12.1   Interval estimation is the process of inferring the range of values that contain the (unknown) population parameter, together with the probability (confidence level) that this estimate does include the parameter.

12.2   A confidence level is the probability that a particular range of values will include the population parameter. As the confidence level increases the width of the confidence interval also increases, and vice versa.

12.3   As sample size increases the width of the confidence interval becomes smaller.

12.4   The standard deviation of the population alters the width of the confidence interval by affecting the standard error of the estimate. As the standard deviation increases so does the standard error, meaning the confidence interval will also widen.

12.5   Age of pre-school children:
90% confidence level: 3.75 [3.64, 3.86]
99% confidence level: 3.75 [3.57, 3.93]

TV watching:
90% confidence level: 150 [145.24, 154.76]
99% confidence level: 150 [142.49, 157.51]

12.6   Economics: 6 [5.26, 6.74]
Sociology: 4 [3.33, 4.67]
History: 4.5 [3.56, 5.44]
Statistics: 3 [2.62, 3.38]

12.7 Increase for all workers across the industry at 95% is $1018 [$907.68, $1128.32], and at the 99% confidence level is $1018 [$871.65, $1164.35].

12.8 (a) 4.3 days [3.79, 4.82] at 99%.
(b) Compared to the other hospital it is about the same since the confidence interval includes the value of 4 days.
(c) To improve the accuracy of the estimate it could include more people in the sample.

12.9 8.5 years [8.28, 8.72]

12.10 (a) $34,420 [$33,127, $35,712]
(b) $34,420 [$32,878, $35,961]
(c) $34,420 [$32,391, $36,448]

13.1 The distribution approaches the normal curve as sample size increases towards infinity, as described by the central limit theorem, regardless of the shape of the population distribution.

13.2 Type I error occurs when the null hypothesis is rejected even though it is true; a type II error occurs when the null hypothesis is accepted when a rejection should have been made. The probability of one happening decreases the possibility of the other occurring increases.

13.3 As the significance level is increased the critical region becomes smaller; that is, the higher the significance level the larger the difference has to be before the null hypothesis is rejected.

13.5

Probability	Test	z-score
0.230	**Two-tail**	±1.2
0.100	Two-tail	**±1.645**
0.018	**One-tail**	±2.1
0.021	Two-tail	±2.3
0.0003	One-tail	±3.4

13.6 (a) $z > 1.645$, $\propto = 0.05$
(b) $z < -1.645$, $\propto = 0.05$
(c) $z > 1.96$ or $z < -1.96$, $\propto = 0.05$

13.7 (a) $z = -1.9$
(b) $z = -20.9$

13.8 (a) The probability of drawing, from a population with a mean of 15 years, a random sample with a mean that differs from the population mean by three or more is 3 in 100.

(b) The probability of drawing, from a population with a mean of 15 years, a random sample with a mean less than the population mean by three or more is 15 in 1000.

13.9 No; significance tests never definitively prove anything about a population. They only indicate the *probability* of drawing a sample with a known mean value from a population with an hypothesized mean value. Even with extremely low significance levels we risk making a type I error.

13.10 $H_0: \mu = 24$
$H_a: \mu > 24$
$\alpha = 0.05$
$z_{sample} = 1.73$, $p = 0.0445$
$z_{critical} = 1.645$, we are using a one-tail (right-tail) test because we are interested in whether this judge has an average greater than the rest.
At an alpha level of 0.05 the probability of the judge being the same as other judges is less than the alpha level, leading the null hypothesis to be rejected. Note that an alpha level of 0.01, or on a two-tail test, the sample score will not be significantly different to the hypothesized value.

14.1 The sample is drawn from a normal population.

14.2

t-score	Probability	Test	*df*
2.015	**0.05**	One-tail	5
2.764	0.02	Two-tail	10
1.708	0.05	One-tail	**25**
2.000	0.05	Two-tail	65
1.282	0.10	One-tail	228

14.3 (a) $t = -3.08$ (reject) two-tail
(b) $t = -3.08$ (reject) one tail
(c) $t = -2.18$ (reject)
(d) $t = -6.11$ (reject)
(e) $t = 1.29$ (fail to reject)
(f) $t = 8.89$ (reject)

14.4 (a) $t_{sample} = -2.35$. At the 0.05 level, $t_{critical} = \pm 1.98$ so the null hypothesis is rejected, the pay rise has not been achieved. However, at the 0.01 level $t_{critical} = \pm 2.617$, so the null hypothesis is not rejected.
(b) Yes, the 95 percent confidence interval does not include the target the pay rise, while at the 99 percent level the interval includes the desired wage increase.

14.5 (a) mean = 63 years; standard deviation = 16.63 years
      (b) $p = 0.045$ (around 45 in every thousand)
      (c) The confidence interval does not include the value of 0, which would indicate no significant difference to 70 years.

14.6 $t_{sample} = -12.96$, $t_{critical} = \pm 2.704$, the null hypothesis is rejected. Hip fractures affect walking speed.

14.7 At an alpha level of 0.05, the following sample scores and decisions regarding the null apply:
      Canada: $t_{sample} = 3.85$ (reject)
      Singapore: $t_{sample} = -6.87$ (reject)
      Australia: $t_{sample} = -1.02$ (do not reject)

14.8 (a) $t_{sample} = -1.151$, significance on a two-tail test = 0.264; therefore do not reject null hypothesis

15.1 The statement is false. The width of an interval estimate is only affected by the sample size, the confidence level, and the sample proportion. No other factor enters into the equation for the confidence interval. Given these factors the interval estimate will be the same regardless of the size of the population from which the sample is drawn.

15.2

	z_{sample}	Two-tail	One-tail
(a)	1.78	Fail to reject	Reject
(b)	−0.36	Fail to reject	Fail to reject

15.3 (a) $z_{sample} = -0.31$, at $\alpha = 0.05$, one tailed, $z_{critical} = -1.645$; therefore the null hypothesis is not rejected: the sample percentage is not significantly different to the target of 40 percent, so that the program was successful.
      (b) The confidence interval supports this because 40 percent is inside the 95 percent confidence interval of [35.6%,42.2%].

15.4 At 95 percent, the confidence interval is [43.6%, 61.4%]. This includes values of less than 50 percent so that the sample does not confirm that the candidate is a certain winner. Similarly, if we conduct a z-test using 50 percent as the test value, the sample percentage is not significantly different.

15.5 At an alpha level of 0.05 the z-score of −3.08 will lead us to reject the null hypothesis so that taping does reduce ankle sprain injury.

15.6   The confidence interval is [51.6%, 60.4%], at a 95 percent confidence level, meaning that a majority of the population supports decriminalization.

15.7   Rounded to whole numbers, (a) [14%, 36%] (b) [16%, 34%]

15.8   (a)   Runs test applicable because the results are in sequence and using a binomial distribution. Runs test is applicable because the research question is interested in whether a *series* of outcomes for a binomial variable is random.
          (b) $z_{sample} = -0.19$, fail to reject.

15.9   (a)   12
          (b)   9.9
          (c)   Not significantly different to the test value; therefore we cannot say the series is non-random.

16.1

	df	$\alpha = 0.10$	$\alpha = 0.05$
Three categories	2	4.605	5.991
Five categories	4	7.779	9.488
Eight categories	7	12.017	14.067

16.2   (a) $\chi^2_{sample} = 5.28,\ df = 4,\ p = 0.35$: do not reject null
          (b) $\chi^2_{sample} = 1.33,\ df = 6,\ p = 0.965$: do not reject null

16.3 $\chi^2_{sample} = 40,\ df = 4,\ p < 0.01$: reject null

16.4 $\chi^2_{sample} = 6.246,\ \chi^2_{critical} = 11.07,\ df = 5$: do not reject null

16.5   (a)   26.8 is the expected value for each school
          (b)   The sample chi-square value is 2.49, which is not significant at the 0.05 level. We cannot reject the statement that these schools have the same percentage of students going on to university.

16.6   Expected frequencies are Clerical 389, Custodial 38, and Manager 47. This is significantly different.

17.1   The samples come from normal populations, and when using the pooled variance estimate, the populations have the same variance.

17.2   (a) $t_{sample} = -1.5,\ t_{critical} = \pm 2.0,\ df = 83$; do not reject null
          (b) $t_{sample} = -3.38,\ t_{critical} = \pm 1.98,\ df = 238$; reject null
          (c) $t_{sample} = -1.5,\ t_{critical} = \pm 2.0,\ df = 83$; do not reject null

(d) $t_{sample} = -2.5$, $t_{critical} = \pm 1.98$, $df = 18$; reject null

17.3 $t_{sample} = -2.2$, $t_{critical} = \pm 1.98$ ($\alpha = 0.05$, two-tail, $df = 196$). Reject null hypothesis.

17.4 $t_{sample} = 3.5$
The utility is interested in whether there is a *reduction* in water use, therefore a one-tail test is appropriate: $t_{critical} = 1.645$ ($\alpha = 0.05$, $df = 198$). Reject null hypothesis.
Important considerations are the number of samples to be compared, interval/ratio data used to describe a mean, and population standard deviations are unknown.

17.5 $t_{sample} = -12.2$
Use one-tail test because we are trying to find an improvement between the pesticides.
$t_{critical} = -1.671$ ($\alpha = 0.05$, $df = 60$)
Reject null hypothesis, the organic pesticide is different and better.

17.6   The sample t-score is 3.2 which is significant at the 0.01 level. Therefore reject the null hypothesis.

18.1   (a)   We are comparing more than two samples in terms of a variable measured at the interval/ratio level.
(b)   There is no difference in the average number of cases handled at each agency.
H_0: $\mu_1 = \mu_2 = \mu_3 = \mu_4 = \mu_5$
(c)   The F-ratio is 0.245. At $\alpha = 0.05$, and $dfb = 4$ and $dfw = 106$, $F_{critical} = 2.52$. Therefore the null hypothesis is not rejected: all means are equal.

18.2   (a)   Method A: mean=20.27   standard deviation=2.05
Method B: mean=22.73   standard deviation=2.87
Method C: mean=29.82   standard deviation=3.95
Looking at the means and the standard deviations it seems that only Method C will be significantly different to each of the others.
(b)   The F-ratio is 29, which is significant at the 0.05 level.

18.3   The F-score is 24.6, which is significant at the 0.01 level. At least one of the populations has a mean not equal to that of the others.

18.4   The significant difference is between Level 1 and all the other Levels of blood alcohol, but no other combinations.

19.1   (a)   2, 6, 9, 10, 11, 17; rank is 4
    (b)   2, 6, 8, 9, 10, 11, 17; rank is 5
    (c)   2, 6, 9, 10, 10, 11, 17; rank is 4.5
    (d)   2, 6, 8, 9, 10, 10, 11, 11, 17; rank is 5.5
    (e)   3, 4, 9, 10, 10, 10, 15, 16, 20, 22; rank is 5

19.2   In the preceding exercise identify and assign the correct rank to the score immediately following 10 in the rank-ordered series.
    (a)   2, 6, 9, 10, 11, 17; 11 is rank 5
    (b)   2, 6, 8, 9, 10, 11, 17; 11 is rank is 6
    (c)   2, 6, 9, 10, 10, 11, 17; 11 is rank is 6
    (d)   2, 6, 8, 9, 10, 10, 11, 11, 17; 11 is rank is 7.5
    (e)   3, 4, 9, 10, 10, 10, 15, 16, 20, 22; 15 is rank is 7

19.3   A rank sum test is used when (i) the test variable is measured at the ordinal level, or (ii) the test variable is measured at the interval/ratio level but the samples come from populations that are not normally distributed.

19.4   (a)
(Ranks in brackets)

Group 1	Group 2
1 (1)	12 (6.5)
15 (8.5)	25 (13)
12 (6.5)	29 (14)
16 (10)	8 (3)
23 (12)	15 (8.5)
9 (4)	20 (11)
11 (23)	7 (2)

    (b)   Group 1: 47, Group 2: 58
    (c)   The smallest rank sum is that for Group 1, $W = 47$
    (d) $\mu_W = 52.5$
    (e) $z_{sample} = -0.7$, do not reject null hypothesis at alpha of 0.05 (or 0.01).

19.5   The sample z-score is -2.15, which is significant at the 0.05 level. Therefore reject the null hypothesis that the exercise program makes no difference.

20.1   (a)   3
    (b)   3
    (c)   15
    (d)   8

20.2   (a)   7.815, 6.251
    (b)   7.815, 6.251

(c) 24.996, 22.307
(d) 15.507, 13.362

20.3 (a) 0.24
(b) 48

20.4 Expected frequencies:

	a	b	c	d	Total
a	1.59	0	6.87	46.54	55
b	1.41	0	6.13	41.46	49
Total	3	0	13	88	104

The shaded cells violate the rules that expected frequencies should not be less than 5.

20.5 $\chi^2_{sample} = 20.9$, which is significant at the 0.05 level with 2 degrees of freedom.

20.6 $\chi^2_{sample} = 0.76$ (your answer may differ slightly due to rounding); we cannot reject the null hypothesis of independence, since this is lower than the critical value with 6 degrees of freedom. There appears to be no relationship between country of residence and amount of TV watched.

20.7 (a) Health level (ordinal), Smoking habit (ordinal)
(e) The significance level for the sample chi-square indicates that we should reject the null hypothesis of independence.

20.8

Can sing anthem?	Job type		
	Blue collar	White collar	Total
Yes	29	22	51
No	21	28	49
Total	50	50	100

$\chi^2_{sample} = 1.96$. With 1 degree of freedom, with $\alpha = 0.05$, the critical score for chi-square is 3.841; therefore do not reject the null hypothesis.

21.1 No; inference tests only apply when generalizing from random samples to the population. Here we have data for the population so there is no need to make an inference.

21.2 The sample *t*-value is 2.14.

21.3   We reject the hypothesis that there is no correlation between these two variables in the population.

22.1   (a)   Mean difference $= -1.3$
           (b) $s_D = 1.212$
           (c) $t_{sample} = -1.07$; $t_{critical} = \pm1.833$ (two-tail test; do not reject null)

22.2   (a) $t_{sample} = 7.16$; $t_{critical} = \pm2.093$; reject null
           (b) $t_{sample} = -1.012$; $t_{critical} = -1.684$; do not reject null

22.3 $t_{sample} = 13.3$, which is significant at the 0.01 level. Therefore the treatment should be adopted.

22.4 $H_0 : \overline{X} = 0$

           $H_a : \overline{X}_D > 0$

           $t_{sample} = 2.5$
           $t_{critical} = 1.833$ ($\alpha = 0.05$, one-tail)
           Reject the null, the changes in workplace have improved productivity.

22.5 $t_{sample} = 1.4$
           The two-tail significance is greater than $\alpha = 0.05$, therefore accept the null hypothesis: people do seem, on average, to get the price they offer.

22.6   (a)   Weight in kg Pre Test; Weight in kg Post Test
           (b)   21
           (c)   70.1 kg
           (d)   66.43 kg
           (e)   3.67 kg
           (f) $t_{sample} = 5.966$, $df = 20$
           (g)   less than 0.0005 (note that SPSS rounds off to 3 decimal places, so that the probability is not actually equal to zero)
           (h)   upper limit $= 4.5$ kg
           (i)   lower limit $= 2.38$ kg
           (j)   Using the t-test, the sample value is lower than any critical value, therefore reject the null – the program is effective in reducing weight. We could also refer to the confidence interval which does not include the value of 0.
                 The 95 percent confidence interval does not include the value of 5. The range of estimated values for weight loss is below the target value; therefore the program is not successful.

22.9   The mean difference is both significantly greater than $0 and also $15,000. We can test the latter by looking at the confidence interval which does not include the test value of $15,000.

23.1 For all tables $\chi^2_{critical} = 3.841$

    (a) $\chi^2_M = 2.16$; do not reject null

    (b) $\chi^2_M = 0.343$; do not reject null

    (c) $\chi^2_M = 14.723$; reject null

23.2   (a) $\chi_M^2 = 0.593$; do not reject null

23.3 $z_{sample} = 0.84$, which has a two-tail probability of 0.4; therefore do not reject the null.

23.4   (a) $z_{sample} = -2.31$, which has a two-tail probability of 0.02; therefore do not reject the null at the 0.01 level. We cannot say that one program is preferred over the other.

24.1 This is an example of a spurious relationship; there is no theoretical basis for concluding that a direct causal relationship exists between these two variables. Rather they are each determined by a child's general state of development.

24.2 The relationship remains the same for each of the partial tables, indicating that the control variable does not alter the direct relationship between X and Y.

24.3 The original relationship is not as strong once the control variable is added (by comparing the original gamma with the partial gamma). This indicates that the relationship is partially spurious or intervening, although some direct relationship also exists between age and concern for the environment. This is stronger for conservatives than for liberals.

25.1   (a)   Days lost

    (b)   It would be reasonable to suspect that days lost decrease as the amount of exercise increases (negative) and that days lost increases as age increases (positive).

    (c)   days lost = 16.99 – 0.942(exercise hours) – 0.06(age in years); note that the sign in front of age is not the one expected.

    (d)   The coefficient for age is not significant, and the value for the adjusted R-squared indicates that it has not improved our predictive ability over the regression equation using exercise alone.

Index